SQL Server Query Tuning and Optimization

Optimize Microsoft SQL Server 2022 queries and applications

Benjamin Nevarez

BIRMINGHAM—MUMBAI

SQL Server Query Tuning and Optimization

Copyright © 2022 Packt Publishing

Publishing Product Manager: Apeksha Shetty
Content Development Editor: Joseph Sunil
Technical Editor: Rahul Limbachiya
Copy Editor: Safis Editing
Project Coordinator: Farheen Fathima
Proofreader: Safis Editing
Indexer: Rekha Nair
Production Designer: Joshua Misquitta
Marketing Coordinator: Nivedita Singh

First published: Aug 2022
Production reference: 1210722

Published by Packt Publishing Ltd.
Livery Place
35 Livery Street
Birmingham
B3 2PB, UK.

ISBN 978-1-80324-262-0
www.packt.com

This book is dedicated to my family, my wife Rocio, and my three boys, Diego, Benjamin and David.

Contributors

About the author

Benjamin Nevarez is a database professional based in Los Angeles, California who specializes in SQL Server query tuning and optimization. He is the author of several books including "SQL Server Query Tuning & Optimization", "High Performance SQL Server", "SQL Server 2017 on Linux", and "Inside the SQL Server Query Optimizer" and has also coauthored other books such as "SQL Server 2012 Internals". Benjamin has also been a speaker at many SQL Server conferences around the world. His blog can be found at `http://www.benjaminnevarez.com` and he can also be reached on twitter at @BenjaminNevarez and Facebook at `https://www.facebook.com/BenjaminNevarez`

About the reviewers

Mark Broadbent is a Microsoft Data Platform MVP and Microsoft Certified Master in SQL Server with over 30 years of IT experience working with data. He is an expert in transaction processing and concurrency control, a lover of Linux, development, Cloud, and Retro computing. In between annoying his long-suffering wife Lorraine and being beaten at video games by his children Lucy and Max, he can be found lurking on Twitter as @retracement.

Brandon Leach is a senior member of the DB Engineering team at Citadel and a recipient of multiple Microsoft Data Platform MVP awards between 2016 and 2022. He puts a high focus on performance tuning and automation at scale. He is also a frequent speaker at events like conferences and user groups.

> *I'd like to thank first and foremost my wonderful wife Anastasia and our two kids Evan and Aiden for all their support. I'd also like to thank Stacia Varga and Thomas Grohser for not only being wonderful friends but also mentors.*

Ajmer Dhariwal is a SQL Server consultant with more than two decades of experience in working for organizations ranging from small start-ups to global software vendors in industries ranging from banking to digital remarketing. Over this time, he has been involved with tuning everything from critical trading systems to clickstream processing applications. Based in St Albans, UK, when not technically reviewing books, he can be found spending his time reading and going for countryside walks.

Artur Wysoczanski works as a senior SQL DBA at Trainline in London, UK. He has spent the last 7 years of his career spanning over 20 years in IT specializing in SQL Server performance tuning and troubleshooting. On a daily basis, he works closely with development and operational teams to make sure that new and existing applications get the best possible database performance. His experience and good analytical skills allow him to help teams troubleshoot and understand problems arising on the company's SQL server estate. He is also well skilled in other database technologies, such as Oracle, PostgreSQL, MySQL, and cloud-native technologies such as AWS Aurora MySQL and Aurora PostgreSQL, DynamoDB, and Amazon Keyspaces. He is a fan of the utilization of new cloud technologies in modern organizations.

Table of Contents

3

The Query Optimizer

4

The Execution Engine

5

Working with Indexes

6

Understanding Statistics

7

In-Memory OLTP

8

Understanding Plan Caching

9

The Query Store

10

Intelligent Query Processing

11

An Introduction to Data Warehouses

12

Understanding Query Hints

Index

Other Books You May Enjoy

Preface

This book covers query tuning and optimization in SQL Server and provides you with the tools and knowledge necessary to get peak performance from your queries and applications. We mostly relate query optimization with the work performed by the query optimizer in which an efficient execution plan is produced for a query. However, sometimes we may not be happy with the query execution performance and may try to improve it by performing additional changes—or what we call query tuning. But even more important, we need to understand that the results we originally get from the query optimizer will greatly depend on all the information we feed it—for example, our database design, the defined indexes, and even some database and server configuration settings.

There are many ways in which we can impact the work performed by the query processor, which is why it is extremely important to understand how we can help this SQL Server component do a superior job. Providing quality information to the query processor will most likely result in high-quality execution plans, which will also improve the performance of your databases. But no query processor is perfect, and it is important to understand the reasons why sometimes we may not, in fact, get an efficient execution plan or good query performance and to know what possible solutions are still available.

Finally, this book covers all the supported versions of SQL Server and has been updated up to SQL Server 2022.

Who this book is for

This book is for SQL Server developers who are struggling with slow query execution, database administrators who are tasked with troubleshooting slow application performance, and database architects who design SQL Server databases in support of line-of-business and data warehousing applications.

What this book covers

This book covers how to get the best performance from your queries and how to use this knowledge to create high-performing applications. It shows how a better understanding of what the SQL Server query processor does behind the scenes can help database developers, administrators, and architects to write better queries and to provide the query processor with the information it needs to produce efficient execution plans. In the same way, this book shows how you can use your newfound knowledge of the query processor's inner workings and SQL Server tools to troubleshoot cases when your queries are not performing as expected.

Chapter 1, An Introduction to Query Tuning and Optimization, starts with an overview of the architecture of the SQL Server relational database engine and then continues by looking in great detail at how to use execution plans, the primary tool we will use to interact with the SQL Server query processor.

Chapter 2, Troubleshooting Queries, continues from *Chapter 1* and provides you with additional tuning tools and techniques, such as SQL trace, extended events, and DMVs, to find out how your queries are using system resources or to root out performance-related problems. The chapter ends with an introduction to the Data Collector, a feature introduced with SQL Server 2008.

Chapters 3 and *4* go deep into the internals of the query optimizer and the query processor operators. *Chapter 3, The Query Optimizer*, explains how the query optimizer works and shows why this knowledge can give you a great background to troubleshoot, optimize, and better tune your application queries. *Chapter 4, The Execution Engine*, tells you about the most used query operators employed in the execution plans created by the query optimizer.

After two chapters talking about the architecture and internals of the query processor, *Chapter 5, Working with Indexes*, puts your feet back on the ground by covering indexes. Indexing is one of the most important techniques used in query tuning and optimization, and one that can dramatically improve the performance of your queries and databases.

Statistics is another essential topic required for query tuning and optimization and troubleshooting. Statistics are used by the query optimizer to make decisions toward producing an efficient execution plan, and this information is also available to you so you can use it to troubleshoot cardinality estimation problems. Statistics are covered in *Chapter 6, Understanding Statistics*.

In-memory OLTP, originally also known as Hekaton, was the most important feature introduced with SQL Server 2014, and *Chapter 7, In-Memory OLTP*, covers how this new technology can help you to develop high-performance applications. In-memory OLTP is, in fact, a new database engine whose main features include optimized tables and indexes for main memory data access, stored procedures compiled to native code, and the elimination of locks and latches.

Query optimization is a relatively expensive operation, so if plans can be cached and reused, this optimization cost can be avoided. How plan caching works and why it is extremely important for the performance of your queries and SQL Server in general are covered in *Chapter 8, Understanding Plan Caching*.

Chapter 9, The Query Store, showcases the Query Store, a feature introduced with SQL Server 2016, which allows you to troubleshoot queries and execution plan-related issues and monitor performance history. The query store collects information about queries, plans, and runtime statistics, helping you pinpoint performance differences by changes in execution plans.

Intelligent query processing is a family of features whose purpose is to improve the performance of existing queries with no application changes or minimal implementation effort. Introduced with SQL Server 2017, it had more features added with each new release, including six in SQL Server 2022. This family of features is covered in *Chapter 10, Intelligent Query Processing.*

Chapter 11, An Introduction to Data Warehouses, is, as its name suggests, an introduction to data warehouses, and explains how the SQL Server Query Optimizer can identify fact and dimension tables and can optimize star join queries. The chapter also covers columnstore indexes, a feature introduced with SQL Server 2012, which is based on columnar storage and new batch processing algorithms that can improve the performance of star join queries by several orders of magnitude.

The last chapter of the book, *Chapter 12, Understanding Query Hints*, discusses the challenges the SQL Server processor still faces today after more than four decades of query optimization research. Recommendations and workarounds for complex queries for which the query optimizer may not be able to provide efficient plans are provided. Finally, hints, which must be used with caution and only as a last resort when no other option is available, are introduced as a way to take explicit control over the execution plan for a given query.

Download the example code files

We also have other code bundles from our rich catalog of books and videos available at https://github.com/PacktPublishing/. Check them out!

Download the color images

We also provide a PDF file that has color images of the screenshots and diagrams used in this book. You can download it here: https://packt.link/06NGV.

Conventions used

There are a number of text conventions used throughout this book.

Code in text: Indicates code words in text, database table names, folder names, filenames, file extensions, pathnames, dummy URLs, user input, and Twitter handles. Here is an example: "Then, it updates any outdated statistics, except in cases where the AUTO_UPDATE_STATISTICS_ASYNC configuration option is used."

A block of code is set as follows:

```
SELECT map_key, map_value FROM sys.dm_xe_map_values
WHERE name = 'statement_recompile_cause'
```

When we wish to draw your attention to a particular part of a code block, the relevant lines or items are set in bold:

```
CREATE OR ALTER PROCEDURE test (@pid int)
AS
SELECT * FROM Sales.SalesOrderDetail
WHERE ProductID = @pid
```

Bold: Indicates a new term, an important word, or words that you see onscreen. For instance, words in menus or dialog boxes appear in **bold**. Here is an example: "You can find the following entry close to the end of the XML plan (or the **Parameter List** property in a graphical plan)."

> **Tips or Important Notes**
> Appear like this.

Get in touch

Feedback from our readers is always welcome.

General feedback: If you have questions about any aspect of this book, email us at customercare@packtpub.com and mention the book title in the subject of your message.

Errata: Although we have taken every care to ensure the accuracy of our content, mistakes do happen. If you have found a mistake in this book, we would be grateful if you would report this to us. Please visit www.packtpub.com/support/errata and fill in the form.

Piracy: If you come across any illegal copies of our works in any form on the internet, we would be grateful if you would provide us with the location address or website name. Please contact us at copyright@packt.com with a link to the material.

If you are interested in becoming an author: If there is a topic that you have expertise in and you are interested in either writing or contributing to a book, please visit authors.packtpub.com.

Share Your Thoughts

Once you've read *SQL Server Query Tuning and Optimization*, we'd love to hear your thoughts! Scan the QR code below to go straight to the Amazon review page for this book and share your feedback.

https://packt.link/r/1-803-24262-0

Your review is important to us and the tech community and will help us make sure we're delivering excellent quality content.

1

An Introduction to Query Tuning and Optimization

We have all been there; suddenly, you get a phone call notifying you of an application outage and asking you to urgently join a conference bridge. After joining the call, you are told that the application is so slow that the company is not able to conduct business; it is losing money and, potentially, customers too. And many times, nobody on the call can provide any additional information that can help you find out what the problem is. So, what you should do? Where do you start? And perhaps more important, how do you avoid these problems from reoccurring in the future?

Although an outage can occur for several different reasons, including a hardware failure or an operating system problem, as a database professional, you should be able to proactively tune and optimize your databases and be ready to quickly troubleshoot any problem that may eventually occur. This book will provide you with the knowledge and tools required to do just that. By focusing on SQL Server performance, and more specifically on query tuning and optimization, this book can help you, first, to avoid these performance problems by optimizing your databases and, second, to quickly troubleshoot and fix them if they happen to appear.

One of the best ways to learn how to improve the performance of your databases is not only to work with the technology, but to understand how the technology works, what it can do for you, how to get the most benefit out of it, and even what its limitations are. The most important SQL Server component that impacts the performance of your queries is the SQL Server query processor, which includes the query optimizer and the execution engine. With a perfect query optimizer, you could just submit any query and you would get a perfect execution plan every time. And with a perfect execution engine, each of your queries would run in just a matter of milliseconds. But the reality is that query optimization is a very complex problem, and no query optimizer can find the best plan all the time – at least, not in a reasonable amount of time. For complex queries, there are so many possible execution plans a query optimizer would need to analyze. And even supposing that a query optimizer could analyze all the possible solutions, the next challenge would be to decide which plan to choose. Which one is the most efficient? Choosing the best plan would require estimating the cost of each solution, which, again, is a very complicated task.

Don't get me wrong: the SQL Server query optimizer does an amazing job and gives you a good execution plan almost all the time. But you still need to understand which information you need to provide to the query optimizer so that it can do a good job, which may include providing the right indexes and adequate statistics, as well as defining the required constraints and a good database design. SQL Server even provides you with tools to help you in some of these areas, including the **Database Engine Tuning Advisor** (**DTA**) and the auto-create and auto-update statistics features. But there is still more you can do to improve the performance of your databases, especially when you are building high-performance applications. Finally, you need to understand the cases where the query optimizer may not give you a good execution plan and what to do in those cases.

So, for you to better understand this technology, this chapter will start by providing you with an overview of how the SQL Server query processor works and introducing the concepts that will be covered in more detail in the rest of the book. We will explain the purpose of both the query optimizer and the execution engine and how they may interact with the plan cache so that you can reuse plans as much as possible. Finally, we will learn how to work with execution plans, which are the primary tools we'll use to interact with the query processor.

We will cover the following topics in this chapter:

- Query processor architecture
- Analyzing execution plans
- Getting plans from a trace or the plan cache
- SET STATISTICS TIME and IO statements

Query Processor Architecture

At the core of the SQL Server database engine are two major components:

- **The storage engine**: The storage engine is responsible for reading data between the disk and memory in a manner that optimizes concurrency while maintaining data integrity.
- **The relational engine** (also called the query processor): The query processor, as the name suggests, accepts all queries submitted to SQL Server, devises a plan for their optimal execution, and then executes the plan and delivers the required results.

Queries are submitted to SQL Server using **SQL** or **Structured Query Language** (or T-SQL, the Microsoft SQL Server extension to SQL). Because SQL is a high-level declarative language, it only defines what data to get from the database, not the steps required to retrieve that data or any of the algorithms for processing the request. Thus, for each query it receives, the first job of the query processor is to devise, as quickly as possible, a plan that describes the best possible way (or, at the very least, an efficient way) to execute the query. Its second job is to execute the query according to that plan. Each of these tasks is delegated to a separate component within the query processor. The query optimizer devises the plan and then passes it along to the execution engine, which will execute the plan and get the results from the database.

The SQL Server query optimizer is cost-based. It analyzes several candidate execution plans for a given query, estimates the cost of each of these plans, and selects the plan with the lowest cost of the choices considered. Given that the query optimizer cannot consider every possible plan for every query, it must find a balance between the optimization time and the quality of the selected plan.

Therefore, the query optimizer is the SQL Server component that has the biggest impact on the performance of your databases. After all, selecting the right or wrong execution plan could mean the difference between a query execution time of milliseconds and one that takes minutes or even hours. Naturally, a better understanding of how the query optimizer works can help both database administrators and developers write better queries and provide the query optimizer with the information it needs to produce efficient execution plans. This book will demonstrate how you can use your newfound knowledge of the query optimizer's inner workings; in addition, it will give you the knowledge and tools to troubleshoot the cases when the query optimizer is not giving you a good execution plan.

To arrive at what it believes to be the best plan for executing a query, the query processor performs several different steps; the entire query-processing process is shown in the following diagram:

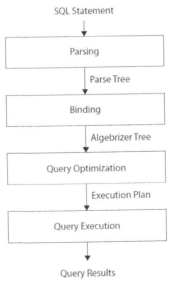

Figure 1.1 – Query processing phases

We will look at this process in more detail in *Chapter 3*, *The Query Optimizer*, but let's just run through the steps briefly now:

1. **Parsing and binding**: The query is parsed and bound. Assuming the query is valid, the output of this phase is a logical tree, with each node in the tree representing a logical operation that the query must perform, such as reading a particular table or performing an inner join.

2. **Query optimization**: The logical tree is then used to run the query optimization process, which roughly consists of the following two steps:

    A. **Generating possible execution plans**: Using the generated logical tree, the query optimizer devises several possible ways to execute the query (that is, several possible execution plans). An execution plan is, in essence, a set of physical operations (such as an Index Seek or a Nested Loop Join) that can be performed to produce the required result, as described by the logical tree.

    B. **Assessing the cost of each plan**: Although the query optimizer does not generate every possible execution plan, it assesses the resource and time cost of each generated plan (or, more exactly, every considered operation). The plan that the query optimizer deems to have the lowest cost is selected and then passed along to the execution engine.

3. **Query execution and plan caching**: The query is executed by the execution engine according to the selected plan; the plan may be stored in memory in the plan cache.

Although the query optimization process will be explained in greater detail in *Chapter 3*, *The Query Optimizer*, let's expand a little bit.

Parsing and binding

Parsing and binding are the first operations that are performed when a query is submitted to a SQL Server instance. Parsing makes sure that the T-SQL query has valid syntax and that it translates the SQL query into an initial tree representation: specifically, a tree of logical operators representing the high-level steps required to execute the query in question. Initially, these logical operators will be closely related to the original syntax of the query and will include such logical operations as *get data from the Customer table*, *get data from the Contact table*, *perform an inner join*, and so on. Different tree representations of the query will be used throughout the optimization process, and the logical tree will receive different names until it is finally used to initialize the Memo structure during the optimization process.

Binding is mostly concerned with name resolution. During the binding operation, SQL Server makes sure that all the object names do exist, and it associates every table and column name on the parse tree with its corresponding object in the system catalog. The output of this second process is called an **algebrizer tree**, which is then sent to the query optimizer to be optimized.

Query optimization

The next step is the optimization process, which involves generating candidate execution plans and selecting the best of these plans according to their cost. As mentioned previously, the SQL Server query optimizer uses a cost-estimation model to estimate the cost of each of the candidate plans.

Query optimization could be also seen, in a simplistic way, as the process of mapping the logical query operations expressed in the original tree representation to physical operations, which can be carried out by the execution engine. So, it's the functionality of the execution engine that is being implemented in the execution plans being created by the query optimizer; that is, the execution engine implements a certain number of different algorithms, and the query optimizer must choose from these algorithms when formulating its execution plans. It does this by translating the original logical operations into the physical operations that the execution engine is capable of performing. Execution plans show both the logical and physical operations of each operator. Some logical operations, such as sorts, translate into the same physical operation, whereas other logical operations map to several possible physical operations. For example, a logical join can be mapped to a Nested Loop Join, Merge Join, or Hash Join physical operator. However, this is not as simple as a one-to-one operator matching and follows a more complicated process, based on transformation rules, which will be explained in more detail in *Chapter 3, The Query Optimizer*.

Thus, the final product of the query optimization process is an execution plan: a tree consisting of several physical operators, which contain a selection of algorithms to be performed by the execution engine to obtain the desired results from the database.

Generating candidate execution plans

As stated previously, the basic purpose of the query optimizer is to find an efficient execution plan for your query. Even for relatively simple queries, there may be a large number of different ways to access the data to produce the same result. As such, the query optimizer must select the best possible plan from what may be a very large number of candidate execution plans. Making a wise choice is important because the time taken to return the results to the user can vary wildly, depending on which plan is selected.

The job of the query optimizer is to create and assess as many candidate execution plans as possible, within certain criteria, to find a good enough plan, which may be (but is not necessarily) the optimal plan. We define the search space for a given query as the set of all possible execution plans for that query, in which any possible plan in this search space returns the same results. Theoretically, to find the optimum execution plan for a query, a cost-based query optimizer should generate all possible execution plans that exist in that search space and correctly estimate the cost of each plan. However, some complex queries may have thousands, or even millions, of possible execution plans, and although the SQL Server query optimizer can typically consider a large number of candidate execution plans, it cannot perform an exhaustive search of all the possible plans for every query. If it did, the time taken to assess all of the plans would be unacceptably long and could start to have a major impact on the overall query execution time.

The query optimizer must strike a balance between optimization time and plan quality. For example, if the query optimizer spends 100 milliseconds finding a good enough plan that executes in 5 seconds, then it doesn't make sense to try to find the perfect or most optimal plan if it is going to take 1 minute of optimization time, plus the execution time. So, SQL Server does not do an exhaustive search. Instead, it tries to find a suitably efficient plan as quickly as possible. As the query optimizer is working within a time constraint, there's a chance that the selected plan may be the optimal plan, but it is also likely that it may just be something close to the optimal plan.

To explore the search space, the query optimizer uses transformation rules and heuristics. Candidate execution plans are generated inside the query optimizer using transformation rules, and the use of heuristics limits the number of choices considered to keep the optimization time reasonable. The set of alternative plans that's considered by the query optimizer is referred to as the plan space, and these plans are stored in memory during the optimization process in a component called the Memo. Transformation rules, heuristics, and the Memo component's structure will be discussed in more detail in *Chapter 3, The Query Optimizer*.

Plan cost evaluation

Searching or enumerating candidate plans is just one part of the optimization process. The query optimizer still needs to estimate the cost of these plans and select the least expensive one. To estimate the cost of a plan, it estimates the cost of each physical operator in that plan, using costing formulas that consider the use of resources such as I/O, CPU, and memory. This cost estimation depends mostly on both the algorithm used by the physical operator and the estimated number of records that will need to be processed. This estimate is known as the cardinality estimation.

To help with this cardinality estimation, SQL Server uses and maintains query optimization statistics, which contain information describing the distribution of values in one or more columns of a table. Once the cost for each operator is estimated using estimations of cardinality and resource demands, the query optimizer will add up all of these costs to estimate the cost for the entire plan. Rather than go into more detail here, we will cover statistics and cost estimation in more detail in *Chapter 6, Understanding Statistics*.

Query execution and plan caching

Once the query has been optimized, the resulting plan is used by the execution engine to retrieve the desired data. The generated execution plan may be stored in memory in the plan cache so that it can be reused if the same query is executed again. SQL Server has a pool of memory that is used to store both data pages and execution plans, among other objects. Most of this memory is used to store database pages, and it is called the buffer pool. A smaller portion of this memory contains the execution plans for queries that were optimized by the query optimizer and is referred to as the plan cache (previously known as the procedure cache). The percentage of memory that's allocated to the plan cache or the buffer pool varies dynamically, depending on the state of the system.

Before optimizing a query, SQL Server first checks the plan cache to see if an execution plan exists for the query or, more exactly, a batch, which may consist of one or more queries. Query optimization is a relatively expensive operation, so if a valid plan is available in the plan cache, the optimization process can be skipped and the associated cost of this step, in terms of optimization time, CPU resources, and so on, can be avoided. If a plan for the batch is not found, the batch is compiled to generate an execution plan for all the queries in the stored procedure, the trigger, or the dynamic SQL batch. Query optimization begins by loading all the interesting statistics. Then, the query optimizer validates if the statistics are outdated. For any outdated statistics, when using the statistics default options, it will update the statistics and proceed with the optimization process.

Once a plan has been found in the plan cache or a new one is created, the plan is validated for schema and data statistics changes. Schema changes are verified for plan correctness. Statistics are also verified: the query optimizer checks for new applicable statistics or outdated statistics. If the plan is not valid for any of these reasons, it is discarded, and the batch or individual query is compiled again. Such compilations are known as **recompilations**. This process is summarized in the following diagram:

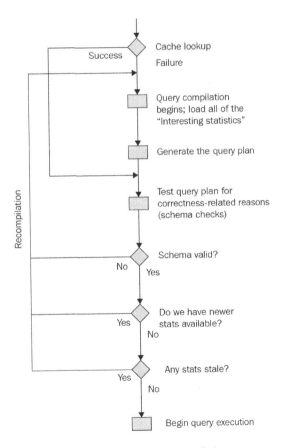

Figure 1.2 – Compilation and recompilation process

Query plans may also be removed from the plan cache when SQL Server is under memory pressure or when certain statements are executed. Changing some configuration options (for example, max degree of parallelism) will clear the entire plan cache. Alternatively, some statements, such as changing the database configuration with certain ALTER DATABASE options, will clear all the plans associated with that particular database.

However, it is also worth noting that reusing an existing plan may not always be the best solution for every instance of a given query, and as a result, some performance problems may appear. For example, depending on the data distribution within a table, the optimal execution plan for a query may differ greatly, depending on the parameters being used to get data from such table. More details about these problems, parameter sniffing, and the plan cache, in general, will be covered in greater detail in *Chapter 8*, Understanding *Plan Caching*.

Now that we have a foundation for the query processor architecture, let's learn how to interact with it using execution plans.

> **Note**
>
> Parameter-sensitive plan optimization, a new feature with SQL Server 2022, will also be covered in *Chapter 8*, Understanding *Plan Caching*.

Analyzing execution plans

Primarily, we'll interact with the query processor through execution plans, which, as mentioned earlier, are ultimately trees consisting of several physical operators that, in turn, contain the algorithms to produce the required results from the database. Given that we will make extensive use of execution plans throughout this book, in this section, we will learn how to display and read them.

You can request either an actual or an estimated execution plan for a given query, and either of these two types can be displayed as a graphic, text, or XML plan. Any of these three formats show the same execution plan – the only difference is how they are displayed and the level of detail they contain.

When an estimated plan is requested, the query is not executed; the plan that's displayed is simply the plan that SQL Server would most probably use if the query were executed, bearing in mind that a recompile, which we'll discuss later, may generate a different plan at execution time. However, when an actual plan is requested, you need to execute the query so that the plan is displayed along with the query results. Nevertheless, using an estimated plan has several benefits, including displaying a plan for a long-running query for inspection without actually running the query, or displaying a plan for update operations without changing the database.

> **Note**
>
> Starting with SQL Server 2014 but using SQL Server Management Studio 2016 (version 13 or later), you can also use Live Query Statistics to view the live execution plan of an active query. Live Query Statistics will be covered in *Chapter 9, The Query Store*.

Graphical plans

You can display graphical plans in SQL Server Management Studio by clicking the **Display Estimated Execution Plan** button or the **Include Actual Execution Plan** button from the **SQL Editor** toolbar. Clicking **Display Estimated Execution Plan** will show the plan immediately, without executing the query. To request an actual execution plan, you need to click **Include Actual Execution Plan** and then execute the query and click the **Execution plan** tab.

As an example, copy the following query to Management Studio Query Editor, select the AdventureWorks2019 database, click the **Include Actual Execution Plan** button, and execute the following query:

```
SELECT DISTINCT(City) FROM Person.Address
```

Then, select the **Execution Plan** tab in the results pane. This will display the plan shown here:

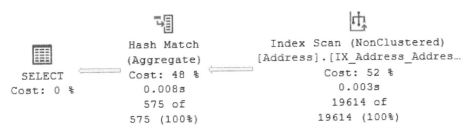

Figure 1.3 – Graphical execution plan

> **Note**
>
> This book contains a large number of sample SQL queries, all of which are based on the AdventureWorks2019 database, although *Chapter 11, An Introduction to Data Warehouses*, additionally uses the AdventureWorksDW2019 database. All code has been tested on SQL Server 2022 CTP (community technology preview) 2.0. Note that these sample databases are not included in your SQL Server installation but instead can be downloaded from https://docs.microsoft.com/en-us/sql/samples/adventureworks-install-configure. You need to download the family of sample databases for SQL Server 2019.

> **Note**
>
> Although you could run the examples in this book using any recent version of SQL Server Management Studio, it is strongly recommended to use version 19.0 or later to work with SQL Server 2022. Although SQL Server Management Studio is not available on a SQL Server installation and must be downloaded separately, every SQL Server version requires a specific version of SQL Server Management Studio. For example, v19.0 must be added, among other things, if you wish to support Contained Always On Availability Groups or the latest showplan XML schema. This book uses SQL Server Management Studio v19.0 Preview 2.

Each node in the tree structure is represented as an icon that specifies a logical and physical operator, such as the Index Scan and the Hash Aggregate operators, as shown in *Figure 1.3*. The first icon is a language element called the Result operator, which represents the `SELECT` statement and is usually the root element in the plan.

Operators implement a basic function or operation of the execution engine; for example, a logical join operation could be implemented by any of three different physical join operators: Nested Loop Join, Merge Join, or Hash Join. Many more operators are implemented in the execution engine. You can find the entire list at `http://msdn.microsoft.com/en-us/library/ms191158(v=sql.110).aspx`.

The query optimizer builds an execution plan and chooses which operations may read records from the database, such as the Index Scan operator shown in the previous plan. Alternatively, it may read records from another operator, such as the Hash Aggregate operator, which reads records from the Index Scan operator.

Each node in the plan is related to a parent node, connected with arrowheads, where data flows from a child operator to a parent operator and the arrow width is proportional to the number of rows. After the operator performs some function on the records it has read, the results are output to its parent. You can hover your mouse pointer over an arrow to get more information about that data flow, which is displayed as a tooltip. For example, if you hover your mouse pointer over the arrow between the Index Scan and Hash Aggregate operators, shown in *Figure 1.3*, you will get the data flow information between these operators, as shown here:

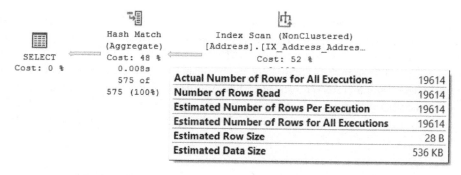

Figure 1.4 – Data flow between the Index Scan and Hash Aggregate operators

By looking at the actual number of rows, you can see that the Index Scan operator is reading 19,614 rows from the database and sending them to the Hash Aggregate operator. The Hash Aggregate operator is, in turn, performing some operation on this data and sending 575 records to its parent, which you can also see by placing your mouse pointer over the arrow between the Hash Aggregate operator and the **SELECT** icon.

Basically, in this plan, the Index Scan operator is reading all 19,614 rows from an index, and the Hash Aggregate operator is processing these rows to obtain the list of distinct cities, of which there are 575, which will be displayed in the **Results** window in Management Studio. Also, notice how you can see the estimated number of rows, which is the query optimizer's cardinality estimation for this operator, as well as the actual number of rows. Comparing the actual and the estimated number of rows can help you detect cardinality estimation errors, which can affect the quality of your execution plans, as will be discussed in *Chapter 6, Understanding Statistics*.

To perform their job, physical operators implement at least the following three methods:

- `Open()` causes an operator to be initialized and may include setting up any required data structures.

- `GetRow()` requests a row from the operator.

- `Close()` performs some cleanup operations and shuts down the operator once it has performed its role.

An operator requests rows from other operators by calling its `GetRow()` method, which also means that execution in a plan starts from left to right. Because `GetRow()` produces just one row at a time, the actual number of rows that's displayed in the execution plan is also the number of times the method was called on a specific operator, plus an additional call to `GetRow()`, which is used by the operator to indicate the end of the result set. In the previous example, the Hash Aggregate operator calls the `Open()` method once, the `GetRow()` operator 19,615 times, and the `Close()` operator once on the Index Scan operator.

> **Note**
>
> For now, and for most of this book, we will be explaining the traditional query-processing mode in which operators process only one row at a time. This processing mode has been used in all versions of SQL Server, at least since SQL Server 7.0, when the current query optimizer was built and released. Later, in *Chapter 11, An Introduction to Data Warehouses*, we will touch on the new batch-processing mode, introduced with SQL Server 2012, in which operators process multiple rows at a time and it is used by operators related to the `columnstore` indexes.

In addition to learning more about the data flow, you can also hover your mouse pointer over an operator to get more information about it. For example, the following screenshot shows information about the Index Scan operator; notice that it includes, among other things, a description of the operator and data on estimated costing information, such as the estimated I/O, CPU, operator, and subtree costs:

Index Scan (NonClustered)	
Scan a nonclustered index, entirely or only a range.	
Physical Operation	Index Scan
Logical Operation	Index Scan
Actual Execution Mode	Row
Estimated Execution Mode	Row
Storage	RowStore
Number of Rows Read	19614
Actual Number of Rows for All Executions	19614
Actual Number of Batches	0
Estimated I/O Cost	0.158681
Estimated Operator Cost	0.180413 (52%)
Estimated CPU Cost	0.0217324
Estimated Subtree Cost	0.180413
Number of Executions	1
Estimated Number of Executions	1
Estimated Number of Rows for All Executions	19614
Estimated Number of Rows Per Execution	19614
Estimated Number of Rows to be Read	19614
Estimated Row Size	28 B
Actual Rebinds	0
Actual Rewinds	0
Ordered	False
Node ID	1

Object
[AdventureWorks2019].[Person].[Address].
[IX_Address_AddressLine1_AddressLine2_City_StateProvinceID_Post
alCode]
Output List
[AdventureWorks2019].[Person].[Address].City

Figure 1.5 – Tooltip for the Index Scan operator

Some of these properties are explained in the following table; others will be explained later in this book:

Property	Description
Physical Operation	Physical implementation algorithm for the node.
Logical Operation	Relational algebraic operator this node represents.
Actual Number of Rows	The actual number of rows produced by the operator.
Estimated I/O Cost	Estimated I/O cost for the operation. Not all operators incur an I/O cost.
Estimated Operator Cost	The query optimizer–estimated cost for executing this operation. This is the estimated I/O and CPU cost. It also includes the cost of operation as a percentage of the total cost of the query displayed in parentheses.
Estimated Subtree Cost	Estimated cumulative cost for executing this operation and all operations preceding it in the same subtree.
Estimated CPU Cost	Estimated CPU cost for the operation.
Estimated Number of Executions	Estimated number of times this operator will be executed while running the current query.
Number of Executions	Number of times this operator was executed after running the query.
Estimated Number of Rows	Estimated number of rows produced by the operator (cardinality estimate).
Estimated Row Size	Estimated average size of the row being passed through this operator.

Table 1.1 – Operator properties

Note

It is worth mentioning that the cost included in these operations is just internal cost units that are not meant to be interpreted in other units, such as seconds or milliseconds. *Chapter 3, The Query Optimizer*, explains the origin of these cost units.

You can also see the relative cost of each operator in the plan as a percentage of the overall plan, as shown previously in *Figure 1.3*. For example, the cost of the Index Scan operator is 52 percent of the cost of the entire plan. Additional information from an operator or the entire query can be obtained by using the **Properties** window. So, for example, choosing the **SELECT** icon and selecting the **Properties** window from the **View** menu (or pressing *F4*) will show some properties for the entire query, as shown in the following screenshot:

Figure 1.6 – The Properties window for the query

The following table lists the most important properties of a plan, most of which are shown in the preceding screenshot. Some other properties may be available, depending on the query (for example, **Parameter List**, **MissingIndexes**, or **Warnings**):

Property	Description
Cached plan size	Plan cache memory in kilobytes used by this query plan.
CompileCPU	CPU time in milliseconds used to compile this query.
CompileMemory	Memory in kilobytes used to compile this query.
CompileTime	Elapsed time in milliseconds used to compile this query.
Degree of Parallelism	Number of threads that can be used to execute the query, should the query processor pick a parallel plan.
Memory Grant	Amount of memory in kilobytes granted to run this query.
MemoryGrantInfo	Memory grant estimate, as well as actual runtime memory grant information.
Optimization Level	Level of optimization used to compile this query. This is shown as StatementOptmLevel on the XML plan. This will be explained in more detail later in this section.
OptimizerHardwareDependentProperties	Hardware-dependent properties that affect the cost estimate (and hence, query plan choice), as seen by the query optimizer.
QueryHash	Binary hash value calculated on the query and used to identify queries with similar logic.
QueryPlanHash	Binary hash value calculated on the query execution plan and used to identify similar query execution plans.

Property	Description
Reason For Early Termination Of Statement Optimization	Shown as StatementOptmEarlyAbortReason on the XML plan. This will be explained in more detail later in this section.
RetrievedFromCache	Indicates if the plan was retrieved from the cache.
Set Options	Shows the status of the set options that affect query cost. These are shown as StatementSetOptions on the XML plan. These SET options are ANSI_NULLS, ANSI_PADDING, ANSI_WARNINGS, ARITHABORT, CONCAT_NULL_YIELDS_NULL, NUMERIC_ROUNDABORT, and QUOTED_IDENTIFIER.
CardinalityEstimationModelVersion	A version of the cardinality estimator used for optimization.
NonParallelPlanReason	The reason a parallel plan may not be chosen for the optimized query.
OptimizerStatsUsage	Statistics used by the query optimizer to produce an execution plan.
QueryTimeStats	Query time statistics. More details about the QueryTimeStats property and SET STATISTICS TIME will be provided later in this chapter.
MissingIndexes	Missing indexes information.
WaitStats	Wait for statistics information.
TraceFlags	Trace flags enabled during query optimization and execution.
Statement	Text of the SQL statement.

Table 1.2 – Query properties

XML plans

Once you have displayed a graphical plan, you can also easily display it in XML format. Simply right-click anywhere on the execution plan window to display a pop-up menu, as shown in *Figure 1.7*, and select **Show Execution Plan XML…**. This will open the XML editor and display the XML plan. As you can see, you can easily switch between a graphical and an XML plan.

If needed, you can save graphical plans to a file by selecting **Save Execution Plan As…** from the pop-up menu shown in *Figure 1.6*. The plan, usually saved with a `.sqlplan` extension, is an XML document containing the XML plan but can be read by Management Studio into a graphical plan. You can load this file again by selecting **File** and then **Open in Management Studio** to immediately display it as a graphical plan, which will behave exactly as it did previously. XML plans can also be used with the USEPLAN query hint, which will be explained in *Chapter 12, Understanding Query Hints*:

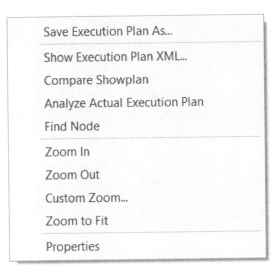

Figure 1.7 – Pop-up menu on the execution plan window

The following table shows the different statements you can use to obtain an estimated or actual execution plan in text, graphic, or XML format:

	Estimated Execution Plan	**Actual Execution Plan**
Text Plan	`SET SHOWPLAN_TEXT   SET SHOWPLAN_ALL`	`SET STATISTICS PROFILE`
Graphic Plan	Management Studio	Management Studio
XML Plan	`SET SHOWPLAN_XML`	`SET STATISTICS XML`

Table 1.3 – Statements for displaying query plans

> **NOTE**
> When you run any of the statements listed in the preceding screenshot using the ON clause, it will apply to all subsequent statements until the option is manually set to OFF again.

To show an XML plan, you can use the following commands:

```
SET SHOWPLAN_XML ON
GO
SELECT DISTINCT(City) FROM Person.Address
GO
SET SHOWPLAN_XML OFF
```

This will display a single-row, single-column (titled Microsoft SQL Server 2005 XML Showplan) result set containing the XML data that starts with the following:

```
<ShowPlanXML xmlns="http://schemas.microsoft.com/sqlserver/2004
...
```

Clicking the link will show you a graphical plan. Then, you can display the XML plan by following the same procedure explained earlier.

You can browse the basic structure of an XML plan via the following exercise. A very simple query can create the basic XML structure, but in this example, we will see a query that can provide two additional parts: the missing indexes and parameter list elements. Run the following query and request an XML plan:

```
SELECT * FROM Sales.SalesOrderDetail
WHERE OrderQty = 1
```

Collapse `<MissingIndexes>`, `<OptimizerStatsUsage>`, `<RelOp>`, `<WaisStats>`, and `<ParameterList>` by clicking the minus sign (-) on the left so that you can easily see the entire structure. You should see something similar to the following:

```
<?xml version="1.0" encoding="utf-16"?>
<ShowPlanXML xmlns:xsi="http://www.w3.org/2001/XMLSchema-instance" xmlns:xsd="http://www.w3.org/2001/XMLSchema"
  <BatchSequence>
    <Batch>
      <Statements>
        <StmtSimple StatementCompId="1" StatementEstRows="348.306" StatementId="1" StatementOptmLevel="FULL" Car
          <StatementSetOptions ANSI_NULLS="true" ANSI_PADDING="true" ANSI_WARNINGS="true" ARITHABORT="true" CONC
          <QueryPlan DegreeOfParallelism="1" CachedPlanSize="32" CompileTime="6" CompileCPU="5" CompileMemory="2
            <MissingIndexes>...</MissingIndexes>
            <MemoryGrantInfo SerialRequiredMemory="0" SerialDesiredMemory="0" GrantedMemory="0" MaxUsedMemory="0
            <OptimizerHardwareDependentProperties EstimatedAvailableMemoryGrant="103269" EstimatedPagesCached="5
            <OptimizerStatsUsage>...</OptimizerStatsUsage>
            <WaitStats>...</WaitStats>
            <QueryTimeStats CpuTime="104" ElapsedTime="603" />
            <RelOp AvgRowSize="112" EstimateCPU="0.0582322" EstimateIO="0" EstimateRebinds="0" EstimateRewinds="
            <ParameterList>...</ParameterList>
          </QueryPlan>
        </StmtSimple>
      </Statements>
    </Batch>
  </BatchSequence>
</ShowPlanXML>
```

Figure 1.8 – XML execution plan

As you can see, the main components of the XML plan are the `<StmtSimple>`, `<StatementSetOptions>`, and `<QueryPlan>` elements. These three elements include several attributes, some of which were already explained when we discussed the graphical plan. In addition, the `<QueryPlan>` element also includes other elements, such as `<MissingIndexes>`, `<MemoryGrantInfo>`, `<OptimizerHardwareDependentProperties>`, `<RelOp>`, `<ParameterList>`, and others not shown in *Figure 1.8*, such as `<Warnings>`, which will be also discussed later in this section. `<StmtSimple>` shows the following for this example:

```
<StmtSimple StatementCompId="1" StatementEstRows="68089"
StatementId="1"
StatementOptmLevel="FULL"
CardinalityEstimationModelVersion="70"
StatementSubTreeCost="1.13478" StatementText="SELECT * FROM
[Sales].[SalesOrderDetail] WHERE [OrderQty]=@1"
StatementType="SELECT"
QueryHash="0x42CFD97ABC9592DD"
QueryPlanHash="0xC5F6C30459CD7C41"
RetrievedFromCache="false">
```

`<QueryPlan>` shows the following:

```
<QueryPlan DegreeOfParallelism="1" CachedPlanSize="32"
CompileTime="3"
CompileCPU="3" CompileMemory="264">
```

As mentioned previously, the attributes of these and other elements were already explained when we discussed the graphical plan. Others will be explained later in this section or in other sections of this book.

Text plans

As shown in *Table 1.3*, there are two commands to get estimated text plans: SET SHOWPLAN_TEXT and SET SHOWPLAN_ALL. Both statements show the estimated execution plan, but SET SHOWPLAN_ALL shows some additional information, including the estimated number of rows, estimated CPU cost, estimated I/O cost, and estimated operator cost. However, recent versions of the documentation indicate that all text versions of execution plans will be deprecated in a future version of SQL Server, so it is recommended that you use the XML versions instead.

You can use the following code to display a text execution plan:

```
SET SHOWPLAN_TEXT ON
GO
```

```
SELECT DISTINCT(City) FROM Person.Address
GO
SET SHOWPLAN_TEXT OFF
GO
```

This code will display two result sets, with the first one returning the text of the T-SQL statement. In the second result set, you will see the following text plan (edited to fit the page), which shows the same Hash Aggregate and Index Scan operators displayed earlier in *Figure 1.3*:

```
|--Hash Match(Aggregate, HASH:([Person].[Address].[City]),
RESIDUAL …
    |--Index Scan(OBJECT:([AdventureWorks].[Person].[Address]. [IX_
Address …
```

SET SHOWPLAN_ALL and SET STATISTICS PROFILE can provide more detailed information than SET SHOWPLAN_TEXT. Also, as shown in *Table 1.3*, you can use SET SHOWPLAN_ALL to get an estimated plan only and SET STATISTICS PROFILE to execute the query. Run the following example:

```
SET SHOWPLAN_ALL ON
GO
SELECT DISTINCT(City) FROM Person.Address
GO
SET SHOWPLAN_ALL OFF
GO
```

The output is shown in the following screenshot:

	StmtText	StmtId	NodeId	Parent	PhysicalOp	LogicalOp
1	SELECT DISTINCT(City) FROM Person.Address	1	1	0	NULL	NULL
2	|--Hash Match(Aggregate, HASH:([AdventureWorks2...	1	2	1	Hash Match	Aggregate
3	|--Index Scan(OBJECT:([AdventureWorks2019].[P...	1	3	2	Index Scan	Index Scan

Figure 1.9 – SET SHOWPLAN_ALL output

Because SET STATISTICS PROFILE executes the query, it provides an easy way to look for cardinality estimation problems because you can easily visually compare multiple operators at a time, which could be complicated to do on a graphical or XML plan. Now, run the following code:

```
SET STATISTICS PROFILE ON
GO
```

```
SELECT * FROM Sales.SalesOrderDetail
WHERE OrderQty * UnitPrice > 25000
GO
SET STATISTICS PROFILE OFF
```

The output is shown in the following screenshot:

	Rows	EstimateRows	Executes	StmtText
1	5	36395.1	1	SELECT * FROM [Sales].[SalesOrderDetail] WHERE [OrderQty]*[UnitPrice]>@1
2	5	36395.1	1	|--Filter(WHERE:([Expr1003]>($25000.0000)))
3	0	121317	0	|--Compute Scalar(DEFINE:([AdventureWorks2019].[Sales].[SalesOrderDetail].[LineTotal]=[A
4	0	121317	0	|--Compute Scalar(DEFINE:([AdventureWorks2019].[Sales].[SalesOrderDetail].[LineTotal]
5	121317	121317	1	|--Clustered Index Scan(OBJECT:([AdventureWorks2019].[Sales].[SalesOrderDetail].[P

Figure 1.10 – SET STATISTICS PROFILE output

Note that the EstimateRows column was manually moved in Management Studio to be next to the column rows so that you can easily compare the actual against the estimated number of rows. For this particular example, you can see a big difference in cardinality estimation on the Filter operator of 36,395.1 estimated versus five actual rows.

Plan properties

One interesting way to learn about the components of an execution plan, including ones of future versions of SQL Server, is to look at the showplan schema. XML plans comply with a published XSD schema, and you can see the current and older versions of this showplan schema at http://schemas.microsoft.com/sqlserver/2004/07/showplan/. You can also find the address or URL at the beginning of each XML execution plan. At the time of writing, accessing that location on a web browser will show you links where you can access the showplan schemas for all the versions of SQL Server since version 2005 (when XML plans were introduced), as shown in the following screenshot. As you can see, a new showplan schema is introduced with every new release and, in some cases, with a new Service Pack.

The only exception could be SQL Server 2008 R2, which even when it is a new version, shares the same schema as SQL Server 2008. A showplan schema for SQL Server 2022 hasn't been published at the time of writing:

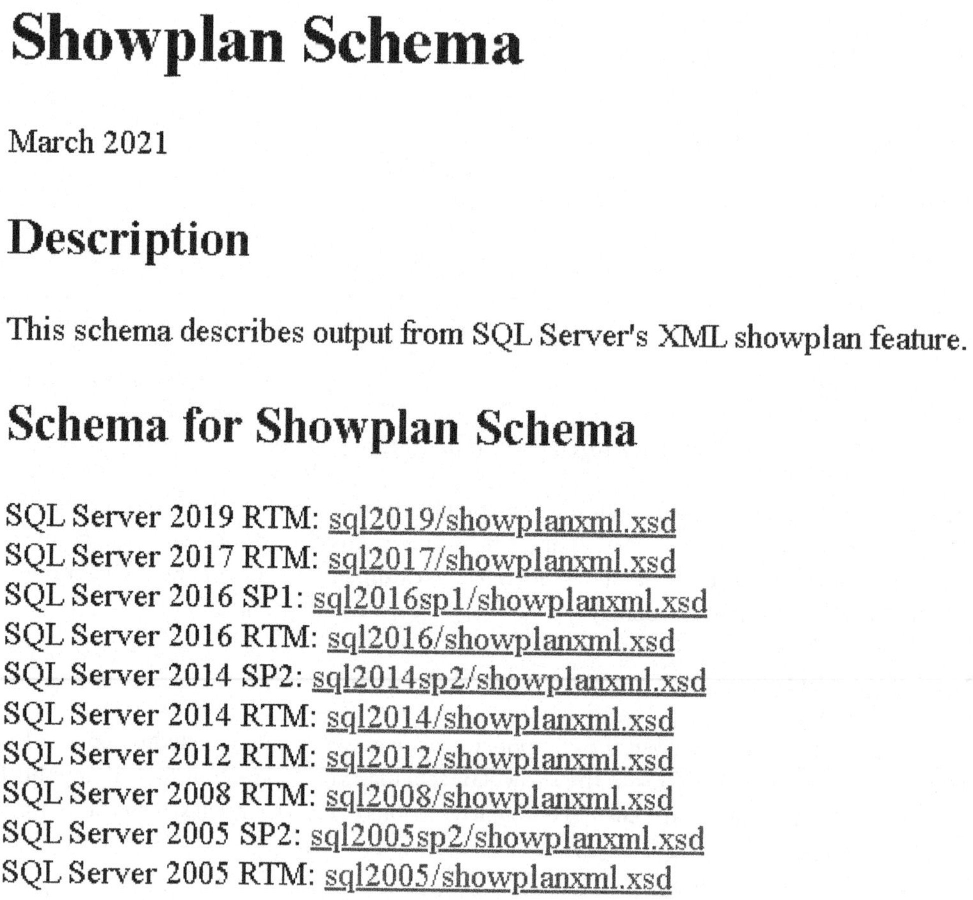

Showplan Schema

March 2021

Description

This schema describes output from SQL Server's XML showplan feature.

Schema for Showplan Schema

SQL Server 2019 RTM: sql2019/showplanxml.xsd
SQL Server 2017 RTM: sql2017/showplanxml.xsd
SQL Server 2016 SP1: sql2016sp1/showplanxml.xsd
SQL Server 2016 RTM: sql2016/showplanxml.xsd
SQL Server 2014 SP2: sql2014sp2/showplanxml.xsd
SQL Server 2014 RTM: sql2014/showplanxml.xsd
SQL Server 2012 RTM: sql2012/showplanxml.xsd
SQL Server 2008 RTM: sql2008/showplanxml.xsd
SQL Server 2005 SP2: sql2005sp2/showplanxml.xsd
SQL Server 2005 RTM: sql2005/showplanxml.xsd

Figure 1.11 – Showplan schema available definitions

Covering all the elements and attributes of an execution plan would take a lot of pages; instead, we will only cover some of the most interesting ones here. *Table 1.2* includes descriptions of query properties. We will use this section to describe some of those properties in more detail.

You can see all these properties, as mentioned earlier, by choosing the **SELECT** icon on a graphical plan and selecting the **Properties** window from the **View** menu. An example of the properties of a query was shown earlier in *Figure 1.6*. The most common operators that are used in execution plans will be covered in more detail in *Chapter 4, The Execution Engine*.

StatementOptmLevel

Although these attributes refer to concepts that will be explained in more detail later in this book, it's worth introducing them here. StatementOptmLevel is the query optimization level, which can be either TRIVIAL or FULL. The optimization process may be expensive to initialize and run for very simple queries that don't require any cost estimation, so to avoid this expensive operation for these simple queries, SQL Server uses the trivial plan optimization. If a query does not apply for a trivial optimization, a full optimization will have to be performed. For example, in SQL Server 2019, the following query will produce a trivial plan:

```
SELECT * FROM Sales.SalesOrderHeader
WHERE SalesOrderID = 43666
```

You can use the undocumented (and therefore unsupported) trace flag 8757 to test the behavior if you want to disable the trivial plan optimization:

```
SELECT * FROM Sales.SalesOrderHeader
WHERE SalesOrderID = 43666
OPTION (QUERYTRACEON 8757)
```

The QUERYTRACEON query hint is used to apply a trace flag at the query level. After running the previous query, SQL Server will run a full optimization, which you can verify by setting StatementOptmLevel to FULL in the resulting plan. You should note that although the QUERYTRACEON query hint is widely known, at the time of writing, it is only supported in a limited number of scenarios. At the time of writing, the QUERYTRACEON query hint is only supported when using the trace flags documented in the following article: http://support.microsoft.com/kb/2801413.

> **Note**
>
> This book shows many undocumented and unsupported features. This is so that you can use them in a test environment for troubleshooting purposes or to learn how the technology works. However, they are not meant to be used in a production environment and are not supported by Microsoft. We will identify when a statement or trace flag is undocumented and unsupported.

StatementOptmEarlyAbortReason

On the other hand, the StatementOptmEarlyAbortReason, or "Reason For Early Termination Of Statement Optimization," attribute can have the GoodEnoughPlanFound, TimeOut, and MemoryLimitExceeded values and only appears when the query optimizer prematurely terminates a query optimization (in older versions of SQL Server, you had to use undocumented trace flag 8675 to see this information). Because the purpose of the query optimizer is to produce a good enough plan as quickly as possible, the query optimizer calculates two values, depending on the query at the beginning of the optimization process. The first of these values is the cost of a good enough plan according to the query, while the second one is the maximum time to spend on the query optimization. During the optimization process, if a plan with a cost lower than the calculated cost threshold is found, the optimization process stops, and the found plan will be returned with the GoodEnoughPlanFound value. If, on the other hand, the optimization process is taking longer than the calculated maximum time threshold, optimization will also stop and the query optimizer will return the best plan found so far, with StatementOptmEarlyAbortReason containing the TimeOut value. The GoodEnoughPlanFound and TimeOut values do not mean that there is a problem, and in all three cases, including MemoryLimitExceeded, the plan that's produced will be correct. However, in the case of MemoryLimitExceeded, the plan may not be optimal. In this case, you may need to simplify your query or increase the available memory in your system. These and other details of the query optimization process will be covered in *Chapter 3, The Query Optimizer*.

For example, even when the following query may seem complex, it still has an early termination and returns Good Enough Plan Found:

```
SELECT pm.ProductModelID, pm.Name, Description, pl.CultureID,
cl.Name AS Language
FROM Production.ProductModel AS pm
JOIN Production.ProductModelProductDescriptionCulture AS pl
ON pm.ProductModelID = pl.ProductModelID
JOIN Production.Culture AS cl
ON cl.CultureID = pl.CultureID
JOIN Production.ProductDescription AS pd
ON pd.ProductDescriptionID = pl.ProductDescriptionID
ORDER BY pm.ProductModelID
```

CardinalityEstimationModelVersion

The CardinalityEstimationModelVersion attribute refers to the version of the cardinality estimation model that's used by the query optimizer. SQL Server 2014 introduced a new cardinality estimator, but you still have the choice of using the old one by changing the database compatibility level or using trace flags 2312 and 9481. More details about both cardinality estimation models will be covered in *Chapter 6, Understanding Statistics*.

Degree of parallelism

This is the number of threads that can be used to execute the query, should the query processor pick a parallel plan. If a parallel plan is not chosen, even when the query estimated cost is greater than the defined "cost threshold for parallelism," which defaults to 5, an additional attribute, NonParallelPlanReason, will be included. NonParallelPlanReason will be covered next.

Starting with SQL Server 2022, DOP_FEEDBACK, a new database configuration option, automatically identifies parallelism inefficiencies for repeating queries based on elapsed time and waits and lowers the degree of parallelism if parallelism usage is deemed inefficient. The degree of parallelism feedback feature will be covered in more detail in *Chapter 10, Intelligent Query Processing.*

NonParallelPlanReason

The NonParallelPlanReason optional attribute of the QueryPlan element, which was introduced with SQL Server 2012, contains a description of why a parallel plan may not be chosen for the optimized query. Although the list of possible values is not documented, the following are popular and easy to obtain:

```
SELECT * FROM Sales.SalesOrderHeader
WHERE SalesOrderID = 43666
OPTION (MAXDOP 1)
```

Because we are using MAXDOP 1, it will show the following:

```
NonParallelPlanReason="MaxDOPSetToOne"
```

It will use the following function:

```
SELECT CustomerID,('AW' + dbo.ufnLeadingZeros(CustomerID))
AS GenerateAccountNumber
FROM Sales.Customer
ORDER BY CustomerID
```

This will generate the following output:

```
NonParallelPlanReason="CouldNotGenerateValidParallelPlan"
```

Now, let's say you try to run the following code on a system with only one CPU:

```
SELECT * FROM Sales.SalesOrderHeader
WHERE SalesOrderID = 43666
OPTION (MAXDOP 8)
```

You will get the following output:

```
<QueryPlan NonParallelPlanReason="EstimatedDOPIsOne"
```

OptimizerHardwareDependentProperties

Finally, also introduced with SQL Server 2012, the showplan XSD schema has the `OptimizerHardwareDependentProperties` element, which provides hardware-dependent properties that can affect the query plan choice. It has the following documented attributes:

- `EstimatedAvailableMemoryGrant`: An estimate of what amount of memory (KB) will be available for this query at execution time to request a memory grant.

- `EstimatedPagesCached`: An estimate of how many pages of data will remain cached in the buffer pool if the query needs to read it again.

- `EstimatedAvailableDegreeOfParallelism`: An estimate of the number of CPUs that can be used to execute the query, should the query optimizer pick a parallel plan.

For example, take a look at the following query:

```
SELECT DISTINCT(CustomerID)
FROM Sales.SalesOrderHeader
```

This will result in the following output:

```
<OptimizerHardwareDependentProperties
EstimatedAvailableMemoryGrant="101808"
EstimatedPagesCached="8877"
EstimatedAvailableDegreeOfParallelism="2" />
```

OptimizerStatsUsage

Starting with SQL Server 2017 and SQL Server 2016 SP2, it is now possible to identify the statistics that are used by the query optimizer to produce an execution plan. This can help you troubleshoot any cardinality estimation problems or may show you that the statistics size sample may be inadequate, or that the statistics are old.

The `OptimizerStatsUsage` element may contain information about one or more statistics. The following code is from an XML plan and shows the name of the statistics object and some other information, such as the sampling percent, the internal modification counter, and the last time the statistics object was last updated. Statistics will be covered in greater detail in *Chapter 6, Understanding Statistics*:

```
<StatisticsInfo
Database="[AdventureWorks2019]"
Schema="[Production]"
Table="[ProductDescription]"
Statistics="[PK_ProductDescription_ProductDescriptionID]"
```

```
ModificationCount="0"
SamplingPercent="100"
LastUpdate="2017-10-27T14:33:07.32" />
```

QueryTimeStats

This property shows the same information that's returned by the SET STATISTICS TIME statement, which will be explained in more detail at the end of this chapter. Additional statistics are returned if the query contains user-defined functions. In such cases, the UdfCpuTime and UdfElapsedTime elements will also be included, which are the same CPU and elapsed time measured in milliseconds for user-defined functions that are included in the query. These elements can be very useful in cases where you want to see how much performance impact a UDF has on the total execution time and cost of the query.

The following example is also from an XML plan:

```
<QueryTimeStats CpuTime="6" ElapsedTime="90" />
```

MissingIndexes

The MissingIndexes element includes indexes that could be useful for the executed query. During query optimization, the query optimizer defines what the best indexes for a query are and if these indexes do not exist, it will make this information available on the execution plan. In addition, SQL Server Management Studio can show you a missing index warning when you request a graphical plan and even show you the syntax to create such indexes.

Alternatively, SQL Server will aggregate the missing indexes information since SQL Server was started and will make it available on the Missing Indexes DMVs. The missing indexes feature will be covered in more detail in *Chapter 5, Working with Indexes.*

For example, another fragment from an XML plan is shown here:

```
<MissingIndexes>
  <MissingIndexGroup Impact="99.6598">
    <MissingIndex Database="[AdventureWorks2019]"
Schema="[Sales]" Table="[SalesOrderDetail]">
      <ColumnGroup Usage="EQUALITY">
        <Column Name="[CarrierTrackingNumber]" ColumnId="3" />
      </ColumnGroup>
    </MissingIndex>
  </MissingIndexGroup>
</MissingIndexes>
```

WaitStats

SQL Server tracks wait statistics information any time a query is waiting on anything and makes this information available in several ways. Analyzing wait statistics is one of the most important tools for troubleshooting performance problems. This information has been available even from the very early releases of SQL Server. Starting with SQL Server 2016 Service Pack 1, however, this information is also available at the query level and included in the query execution plan. Only the top 10 waits are included.

The following is an example:

```
<WaitStats>
  <Wait WaitType="ASYNC_NETWORK_IO" WaitTimeMs="58"
WaitCount="35" />
  <Wait WaitType="PAGEIOLATCH_SH" WaitTimeMs="1" WaitCount="6"
/>
</WaitStats>
```

For more information about wait statistics, see the SQL Server documentation or my book *High-Performance SQL Server*.

Trace flags

A trace flag is a mechanism that's used to change the behavior of SQL Server. Note, however, that some of these trace flags may impact query optimization and execution. As an additional query performance troubleshooting mechanism, starting with SQL Server 2016 Service Pack 1 (and later, with SQL Server 2014 Service Pack 3 and SQL Server 2012 Service Pack 4), trace flags that can impact query optimization and execution are included in the query plan.

For example, let's assume you've enabled the following trace flags:

```
DBCC TRACEON (2371, -1)
DBCC TRACEON (4199, -1)
```

You may get the following entry on your query XML execution plan:

```
<TraceFlags IsCompileTime="true">
  <TraceFlag Value="2371" Scope="Global" />
  <TraceFlag Value="4199" Scope="Global" />
</TraceFlags>
<TraceFlags IsCompileTime="false">
  <TraceFlag Value="2371" Scope="Global" />
  <TraceFlag Value="4199" Scope="Global" />
</TraceFlags>
```

This shows that both trace flags were active during optimization and execution times, indicated by the `IsCompileTime` values of `true` and `false`, respectively. `Scope` could be `Global`, as shown in our example, or `Session`, if you're using, for example, `DBCC TRACEON` without the `-1` argument or using the QUERYTRACEON hint.

Don't forget to disable these trace flags if you tested them in your system:

```
DBCC TRACEOFF (2371, -1)
DBCC TRACEOFF (4199, -1)
```

Warnings on execution plans

Execution plans can also show warning messages. Plans that contain these warnings should be carefully reviewed because they may be a sign of a performance problem. Before SQL Server 2012, only the `ColumnsWithNoStatistics` and `NoJoinPredicate` warnings were available. The SQL Server 2012 showplan schema added six more iterator- or query-specific warnings to make a total of 13 in SQL Server 2019. As mentioned earlier, no showplan schema for SQL Server 2022 has been published at the time of writing. The entire list can be seen here:

- `SpillOccurred`
- `ColumnsWithNoStatistics`
- `SpillToTempDb`
- `Wait`
- `PlanAffectingConvert`
- `SortSpillDetails`
- `HashSpillDetails`
- `ExchangeSpillDetails`
- `MemoryGrantWarning`
- `NoJoinPredicate`
- `SpatialGuess`
- `UnmatchedIndexes`
- `FullUpdateForOnlineIndexBuild`

Let's examine some of them in this section.

> **Note**
>
> You can inspect this list yourself by opening the showplan schema document located at `http://schemas.microsoft.com/sqlserver/2004/07/showplan`, as explained in the previous section, and search for the `WarningsType` section.

ColumnsWithNoStatistics

This warning means that the query optimizer tried to use statistics, but none were available. As explained earlier in this chapter, the query optimizer relies on statistics to produce an optimal plan. Follow these steps to simulate this warning:

1. Run the following statement to drop the existing statistics for the `VacationHours` column, if available:

    ```
    DROP STATISTICS HumanResources.Employee._WA_
    Sys_0000000C_70DDC3D8
    ```

2. Next, temporarily disable the automatic creation of statistics at the database level:

    ```
    ALTER DATABASE AdventureWorks2019 SET AUTO_CREATE_
    STATISTICS OFF
    ```

3. Then, run the following query:

    ```
    SELECT * FROM HumanResources.Employee
    WHERE VacationHours = 48
    ```

You will get the partial plan shown in the following screenshot:

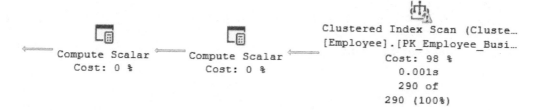

Figure 1.12 – Plan showing a ColumnsWithNoStatistics warning

Notice the warning (the symbol with an exclamation mark) on the Clustered Index Scan operator. If you look at its properties, you will see **Columns With No Statistics: [AdventureWorks2019]. [HumanResources].[Employee].VacationHours.**

> **Note**
>
> Throughout this book, we may decide to show only part of the execution plan. Although you can see the entire plan on SQL Server Management Studio, our purpose is to improve the quality of the image by just showing the required operators.

Don't forget to reenable the automatic creation of statistics by running the following command. There is no need to create the statistics object that was dropped previously because it can be created automatically if needed:

```
ALTER DATABASE AdventureWorks2019 SET AUTO_CREATE_STATISTICS ON
```

NoJoinPredicate

A possible problem while using the old-style ANSI SQL-89 join syntax is accidentally missing the join predicate and getting a `NoJoinPredicate` warning. Let's suppose you intend to run the following query but forgot to include the WHERE clause:

```
SELECT * FROM Sales.SalesOrderHeader soh, Sales.
SalesOrderDetail sod
WHERE soh.SalesOrderID = sod.SalesOrderID
```

The first indication of a problem could be that the query takes way too long to execute, even for small tables. Later, you will see that the query also returns a huge result set.

Sometimes, a way to troubleshoot a long-running query is to just stop its execution and request an estimated plan instead. If you don't include the join predicate (in the WHERE clause), you will get the following plan:

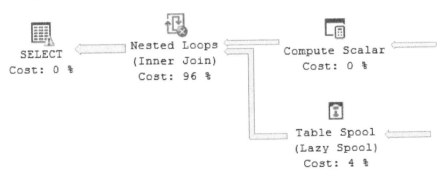

Figure 1.13 – Plan with a NoJoinPredicate warning

This time, you can see the warning on the Nested Loop Join as "No Join Predicate" with a different symbol. Notice that you cannot accidentally miss a join predicate if you use the ANSI SQL-92 join syntax because you get an error instead, which is why this syntax is recommended. For example, missing the join predicate in the following query will return an incorrect syntax error:

```
SELECT * FROM Sales.SalesOrderHeader soh JOIN Sales.
SalesOrderDetail sod
-- ON soh.SalesOrderID = sod.SalesOrderID
```

> **Note**
>
> You can still get, if needed, a join whose result set includes one row for each possible pairing of rows from the two tables, also called a Cartesian product, by using the CROSS JOIN syntax.

PlanAffectingConvert

This warning shows that type conversions were performed that may impact the performance of the resulting execution plan. Run the following example, which declares the nvarchar variable and then uses it in a query to compare against a varchar column, CreditCardApprovalCode:

```
DECLARE @code nvarchar(15)
SET @code = '95555Vi4081'
SELECT * FROM Sales.SalesOrderHeader
WHERE CreditCardApprovalCode = @code
```

The query returns the following plan:

Figure 1.14 – Plan with a PlanAffectingConvert warning

The following two warnings are shown on the **SELECT** icon:

- The type conversion in the (CONVERT_IMPLICIT(nvarchar(15), [AdventureWorks2019].
  [Sales].[SalesOrderHeader].[CreditCardApprovalCode],0)) expression
  may affect CardinalityEstimate in the query plan choice.

- Type conversion in the (CONVERT_IMPLICIT(nvarchar(15),[AdventureWorks2019].[Sales].[SalesOrderHeader].[CreditCardApprovalCode],0)=[@code]) expression may affect SeekPlan in the query plan choice.

The recommendation is to use similar data types for comparison operations.

SpillToTempDb

This warning shows that an operation didn't have enough memory and had to spill data to disk during execution, which can be a performance problem because of the extra I/O overhead. To simulate this problem, run the following example:

```
SELECT * FROM Sales.SalesOrderDetail
ORDER BY UnitPrice
```

This is a very simple query, and depending on the memory available on your system, you may not get the warning in your test environment, so you may need to try with a larger table instead. The plan shown in *Figure 1.15* will be generated.

This time, the warning is shown on the Sort operator, which in my test included the message **Operator used tempdb to spill data during execution with spill level 2 and 8 spilled thread(s), Sort wrote 2637 pages to and read 2637 pages from tempdb with granted memory 4096KB and used memory 4096KB**. The XML plan also shows this:

```
<SpillToTempDb SpillLevel="2" SpilledThreadCount="8" />
<SortSpillDetails GrantedMemory="4096" UsedMemory="4096"
WritesToTempDb="2637" ReadsFromTempDb="2637" />
```

This is shown here:

Figure 1.15 – Plan with a SpillToTempDb warning

UnmatchedIndexes

Finally, the UnmatchedIndexes element can show that the query optimizer was unable to match a filtered index for a particular query (for example, when it is unable to see the value of a parameter). Suppose you create the following filtered index:

```
CREATE INDEX IX_Color ON Production.Product(Name,
ProductNumber)
WHERE Color = 'White'
```

Then, you run the following query:

```
DECLARE @color nvarchar(15)
SET @color = 'White'
SELECT Name, ProductNumber FROM Production.Product
WHERE Color = @color
```

The IX_Color index is not used at all, and you will get a warning on the plan, as shown here:

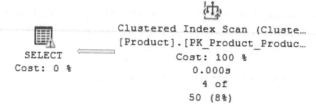

Figure 1.16 – Plan with an UnmatchedIndexes warning

Unfortunately, if you inspect the **SELECT** item in the graphical plan, it will not show any information about the warning at all. You will have to see the following on the XML plan (or by looking at the UnmatchedIndexes property of the SELECT operator's properties window):

```
<UnmatchedIndexes>
<Parameterization>
<Object Database="[AdventureWorks2019]" Schema="[Production]"
Table="[Product]" Index="[IX_Color]" />
</Parameterization>
</UnmatchedIndexes>
<Warnings UnmatchedIndexes="true" />
```

However, the following query will use the index:

```
SELECT Name, ProductNumber FROM Production.Product
WHERE Color = 'White'
```

Filtered indexes and the `UnmatchedIndexes` element will be covered in detail in *Chapter 5, Working with Indexes*. For now, remove the index we just created:

```
DROP INDEX Production.Product.IX_Color
```

> **Note**
>
> Many exercises in this book will require you to make changes in the `AdventureWorks` databases. Although the database is reverted to its original state at the end of every exercise, you may also consider refreshing a copy of the database after several changes or tests, especially if you are not getting the expected results.

Getting plans from a trace or the plan cache

So far, we have been testing getting execution plans by directly using the query code in SQL Server Management Studio. However, this method may not always produce the plan you want to troubleshoot or the plan creating the performance problem. One of the reasons for this is that your application might be using a different `SET` statement option than SQL Server Management Studio and producing an entirely different execution plan for the same query. This behavior, where two plans may exist for the same query, will be covered in more detail in *Chapter 8*, Understanding *Plan Caching*.

Because of this behavior, sometimes, you may need to capture an execution plan from other locations, for example, the plan cache or current query execution. In these cases, you may need to obtain an execution plan from a trace, for example, using SQL trace or extended events, or the plan cache using the `sys.dm_exec_query_plan` **dynamic management function** (**DMF**) or perhaps using some collected data, as in the case of SQL Server Data Collector. Let's take a look at some of these sources.

sys.dm_exec_query_plan DMF

As mentioned earlier, when a query is optimized, its execution plan may be kept in the plan cache. The `sys.dm_exec_query_plan` DMF can be used to return such cached plans, as well as any plan that is currently executing. However, when a plan is removed from the cache, it will no longer be available and the `query_plan` column of the returned table will be null.

For example, the following query shows the execution plans for all the queries currently running in the system. The `sys.dm_exec_requests` **dynamic management view** (**DMV**), which returns information about each request that's currently executing, is used to obtain the `plan_handle` value, which is needed to find the execution plan using the `sys.dm_exec_query_plan` DMF.

A `plan_handle` is a hash value that represents a specific execution plan, and it is guaranteed to be unique in the system:

```
SELECT * FROM sys.dm_exec_requests
CROSS APPLY sys.dm_exec_query_plan(plan_handle)
```

The output will be a result set containing the `query_plan` column, which shows links similar to the one shown in the *XML plans* section. As explained previously, clicking the link shows you requested the graphical execution plan.

In the same way, the following example shows the execution plans for all cached query plans. The `sys.dm_exec_query_stats` DMV contains one row per query statement within the cached plan and, again, provides the `plan_handle` value needed by the `sys.dm_exec_query_plan` DMF:

```
SELECT * FROM sys.dm_exec_query_stats
CROSS APPLY sys.dm_exec_query_plan(plan_handle)
```

Now, suppose you want to find the 10 most expensive queries by CPU usage. You can run the following query to get this information, which will return the average CPU time in microseconds per execution, along with the query execution plan:

```
SELECT TOP 10
total_worker_time/execution_count AS avg_cpu_time, plan_handle,
query_plan
FROM sys.dm_exec_query_stats
CROSS APPLY sys.dm_exec_query_plan(plan_handle)
ORDER BY avg_cpu_time DESC
```

SQL Trace/Profiler

You can also use SQL Trace and/or Profiler to capture the execution plans of queries that are currently executing. You can use the **Performance event** category in Profiler, which includes the following events:

- **Performance Statistics**
- **Showplan All**
- **Showplan All For Query Compile**
- **Showplan Statistics Profile**
- **Showplan Text**
- **Showplan Text (Unencoded)**
- **Showplan XML**

- **Showplan XML For Query Compile**

- **Showplan XML Statistics Profile**

To trace any of these events, run Profiler, connect to your SQL Server instance, click **Events Selection**, expand the **Performance event** category, and select any of the required events. You can select all the columns or only a subset of the columns, specify a column filter, and so on. Click **Run** to start the trace. The following screenshot shows an example of a trace with the Showplan XML event:

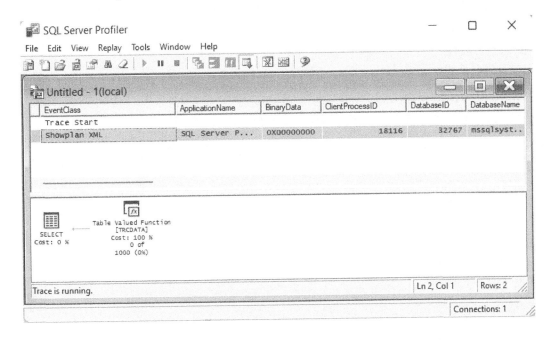

Figure 1.17 – A trace in Profiler showing the Showplan XML event

Optionally, you can create a server trace using a script, and even use Profiler as a scripting tool. To do that, define the events for your trace, run and stop the trace, and select **File | Export | Script Trace Definition | For SQL Server 2005 – vNext…**. This will produce the code to run a server trace, which will only be required to specify a filename to capture the trace. Part of the generated code is shown here:

```
/************************************************/
/* Created by: SQL Server vNext CTP1.0 Profiler */
/* Date: 05/29/2022 08:37:22 AM */
/************************************************/
-- Create a Queue
declare @rc int
declare @TraceID int
```

```
declare @maxfilesize bigint
set @maxfilesize = 5
-- Please replace the text InsertFileNameHere, with an
appropriate
-- filename prefixed by a path, e.g., c:\MyFolder\MyTrace. The
.trc extension
-- will be appended to the filename automatically. If you are
writing from
-- remote server to local drive, please use UNC path and make
sure server has
-- write access to your network share
exec @rc = sp_trace_create @TraceID output, 0,
N'InsertFileNameHere', @maxfilesize,
NULL
if (@rc != 0) goto error
-- Client side File and Table cannot be scripted
-- Set the events
declare @on bit
set @on = 1
exec sp_trace_setevent @TraceID, 10, 1, @on
exec sp_trace_setevent @TraceID, 10, 9, @on
exec sp_trace_setevent @TraceID, 10, 2, @on
exec sp_trace_setevent @TraceID, 10, 66, @on
exec sp_trace_setevent @TraceID, 10, 10, @on
exec sp_trace_setevent @TraceID, 10, 3, @on
exec sp_trace_setevent @TraceID, 10, 4, @on
exec sp_trace_setevent @TraceID, 10, 6, @on
exec sp_trace_setevent @TraceID, 10, 7, @on
exec sp_trace_setevent @TraceID, 10, 8, @on
exec sp_trace_setevent @TraceID, 10, 11, @on
exec sp_trace_setevent @TraceID, 10, 12, @on
exec sp_trace_setevent @TraceID, 10, 13, @on
```

You may notice SQL Server vNext in a couple of places and even CTP1.0 being incorrectly shown. This was tested with SQL Server Profiler v19.0 Preview 2 and SQL Server 2022 CTP 2.0.

> **Note**
>
> As of SQL Server 2008, all non-XML events mentioned earlier, such as `Showplan All`, `Showplan Text`, and so on, are deprecated. Microsoft recommends using the XML events instead. SQL Trace has also been deprecated as of SQL Server 2012. Instead, Microsoft recommends using extended events.

For more details about using Profiler and SQL Trace, please refer to the SQL Server documentation.

> **Note**
>
> The SQL Server documentation used to be referred to as *SQL Server Books Online*, which was a component that could be optionally installed on your server. Recently, you are more likely to find such documentation on the web, such as at `docs.microsoft.com/en-us/sql`.

Extended events

You can also use extended events to capture execution plans. Although in general, Microsoft recommends using extended events over SQL Trace, as mentioned earlier, the events to capture execution plans are expensive to collect on the current releases of SQL Server. The documentation shows the following warning for all three extended events available to capture execution plans: *Using this event can have a significant performance overhead so it should only be used when troubleshooting or monitoring specific problems for brief periods of time.*

You can create and start an extended events session by using `CREATE EVENT SESSION` and `ALTER EVENT SESSION`. You can also use the new graphic user interface introduced in SQL Server 2012. Here are the events related to execution plans:

- `query_post_compilation_showplan`: Occurs after a SQL statement is compiled. This event returns an XML representation of the estimated query plan that is generated when the query is compiled.

- `query_post_execution_showplan`: Occurs after a SQL statement is executed. This event returns an XML representation of the actual query plan.

- `query_pre_execution_showplan`: Occurs after a SQL statement is compiled. This event returns an XML representation of the estimated query plan that is generated when the query is optimized.

For example, let's suppose you want to start a session to trace the `query_post_execution_showplan` event. You could use the following code to create the extended event session:

```
CREATE EVENT SESSION [test] ON SERVER
ADD EVENT sqlserver.query_post_execution_showplan(
ACTION(sqlserver.plan_handle)
WHERE ([sqlserver].[database_name]=N'AdventureWorks2019'))
ADD TARGET package0.ring_buffer
WITH (STARTUP_STATE=OFF)
GO
```

More details about extended events will be covered in *Chapter 2, Troubleshooting Queries*. In the meantime, you can notice that the `ADD EVENT` argument shows the event name (in this case, `query_post_execution_showplan`), `ACTION` refers to global fields you want to capture in the event session (in this case, `plan_handle`), and `WHERE` is used to apply a filter to limit the data you want to capture. The `[sqlserver].[database_name]=N'AdventureWorks2019'` predicate indicates that we want to capture events for the `AdventureWorks2019` database only. `TARGET` is the event consumer, and we can use it to collect the data for analysis. In this case, we are using the ring buffer target. Finally, `STARTUP_STATE` is one of the extended event options, and it is used to specify whether or not this event session is automatically started when SQL Server starts.

Once the event session has been created, you can start it using the `ALTER EVENT SESSION` statement, as shown in the following example:

```
ALTER EVENT SESSION [test]
ON SERVER
STATE=START
```

You can use the **Watch Live Data** feature, introduced with SQL Server 2012, to view the data that's been captured by the event session. To do that, expand the **Management** folder in **Object Explorer | Extended Events | Sessions**, right-click the extended event session, and select **Watch Live Data**.

You can also run the following code to see this data:

```
SELECT
event_data.value('(event/@name)[1]', 'varchar(50)') AS event_
name,
event_data.value('(event/action[@name="plan_handle"]/value)
[1]',
'varchar(max)') as plan_handle,
event_data.query('event/data[@name="showplan_xml"]/value/*') as
showplan_xml,
```

```
event_data.value('(event/action[@name="sql_text"]/value)[1]',
'varchar(max)') AS sql_text
FROM ( SELECT evnt.query('.') AS event_data
FROM
( SELECT CAST(target_data AS xml) AS target_data
FROM sys.dm_xe_sessions AS s
JOIN sys.dm_xe_session_targets AS t
ON s.address = t.event_session_address
WHERE s.name = 'test'
AND t.target_name = 'ring_buffer'
) AS data
CROSS APPLY target_data.nodes('RingBufferTarget/event') AS
xevent(evnt)
) AS xevent(event_data)
```

Once you've finished testing, you need to stop and delete the event session. Run the following statements:

```
ALTER EVENT SESSION [test]
ON SERVER
STATE=STOP
GO
DROP EVENT SESSION [test] ON SERVER
```

Finally, some other SQL Server tools can allow you to see plans, including the Data Collector. The Data Collector was introduced with SQL Server 2008 and will be covered in *Chapter 2, Troubleshooting Queries.*

Removing plans from the plan cache

You can use a few different commands to remove plans from the plan cache. These commands, which will be covered in more detail in *Chapter 8,* Understanding *Plan Caching,* can be useful during your testing and should not be executed in a production environment unless the requested effect is desired. The DBCC FREEPROCCACHE statement can be used to remove all the entries from the plan cache. It can also accept a plan handle or a SQL handle to remove only specific plans, or a Resource Governor pool name to remove all the cache entries associated with it. The DBCC FREESYSTEMCACHE statement can be used to remove all the elements from the plan cache or only the elements associated with a Resource Governor pool name. DBCC FLUSHPROCINDB can be used to remove all the cached plans for a particular database.

Finally, although not related to the plan cache, the DBCC DROPCLEANBUFFERS statement can be used to remove all the buffers from the buffer pool. You can use this statement in cases where you want to simulate a query starting with a cold cache, as we will do in the next section.

SET STATISTICS TIME and IO statements

We will close this chapter with two statements that can give you additional information about your queries and that you can use as an additional tuning technique. These can be a great complement to execution plans to get additional information about your queries' optimization and execution. One common misunderstanding we sometimes see is developers trying to compare plan cost to plan performance. You should not assume a direct correlation between a query-estimated cost and its actual runtime performance. Cost is an internal unit used by the query optimizer and should not be used to compare plan performance; SET STATISTICS TIME and SET STATISTICS IO can be used instead. This section explains both statements.

You can use SET STATISTICS TIME to see the number of milliseconds required to parse, compile, and execute each statement. For example, run the following command:

```
SET STATISTICS TIME ON
```

Then, run the following query:

```
SELECT DISTINCT(CustomerID)
FROM Sales.SalesOrderHeader
```

To see the output, you will have to look at the **Messages** tab of the **Edit** window, which will show an output similar to the following:

```
SQL Server parse and compile time:
CPU time = 16 ms, elapsed time = 226 ms.
SQL Server Execution Times:
CPU time = 16 ms, elapsed time = 148 ms.
```

parse and compile time refers to the time SQL Server takes to optimize the SQL statement, as explained earlier. You can get similar information by looking at the QueryTimeStats query property, as shown earlier in this chapter. SET STATISTICS TIME will continue to be enabled for any subsequently executed queries. You can disable it like so:

```
SET STATISTICS TIME OFF
```

As mentioned previously, parse and compile information can also be seen on the execution plan, as shown here:

```
<QueryPlan DegreeOfParallelism="1" CachedPlanSize="16"
CompileTime="226"
CompileCPU="9" CompileMemory="232">
```

If you only need the execution time of each query, you can see this information in Management Studio Query Editor.

SET STATISTICS IO displays the amount of disk activity generated by a query. To enable it, run the following statement:

```
SET STATISTICS IO ON
```

Run the following statement to clean all the buffers from the buffer pool to make sure that no pages for this table are loaded in memory:

```
DBCC DROPCLEANBUFFERS
```

Then, run the following query:

```
SELECT * FROM Sales.SalesOrderDetail
WHERE ProductID = 870
```

You will see an output similar to the following:

```
Table 'SalesOrderDetail'. Scan count 1, logical reads 1246,
physical reads 3,
read-ahead reads 1277, lob logical reads 0, lob physical reads
0,
lob read-ahead reads 0.
```

Here are the definitions of these items, which all use 8K pages:

- **Logical reads**: Number of pages read from the buffer pool.
- **Physical reads**: Number of pages read from disk.
- **Read-ahead reads**: Read-ahead is a performance optimization mechanism that anticipates the needed data pages and reads them from disk. It can read up to 64 contiguous pages from one data file.
- **Lob logical reads**: Number of **large object** (**LOB**) pages read from the buffer pool.

- **Lob physical reads**: Number of LOB pages read from disk.

- **Lob read-ahead reads**: Number of LOB pages read from disk using the read-ahead mechanism, as explained earlier.

Now, if you run the same query again, you will no longer get physical and read-ahead reads. Instead, you will get an output similar to the following:

```
Table 'SalesOrderDetail'. Scan count 1, logical reads 1246,
physical reads 0,
read-ahead reads 0, lob logical reads 0, lob physical reads 0,
lob read-ahead reads 0.
```

`Scan count` is defined as the number of seeks or scans started after reaching the leaf level (that is, the bottom level of an index). The only case when `Scan count` will return 0 is when you're seeking only one value on a unique index, as shown in the following example:

```
SELECT * FROM Sales.SalesOrderHeader
WHERE SalesOrderID = 51119
```

If you try running the following query, in which `SalesOrderID` is defined in a non-unique index and can return more than one record, you will see that `Scan count` now returns 1:

```
SELECT * FROM Sales.SalesOrderDetail
WHERE SalesOrderID = 51119
```

Finally, in the following example, the scan count is 4 because SQL Server must perform four seeks:

```
SELECT * FROM Sales.SalesOrderHeader
WHERE SalesOrderID IN (51119, 43664, 63371, 75119)
```

Summary

In this chapter, we showed you how a better understanding of what the query processor does behind the scenes can help both database administrators and developers write better queries, as well as provide the query optimizer with the information it needs to produce efficient execution plans. In the same way, we showed you how to use your newfound knowledge of the query processor's inner workings and SQL Server tools to troubleshoot cases when your queries are not performing as expected. Based on this, the basics of the query optimizer, the execution engine, and the plan cache were explained. These SQL Server components will be covered in greater detail later in this book.

Because we will be using execution plans throughout this book, we also introduced you to how to read them, their more important properties, and how to obtain them from sources such as the plan cache and a server trace. This should have given you enough background to follow along with the rest of this book. Query operators were also introduced but will be covered in a lot more detail in *Chapter 4, The Execution Engine*, and other sections of this book.

In the next chapter, we will explore additional tuning tools and techniques, such as using SQL Trace, extended events, and DMVs, to find out which queries are consuming the most resources or investigate some other performance-related problems.

2
Troubleshooting Queries

In *Chapter 1, An Introduction to Query Tuning and Optimization*, we introduced you to reading execution plans as the primary tool we'll use to interact with the SQL Server query processor. We also checked out the `SET STATISTICS TIME` and `SET STATISTICS IO` statements, which can provide you with additional performance information about your queries. In this chapter, we continue where we left off in the previous chapter. We will look into additional tuning tools and techniques you can use to find out how many server resources your queries are using and how to find the most expensive queries on your system.

Dynamic management views (**DMVs**) were introduced with SQL Server 2005 as a great tool to diagnose problems, tune performance, and monitor the health of a SQL Server instance. There are many DMVs available, and the first section in this chapter focuses on `sys.dm_exec_requests`, `sys.dm_exec_sessions`, and `sys.dm_exec_query_stats`, which you can use to find out the server resources, such as CPU and I/O, that are used by queries running on the system. Many more DMVs will be introduced in other chapters of this book, including later in this chapter, when we cover extended events.

Although SQL Trace has been deprecated as of SQL Server 2012, it's still widely used and will be available in some of the next versions of SQL Server. SQL Trace is usually related to SQL Server Profiler because using this tool is the easiest way to define and run a trace, and it is also the tool of choice for scripting and creating a server trace, which is used in some scenarios where running Profiler directly may be expensive. In this chapter, we'll cover some of the trace events we would be more interested in when tracing query execution for performance problems.

Following on from the same concept as SQL Trace, in the next section, we will explore extended events. All the basic concepts and definitions will be explained first, including events, predicates, actions, targets, and sessions. Then, we will create some sessions to obtain performance information about queries. Because most SQL Server professionals are already familiar with SQL Trace or Profiler, we will also learn how to map the old trace events to the new extended events.

Finally, the Data Collector, a feature introduced with SQL Server 2008, will be shown as a tool that can help you proactively collect performance data that can be used to troubleshoot performance problems when they occur.

In this chapter, we will cover the following topics:

- DMVs and DMFs
- SQL Trace
- Extended events
- The Data Collector

DMVs and DMFs

In this section, we will show you several **dynamic management views (DMVs)** and **dynamic management functions (DMFs)** that can help you to find out the number of server resources that are being used by your queries and to find the most expensive queries in your SQL Server instance.

sys.dm_exec_requests and sys.dm_exec_sessions

The `sys.dm_exec_requests` DMV can be used to display the requests currently executing on SQL Server, whereas `sys.dm_exec_sessions` shows the authenticated sessions on the instance. Although these DMVs include many columns, in this section, we will focus on the ones related to resource usage and query performance. You can look at the definitions of the other columns on the SQL Server documentation.

Both DMVs share several columns, as shown in the following table:

Column	Definition
cpu_time	CPU time in milliseconds used by this request or by the requests in this session.
total_elapsed_time	Total time elapsed in milliseconds since the request arrived or the session was established.
reads	The number of reads performed by this request or by the requests in this session.
writes	The number of writes performed by this request or by the requests in this session.
logical_reads	The number of logical reads that have been performed by the request or by the requests in this session.
row_count	The number of rows that have been returned to the client by this request.

Table 2.1 – The sys.dm_exec_requests and sys.dm_exec_sessions columns

`sys.dm_exec_requests` will show the resources that are used by a specific request currently executing, whereas `sys.dm_exec_sessions` will show the accumulated resources of all the requests completed by a session. To understand how these two DMVs collect resource usage information, we can use a query that takes at least a few seconds. Open a new query in Management Studio and get its session ID (for example, using `SELECT @@SPID`), but make sure you don't run anything on it yet – the resource usage will be accumulated on the `sys.dm_exec_sessions` DMV. Copy and be ready to run the following code on that window:

```
DBCC FREEPROCCACHE
DBCC DROPCLEANBUFFERS
GO
SELECT * FROM Production.Product p1 CROSS JOIN Production.
Product p2
```

Copy the following code to a second window, replacing `session_id` with the value you obtained in the first window:

```
SELECT cpu_time, reads, total_elapsed_time, logical_reads, row_
count
FROM sys.dm_exec_requests
WHERE session_id = 56
GO
SELECT cpu_time, reads, total_elapsed_time, logical_reads, row_
count
FROM sys.dm_exec_sessions
WHERE session_id = 56
```

Run the query on the first session and, at the same time, run the code on the second session several times to see the resources used. The following output shows a sample execution while the query is still running and has not been completed yet. Notice that the `sys.dm_exec_requests` DMV shows the partially used resources and that `sys.dm_exec_sessions` shows no used resources yet. Most likely, you will not see the same results for `sys.dm_exec_requests`:

cpu_time	reads	total_elapsed_time	logical_reads	row_count
468	62	4767	5868	1

cpu_time	reads	total_elapsed_time	logical_reads	row_count
0	0	5	0	1

After the query completes, the original request no longer exists and `sys.dm_exec_requests` returns no data at all. `sys.dm_exec_sessions` now records the resources used by the first query:

cpu_time	reads	total_elapsed_time	logical_reads	row_count
671	62	6996	8192	254016

If you run the query on the first session again, `sys.dm_exec_sessions` will accumulate the resources used by both executions, so the values of the results will be slightly more than twice their previous values, as shown here:

cpu_time	reads	total_elapsed_time	logical_reads	row_count
1295	124	14062	16384	254016

Keep in mind that CPU time and duration may vary slightly during different executions and that you will likely get different values as well. The number of reads for this execution is 8,192, and we can see the accumulated value of 16,384 for two executions. In addition, the `sys.dm_exec_requests` DMV only shows information of currently executing queries, so you may not see this particular data if a query completes before you can query it.

In summary, `sys.dm_exec_requests` and `sys.dm_exec_sessions` are useful for inspecting the resources being used by a request or the accumulation of resources being used by requests on a session since its creation.

Sys.dm_exec_query_stats

If you've ever worked with any version of SQL Server older than SQL Server 2005, you may remember how difficult it was to find the most expensive queries in your instance. Performing that kind of analysis usually required running a server trace in your instance for some time and then analyzing the collected data, usually in the size of gigabytes, using third-party tools or your own created methods (a very time-consuming process). Not to mention the fact that running such a trace could also affect the performance of a system, which most likely is having a performance problem already.

DMVs were introduced with SQL Server 2005 and are a great help to diagnose problems, tune performance, and monitor the health of a server instance. In particular, `sys.dm_exec_query_stats` provides a rich amount of information not available before in SQL Server regarding aggregated performance statistics for cached query plans. This information helps you avoid the need to run a trace, as mentioned earlier, in most cases. This view returns a row for each statement available in the plan cache, and SQL Server 2008 added enhancements such as the query hash and plan hash values, which will be explained shortly.

Let's take a quick look at understanding how `sys.dm_exec_query_stats` works and the information it provides. Create the following stored procedure with three simple queries:

```
CREATE PROC test
AS
SELECT * FROM Sales.SalesOrderDetail WHERE SalesOrderID = 60677
SELECT * FROM Person.Address WHERE AddressID = 21
SELECT * FROM HumanResources.Employee WHERE BusinessEntityID =
229
```

Run the following code to clean the plan cache (so that it is easier to inspect), remove all the clean buffers from the buffer pool, execute the created test stored procedure, and inspect the plan cache. Note that the code uses the `sys.dm_exec_sql_text` DMF, which requires a `sql_handle` or `plan_handle` value and returns the text of the SQL batch:

```
DBCC FREEPROCCACHE
DBCC DROPCLEANBUFFERS
GO
EXEC test
GO
SELECT * FROM sys.dm_exec_query_stats
CROSS APPLY sys.dm_exec_sql_text(sql_handle)
WHERE objectid = OBJECT_ID('dbo.test')
```

Examine the output. Because the number of columns is too large to show in this book, only some of the columns are shown here:

statement_ start_offset	statement_ end_offset	execution_ count	total_ worker_ time	last_ worker_ time	min_ worker_ time	max_ worker_ time	Text
44	168	1	532	532	532	532	CREATE PROC test AS ...
174	270	1	622	622	622	622	CREATE PROC test AS ...
276	406	1	667	667	667	667	CREATE PROC test AS ...

As you can see by looking at the query text, all three queries were compiled as part of the same batch, which we can also verify by validating they have the same `plan_handle` and `sql_handle`. `statement_start_offset` and `statement_end_offset` can be used to identify the particular queries in the batch, a process that will be explained later in this section. You can also see the number of times the query was executed and several columns showing the CPU time used by each query, such as `total_worker_time`, `last_worker_time`, `min_worker_time`, and `max_worker_time`. Should the query be executed more than once, the statistics would show the accumulated CPU time on `total_worker_time`. Not shown in the previous output are additional performance statistics for physical reads, logical writes, logical reads, CLR time, and elapsed time. The following table shows the list of columns, including performance statistics and their documented description:

Column	Description
total_worker_time	The total amount of CPU time, reported in microseconds (but only accurate to milliseconds), that was consumed by executions of this plan since it was compiled.
last_worker_time	CPU time, reported in microseconds (but only accurate to milliseconds), that was consumed the last time the plan was executed.
min_worker_time	Minimum CPU time, reported in microseconds (but only accurate to milliseconds), that this plan has ever consumed during a single execution.
max_worker_time	Maximum CPU time, reported in microseconds (but only accurate to milliseconds), that this plan has ever consumed during a single execution.
total_physical_reads	The total number of physical reads performed by executions of this plan since it was compiled.
last_physical_reads	The number of physical reads performed the last time the plan was executed.
min_physical_reads	The minimum number of physical reads that this plan has ever performed during a single execution.
max_physical_reads	The maximum number of physical reads that this plan has ever performed during a single execution.
total_logical_writes	The total number of logical writes performed by executions of this plan since it was compiled.
last_logical_writes	The number of logical writes performed the last time the plan was executed.
min_logical_writes	The minimum number of logical writes that this plan has ever performed during a single execution.
max_logical_writes	The maximum number of logical writes that this plan has ever performed during a single execution.

Column	Description
total_logical_reads	The total number of logical reads performed by executions of this plan since it was compiled.
last_logical_reads	The number of logical reads performed the last time the plan was executed.
min_logical_reads	The minimum number of logical reads that this plan has ever performed during a single execution.
max_logical_reads	The maximum number of logical reads that this plan has ever performed during a single execution.
total_clr_time	Time, reported in microseconds (but only accurate to milliseconds), consumed inside Microsoft .NET Framework **common language runtime (CLR)** objects by executions of this plan since it was compiled. The CLR objects can be stored procedures, functions, triggers, types, and aggregates.
last_clr_time	Time, reported in microseconds (but only accurate to milliseconds), consumed by execution inside .NET Framework CLR objects during the last execution of this plan. The CLR objects can be stored procedures, functions, triggers, types, and aggregates.
min_clr_time	Minimum time, reported in microseconds (but only accurate to milliseconds), that this plan has ever consumed inside .NET Framework CLR objects during a single execution. The CLR objects can be stored procedures, functions, triggers, types, and aggregates.
max_clr_time	Maximum time, reported in microseconds (but only accurate to milliseconds), that this plan has ever consumed inside the .NET Framework CLR during a single execution. The CLR objects can be stored procedures, functions, triggers, types, and aggregates.
total_elapsed_time	Total elapsed time, reported in microseconds (but only accurate to milliseconds), for completed executions of this plan.
last_elapsed_time	Elapsed time, reported in microseconds (but only accurate to milliseconds), for the most recently completed execution of this plan.
min_elapsed_time	Minimum elapsed time, reported in microseconds (but only accurate to milliseconds), for any completed execution of this plan.
max_elapsed_time	Maximum elapsed time, reported in microseconds (but only accurate to milliseconds), for any completed execution of this plan.

Table 2.2 – The sys.dm_exec_query_stats columns

Keep in mind that this view only shows statistics for completed query executions. You can look at `sys.dm_exec_requests`, as explained earlier, for information about queries currently executing. Finally, as explained in the previous chapter, certain types of execution plans may never be cached, and some cached plans may also be removed from the plan cache for several reasons, including internal or external memory pressure on the plan cache. Information for these plans will not be available on `sys.dm_exec_query_stats`.

Now, let's look at the `statement_start_offset` and `statement_end_offset` values.

Understanding statement_start_offset and statement_end_offset

As shown from the previous output of `sys.dm_exec_query_stats`, the `sql_handle`, `plan_handle`, and `text` columns showing the code for the stored procedure are the same in all three records. The same plan and query are used for the entire batch. So, how do we identify each of the SQL statements, for example, supposing that only one of them is expensive? We must use the `statement_start_offset` and `statement_end_offset` columns. `statement_start_offset` is defined as the starting position of the query that the row describes within the text of its batch, whereas `statement_end_offset` is the ending position of the query that the row describes within the text of its batch. Both `statement_start_offset` and `statement_end_offset` are indicated in bytes, starting with 0. A value of –1 indicates the end of the batch.

We can easily extend our previous query to inspect the plan cache to use `statement_start_offset` and `statement_end_offset` and get something like the following:

```
DBCC FREEPROCCACHE
DBCC DROPCLEANBUFFERS
GO
EXEC test
GO
SELECT SUBSTRING(text, (statement_start_offset/2) + 1,
((CASE statement_end_offset
WHEN -1
THEN DATALENGTH(text)
ELSE
statement_end_offset
END
- statement_start_offset)/2) + 1) AS statement_text, *
FROM sys.dm_exec_query_stats
CROSS APPLY sys.dm_exec_sql_text(sql_handle)
WHERE objectid = OBJECT_ID('dbo.test')
```

This would produce output similar to the following (only a few columns are shown here):

statement_text	statement_start_offset	statement_end_offset
SELECT * FROM Sales.SalesOrderDetail WHERE SalesOrderID = 60677	44	168
SELECT * FROM Person.Address WHERE AddressID = 21	174	270
SELECT * FROM HumanResources.Employee WHERE BusinessEntityID = 229	276	406

The query makes use of the SUBSTRING function, as well as `statement_start_offset` and `statement_end_offset` values, to obtain the text of the query within the batch. Division by 2 is required because the text data is stored as Unicode.

To test the concept for a particular query, you can replace the values for `statement_start_offset` and `statement_end_offset` directly for the first statement (44 and 168, respectively) and provide `sql_handle` or `plan_handle`, (returned in the previous query and not printed in the book) as shown here, to get the first statement that was returned:

```
SELECT SUBSTRING(text, 44 / 2 + 1, (168 - 44) / 2 + 1)
FROM sys.dm_exec_sql_
text(0x03000500996DB224E0B27201B7A1000001000000000000
000000000000000000000000000000000000000000000)
```

sql_handle and plan_handle

The `sql_handle` value is a hash value that refers to the batch or stored procedure the query is part of. It can be used in the `sys.dm_exec_sql_text` DMF to retrieve the text of the query, as demonstrated previously. Let's use the example we used previously:

```
SELECT * from sys.dm_exec_sql_
text(0x03000500996DB224E0B27201B7A1000001000000
000000000000000000000000000000000000000000000)
```

We would get the following in return:

dbid	objectid	number	encrypted	text
5	615673241	1	0	CREATE PROC test AS SELECT * FROM …

The `sql_handle` hash is guaranteed to be unique for every batch in the system. The text of the batch is stored in the SQL Manager Cache or SQLMGR, which you can inspect by running the following query:

```
SELECT * FROM sys.dm_os_memory_objects
WHERE type = 'MEMOBJ_SQLMGR'
```

Because a `sql_handle` has a 1:N relationship with a `plan_handle` (that is, there can be more than one generated executed plan for a particular query), the text of the batch will remain on the SQLMGR cache store until the last of the generated plans is evicted from the plan cache.

The `plan_handle` value is a hash value that refers to the execution plan the query is part of and can be used in the `sys.dm_exec_query_plan` DMF to retrieve such an execution plan. It is guaranteed to be unique for every batch in the system and will remain the same, even if one or more statements in the batch are recompiled. Here is an example:

```
SELECT * FROM sys.dm_exec_query_
plan(0x05000500996DB224B0C9B8F8010000000100
00000000000000000000000000000000000000000000000000000)
```

Running the preceding code will return the following output, and clicking the `query_plan` link will display the requested graphical execution plan. Again, make sure you are using a valid `plan_handle` value:

dbid	objectid	number	encrypted	query_plan
5	615673241	1	0	`<ShowPlanXML xmlns="http://schemas.microsoft.com/sqlserver/2004/07/showplan"` ...

Cached execution plans are stored in the SQLCP and OBJCP cache stores: object plans, including stored procedures, triggers, and functions, are stored in the OBJCP cache store, whereas plans for ad hoc, auto parameterized, and prepared queries are stored in the SQLCP cache store.

query_hash and plan_hash

Although `sys.dm_exec_query_stats` was a great resource that provided performance statistics for cached query plans when it was introduced in SQL Server 2005, one of its limitations was that it was not easy to aggregate the information for the same query when this query was not parameterized. The `query_hash` and `plan_hash` columns, introduced with SQL Server 2008, provide a solution to this problem. To understand the problem, let's look at an example of the behavior of `sys.dm_exec_query_stats` when a query is auto-parameterized:

```
DBCC FREEPROCCACHE
DBCC DROPCLEANBUFFERS
GO
SELECT * FROM Person.Address
WHERE AddressID = 12
GO
SELECT * FROM Person.Address
WHERE AddressID = 37
GO
SELECT * FROM sys.dm_exec_query_stats
```

Because `AddressID` is part of a unique index, the `AddressID = 12` predicate would always return a maximum of one record, so it is safe for the query optimizer to auto-parameterize the query and use the same plan. Here is the output:

sql_handle	execution_count	query_hash	query_plan_hash
0x020000002D83010497EDC81695 B0146B2F0000B7B2D28D19000000 0000000000000000000000000000000000	2	0x10E4AFA44470632D	0x1C9E602B6F826BBC

In this case, we only have one plan that's been reused for the second execution, as shown in the `execution_count` value. Therefore, we can also see that plan reuse is another benefit of parameterized queries. However, we can see a different behavior by running the following query:

```
DBCC FREEPROCCACHE
DBCC DROPCLEANBUFFERS
GO
SELECT * FROM Person.Address
WHERE StateProvinceID = 79
GO
SELECT * FROM Person.Address
WHERE StateProvinceID = 59
GO
SELECT * FROM sys.dm_exec_query_stats
```

Because a filter with an equality comparison on `StateProvinceID` could return zero, one, or more values, it is not considered safe for SQL Server to auto-parameterize the query; in fact, both executions return different execution plans. Here is the output:

sql_handle	query_hash	query_plan_hash
0x020000000E311524E986FAF37BD4D922A18E2A758EFF1A23 0000000000000000000000000000000000000000	0x1891A5DAEB303AE2	0x03D4D190651B0551
0x02000000EBFDF423379C4875CCC482ACD143308C504C72F 10000000000000000000000000000000000000000	0x1891A5DAEB303AE2	0xAE5E89B0A490F3C9

As you can see, `sql_handle`, `plan_handle` (not shown), and `query_plan_hash` have different values because the generated plans are different. However, `query_hash` is the same because it is the same query, only with a different parameter. Supposing that this was the most expensive query in the system and there are multiple executions with different parameters, it would be very difficult to find out that all those execution plans do belong to the same query. This is where `query_hash` can help. You can use `query_hash` to aggregate performance statistics of similar queries that are not explicitly or implicitly parameterized. Both `query_hash` and `plan_hash` are available on the `sys.dm_exec_query_stats` and `sys.dm_exec_requests` DMVs.

The query_hash value is calculated from the tree of logical operators that was created after parsing just before query optimization. This logical tree is used as the input to the query optimizer. Because of this, two or more queries do not need to have the same text to produce the same query_hash value since parameters, comments, and some other minor differences are not considered. And, as shown in the first example, two queries with the same query_hash value can have different execution plans (that is, different query_plan_hash values). On the other hand, query_plan_hash is calculated from the tree of physical operators that makes up an execution plan. If two plans are the same, although very minor differences are not considered, they will produce the same plan hash value as well.

Finally, a limitation of the hashing algorithms is that they can cause collisions, but the probability of this happening is extremely low. This means that two similar queries may produce different query_hash values or that two different queries may produce the same query_hash value, but again, the probability of this happening is extremely low, and it should not be a concern.

Finding expensive queries

Now, let's apply some of the concepts explained in this section and use the sys.dm_exec_query_stats DMV to find the most expensive queries in your system. A typical query to find the most expensive queries on the plan cache based on CPU is shown in the following code. Note that the query is grouped on the query_hash value to aggregate similar queries, regardless of whether or not they are parameterized:

```
SELECT TOP 20 query_stats.query_hash,
SUM(query_stats.total_worker_time) / SUM(query_stats.execution_
count)
AS avg_cpu_time,
MIN(query_stats.statement_text) AS statement_text
FROM
(SELECT qs.*,
SUBSTRING(st.text, (qs.statement_start_offset/2) + 1,
((CASE statement_end_offset
WHEN -1 THEN DATALENGTH(ST.text)
ELSE qs.statement_end_offset END
- qs.statement_start_offset)/2) + 1) AS statement_text
FROM sys.dm_exec_query_stats qs
CROSS APPLY sys.dm_exec_sql_text(qs.sql_handle) AS st) AS
query_stats
```

```
GROUP BY query_stats.query_hash
ORDER BY avg_cpu_time DESC
```

You may also notice that each returned row represents a query in a batch (for example, a batch with five queries would have five records on the `sys.dm_exec_query_stats` DMV, as explained earlier). We could trim the previous query into something like the following query to focus on the batch and plan level instead. Notice that there is no need to use the `statement_start_offset` and `statement_end_offset` columns to separate the particular queries and that this time, we are grouping on the `query_plan_hash` value:

```
SELECT TOP 20 query_plan_hash,
SUM(total_worker_time) / SUM(execution_count) AS avg_cpu_time,
MIN(plan_handle) AS plan_handle, MIN(text) AS query_text
FROM sys.dm_exec_query_stats qs
CROSS APPLY sys.dm_exec_sql_text(qs.plan_handle) AS st
GROUP BY query_plan_hash
ORDER BY avg_cpu_time DESC
```

These examples are based on CPU time (worker time). Therefore, in the same way, you can update these queries to look for other resources listed on `sys.dm_exec_query_stats`, such as physical reads, logical writes, logical reads, CLR time, and elapsed time.

Finally, we could also apply the same concept to find the most expensive queries that are currently executing, based on `sys.dm_exec_requests`, as shown in the following query:

```
SELECT TOP 20 SUBSTRING(st.text, (er.statement_start_offset/2)
+ 1,
((CASE statement_end_offset
WHEN -1
THEN DATALENGTH(st.text)
ELSE
er.statement_end_offset
END
- er.statement_start_offset)/2) + 1) AS statement_text
, *
FROM sys.dm_exec_requests er
CROSS APPLY sys.dm_exec_sql_text(er.sql_handle) st
ORDER BY total_elapsed_time DESC
```

Blocking and waits

We have talked about queries using resources such as CPU, memory, or disk and measured as CPU time, logical reads, and physical reads, among other performance counters. In SQL Server, however, those resources may not available immediately and your queries may have to wait until they are, causing delays and other performance problems. Although those waits are expected and could be unnoticeable, in some cases, this could be unacceptable, requiring additional troubleshooting. SQL Server provides several ways to track these waits, including several DMVs, which we will cover next, or the WaitsStat element, which we covered in *Chapter 1, An Introduction to Query Tuning and Optimization.*

Blocking can be seen as a type of wait and occurs all the time on relational databases, as it is required for applications to correctly access and change data. But its duration should be unnoticeable and should not impact applications. So, similar to most other wait types, excessive blocking could be a common performance problem too.

Finally, there are some wait types that, even in large wait times, never impact the performance of some other queries. A few examples of such wait types are LAZYWRITER_SLEEP, LOGMGR_QUEUE, and DIRTY_PAGE_POOL and they are typically filtered out when collecting wait information.

Let me show you a very simple example of blocking so that you can understand how to detect it and troubleshoot it. Using the default isolation level, which is read committed, the following code will block any operation trying to access the same data:

```
BEGIN TRANSACTION
UPDATE Sales.SalesOrderHeader
SET Status = 1
WHERE SalesOrderID = 43659
```

If you open a second window and run the following query, it will be blocked until the UPDATE transaction is either committed or rolled back:

```
SELECT * FROM Sales.SalesOrderHeader
```

Two very simple ways to see if blocking is the problem, and to get more information about it, is to run any of the following queries. The first uses the traditional but now deprecated catalog view – that is, sysprocesses:

```
SELECT * FROM sysprocesses
WHERE blocked <> 0
```

The second method uses the `sys.dm_exec_requests` DMV, as follows:

```
SELECT * FROM sys.dm_exec_requests
WHERE blocking_session_id <> 0
```

In both cases, the blocked or `blocking_session_id` columns will show the session ID of the blocking process. They will also provide information about the wait type, which in this case is LCK_M_S, the wait resource, which in this case is the data page number (10:1:16660), and the waiting time so far in milliseconds. LCK_M_S is only one of the multiple lock modes available in SQL Server.

Notice that in the preceding example, `sysprocesses` and `sys.dm_requests` only return the row for the blocked process, but you can use the same catalog view and DMV, respectively, to get additional information about the blocking process.

An additional way to find the blocking statement could be to use the DBCC INPUTBUFFER statement or the `sys.dm_exec_input_buffer` DMF and prove it with the blocking session ID. This can be seen here:

```
SELECT * FROM sys.dm_exec_input_buffer(70, 0)
```

Finally, roll back the current transaction to cancel the current UPDATE statement:

```
ROLLBACK TRANSACTION
```

Let's extend our previous example to show a CXPACKET and other waits but this time while blocking the first record of `SalesOrderDetail`. We need a bigger table to encourage a parallel plan:

```
BEGIN TRANSACTION
UPDATE Sales.SalesOrderDetail
SET OrderQty = 3
WHERE SalesOrderDetailID = 1
```

Now, open a second query window and run the following query. Optionally, request an actual execution plan:

```
SELECT * FROM Sales.SalesOrderDetail
ORDER BY OrderQty
```

Now, open yet another query window and run the following, replacing 63 with the session ID from running your SELECT statement:

```
SELECT * FROM sys.dm_os_waiting_tasks
WHERE session_id = 63
```

This time, you may see a row per session ID and execution context ID. In my test, there is only one process waiting on LCK_M_S, as in our previous example, plus eight context IDs waiting on CXPACKET waits.

Complete this exercise by canceling the transaction again:

```
ROLLBACK TRANSACTION
```

You can also examine the execution plan, as covered in the previous chapter, to see the wait information, as shown in the following plan extract. My plan returned eight wait types, four of which are shown here:

```
<WaitStats>
    <Wait WaitType="CXPACKET" WaitTimeMs="2004169"
WaitCount="1745" />
    <Wait WaitType="LCK_M_S" WaitTimeMs="249712" WaitCount="1"
/>
    <Wait WaitType="ASYNC_NETWORK_IO" WaitTimeMs="746"
WaitCount="997" />
    <Wait WaitType="LATCH_SH" WaitTimeMs="110" WaitCount="5" />
...
</WaitStats>
```

Blocking and waits could be more complicated topics. For more details, please refer to the SQL Server documentation.

Now that we have covered DMVs and DMFs, it is time to explore SQL Trace, which can also be used to troubleshoot queries in SQL Server.

SQL Trace

SQL Trace is a SQL Server feature you can use to troubleshoot performance issues. It has been available since the early versions of SQL Server, so it is well-known by database developers and administrators. However, as noted in the previous chapter, SQL Trace has been deprecated as of SQL Server 2012, and Microsoft recommends using extended events instead.

Although you can trace dozens of events using SQL Trace, in this section, we will focus on the ones you can use to measure query resource usage. Because running a trace can take some resources itself, usually, you would only want to run it when you are troubleshooting a query problem, instead of running it all the time. Here are the main trace events we are concerned with regarding query resources usage:

Stored Procedures	RPC:Completed	Occurs when a remote procedure call has been completed
	SP:Completed	Indicates when the stored procedure has been completed
	SP:StmtCompleted	Indicates that a SQL statement within a stored procedure has been completed
T-SQL	SQL:BatchCompleted	Occurs when a SQL batch has been completed
	SQL:StmtCompleted	Occurs when the SQL statement has been completed

The following screenshot shows an example of such a trace configuration on SQL Server Profiler. Usually, you would want to use Profiler to run the trace for a very short time. If you need to run the trace for, say, hours or a few days, a server trace may be a better choice because it uses fewer resources. The previous chapter showed how you can use Profiler to script and run a server trace:

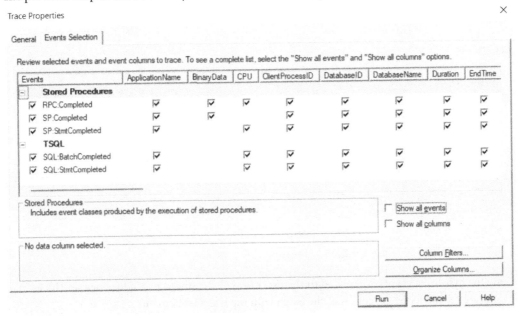

Figure 2.1 – Trace configuration using SQL Server Profiler

Now, let's see how it works. Run **Profiler** and select the previous five listed events. Run the trace and then execute the following ad hoc query in Management Studio:

```
SELECT * FROM Sales.SalesOrderDetail WHERE SalesOrderID = 60677
```

This query execution will trigger the following events:

```
SQL:StmtCompleted. SELECT * FROM Sales.SalesOrderDetail WHERE
SalesOrderID = 60677

SQL:BatchCompleted. SELECT * FROM Sales.SalesOrderDetail WHERE
SalesOrderID = 60677
```

You could look for ApplicationName under **Microsoft SQL Server Management Studio – Query** in case you see more events. You may also consider filtering by SPID using Profiler's filtering capabilities.

Now, let's say we create and execute the same query as part of a simple stored procedure, like so:

```
CREATE PROC test
AS
SELECT * FROM HumanResources.Employee WHERE BusinessEntityID =
229
```

Let's run it:

```
EXEC test
```

Here, we would hit the following events:

```
SP:StmtCompleted. SELECT * FROM HumanResources.Employee WHERE
BusinessEntityID = 229

SP:Completed. SELECT * FROM HumanResources.Employee WHERE
BusinessEntityID = 229

SP:Completed. EXEC test

SQL:StmtCompleted. EXEC test

SQL:BatchCompleted. EXEC test
```

Only the first three events are related to the execution of the stored procedure per se. The last two events are related to the execution of the batch with the EXEC statement.

So, when would we see an RPC:Completed event? For this, we need a remote procedure call (for example, using a .NET application). For this test, we will use the C# code given in the **C# Code for RPS Test** sidebar. Compile the code and run the created executable file. Because we are calling a stored procedure inside the C# code, we will have the following events:

```
SP:Completed. SELECT * FROM HumanResources.Employee WHERE
BusinessEntityID = 229

SP:StmtCompleted. SELECT * FROM HumanResources.Employee WHERE
BusinessEntityID = 229
```

```
SP:Completed. exec dbo.test
RPC:Completed. exec dbo.test
```

Again, you can look for `ApplicationName` under **.Net SqlClient Data Provider** in Profiler in case you see additional events:

```
C# Code for RPC Test
```

Although looking at .NET code is outside the scope of this book, you can use the following code for the test:

```
using System;
using System.Data;
using System.Data.SqlClient;
class Test
{
    static void Main()
    {
        SqlConnection cnn = null;
        SqlDataReader reader = null;
        try
            {
            cnn = new SqlConnection("Data Source=(local);
            Initial Catalog=AdventureWorks2019;Integrated
            Security=SSPI");
            SqlCommand cmd = new SqlCommand();
            cmd.Connection = cnn;
            cmd.CommandText = "dbo.test";
            cmd.CommandType = CommandType.StoredProcedure;
            cnn.Open();
            reader = cmd.ExecuteReader();
            while (reader.Read())
            {
                Console.WriteLine(reader[0]);
            }
            return;
        }
        catch (Exception e)
```

```
        {
            throw e;
        }
        finally
        {
            if (cnn != null)
            {
                if (cnn.State != ConnectionState.Closed)
                cnn.Close();
            }
        }
    }
}
```

To compile the C# code, run the following in a command prompt window:

```
csc test.cs
```

You don't need Visual Studio installed, just Microsoft .NET Framework, which is required to install SQL Server, so it will already be available on your system. You may need to find the CSC executable, though, if it is not included on the system's PATH, although it is usually inside the C:\Windows\ Microsoft.NET directory. You may also need to edit the used connection string, which assumes you are connecting to a default instance of SQL Server using Windows authentication.

Extended events

We briefly introduced extended events in the previous chapter to show you how to capture execution plans. In this section, we'll gain more information about this feature, which was introduced with SQL Server 2008. There is another important reason for this: as of SQL Server 2012, SQL Trace has been deprecated, making extended events the tool of choice to provide debugging and diagnostic capabilities in SQL Server. Although explaining extended events in full detail is beyond the scope of this book, this section will give you enough background to get started using this feature to troubleshoot your queries.

In this section, you will be introduced to the basic concepts surrounding extended events, including events, predicates, actions, targets, and sessions. Although we mainly use code for the examples in this book, it is worth showing you the new extended events graphical user interface too, which is useful if you are new to this technology and can also help you script the definition of extended events sessions in pretty much the same way we use Profiler to script a server trace. The extended events graphical user interface was introduced in SQL Server 2012.

One of my favorite things to do with SQL Trace – and now with extended events – is to learn how other SQL Server tools work. You can run a trace against your instance and run any one of the tools to capture all the T-SQL statements sent from the tool to the database engine. For example, I recently troubleshooted a problem with Replication Monitor by capturing all the code this tool was sending to SQL Server. Interestingly, the extended events graphical user interface is not an exception, and you can use it to see how the tool itself works. When you start the tool, it loads all the required extended events information. By tracing it, you can see where the information is coming from. You don't have to worry about this for now as we will cover it next.

Extended events are designed to have a low impact on server performance. They correspond to well-known points in the SQL Server code, so when a specific task is executing, SQL Server will perform a quick check to find out if any sessions have been configured to listen to this event. If no sessions are active, the event will not fire, and the SQL Server task will continue with no overhead. If, on the other hand, there are active sessions that have the event enabled, SQL Server will collect the required data associated with the event. Then, it will validate the predicate, if any, that was defined for the session. If the predicate evaluates to `false`, the task will continue with minimal overhead. If the predicate evaluates to `true`, the actions defined in the session will be executed. Finally, all the event data is collected by the defined targets for later analysis.

You can use the following statement to find out the list of events that are available on the current version of SQL Server. You can create an extended events session by selecting one or more of the following events:

```
SELECT name, description
FROM sys.dm_xe_objects
WHERE object_type = 'event' AND
(capabilities & 1 = 0 OR capabilities IS NULL)
ORDER BY name
```

Note that 2,408 events are returned with SQL Server 2022 CTP 2.0, including `sp_statement_completed`, `sql_batch_completed`, and `sql_statement_completed`, which we will discuss later.

Each event has a set of columns that you can display by using the `sys.dm_xe_object_columns` DMV, as shown in the following code:

```
SELECT o.name, c.name as column_name, c.description
FROM sys.dm_xe_objects o
JOIN sys.dm_xe_object_columns c
ON o.name = c.object_name
WHERE object_type = 'event' AND
c.column_type <> 'readonly' AND
```

```
(o.capabilities & 1 = 0 OR o.capabilities IS NULL)
ORDER BY o.name, c.name
```

An action is a programmatic response to an event and allows you to execute additional code. Although you can use actions to perform operations such as capturing a stack dump or inserting a debugger break into SQL Server, most likely, they will be used to capture global fields that are common to all the events, such as `plan_handle` and `database_name`. Actions are also executed synchronously. You can run the following code to find the entire list of available actions:

```
SELECT name, description
FROM sys.dm_xe_objects
WHERE object_type = 'action' AND
(capabilities & 1 = 0 OR capabilities IS NULL)
ORDER BY name
```

Predicates are used to limit the data you want to capture, and you can filter against event data columns or any of the global state data returned by the following query:

```
SELECT name, description
FROM sys.dm_xe_objects
WHERE object_type = 'pred_source' AND
(capabilities & 1 = 0 OR capabilities IS NULL)
ORDER BY name
```

The query returns 50 values, including `database_id`, `session_id`, and `query_hash`. Predicates are Boolean expressions that evaluate to either true or false, and they also support short-circuiting, in which an entire expression will evaluate to false as soon as any of its predicates evaluates to false.

Finally, you can use targets to specify how you want to collect the data for analysis; for example, you can store event data in a file or keep it in the ring buffer (a ring buffer is a data structure that briefly holds event data in memory in a circular way). These targets are named `event_file` and `ring_buffer`, respectively. Targets can consume event data both synchronously and asynchronously, and any target can consume any event. You can list the six available targets by running the following query:

```
SELECT name, description
FROM sys.dm_xe_objects
WHERE object_type = 'target' AND
(capabilities & 1 = 0 OR capabilities IS NULL)
ORDER BY name
```

We will cover how to use all these concepts to create event sessions later in this chapter, but first, we will check out how to find the names of events you may be already familiar with when using SQL Trace.

Mapping SQL Trace events to extended events

You are probably already familiar with some SQL Trace events or even have trace definitions already configured in your environment. You can use the sys.trace_xe_event_map extended events system table to help you map SQL Trace event classes to extended events. sys.trace_xe_event_map contains one row for each extended event that is mapped to a SQL Trace event class. To see how it works, run the following query:

```
SELECT te.trace_event_id, name, package_name, xe_event_name
FROM sys.trace_events te
JOIN sys.trace_xe_event_map txe ON te.trace_event_id = txe.
trace_event_id
WHERE te.trace_event_id IS NOT NULL
ORDER BY name
```

The query returns 139 records, some of which are shown here:

trace_event_id	name	package_name	xe_event_name
196	Assembly Load	sqlserver	assembly_load
16	Attention	sqlserver	attention
14	Audit Login	sqlserver	login
15	Audit Logout	sqlserver	logout
18	Audit Server Starts And Stops	sqlserver	server_start_stop
58	Auto Stats	sqlserver	auto_stats
193	Background Job Error	sqlserver	background_job_error
212	Bitmap Warning	sqlserver	bitmap_disabled_warning
137	Blocked process report	sqlserver	blocked_process_report

In addition, you can use the sys.trace_xe_event_map system table in combination with the sys.fn_trace_geteventinfo function to map the events that have been configured on an existing trace to extended events. The sys.fn_trace_geteventinfo function returns information about a trace currently running and requires its trace ID. To test it, run your trace (explained previously) and run the following statement to get its trace ID. trace_id 1 is usually the default trace. You can easily identify your trace by looking at the path column on the output, where NULL is shown if you are running a Profiler trace:

```
SELECT * FROM sys.traces
```

Once you get the trace ID, you can run the following code. In this case, we are using a trace_id value of 2 (used by the sys.fn_trace_geteventinfo function):

```
SELECT te.trace_event_id, name, package_name, xe_event_name
FROM sys.trace_events te
```

```
JOIN sys.trace_xe_event_map txe ON te.trace_event_id = txe.
trace_event_id
WHERE te.trace_event_id IN (
SELECT DISTINCT(eventid) FROM sys.fn_trace_geteventinfo(2))
ORDER BY name
```

If we run the trace we created previously in the *SQL Trace* section, we will get the following output:

trace_event_id	name	package_name	xe_event_name
10	RPC:Completed	sqlserver	rpc_completed
43	SP:Completed	sqlserver	module_end
45	SP:StmtCompleted	sqlserver	sp_statement_completed
12	SQL:BatchCompleted	sqlserver	sql_batch_completed
41	SQL:StmtCompleted	sqlserver	sql_statement_completed

As you can see, the event names of our selected SQL Trace events are very similar to their extended events counterparts, except for SP:Completed, whose extended events name is module_end. Here are the definitions of these events:

rpc_completed	Occurs when a remote procedure call has been completed
module_end	Indicates when the stored procedure has been completed
sp_statement_completed	Indicates that a SQL statement within a stored procedure has been completed
sql_batch_completed	Occurs when a SQL batch has been completed
sql_statement_completed	Occurs when the SQL statement has been completed

> **Note**
>
> SQL Server comes with several extended events templates. One of them, called Query Detail Sampling, collects detailed statement and error information and includes the five listed events, plus error_reported. It also has some predefined actions and predicates, and it uses the ring_buffer target to collect its data. Its predefined predicated filters only collect 20 percent of the active sessions on the server at any given time, so perhaps that is something you may decide to change.

Working with extended events

At this point, we have enough information to create an extended events session. Extended events include different DDL commands to work with sessions, such as CREATE EVENT SESSION, ALTER EVENT SESSION, and DROP EVENT SESSION. But first, we will learn how to create a session using the extended events graphical user interface, which you can use to easily create and manage extended events sessions, as well as script the generated CREATE EVENT code. To start, in Management Studio, expand the **Management** and **Extended Event** nodes and right-click **Sessions**.

> **Note**
>
> By expanding the **Sessions** node, you will see three extended events sessions that are defined by default: `AlwaysOn_health`, `telemetry_xevents`, and `system_health`. `system_health` is started by default every time SQL Server starts, and it is used to collect several predefined events to troubleshoot performance issues. `AlwaysOn_health`, which is `off` by default, is a session designed to provide monitoring for Availability Groups, a feature introduced with SQL Server 2012. `telemetry_xevents`, introduced with SQL Server 2016, is also started by default and includes a large number of events that can also be used to troubleshoot problems with SQL Server. You can see the events, actions, predicates, targets, and configurations that have been defined for these sessions by looking at their properties or scripting them. To script an extended events session in Management Studio, right-click the session and select both **Script Session As** and **CREATE To**.

You should see the **New Session** wizard and the **New Session** dialog. In this section, we will be briefly introduced to the **New Session** dialog. Once you select it, you should see the following screen, along with four different pages: **General**, **Events**, **Data Storage**, and **Advanced**:

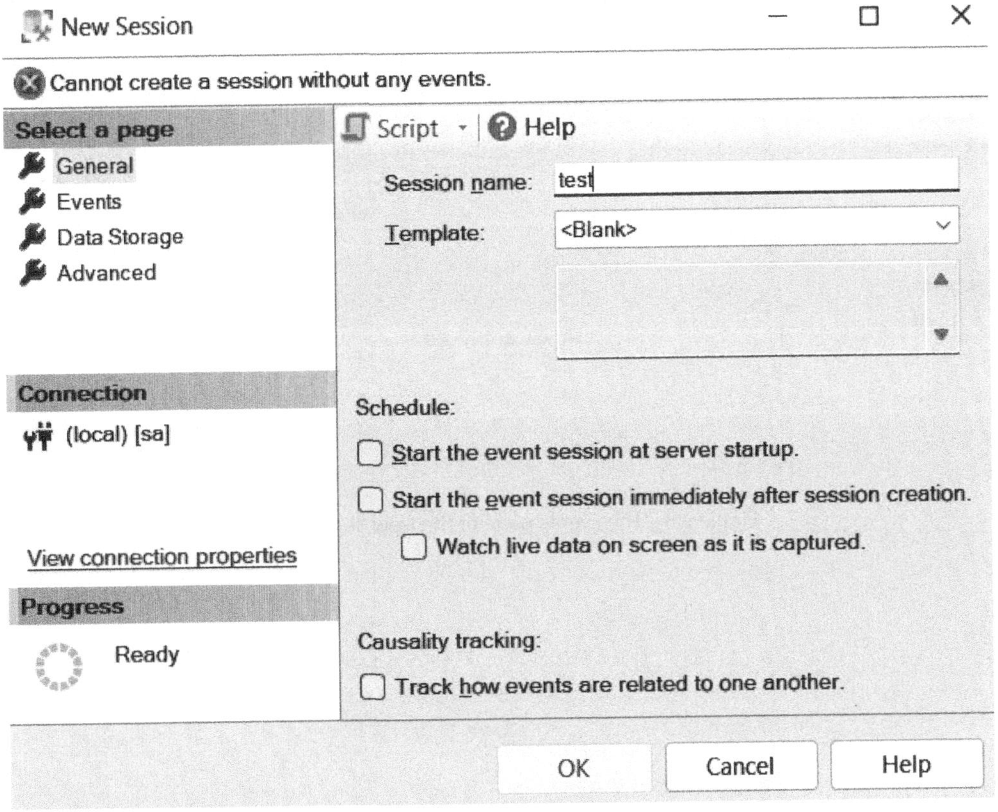

Figure 2.2 – The General page of the New Session dialog

Name the session `Test` and click the **Events** page in the selection area on the left.

The **Events** page allows you to select the events for your session. Because this page may contain a lot of information, you may want to maximize this window. Searching for events in the event library is allowed; for example, because four of the five events we are looking for contain the word `completed`, you could just type this word to search for them, as shown here:

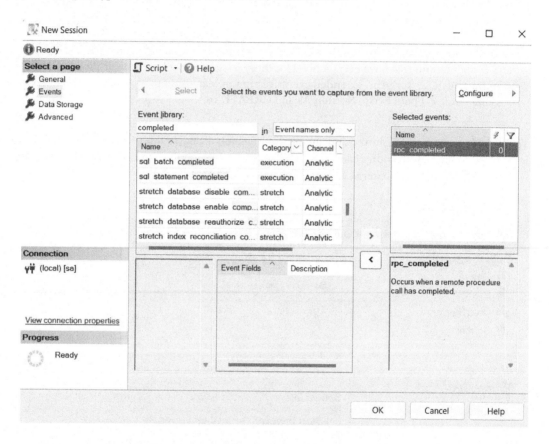

Figure 2.3 – The Events page of the New Session dialog

Click the > button to select the **rpc_completed**, **sp_statement_completed**, **sql_batch_completed**, and **sql_statement_completed** events. Do a similar search and add the **module_end** event. The **Events** page also allows you to define actions and predicates (filters) by clicking the **Configure** button, which shows the **Event Configuration Options** section. Click the **Configure** button, and in addition to selecting our five chosen extended events, check the boxes for the following actions in the **Global Fields (Actions)** tab: **plan_handle**, **query_hash**, **query_plan_hash**, and **sql_text**. Your current selection should look as follows:

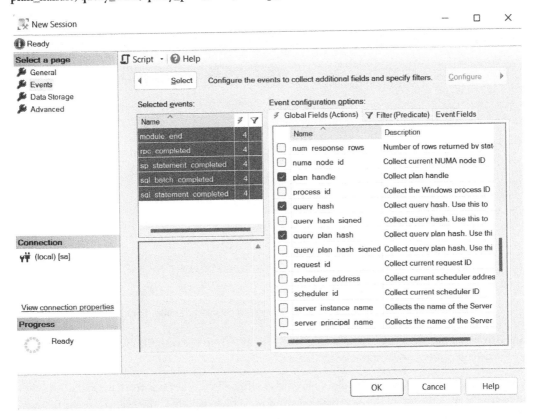

Figure 2.4 – The Event configuration options section of the Events page

Clicking the **Data Storage** page allows you to select one or more targets to collect your event data. Select the **ring_buffer** target, as shown in the following screenshot:

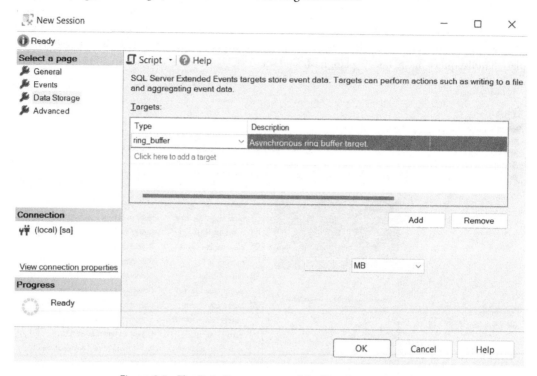

Figure 2.5 – The Data Storage page of the New Session dialog

The **Advanced** page allows you to specify additional options to use with the event session. Let's keep all the default options as-is on this page.

Finally, as usual in Management Studio, you can also script all the selections you have made by clicking the **Script** icon at the top of the **New Session** window. Let's do just that. This will create the following code, which we can use to create our extended events session:

```
CREATE EVENT SESSION test ON SERVER
ADD EVENT sqlserver.module_end(
ACTION(sqlserver.plan_handle,sqlserver.query_hash,sqlserver.
query_plan_hash,
sqlserver.sql_text)),
ADD EVENT sqlserver.rpc_completed(
ACTION(sqlserver.plan_handle,sqlserver.query_hash,sqlserver.
query_plan_hash,
sqlserver.sql_text)),
```

```
ADD EVENT sqlserver.sp_statement_completed(
ACTION(sqlserver.plan_handle,sqlserver.query_hash,sqlserver.
query_plan_hash,
sqlserver.sql_text)),
ADD EVENT sqlserver.sql_batch_completed(
ACTION(sqlserver.plan_handle,sqlserver.query_hash,sqlserver.
query_plan_hash,
sqlserver.sql_text)),
ADD EVENT sqlserver.sql_statement_completed(
ACTION(sqlserver.plan_handle,sqlserver.query_hash,sqlserver.
query_plan_hash,
sqlserver.sql_text))
ADD TARGET package0.ring_buffer
WITH (STARTUP_STATE=OFF)
```

As shown in the previous chapter, we also need to start the extended events session by running the following code:

```
ALTER EVENT SESSION [test]
ON SERVER
STATE=START
```

So, at the moment, our session is active, and we just need to wait for the events to occur. To test it, run the following statements:

```
SELECT * FROM Sales.SalesOrderDetail WHERE SalesOrderID = 60677
GO
SELECT * FROM Person.Address WHERE AddressID = 21
GO
SELECT * FROM HumanResources.Employee WHERE BusinessEntityID =
229
GO
```

Once you have captured some events, you may want to read and analyze their data. You can use the **Watch Live Data** feature that was introduced with SQL Server 2012 to view and analyze the extended events data that was captured by the event session, as introduced in the previous chapter. Alternatively, you can use XQuery to read the data from any of the targets. To read the current captured events, run the following code:

```
SELECT name, target_name, execution_count, CAST(target_data AS
xml)
```

```
AS target_data
FROM sys.dm_xe_sessions s
JOIN sys.dm_xe_session_targets t
ON s.address = t.event_session_address
WHERE s.name = 'test'
```

This will produce an output similar to the following:

name	target_name	execution_count	target_data
test	ring_buffer	68	<RingBufferTarget truncated="1" processingTime="267"...

You can open the link to see the captured data in XML format. Because the XML file would be too large to show in this book, only a small sample of the first event that was captured, showing cpu_time, duration, physical_reads, and logical_reads, and writes, is included here:

```
<RingBufferTarget truncated="0" processingTime="0"
totalEventsProcessed="12"
eventCount="12" droppedCount="0" memoryUsed="5810">
<event name="sql_batch_completed" package="sqlserver"
timestamp="2022-06-01T20:08:42.240Z">
<data name="cpu_time">
<type name="uint64" package="package0" />
<value>0</value>
</data>
<data name="duration">
<type name="uint64" package="package0" />
<value>1731</value>
</data>
<data name="physical_reads">
<type name="uint64" package="package0" />
<value>0</value>
</data>
<data name="logical_reads">
<type name="uint64" package="package0" />
<value>4</value>
</data>
<data name="writes">
<type name="uint64" package="package0" />
```

```
<value>0</value>
</data>
```

However, because reading XML directly is not much fun, we can use XQuery to extract the data from the XML document and get a query like this:

```
SELECT
event_data.value('(event/@name)[1]', 'varchar(50)') AS event_
name,
event_data.value('(event/action[@name="query_hash"]/value)[1]',
'varchar(max)') AS query_hash,
event_data.value('(event/data[@name="cpu_time"]/value)[1]',
'int')
AS cpu_time,
event_data.value('(event/data[@name="duration"]/value)[1]',
'int')
AS duration,
event_data.value('(event/data[@name="logical_reads"]/value)
[1]', 'int')
AS logical_reads,
event_data.value('(event/data[@name="physical_reads"]/value)
[1]', 'int')
AS physical_reads,
event_data.value('(event/data[@name="writes"]/value)[1]',
'int') AS writes,
event_data.value('(event/data[@name="statement"]/value)[1]',
'varchar(max)')
AS statement
FROM(SELECT evnt.query('.') AS event_data
FROM
(SELECT CAST(target_data AS xml) AS target_data
FROM sys.dm_xe_sessions s
JOIN sys.dm_xe_session_targets t
ON s.address = t.event_session_address
WHERE s.name = 'test'
AND t.target_name = 'ring_buffer'
) AS data
```

```
CROSS APPLY target_data.nodes('RingBufferTarget/event') AS
xevent(evnt)
) AS xevent(event_data)
```

This will show an output similar to the following:

event_name	cpu_time	duration	logical_reads	physical_reads	writes	statement
sql_statement_completed	0	42522	3	24	0	SELECT * FROM Sales.SalesOrderDetail WHERE SalesOrderID = 60677
sql_batch_completed	0	80265	13	48	0	NULL
sql_statement_completed	0	23970	2	16	0	SELECT * FROM Person.Address WHERE AddressID = 21
sql_batch_completed	0	53971	4	24	0	NULL
sql_statement_completed	0	29976	2	16	0	SELECT * FROM HumanResources.Employee WHERE BusinessEntityID = 229
sql_batch_completed	0	64189	20	31	0	NULL

However, using that query, you get all the data for each event, and sometimes, you may want to aggregate the data. For example, sorting the data to look for the greatest CPU consumers may not be enough. As you will also see in other areas of this book, sometimes, a performance problem may be caused by some query that, even if it does not show up on the top 10 consumers, or even the top 100, is executed so many times that its aggregated CPU usage can make it one of the top CPU consumers. You can update the previous query to aggregate this data directly, or you can change it to save the information to a temporary table (for example, using SELECT ... INTO) and then group by query_hash and, optionally, sort as needed, as shown here:

```
SELECT query_hash, SUM(cpu_time) AS cpu_time, SUM(duration) AS
duration,
SUM(logical_reads) AS logical_reads, SUM(physical_reads) AS
physical_reads,
SUM(writes) AS writes, MAX(statement) AS statement
FROM #eventdata
GROUP BY query_hash
```

Again, as covered in the previous chapter, after you finish your test, you need to stop and delete the event session. Run the following statements:

```
ALTER EVENT SESSION [test]
ON SERVER
STATE=STOP
GO
DROP EVENT SESSION [test] ON SERVER
```

You could also use the file target when collecting large amounts of data or running the session for a long time. The following example is exactly the same as before, but using the file target (note the file definition on the C:\Data folder):

```
CREATE EVENT SESSION test ON SERVER
ADD EVENT sqlserver.module_end(
ACTION(sqlserver.plan_handle,sqlserver.query_hash,sqlserver.
query_plan_hash,
sqlserver.sql_text)),
ADD EVENT sqlserver.rpc_completed(
ACTION(sqlserver.plan_handle,sqlserver.query_hash,sqlserver.
query_plan_hash,
sqlserver.sql_text)),
ADD EVENT sqlserver.sp_statement_completed(
ACTION(sqlserver.plan_handle,sqlserver.query_hash,sqlserver.
query_plan_hash,
sqlserver.sql_text)),
ADD EVENT sqlserver.sql_batch_completed(
ACTION(sqlserver.plan_handle,sqlserver.query_hash,sqlserver.
query_plan_hash,
sqlserver.sql_text)),
ADD EVENT sqlserver.sql_statement_completed(
ACTION(sqlserver.plan_handle,sqlserver.query_hash,sqlserver.
query_plan_hash,
sqlserver.sql_text))
ADD TARGET package0.event_file(SET filename=N'C:\Data\test.
xel')
WITH (STARTUP_STATE=OFF)
```

After starting the session and capturing some events, you can query its data by using the following query and the sys.fn_xe_file_target_read_file function:

```
SELECT
event_data.value('(event/@name)[1]', 'varchar(50)') AS event_
name,
event_data.value('(event/action[@name="query_hash"]/value)[1]',
'varchar(max)') AS query_hash,
event_data.value('(event/data[@name="cpu_time"]/value)[1]',
'int')
AS cpu_time,
event_data.value('(event/data[@name="duration"]/value)[1]',
'int')
AS duration,
event_data.value('(event/data[@name="logical_reads"]/value)
[1]', 'int')
AS logical_reads,
event_data.value('(event/data[@name="physical_reads"]/value)
[1]', 'int')
AS physical_reads,
event_data.value('(event/data[@name="writes"]/value)[1]',
'int') AS writes,
event_data.value('(event/data[@name="statement"]/value)[1]',
'varchar(max)')
AS statement
FROM
(
SELECT CAST(event_data AS xml)
FROM sys.fn_xe_file_target_read_file
(
'C:\Data\test*.xel',
NULL,
NULL,
NULL
)
) AS xevent(event_data)
```

If you inspect the `C:\Data` folder, you will find a file with a name similar to `test_0_130133932321310000.xel`. SQL Server adds "`_0_`" plus an integer representing the number of milliseconds since January 1, 1600, to the specified filename. You can inspect the contents of a particular file by providing the assigned filename or by using a wildcard (such as the asterisk shown in the preceding code) to inspect all the available files. For more details on using the file target, see the SQL Server documentation. Again, don't forget to stop and drop your session when you finish testing.

Finally, we will use extended events to show you how to obtain the waits for a specific query, something that was not even possible before extended events. You must use the `wait_info` event and select any of the many available fields (such as `username` or `query_hash`) or selected actions to apply a filter (or predicate) to it. In this example, we will use `session_id`. Make sure to replace `session_id` as required if you are testing this code:

```
CREATE EVENT SESSION [test] ON SERVER
ADD EVENT sqlos.wait_info(
WHERE ([sqlserver].[session_id]=(61)))
ADD TARGET package0.ring_buffer
WITH (STARTUP_STATE=OFF)
```

Start the event:

```
ALTER EVENT SESSION [test]
ON SERVER
STATE=START
```

Run some transactions but note that they need to be executed in the session ID you specified (and they need to create waits). For example, run the following query:

```
SELECT * FROM Production.Product p1 CROSS JOIN
Production.Product p2
```

Then, you can read the captured data:

```
SELECT
event_data.value('(event/@name)[1]', 'varchar(50)') AS event_
name,
event_data.value('(event/data[@name="wait_type"]/text)[1]',
'varchar(40)')
AS wait_type,
```

```
event_data.value('(event/data[@name="duration"]/value)[1]',
'int')
AS duration,
event_data.value('(event/data[@name="opcode"]/text)[1]',
'varchar(40)')
AS opcode,
event_data.value('(event/data[@name="signal_duration"]/value)
[1]', 'int')
AS signal_duration
FROM(SELECT evnt.query('.') AS event_data
FROM
(SELECT CAST(target_data AS xml) AS target_data
FROM sys.dm_xe_sessions s
JOIN sys.dm_xe_session_targets t
ON s.address = t.event_session_address
WHERE s.name = 'test'
AND t.target_name = 'ring_buffer'
) AS data
CROSS APPLY target_data.nodes('RingBufferTarget/event') AS
xevent(evnt)
) AS xevent(event_data)
```

Here is the output on my system:

event_name	wait_type	wait_type	opcode	signal_duration
wait_info	NETWORK_IO	0	Begin	0
wait_info	NETWORK_IO	0	End	0
wait_info	NETWORK_IO	0	Begin	0
wait_info	NETWORK_IO	0	End	0

Again, this is another example where aggregating the captured data would be beneficial. Finally, don't forget to stop and drop your event session, as indicated previously.

So, now that we have covered several features that we can use to collect query performance information, such as DMVs, DMFs, SQL Trace, and extended events, let's close this chapter with the Data Collector. The Data Collector is a tool that's designed to collect performance data and is especially useful in cases where you do not have access to a dedicated third-party tool.

The Data Collector

There may be cases when a performance problem occurs and there is little or no information available to troubleshoot it. For example, you may receive a notification that CPU percentage usage was 100 percent for a few minutes, thus slowing down your application, but by the time you connected to the system to troubleshoot, the problem is already gone. Many times, a specific problem is difficult to reproduce, and the only choice is to enable a trace or some other collection of data and wait until the problem happens again.

This is where proactively collecting performance data is extremely important, and the Data Collector, a feature introduced with SQL Server 2008, can help you to do just that. The Data Collector allows you to collect performance data, which you can use immediately after a performance problem occurs. You only need to know the time the problem occurred and start looking at the collected data around that period.

Explaining the Data Collector would take an entire chapter, if not an entire book. Therefore, this section aims to show you how to get started. You can find more details about the Data Collector by reading the SQL Server documentation or by reading the Microsoft white paper *Using Management Data Warehouse for Performance Monitoring* by Ken Lassesen.

Configuration

The Data Collector is not enabled by default after you install SQL Server. To configure it, you need to follow a two-step process:

1. To configure the first part, expand the **Management** folder in Management Studio, right-click the **Data Collection** node, and select **Tasks**, followed by **Configure Management Data Warehouse**. This will run the **Configure Management Data Warehouse** Wizard. Click **Next** on the **Welcome** screen. This will take you to the **Configure Management Data Warehouse Storage** screen, as shown in the following screenshot. This screen allows you to select the database you will use to collect data. Optionally, you can create a new database by selecting the **New** button:

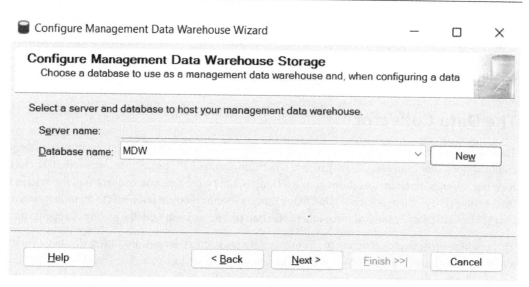

Figure 2.6 – The Configure Management Data Warehouse Storage screen

2.   Select an existing database, or create a new one, and then click **Next**. The following screen, **Map Logins and Users**, as shown in the following screenshot, allows you to map logins and users to management data warehouse roles:

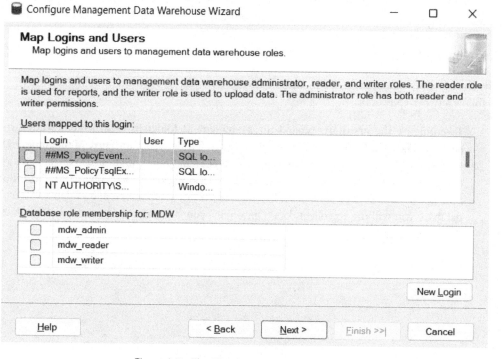

Figure 2.7 – The Map Logins and Users screen

3. Click **Next**. The **Complete the Wizard** screen will appear.

4. On the **Complete the Wizard** screen, click **Finish**. You will see the **Configure Data Collection Wizard Progress** screen. Make sure all the steps shown are executed successfully and click the **Close** button. This step configures the management data warehouse database, and, among other objects, it will create a collection of tables, some of which we will query directly later in this section.

5. To configure the second step, right-click **Data Collection** again and select **Tasks**, followed by **Configure Data Collection**. This will open the **Configure Data Collection Wizard** screen. Click **Next**. You should see **Setup Data Collection Sets**, as shown in the following screenshot:

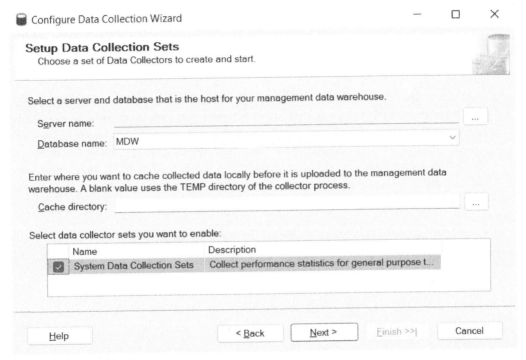

Figure 2.8 – The Setup Data Collection Sets screen

This is where you select the database to be used as the management data warehouse, which is the database you configured in *Step 1*. You can also configure the cache directory, which is used to collect the data before it is uploaded to the management data warehouse.

6. Finally, you need to select the Data Collector sets that you want to enable, which in our case requires selecting **System Data Collection Sets**. Although it is the only data collector set available on SQL Server 2022, some others have been available on previous versions, such as the Transaction Performance Collection Set, which was used by the In-Memory OLTP feature. Click **Next** and then **Finish** on the **Complete the Wizard** screen.

Once you've configured the Data Collector, among other items, you will see the three enabled system data collection sets: **Disk Usage**, **Query Statistics**, and **Server Activity**. The Utility Information collection set is disabled by default, and it will not be covered in this book. The following data was collected by the System Data Collection Sets:

Disk Usage	Collects data about disk and log usage for all the databases installed on the SQL Server instance
Query Statistics	Collects query statistics, individual query text, query plans, and specific queries
Server Activity	Collects resource usage statistics and performance data from the server and the SQL Server instance

In addition, it is strongly recommended that you install the optional Query Hash Statistics collection set, which you can download from `http://blogs.msdn.com/b/bartd/archive/2010/11/03/query-hash-statistics-a-query-cost-analysis-tool-now-available-for-download.aspx`. The Query Hash Statistics collection set, which unfortunately is not included as part of SQL Server 2022, is based on the `query_hash` and `plan_hash` values, as explained earlier in this chapter. It collects historical query and query plan fingerprint statistics, allowing you to easily see the true cumulative cost of the queries in each of your databases. After you install the Query Hash Statistics collection set, you will need to disable the Query Statistics collection set because it collects the same information.

7. Finally, you need to be aware of the following SQL Server Agent jobs that were created:

- `collection_set_1_noncached_collect_and_upload`
- `collection_set_2_collection`
- `collection_set_2_upload`
- `collection_set_3_collection`
- `collection_set_3_upload`
- `mdw_purge_data_[MDW]`
- `syspolicy_purge_history`

Using the Data Collector

The next thing you want to do is become familiar with the Data Collector – mostly, the reports available and the information that's collected on each table. To start looking at the reports, right-click **Data Collection** and select **Reports**, **Management Data Warehouse**, and **Server Activity History**. Assuming enough data has already been collected, you should see a report similar to the one shown in the following screenshot (only partly shown):

Navigate through the historical snapshots of data using the time line below:

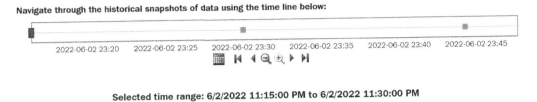

Selected time range: 6/2/2022 11:15:00 PM to 6/2/2022 11:30:00 PM

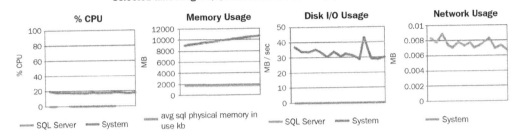

Figure 2.9 – The Server Activity History report

Clicking the **SQL Server** section of the **% CPU** graph will take you to the **Query Statistics History** report. You can also reach this report by right-clicking **Data Collection** and then selecting **Reports**, **Management Data Warehouse**, and **Query Statistics History**. In both cases, you will end up with the report shown in the following screenshot (only partly shown):

Navigate through the historical snapshots of data using the time line below:

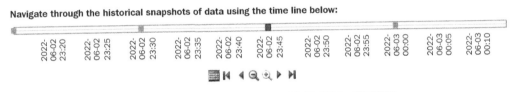

Selected time range: 6/2/2022 11:45:00 PM to 6/3/2022

Top Queries by Total CPU

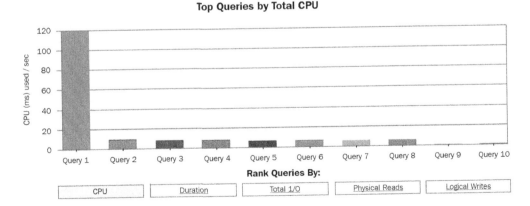

Figure 2.10 – The Query Statistics History report

Running the **Query Statistics History** report will show you the top 10 most expensive queries ranked by CPU usage, though you also have the choice of selecting the most expensive queries by duration, total I/O, physical reads, and logical writes. The Data Collector includes other reports, and as you've seen already, some reports include links to navigate to other reports for more detailed information.

Querying the Data Collector tables

More advanced users will want to query the Data Collector tables directly to create reports or look deeper into the collected data. Creating custom collection sets is also possible and may be required when you need to capture data that the default installation is not collecting. Having custom collection sets would, again, require you to create your own queries and reports.

For example, the Data Collector collects multiple performance counters, which you can see by looking at the properties of the Server Activity collection set. To do this, expand both the **Data Collection** and **System Data Collection** sets, right-click the **Server Activity** collection set, and select **Properties**. In the **Data Collection Set Properties** window, select **Server Activity – Performance Counters** in the **Collection Items** list box and look at the **Input Parameters** window. Here is a small sample of these performance counters:

```
\Memory \% Committed Bytes In Use
\Memory \Available Bytes
\Memory \Cache Bytes
\Memory \Cache Faults/sec
\Memory \Committed Bytes
\Memory \Free & Zero Page List Bytes
\Memory \Modified Page List Bytes
\Memory \Pages/sec
\Memory \Page Reads/sec
\Memory \Page Write/sec
\Memory \Page Faults/sec
\Memory \Pool Nonpaged Bytes
\Memory \Pool Paged Bytes
```

You can also see a very detailed definition of the performance counters that have been collected in your instance by looking at the `snapshots.performance_counter_instances` table. Performance counters' data is then stored in the `snapshots.performance_counter_values` table. One of the most used performance counters by database administrators is `'\Processor(_Total)\% Processor Time'`, which allows you to collect the processor percentage usage. We can use the following query to get the collected data:

```
SELECT sii.instance_name, collection_time, [path] AS counter_
name,
```

```
formatted_value AS counter_value_percent
FROM snapshots.performance_counter_values pcv
JOIN snapshots.performance_counter_instances pci
ON pcv.performance_counter_instance_id = pci.performance_
counter_id
JOIN core.snapshots_internal si ON pcv.snapshot_id =
si.snapshot_id
JOIN core.source_info_internal sii ON sii.source_id =
si.source_id
WHERE pci.[path] = '\Processor(_Total)\% Processor Time'
ORDER BY pcv.collection_time desc
```

An output similar to the following will be shown:

There are some other interesting tables, at least from the point of view of query data collection, you may need to query directly. The Query Statistics collection set uses queries defined in the `QueryActivityCollect.dtsx` and `QueryActivityUpload.dtsx` SSIS packages, and the collected data is loaded into the `snapshots.query_stats`, `snapshots.notable_query_text`, and `snapshots.notable_query_plan` tables. These tables collect query statistics, query text, and query plans, respectively. If you installed the Query Hash Statistics collection set, the `QueryHashStatsPlanCollect` and `QueryHashStatsPlanUpload` packages will be used instead. Another interesting table is `snapshots.active_sessions_and_requests`, which collects information about SQL Server sessions and requests.

collection_time	counter_name	counter_value_percent
2022-06-02 23:33:42.0000000 -07:00	\Processor(_Total)\% Processor Time	17.35051722
2022-06-02 23:32:42.0000000 -07:00	\Processor(_Total)\% Processor Time	17.47507888
2022-06-02 23:31:42.0000000 -07:00	\Processor(_Total)\% Processor Time	17.97797844
2022-06-02 23:30:42.0000000 -07:00	\Processor(_Total)\% Processor Time	20.02577005
2022-06-02 23:29:42.0000000 -07:00	\Processor(_Total)\% Processor Time	18.0100147
2022-06-02 23:28:42.0000000 -07:00	\Processor(_Total)\% Processor Time	17.32953855
2022-06-02 23:27:42.0000000 -07:00	\Processor(_Total)\% Processor Time	17.95348552
2022-06-02 23:26:42.0000000 -07:00	\Processor(_Total)\% Processor Time	18.7135785

Summary

This chapter has provided you with several tuning techniques you can use to find out how your queries are using system resources such as disk and CPU. First, we explained some essential DMVs and DMFs that are very useful for tracking expensive queries. Two features that were introduced with SQL Server 2008, extended events and the Data Collector, were explained as well, along with how they can help capture events and performance data. We also discussed SQL Trace, a feature that has been around in all the SQL Server versions as far as any of us can remember.

So, now that we know how to find the expensive queries in SQL Server, what's next? Our final purpose is to do something to improve the performance of the query. To achieve that, we will cover different approaches in the coming chapters. Is just a better index needed? Maybe your query is sensitive to different parameters, or maybe the query optimizer is not giving you a good execution plan because a used feature does not have good support for statistics. We will cover these and many other issues in the following chapters.

Once we have found the query that may be causing the problem, we still need to troubleshoot what the problem is and find a solution to it. Many times, we can troubleshoot what the problem is just by inspecting all the rich information that's available in the query execution plan. To do that, we need to dive deeper into how the query optimizer works and what the different operators the execution engine provides. We will cover those topics in detail in the following two chapters.

3

The Query
Optimizer

In this chapter, we will cover how the SQL Server Query Optimizer works and introduce the steps it performs in the background. This covers everything, from the time a query is submitted to SQL Server until an execution plan is generated and is ready to be executed. This includes steps such as parsing, binding, simplification, trivial plan optimization, and full optimization. Important components and mechanisms that are part of the Query Optimizer architecture, such as transformation rules and the Memo structure, are also introduced.

The purpose of the Query Optimizer is to provide an optimum execution plan, or at least a good enough execution plan, and to do so, it generates many possible alternatives through the use of transformation rules. These alternative plans are stored for the duration of the optimization process in a structure called the Memo. Unfortunately, a drawback of cost-based optimization is the cost of optimization itself. Given that finding the optimum plan for some queries would take an unacceptably long optimization time, some heuristics are used to limit the number of alternative plans considered instead of using the entire search space—remember that the goal is to find a good enough plan as quickly as possible. Heuristics help the Query Optimizer to cope with the combinatorial explosion that occurs in the search space as queries get progressively more complex. However, the use of transformation rules and heuristics does not necessarily reduce the cost of the available alternatives, so the cost of each candidate plan is also determined, and the best alternative is chosen based on those costs.

This chapter covers the following topics:

- Query optimization research
- Introduction to query processing
- The sys.dm_exec_query_optimizer_info DMV
- Parsing and binding

- Simplification

- Trivial plan

- Joins

- Transformation rules

- The memo

- Statistics

- Full optimization

Query optimization research

Query optimization research dates back to the early 1970s. One of the earliest works describing a cost-based query optimizer was *Access Path Selection in a Relational Database Management System*, published in 1979 by Pat Selinger et al, to describe the query optimizer for an experimental database management system developed in 1975 at what is now the IBM Almaden Research Center. This database management system, called **System R**, advanced the field of query optimization by introducing the use of cost-based query optimization, the use of statistics, an efficient method of determining join orders, and the addition of CPU cost to the optimizer's cost estimation formulae.

Yet, despite being an enormous influence in the field of query optimization research, it suffered a major drawback: its framework could not be easily extended to include additional transformations. This led to the development of more extensible optimization architectures that facilitated the gradual addition of new functionality to query optimizers. The trailblazers in this field were the Exodus Optimizer Generator, defined by Goetz Graefe and David DeWitt, and, later, the Volcano Optimizer Generator, defined by Goetz Graefe and William McKenna. Goetz Graefe then went on to define the Cascades Framework, resolving errors that were present in his previous two endeavors.

What is most relevant for us about this previous research is that SQL Server implemented a new cost-based query optimizer, based on the Cascades Framework, in 1999, when its database engine was re-architected for the release of SQL Server 7.0. The extensible architecture of the Cascades Framework has made it much easier for new functionality, such as new transformation rules or physical operators, to be implemented in the Query Optimizer. We will now check out the *what* and *how* of query processing.

Introduction to query processing

The query optimization and execution process was introduced in *Chapter 1, An Introduction to Query Tuning and Optimization*, and will be explained in more detail throughout this chapter. However, before we get started, we'll briefly explore the inner workings of the query optimization process, which extends both before and after the Query Optimizer itself. The diagram in *Figure 3.1* shows the major phases of the query processing process, and each phase will be explained in more detail in the remaining sections of this chapter.

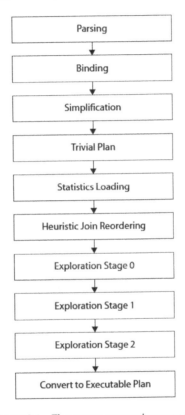

Figure 3.1 – The query-processing process

Parsing and binding are the first operations performed when a query is submitted to a SQL Server database engine. Parsing and binding produce a tree representation of the query, which is then sent to the Query Optimizer to perform the optimization process. At the beginning of this optimization process, this logical tree will be simplified, and the Query Optimizer will check whether the query qualifies for a trivial plan. If it does, a trivial execution plan is returned and the optimization process immediately ends. The parsing, binding, simplification, and trivial plan processes do not depend on the contents of the database (such as the data itself), but only on the database schema and query definition. Because of this, these processes also do not use statistics, cost estimation, or cost-based decisions, all of which are only employed during the full optimization process.

If the query does not qualify for a trivial plan, the Query Optimizer will run the full optimization process, which is executed in up to three stages, and a plan may be produced at the end of any of these stages. In addition, to consider all of the information gathered in the previous phases, such as the query definition and database schema, the full optimization process will use statistics and cost estimation and will then select the best execution plan (within the available time) based solely on that plan's cost

The Query Optimizer has several optimization phases designed to try to optimize queries as quickly and simply as possible and to not use more expensive and sophisticated options unless absolutely necessary. These phases are called the simplification, trivial plan optimization, and full optimization stages. In the same way, the full optimization phase itself consists of up to three stages, as follows:

- Transaction processing

- Quick plan

- Full optimization phases

These three stages are also simply called search 0, search 1, and search 2 phases, respectively. Plans can be produced in any of these stages, except for the simplification phase, which we will discuss in a moment.

> **Caution**
>
> This chapter contains many undocumented and unsupported features, and they are identified in each section as such. They are included in the book and intended for educational purposes so you can use them to better understand how the Query Optimizer works. These undocumented and unsupported features are not supposed to be used in a production environment. Use them carefully, if possible, and only on your own isolated non-production SQL Server instance.

Now that we have explored query processing, we will now check out a unique DMV that can be used for more insights about the Query Optimizer.

The sys.dm_exec_query_optimizer_info DMV

You can use the sys.dm_exec_query_optimizer_info DMV to gain additional insight into the work being performed by the Query Optimizer. This DMV, which is only partially documented, provides information regarding the optimizations performed on the SQL Server instance. Although this DMV contains cumulative statistics recorded since the given SQL Server instance was started, it can also be used to get optimization information for a specific query or workload, as we'll see in a moment.

As mentioned, you can use this DMV to obtain statistics regarding the operation of the Query Optimizer, such as how queries have been optimized and how many of them have been optimized since the instance started. This DMV returns three columns:

- **Counter**: The name of the optimizer event
- **Occurrence**: The number of occurrences of the optimization event for this counter
- **Value**: The average value per event occurrence

Thirty-eight counters were originally defined for this DMV when it was originally introduced with SQL Server 2005, and a new counter called merge stmt was added in SQL Server 2008, giving a total of 39, which continues through SQL Server 2022. To view the statistics for all the query optimizations since the SQL Server instance was started, we can just run the following:

```
SELECT * FROM sys.dm_exec_query_optimizer_info
```

Here is the partial output we get from one production instance:

Counter	Occurrence	Value
optimizations	691,473	1
elapsed time	691,465	0.007806012
final cost	691,465	1.398120739
trivial plan	29,476	1
tasks	661,989	332.5988816
no plan	0	NULL
search 0	26,724	1
search 0 time	31,420	0.01646922
search 0 tasks	31,420	1198.811617

The output shows that there have been 691,473 optimizations since the instance was started, that the average elapsed time for each optimization was 0.0078 seconds, and that the average estimated cost of each optimization, in internal cost units, was about 1.398. This particular example shows optimizations of inexpensive queries typical of an OLTP system.

Although the `sys.dm_exec_query_optimizer_info` DMV was completely documented in the original version of SQL Server 2005 documentation (originally called *Books Online*), more recent versions of the documentation omit descriptions of nearly half (18 out of 39) of the counters, and instead label them as *Internal only*. Therefore, in *Table 3.1*, you can see the currently documented descriptions plus descriptions of the 18 undocumented counters, according to their original documentation, which is still valid for SQL Server 2022:

Counter	Occurrence	Value
optimizations	Total number of optimizations.	Not applicable.
elapsed time	Total number of optimizations.	Average elapsed time per optimization of an individual statement (query), in seconds.
final cost	Total number of optimizations.	Average estimated cost for an optimized plan, in internal cost units.
trivial plan	Total number of trivial plans (used as final plan).	Not applicable.
tasks	Number of optimizations that applied tasks (exploration, implementation, and property derivation).	Average number of tasks executed.
no plan	Number of optimizations for which no plan was found after a full optimization run, and where no other errors were issued during query compilation.	Not applicable.
search 0	Total number of final plans found in the search 0 phase.	Not applicable.
search 0 time	Number of optimizations that entered search 0.	Average time spent in search 0, in seconds.
search 0 tasks	Number of optimizations that entered search 0.	Average number of tasks run in search 0.
search 1	Total number of final plans found in the search 1 phase.	Not applicable.
search 1 time	Number of optimizations that entered search 1.	Average time spent in search 1, in seconds.
search 1 tasks	Number of optimizations that entered search 1.	Average number of tasks run in search 1.
search 2	Total number of final plans found in the search 2 phase.	Not applicable.
search 2 time	Total number of final plans found in the search 2 phase.	Average time spent in search 2.
search 2 tasks	Number of optimizations that entered search 2.	Average number of tasks run in search 2.

gain stage 0 to stage 1	Number of times search 1 was run after search 0.	Average gain from stage 0 to stage 1 as (MinimumPlanCost(search 0) – MinimumPlanCost(search 1)) / MinimumPlanCost(search 0).
gain stage 1 to stage 2	Number of times search 2 was run after search 1.	Average gain from stage 1 to stage 2 as (MinimumPlanCost(search 1) – MinimumPlanCost(search 2)) / MinimumPlanCost(search 1).
timeout	Number of optimizations for which internal timeout occurred.	Not applicable.
memory limit exceeded	Number of optimizations for which an internal memory limit was exceeded.	Not applicable.
insert stmt	Number of optimizations that are for INSERT statements.	Not applicable.
delete stmt	Number of optimizations that are for DELETE statements.	Not applicable.
update stmt	Number of optimizations that are for UPDATE statements.	Not applicable.
merge stmt	Number of optimizations that are for MERGE statements.	Not applicable.
contains subquery	Number of optimizations for a query that contains at least one subquery.	Not applicable.
unnest failed	Number of times where subquery unnesting could not remove the subquery.	Not applicable.
tables	Total number of optimizations.	Average number of tables referenced per query optimized.
hints	Number of times some hint was specified. Hints counted include JOIN, GROUP, UNION, and FORCE ORDER query hints, FORCE PLAN set option, and join hints.	Not applicable.
order hint	Number of times a force order hint was specified.	Not applicable.
join hint	Number of times the join algorithm was forced by a join hint.	Not applicable.
view reference	Number of times a view has been referenced in a query.	Not applicable.

remote query	Number of optimizations where the query referenced at least one remote data source, such as a table with a four-part name or an OPENROWSET result.	Not applicable.
maximum DOP	Total number of optimizations.	Average effective MAXDOP value for an optimized plan. By default, effective MAXDOP is determined by the maximum degree of parallelism server configuration option and may be overridden for a specific query by the value of the MAXDOP query hint.
maximum recursion level	Number of optimizations in which a MAXRECURSION level greater than 0 has been specified with the query hint.	Average MAXRECURSION level in optimizations where a maximum recursion level is specified with the query hint.
indexed views loaded	Number of queries for which one or more indexed views were loaded for consideration for matching.	Average number of views loaded.
indexed views matched	Number of optimizations where one or more indexed views have been matched.	Average number of views matched.
indexed views used	Number of optimizations where one or more indexed views are used in the output plan after being matched.	Average number of views used.
indexed views updated	Number of optimizations of a DML statement that produce a plan that maintains one or more indexed views.	Average number of views maintained.
dynamic cursor request	Number of optimizations in which a dynamic cursor request has been specified.	Not applicable.
fast forward cursor request	Number of optimizations in which a fast-forward cursor request has been specified.	Not applicable.

Table 3.1 – The sys.dm_exec_query_optimizer_info DMV with undocumented counters

The counters can be used in several ways to show important insights about the optimizations being performed in your instance. For example, the next query displays the percentage of optimizations in the instance that includes hints. This information could be useful to show how extensive the use of hints in your databases is, which in turn can demonstrate that your code may be less flexible than anticipated and may require additional maintenance. Hints are explained in detail in the last chapter of this book. *Table 3.1* showcases the various counters, which we can find out using the following code as well:

```
SELECT (SELECT occurrence FROM sys.dm_exec_query_optimizer_info
WHERE counter =
'hints') * 100.0 / (SELECT occurrence FROM sys.dm_exec_query_
optimizer_info
WHERE counter = 'optimizations')
```

As mentioned previously, you can use this DMV in two different ways: you can use it to get information regarding the history of accumulated optimizations on the system since the instance was started, or you can use it to get optimization information for a particular query or a workload. To capture data on the latter, you need to take two snapshots of the DMV—one before optimizing your query and another one after the query has been optimized—and manually find the difference between them. Unfortunately, there is no way to initialize the values of this DMV, which could make this process easier.

However, there may still be several issues to consider when capturing two snapshots of this DMV. First, you need to eliminate the effects of system-generated queries and queries executed by other users that may be running at the same time as your sample query. Try to isolate the query or workload on your own instance, and make sure that the number of optimizations reported is the same as the number of optimizations you are requesting to optimize by checking the optimizations counter. If the former is greater, the data probably includes some of those queries submitted by the system or other users. Of course, it's also possible that your own query against the sys.dm_exec_query_optimizer_info DMV may count as an optimization.

Second, you need to make sure that query optimization is actually taking place. For example, if you run the same query more than once, SQL Server may simply use an existing plan from the plan cache, without performing any query optimization. You can force an optimization by using the RECOMPILE hint (as shown later), using sp_recompile, or by manually removing the plan from the plan cache. For instance, starting with SQL Server 2008, the DBCC FREEPROCCACHE statement can be used to remove a specific plan, all the plans related to a specific resource pool, or the entire plan cache. It is worth warning you at this point not to run commands to clear the entire plan cache of a production environment.

With all of this in mind, the script shown next will display the optimization information for a specific query, while avoiding all the aforementioned issues. The script has a section to include the query you want the optimization information from:

```
-- optimize these queries now
-- so they do not skew the collected results
GO
SELECT *
INTO after_query_optimizer_info
FROM sys.dm_exec_query_optimizer_info
GO
SELECT *
INTO before_query_optimizer_info
FROM sys.dm_exec_query_optimizer_info
GO
DROP TABLE before_query_optimizer_info
```

```
DROP TABLE after_query_optimizer_info
GO
-- real execution starts
GO
SELECT *
INTO before_query_optimizer_info
FROM sys.dm_exec_query_optimizer_info
GO
-- insert your query here
SELECT *
FROM Person.Address
-- keep this to force a new optimization
OPTION (RECOMPILE)
GO
SELECT *
INTO after_query_optimizer_info
FROM sys.dm_exec_query_optimizer_info
GO
SELECT a.counter,
(a.occurrence - b.occurrence) AS occurrence,
(a.occurrence * a.value - b.occurrence *
b.value) AS value
FROM before_query_optimizer_info b
JOIN after_query_optimizer_info a
ON b.counter = a.counter
WHERE b.occurrence <> a.occurrence
DROP TABLE before_query_optimizer_info
DROP TABLE after_query_optimizer_info
```

Note that some queries are listed twice in the code. The purpose of this is to optimize them the first time they are executed so that their plan can be available in the plan cache for all the executions after that. In this way, we aim as far as possible to isolate the optimization information from the queries we are trying to analyze. Care must be taken that both queries are exactly the same, including case, comments, and so on, and separated in their own batch for the GO statements.

If you run this script against the `AdventureWorks2019` database, the output (after you have scrolled past the output of your query) should look like what is shown next. Note that the times shown obviously may be different from the ones you get in your system, for both this and other examples in this chapter. The output indicates, among other things, that there was one optimization, referencing one table, with a cost of 0.278931474:

Certainly, for this simple query, we could find the same information in some other places, such as in an execution plan. However, as I will show later in this chapter, this DMV can provide optimization information that is not available anywhere else. I will be using this DMV later in this chapter to show you why it is very useful in providing additional insight into the work being performed by the Query Optimizer. With that, we will move on to two of the initial operations that SQL Server executes when you query it.

Counter	Occurrence	Value
elapsed time	1	0
final cost	1	0.278931474
maximum DOP	1	0
optimizations	1	1
tables	1	1
trivial plan	1	1

Parsing and binding

Parsing and binding are the first operations that SQL Server executes when you submit a query to the database engine and are performed by a component called the **Algebrizer**. Parsing first makes sure that the **Transact-SQL (T-SQL)** query has a valid syntax and then uses the query information to build a tree of relational operators. By that, I mean the parser translates the SQL query into an algebra tree representation of logical operators, which is called a **parse tree**. Parsing only checks for valid T-SQL syntax, not for valid table or column names, which are verified in the next phase: binding.

Parsing is similar to the **Parse** functionality available in Management Studio (by clicking the **Parse** button on the default toolbar) or the SET PARSEONLY statement. For example, the following query will successfully parse on the `AdventureWorks2019` database, even when the listed columns and table do not exist in the said database:

```
SELECT lname, fname FROM authors
```

However, if you incorrectly write the SELECT or FROM keyword, like in the next query, SQL Server will return an error message complaining about the incorrect syntax:

```
SELECT lname, fname FRXM authors
```

Once the parse tree has been constructed, the Algebrizer performs the binding operation, which is mostly concerned with name resolution. During this operation, the Algebrizer makes sure that all of the objects named in the query do actually exist, confirms that the requested operations between them are valid, and verifies that the objects are visible to the user running the query (in other words, the user has the proper permissions). It also associates every table and column name on the parse tree with their corresponding object in the system catalog. Name resolution for views includes the process of view substitution, where a view reference is expanded to include the view definition—for example, to directly include the tables used in the view. The output of the binding operation, which is called an algebrizer tree, is then sent to the Query Optimizer, as you'll have guessed, for optimization.

Originally, this tree will be represented as a series of logical operations that are closely related to the original syntax of the query. These include such logical operations as *get data from the Customer table*, *get data from the Contact table*, *perform an inner join*, and so on. Different tree representations of the query will be used throughout the optimization process, and this logical tree will receive different names until it is finally used to initialize the Memo structure, which we will check later.

There is no documented information about these logical trees in SQL Server, but interestingly, the following query returns the names used by those trees:

```
SELECT * FROM sys.dm_xe_map_values WHERE name = 'query_
optimizer_tree_id'
```

The query returns the following output:

map_key	map_value
0	CONVERTED_TREE
1	INPUT_TREE
2	SIMPLIFIED_TREE
3	JOIN_COLLAPSED_TREE
4	TREE_BEFORE_PROJECT_NORM
5	TREE_AFTER_PROJECT_NORM
6	OUTPUT_TREE
7	TREE_COPIED_OUT

We will look at some of these logical trees later in this chapter.

For example, the following query will have the tree representation shown in *Figure 3.2*:

```
SELECT c.CustomerID, COUNT(*)
FROM Sales.Customer c JOIN Sales.SalesOrderHeader s
ON c.CustomerID = s.CustomerID
WHERE c.TerritoryID = 4
GROUP BY c.CustomerID
```

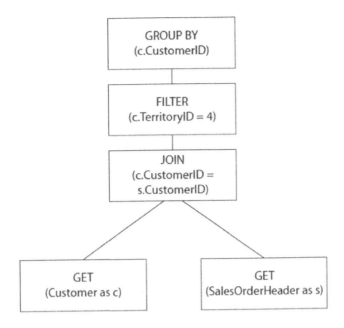

Figure 3.2 – Query tree representation

There are also several undocumented trace flags that can allow you to see these different logical trees used during the optimization process. For example, you can try the following query with the undocumented 8605 trace flag. But first, enable the 3604 trace flag, as shown next:

```
DBCC TRACEON(3604)
```

The 3604 trace flag allows you to redirect the trace output to the client executing the command, in this case, SQL Server Management Studio. You will be able to see its output on the query window **Messages** tab:

```
SELECT ProductID, name FROM Production.Product
WHERE ProductID = 877
OPTION (RECOMPILE, QUERYTRACEON 8605)
```

> **NOTE**
>
> QUERYTRACEON is a query hint used to apply a trace flag at the query level and was introduced in *Chapter 1*.

This shows the following output:

```
*** Converted Tree: ***
LogOp_Project QCOL: [AdventureWorks2012].[Production].
[Product].ProductID
QCOL: [AdventureWorks2012].[Production].[Product].Name
LogOp_Select
LogOp_Get TBL: Production.Product Production.Product
TableID=1973582069 TableReferenceID=0 IsRow: COL: IsBaseRow1001
ScaOp_Comp x_cmpEq
ScaOp_Identifier QCOL:
[AdventureWorks2012].[Production].[Product].ProductID
ScaOp_Const TI(int,ML=4) XVAR(int,Not Owned,Value=877)
AncOp_PrjList
```

The output for these trace flags gets very verbose quickly, even for simple queries; unfortunately, there is no documented information to help understand these output trees and their operations. These operations are, in fact, relational algebra operations. For example, the Select operation, shown as LogOp_Select, selects the records that satisfy a given predicate and should not be confused with the SQL SELECT statement. The SELECT operation is more like the WHERE clause in a SQL statement. The Project operation, shown as LogOp_Project, is used to specify the columns required in the result. In the query, we are only requesting ProductID and Name, and you can verify those columns on the LogOp_Project operation. You can read more about relational algebra operations in *Database System Concepts* by *Abraham Silberschatz, Henry F. Korth, and S. Sudarshan (McGraw-Hill, 2010)*.

Now that we have a basic understanding of the created logical trees, in the next section, we will show you how SQL Server tries to simplify the current input tree.

Simplification

Query rewrites or, more exactly, tree rewrites are performed at this stage to reduce the query tree into a simpler form to make the optimization process easier. Some of these simplifications include the following:

- Subqueries are converted into joins, but because a subquery does not always translate directly to an inner join, outer join and group-by operations may be added as necessary.

- Redundant inner and outer joins may be removed. A typical example is the **Foreign Key Join** elimination, which occurs when the SQL Server can detect that some joins may not be needed, as foreign key constraints are available and only columns of the referencing table are requested. An example of Foreign Key Join elimination is shown later.

- Filters in WHERE clauses are pushed down in the query tree to enable early data filtering as well as potentially better matching of indexes and computed columns later in the optimization process (this simplification is known as **predicate pushdown**).

- Contradictions are detected and removed. Because these parts of the query are not executed at all, SQL Server saves resources such as I/O, locks, memory, and CPU, thus making the query execute faster. For example, the Query Optimizer may know that no records can satisfy a predicate even before touching any page of data. A contradiction may be related to a check constraint or may be related to the way the query is written. Both scenarios will be shown in the next section.

The output of the simplification process is a simplified logical operator tree. Let's see a couple of examples of the simplification process, starting with contradiction detection.

Contradiction detection

For this example, I need a table with a check constraint, and, handily, the Employee table has the following check constraint definition (obviously, there is no need to run the code; the constraint already exists):

```
ALTER TABLE HumanResources.Employee WITH CHECK ADD CONSTRAINT
CK_Employee_VacationHours CHECK (VacationHours>=-40 AND
VacationHours<=240)
```

This check constraint makes sure that the number of vacation hours is a number between –40 and 240. Therefore, if I request the following:

```
SELECT * FROM HumanResources.Employee WHERE VacationHours > 80
```

SQL Server will use a Clustered Index Scan operator, as shown in *Figure 3.3*:

Figure 3.3 – Plan without contradiction detection

However, if I request all employees with more than 300 vacation hours, because of this check constraint, the Query Optimizer must immediately know that no records qualify for the predicate. Run the following query:

```
SELECT * FROM HumanResources.Employee WHERE VacationHours > 300
```

As expected, the query will return no records, but this time, it will produce a very different execution plan, as shown in *Figure 3.4*:

Figure 3.4 – Contradiction detection example

Note that, this time, instead of a Clustered Index Scan, SQL Server is using a Constant Scan operator. The Constant Scan operator introduces one or more constant rows into a query and has virtually no cost. Because there is no need to access the table at all, SQL Server saves resources such as I/O, locks, memory, and CPU, thus making the query execute faster.

Now, let's see what happens if I disable the check constraint. Run the following statement:

```
ALTER TABLE HumanResources.Employee NOCHECK CONSTRAINT CK_
Employee_VacationHours
```

This time, running the previous SELECT query once again uses a Clustered Index Scan operator, as the Query Optimizer can no longer use the check constraint to guide its decisions. In other words, it has to scan the entire table, which at this point, has no records that qualify for the VacationHours > 300 predicate.

Don't forget to enable the constraint again by running the following statement:

```
ALTER TABLE HumanResources.Employee WITH CHECK CHECK CONSTRAINT
CK_Employee_VacationHours
```

The second type of contradiction case is when the query itself explicitly contains a contradiction. Take a look at the following query:

```
SELECT * FROM HumanResources.Employee WHERE VacationHours > 10
AND VacationHours < 5
```

In this case, no check constraint is involved; both predicates are valid, and each will individually return records. But, they contradict each other when they are run together with an AND operator. As a result, the query returns no records and the plan shows a Constant Scan operator similar to the plan in *Figure 3.4*.

This may just look like a badly written query that just needs to be fixed. But, remember that some predicates may already be included in, for example, view definitions, and the developer of the query calling the view may be unaware of them. For example, a view may include the VacationHours > 10 predicate, and a developer may call the view using the VacationHours < 5 predicate. Because both predicates contradict each other, a Constant Scan operator will be used again instead. A contradiction may be also difficult to detect by the developer on some complex queries, which we all have in our production environments, even if the contradicting predicates are in the same query.

The following example illustrates the view scenario. Create the following view:

```
CREATE VIEW VacationHours
AS
SELECT * FROM HumanResources.Employee WHERE VacationHours > 10
```

Run the following statement using our new view:

```
SELECT * FROM VacationHours
```

Nothing out of the ordinary so far. But, the following statement will show again a contradiction detection, even when you cannot see the problem directly in the call to the view. Again, the plan will have a Constant Scan operator as shown in *Figure 3.4*:

```
SELECT * FROM VacationHours
WHERE VacationHours < 5
```

> **Note**
>
> You may try some simple similar queries on your own and not get a contradiction detection behavior. In some cases, a trivial plan may block this behavior.

Now, let's see the logical trees created during contradiction detection, again using the undocumented 8606 trace flag (enable the 3604 trace flag if needed):

```
SELECT * FROM HumanResources.Employee WHERE VacationHours > 300
OPTION (RECOMPILE, QUERYTRACEON 8606)
```

We get the following output (edited to fit the page):

```
*** Input Tree: ***
LogOp_Project QCOL:[HumanResources].[Employee].BusinessEntityID
LogOp_Select
LogOp_Project
LogOp_Get TBL: HumanResources.Employee TableID=1237579447
TableReferenceID=0 IsRow: COL: IsBaseRow1001
AncOp_PrjList
AncOp_PrjEl QCOL:
[HumanResources].[Employee].OrganizationLevel
ScaOp_UdtFunction EClrFunctionType_UdtMethodGetLevel
IsDet NoDataAccess TI(smallint,Null,ML=2)
ScaOp_Identifier QCOL:
[HumanResources].[Employee].OrganizationNode
ScaOp_Comp x_cmpGt
ScaOp_Identifier QCOL:
[HumanResources].[Employee].VacationHours
ScaOp_Const TI(smallint,ML=2)
AncOp_PrjList
*** Simplified Tree: ***
LogOp_ConstTableGet (0) COL: Chk1000 COL: IsBaseRow1001 QCOL:
[HumanResources].[Employee].BusinessEntityID
```

The important part to notice is that all the logical operators of the entire input tree are replaced by the simplified tree, consisting only of a LogOp_ConstTableGet operator, which will be later translated into the logical and physical Constant Scan operator we saw previously.

Foreign Key Join elimination

Now, I will show you an example of Foreign Key Join elimination. The following query joins two tables and shows the execution plan in *Figure 3.5*:

```
SELECT soh.SalesOrderID, c.AccountNumber
FROM Sales.SalesOrderHeader soh
JOIN Sales.Customer c ON soh.CustomerID = c.CustomerID
```

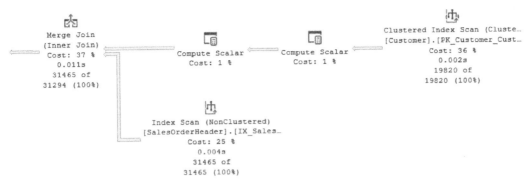

Figure 3.5 – Original plan joining two tables

Let's see what happens if we comment out the AccountNumber column:

```
SELECT soh.SalesOrderID --, c.AccountNumber
FROM Sales.SalesOrderHeader soh
JOIN Sales.Customer c ON soh.CustomerID = c.CustomerID
```

If you run the query again, the Customer table and obviously the join operation are eliminated, as can be seen in the execution plan in *Figure 3.6*:

Figure 3.6 – Foreign Key Join elimination example

There are two reasons for this change in the execution plan. First, because the AccountNumber column is no longer required, no columns are requested from the Customer table. However, it seems like the Customer table has to be included as it is required as part of the equality operation on a join condition. That is, SQL Server needs to make sure that a Customer record exists for each related record in the Individual table.

In reality, this join validation is performed by an existing foreign key constraint, so the Query Optimizer realizes that there is no need to use the Customer table at all. This is the defined forcign key (again, there is no need to run this code):

```
ALTER TABLE Sales.SalesOrderHeader WITH CHECK ADD CONSTRAINT
FK_SalesOrderHeader_Customer_CustomerID FOREIGN KEY(CustomerID)
REFERENCES Sales.Customer(CustomerID)
```

As a test, temporarily disable the foreign key by running the following statement:

```
ALTER TABLE Sales.SalesOrderHeader NOCHECK CONSTRAINT
FK_SalesOrderHeader_Customer_CustomerID
```

Now, run the previous query with the commented column again. Without the foreign key constraint, SQL Server has no choice but to perform the join operation to make sure that the join condition is executed. As a result, it will use a plan joining both tables again, very similar to the one shown previously in *Figure 3.5*. Do not forget to re-enable the foreign key by running the following statement:

```
ALTER TABLE Sales.SalesOrderHeader WITH CHECK CHECK CONSTRAINT
FK_SalesOrderHeader_Customer_CustomerID
```

Finally, you can also see this behavior on the created logical trees. To see this, use again the undocumented 8606 trace flag, as shown next:

```
SELECT soh.SalesOrderID --, c.AccountNumber
FROM Sales.SalesOrderHeader soh
JOIN Sales.Customer c ON soh.CustomerID = c.CustomerID
OPTION (RECOMPILE, QUERYTRACEON 8606)
```

You can see an output similar to this, edited to fit the page:

```
*** Input Tree: ***
LogOp_Project QCOL: [soh].SalesOrderID
LogOp_Select
LogOp_Join
LogOp_Project
LogOp_Get TBLW: Sales.SalesOrderHeader(alias TBL: soh)
Sales.SalesOrderHeader TableID=1266103551
TableReferenceID=0 IsRow: COL: IsBaseRow1001
AncOp_PrjList
AncOp_PrjEl QCOL: [soh].SalesOrderNumber
ScaOp_Intrinsic isnull
ScaOp_Arithmetic x_aopAdd
...
LogOp_Project
LogOp_Get TBL: Sales.Customer(alias TBL: c)
```

```
Sales.Customer TableID=997578592 TableReferenceID=0
IsRow: COL: IsBaseRow1003
AncOp_PrjList
AncOp_PrjEl QCOL: [c].AccountNumber
ScaOp_Intrinsic isnull
ScaOp_Arithmetic x_aopAdd
ScaOp_Const TI(varchar collate
872468488,Var,Trim,ML=2)
ScaOp_Udf dbo.ufnLeadingZeros IsDet
ScaOp_Identifier QCOL: [c].CustomerID
...
*** Simplified Tree: ***
LogOp_Join
LogOp_Get TBL: Sales.SalesOrderHeader(alias TBL: soh)
Sales.SalesOrderHeader TableID=1266103551 TableReferenceID=0
IsRow: COL: IsBaseRow1001
LogOp_Get TBL: Sales.Customer(alias TBL: c) Sales.Customer
TableID=997578592 TableReferenceID=0 IsRow: COL: IsBaseRow1003
ScaOp_Comp x_cmpEq
ScaOp_Identifier QCOL: [c].CustomerID
ScaOp_Identifier QCOL: [soh].CustomerID
*** Join-collapsed Tree: ***
LogOp_Get TBL: Sales.SalesOrderHeader(alias TBL: soh)
Sales.SalesOrderHeader TableID=1266103551 TableReferenceID=0
IsRow: COL:
IsBaseRow1001
```

In the output, although edited to fit the page, you can see that both the input and the simplified tree still have logical Get operators, or LogOp_Get, for the Sales.SalesOrderHeader and Sales.Customer tables. However, the join-collapsed tree at the end has eliminated one of the tables, showing only Sales.SalesOrderHeader. Notice that the tree was simplified after the original input tree and, after that, the join was eliminated on the join-collapsed tree. We will now check out what trivial plan optimization is.

Trivial plan optimization

The optimization process may be expensive to initialize and run for simple queries that don't require any cost estimation. To avoid this expensive operation for simple queries, SQL Server uses trivial plan optimization. In short, if there's only one way, or one obvious best way, to execute the query, depending on the query definition and available metadata, a lot of work can be avoided. For example, the following AdventureWorks2019 query will produce a trivial plan:

```
SELECT * FROM Sales.SalesOrderDetail
WHERE SalesOrderID = 43659
```

The execution plan will show whether a trivial plan optimization was performed; the Optimization Level entry in the Properties window of a graphical plan will show TRIVIAL. In the same way, an XML plan will show the StatementOptmLevel attribute as TRIVIAL, as you can see in the next XML fragment:

```
<StmtSimple StatementCompId="1" StatementEstRows="12"
StatementId="1" StatementOptmLevel="TRIVIAL"
StatementSubTreeCost="0.0032976" StatementText="SELECT *
FROM [Sales].[SalesOrderDetail] WHERE [SalesOrderID]=@1"
StatementType="SELECT" QueryHash="0x801851E3A6490741"
QueryPlanHash="0x3E34C903A0998272" RetrievedFromCache="true">
```

As I mentioned at the start of this chapter, additional information regarding the optimization process can be shown using the sys.dm_exec_query_optimizer_info DMV, which will produce an output similar to the following for this query:

Counter	Occurrence	Value
elapsed time	1	0.076
final cost	1	0.0032976
maximum DOP	1	0
optimizations	1	1
tables	1	1
trivial plan	1	1

The output shows that this is in fact a trivial plan optimization, using one table and a maximum DOP of 0, and it also displays the elapsed time and final cost. However, if we slightly change the query to the following, looking up on ProductID rather than SalesOrderID, we now get a full optimization:

```
SELECT * FROM Sales.SalesOrderDetail
WHERE ProductID = 870
```

In this case, the Optimization Level or StatementOptLevel property is FULL, which obviously means that the query did not qualify for a trivial plan, and a full optimization was performed instead. Full optimization is used for more complicated queries or queries using more complex features, which will require comparisons of candidate plans' costs to guide decisions; this will be explained in the next section. In this particular example, because the ProductID = 870 predicate can return zero, one, or more records, different plans may be created depending on cardinality estimations and the available navigation structures. This was not the case in the previous query using the SalesOrderID query, which is part of a unique index, and so it can return only zero or one record.

Finally, you can use an undocumented trace flag, 8757, to disable the trivial plan optimization, which you can use for testing purposes. Let's try this flag with our previous trivial plan query:

```
SELECT * FROM Sales.SalesOrderDetail
WHERE SalesOrderID = 43659
OPTION (RECOMPILE, QUERYTRACEON 8757)
```

If we use the sys.dm_exec_query_optimizer_info DMV again, we can see that now, instead of a trivial plan, we have a hint and the optimization goes to the search 1 phase, which will be explained later in the chapter:

Counter	Occurrence	Value
elapsed time	1	0.001
final cost	1	0.0032976
hints	1	1
maximum DOP	1	0
optimizations	1	1
search 1	1	1
search 1 tasks	1	131
search 1 time	1	0
tables	1	1
tasks	1	131

Now that we have learned about trivial plans, we will now check out what joins are and how they help.

Joins

Join ordering is one of the most complex problems in query optimization and one that has been the subject of extensive research since the 1970s. It refers to the process of calculating the optimal join order (that is, the order in which the necessary tables are joined) when executing a query. Because the order of joins is a key factor in controlling the amount of data flowing between each operator in an execution plan, it's a factor to which the Query Optimizer needs to pay close attention. As suggested earlier, join order is directly related to the size of the search space because the number of possible plans for a query grows very rapidly, depending on the number of tables joined.

A join operation combines records from two tables based on some common information, and the predicate that defines which columns are used to join the tables is called a join predicate. A join works with only two tables at a time, so a query requesting data from *n* tables must be executed as a sequence of *n – 1* joins, although it should be noted that a join does not have to be completed (that is, joined all the required data from both tables) before the next join can be started.

The Query Optimizer needs to make two important decisions regarding joins: the selection of a join order and the choice of a join algorithm. The selection of join algorithms will be covered in *Chapter 4, The Execution Engine*, so in this section, we will talk about join order. As mentioned, the order in which the tables are joined can greatly impact the cost and performance of a query. Although the results of the query are the same, regardless of the join order, the cost of each different join order can vary dramatically.

As a result of the commutative and associative properties of joins, even simple queries offer many different possible join orders, and this number increases exponentially with the number of tables that need to be joined. The task of the Query Optimizer is to find the optimal sequence of joins between the tables used in the query.

The commutative property of a join between tables A and B states that A JOIN B is logically equivalent to B JOIN A. This defines which table will be accessed first or, said in a different way, which role each table will play in the join. In a Nested Loops Join, for example, the first accessed table is called the outer table and the second one the inner table. In a Hash Join, the first accessed table is the build input, and the second one is the probe input. As we will see in *Chapter 4, The Execution Engine*, correctly defining which table will be the inner table and which will be the outer table in a Nested Loops Join, or the build input or probe input in a Hash Join, has significant performance and cost implications, and it is a choice made by the Query Optimizer.

The associative property of a join between tables A, B, and C states that (A JOIN B) JOIN C is logically equivalent to A JOIN (B JOIN C). This defines the order in which the tables are joined. For example, (A JOIN B) JOIN C specifies that table A must be joined to table B first, and then the result must be joined to table C. A JOIN (B JOIN C) means that table B must be joined to table C first, and then the result must be joined to table A. Each possible permutation may have different cost and performance results depending, for example, on the size of their temporary results.

As noted earlier, the number of possible join orders in a query increases exponentially with the number of tables joined. In fact, with just a handful of tables, the number of possible join orders could be in the thousands or even millions, although the exact number of possible join orders depends on the overall shape of the query tree. It is impossible for the Query Optimizer to look at all those combinations; it would take far too long. Instead, the SQL Server Query Optimizer uses heuristics to help narrow down the search space.

As mentioned before, queries are represented as trees in the query processor, and the shape of the query tree, as dictated by the nature of the join order, is so important in query optimization that some of these trees have names, such as left-deep, right-deep, and bushy trees. *Figure 3.7* shows left-deep and bushy trees for a join of four tables. For example, the left-deep tree could be JOIN(JOIN(JOIN(A, B), C), D), and the bushy tree could be JOIN(JOIN(A, B), JOIN(C, D)):

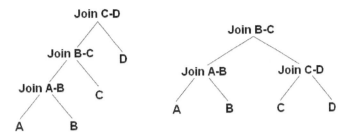

Figure 3.7 – Left-deep and bushy trees

Left-deep trees are also called linear trees or linear processing trees, and you can see how their shapes lead to that description. Bushy trees, on the other hand, can take any arbitrary shape, and so the set of bushy trees includes the sets of both left-deep and right-deep trees.

The number of left-deep trees is calculated as *n!* (or n factorial), where *n* is the number of tables in the relation. A factorial is the product of all positive integers less than or equal to *n*. For example, for a five-table join, the number of possible join orders is *5! = 5 × 4 × 3 × 2 × 1 = 120*. The number of possible join orders for a bushy tree is more complicated and can be calculated as *(2n – 2)!/(n – 1)!*.

The important point to remember here is that the number of possible join orders grows very quickly as the number of tables increases, as highlighted in *Table 3.2*. For example, in theory, if we had a six-table join, a query optimizer would potentially need to evaluate 30,240 possible join orders. Of course, we should also bear in mind that this is just the number of permutations for the join order. On top of this, a query optimizer also has to evaluate physical join operators and data access methods, as well as optimize other parts of the query, such as aggregations, subqueries, and so on.

Tables	Left-Deep Trees	Bushy Trees
2	2	2
3	6	12
4	24	120
5	120	1,680
6	720	30,240
7	5,040	665,280
8	40,320	17,297,280
9	362,880	518,918,400
10	3,628,800	17,643,225,600
11	39,916,800	670,442,572,800
12	479,001,600	28,158,588,057,600

Table 3.2 – Possible join orders for left-deep and bushy trees

So, how does the SQL Server Query Optimizer analyze all these possible plan combinations? The answer is it doesn't. Performing an exhaustive evaluation of all possible combinations for many queries would take too long to be useful, so the Query Optimizer must find a balance between the optimization time and the quality of the resulting plan. As mentioned earlier in the book, the goal of the Query Optimizer is to find a good enough plan as quickly as possible. Rather than exhaustively evaluate every single combination, the Query Optimizer tries to narrow the possibilities down to the most likely candidates, using heuristics (some of which we've already touched upon) to guide the process.

Transformation rules

As we've seen earlier, the SQL Server Query Optimizer uses transformation rules to explore the search space—that is, to explore the set of possible execution plans for a specific query. Transformation rules are based on relational algebra, taking a relational operator tree and generating equivalent alternatives, in the form of equivalent relational operator trees. At the most fundamental level, a query consists of logical expressions, and applying these transformation rules will generate equivalent logical and physical alternatives, which are stored in memory (in a structure called the Memo) for the entire duration of the optimization process. As explained in this chapter, the Query Optimizer uses up to three optimization stages, and different transformation rules are applied in each stage.

Each transformation rule has a pattern and a substitute. The pattern is the expression to be analyzed and matched, and the substitute is the equivalent expression that is generated as an output. For example, for the commutativity rule, which is explained next, a transformation rule can be defined as follows:

```
Expr1 join Expr2 - > Expr2 join Expr1
```

This means that SQL Server will match the `Expr1 join Expr2` pattern, as in *Individual join Customer*, and will produce the equivalent expression, `Expr2 join Expr1`, or in our case, *Customer join Individual*. The two expressions are logically equivalent because both return the same results.

Initially, the query tree contains only logical expressions, and transformation rules are applied to these logical expressions to generate either logical or physical expressions. As an example, a logical expression can be the definition of a logical join, whereas a physical expression could be an actual join implementation, such as a **Merge Join** or a **Hash Join**. Bear in mind that transformation rules cannot be applied to physical expressions.

The main types of transformation rules include simplification, exploration, and implementation rules. Simplification rules produce simpler logical trees as their outputs and are mostly used during the simplification phase, before the full optimization, as explained previously. Exploration rules, also called logical transformation rules, generate logical equivalent alternatives. Finally, implementation rules, or physical transformation rules, are used to obtain physical alternatives. Both exploration and implementation rules are executed during the full optimization phase.

Examples of exploration rules include the *commutativity* and *associativity* rules, which are used in join optimization, and are shown in *Figure 3.8*:

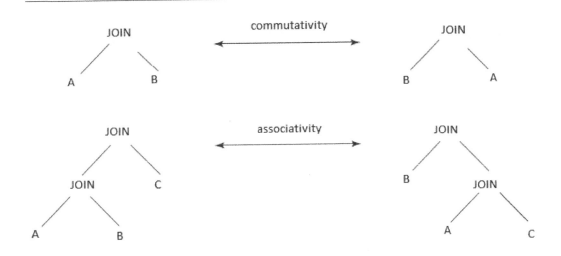

Figure 3.8 – Commutativity and associativity rules

Commutativity and associativity rules are, respectively, defined as follows:

```
A join B - > B join A
and
(A join B) join C - > B join (A join C)
```

The commutativity rule (A join B - > B join A) means that A join B is equivalent to B join A and joining the tables A and B in any order will return the same results. Also, note that applying the commutativity rule twice will generate the original expression again; that is, if you initially apply this transformation to obtain B join A, and then later apply the same transformation, you can obtain A join B again. However, the Query Optimizer can handle this problem to avoid duplicated expressions. In the same way, the associativity rule shows that (A join B) join C is equivalent to B join (A join C) because they also both produce the same results. An example of an implementation rule would be selecting a physical algorithm for a logical join, such as a Merge Join or a Hash Join.

So, the Query Optimizer is using sets of transformation rules to generate and examine possible alternative execution plans. However, it's important to remember that applying rules does not necessarily reduce the cost of the generated alternatives, and the costing component still needs to estimate their costs. Although both logical and physical alternatives are kept in the Memo structure, only the physical alternatives have their costs determined. It's important, then, to bear in mind that although these alternatives may be equivalent and return the same results, their physical implementations may have very different costs. The final selection, as is hopefully clear now, will be the best (or, if you like, the *cheapest*) physical alternative stored in the Memo.

For example, implementing A join B may have different costs depending on whether a Nested Loops Join or a Hash Join is selected. In addition, for the same physical join, implementing the A join B expression may have a different performance from B join A. As explained in *Chapter 4, The Execution Engine*, the performance of a join is different depending on which table is chosen as the inner or outer table in a Nested Loops Join, or the build and the probe inputs in a Hash Join. If you want to find out why the Query Optimizer might not choose a specific join algorithm, you can test using a hint to force a specific physical join and compare the cost of both the hinted and the original plans.

Those are the foundation principles of transformation rules, and the sys.dm_exec_query_transformation_stats DMV provides information about the existing transformation rules and how they are being used by the Query Optimizer. According to this DMV, SQL Server 2022 CTP 2.0 currently has 439 transformation rules, and more can be added in future updates or versions of the product.

Similar to sys.dm_exec_query_optimizer_info, this DMV contains information regarding the optimizations performed since the time the given SQL Server instance was started and can also be used to get optimization information for a particular query or workload by taking two snapshots of the DMV (before and after optimizing your query) and manually finding the difference between them.

To start looking at this DMV, run the following query:

```
SELECT * FROM sys.dm_exec_query_transformation_stats
```

Here is some sample output from my test system using SQL Server 2022, showing the first few records out of 439 (edited to fit the page):

Name	promise_total	promise_avg	promised	built_substitute	Succeeded
JNtoNL	203352155	92.96051768	2187511	350792	285,532
LOJNtoNL	35938188	449.0701754	80028	80028	79,504
LSJNtoNL	40614706	450.6936171	90116	90116	90,116
LASJNtoNL	4029039	451.6353548	8921	8921	8,921
JNtoSM	366499276	418.7495941	875223	814754	441,413
FOJNtoSM	6356	454	14	14	4
LOJNtoSM	11180944	443.3891422	25217	24996	17,098
ROJNtoSM	11179128	443.3874589	25213	24992	17,094
LSJNtoSM	4263232	443.2094812	9619	9453	1,495
RSJNtoSM	4263232	443.2094812	9619	9453	6,922

The sys.dm_exec_query_transformation_stats DMV includes what is known as the promise information, which tells the Query Optimizer how useful a given transformation rule might be. The first field in the results output is the name of the rule; for example, the first three rules listed are JNtoNL (**Join to Nested Loops Join**), LOJNtoNL (**Left Outer Join to Nested Loops Join**), and JNtoSM (**Join to Sort Merge Join**), where Sort Merge Join is the academic name of the SQL Server Merge Join operator.

The same issues are shown for the `sys.dm_exec_query_optimizer_info` DMV regarding collecting data also applies to the `sys.dm_exec_query_transformation_stats` DMV, so the query shown next can help you to isolate the optimization information for a specific query while avoiding data from related queries as much as possible. The query is based on the succeeded column, which keeps track of the number of times a transformation rule was used and successfully produced a result:

```
-- optimize these queries now
-- so they do not skew the collected results
GO
SELECT *
INTO before_query_transformation_stats
FROM sys.dm_exec_query_transformation_stats
GO
SELECT *
INTO after_query_transformation_stats
FROM sys.dm_exec_query_transformation_stats
GO
DROP TABLE after_query_transformation_stats
DROP TABLE before_query_transformation_stats
-- real execution starts
GO
SELECT *
INTO before_query_transformation_stats
FROM sys.dm_exec_query_transformation_stats
GO
-- insert your query here
SELECT * FROM Sales.SalesOrderDetail
WHERE SalesOrderID = 43659
-- keep this to force a new optimization
OPTION (RECOMPILE)
GO
SELECT *
INTO after_query_transformation_stats
FROM sys.dm_exec_query_transformation_stats
GO
SELECT a.name, (a.promised - b.promised) as promised
```

```
FROM before_query_transformation_stats b
JOIN after_query_transformation_stats a
ON b.name = a.name
WHERE b.succeeded <> a.succeeded
DROP TABLE before_query_transformation_stats
DROP TABLE after_query_transformation_stats
```

For example, let's test with a very simple `AdventureWorks2019` query, such as the following (which is already included in the previous code):

```
SELECT * FROM Sales.SalesOrderDetail
WHERE SalesOrderID = 43659
```

This will show that the following transformation rules are being used:

Name	promised
ProjectToComputeScalar	1
SelIdxToRng	1
SelPrjGetToTrivialScan	1
SelToTrivialFilter	1

The plan produced is a trivial plan. Let's again add the undocumented 8757 trace flag to avoid a trivial plan (just for testing purposes):

```
SELECT * FROM Sales.SalesOrderDetail
WHERE SalesOrderID = 43659
OPTION (RECOMPILE, QUERYTRACEON 8757)
```

We would then get the following output:

Name	promised
AddCCPrjToGet	2
GetIdxToRng	1
GetToIdxScan	2
GetToScan	2
ProjectToComputeScalar	2
SelectToFilter	1
SelIdxToRng	1
SelToIdxStrategy	1

Let's now test a more complicated query. Include the following query in the code to explore the transformation rules it uses:

```
SELECT c.CustomerID, COUNT(*)
FROM Sales.Customer c JOIN Sales.SalesOrderHeader o
ON c.CustomerID = o.CustomerID
GROUP BY c.CustomerID
```

As shown in the following output, 17 transformation rules were exercised during the optimization process:

Name	promised
AppIdxToApp	0
EnforceSort	23
GbAggBeforeJoin	4
GbAggToHS	8
GbAggToStrm	8
GenLGAgg	2
GetIdxToRng	0
GetToIdxScan	4
GetToScan	4
ImplRestrRemap	3
JNtoHS	6
JNtoIdxLookup	6
JNtoSM	6
JoinCommute	2
ProjectToComputeScalar	2
SelIdxToRng	6
SELonJN	1

The previous query gives us an opportunity to show an interesting transformation rule, GbAggBeforeJoin (or *Group By Aggregate Before Join*), which is included in the previous list.

The *Group By Aggregate Before Join* can be used in cases where we have joins and aggregations. A traditional query optimization for this kind of query is to perform the join operation first, followed by the aggregation. An alternative optimization is to push down a group by aggregate before the join. This is represented in *Figure 3.9*. In other words, if our original logical tree has the shape of the tree on the left in *Figure 3.9*, after applying GbAggBeforeJoin, we can get the alternate tree on the right, which as expected produces the same query results:

Figure 3.9 – Group By Aggregate Before Join optimization

We can see that `GbAggBeforeJoin` was applied, as shown on the list of transformation rules earlier, and that the tree on the right was selected, as shown on the final execution plan shown in *Figure 3.10*:

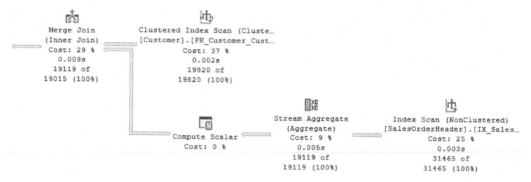

Figure 3.10 – Original execution plan

Here you can see, among other things, that SQL Server is pushing an aggregate below the join (a Stream Aggregate before the Merge Join). The Query Optimizer can push aggregations that significantly reduce cardinality estimation as early in the plan as possible. As mentioned, this is performed by the `GbAggBeforeJoin` transformation rule (or *Group By Aggregate Before Join*). This specific transformation rule is used only if certain requirements are met—for example, when the GROUP BY clause includes the joining columns, which is the case in our example.

Now, as I will explain in more detail in *Chapter 12, Understanding Query Hints*, you may disable some of these transformation rules in order to obtain a specific desired behavior. As a way of experimenting with the effects of these rules, you can also use the undocumented DBCC RULEON and DBCC RULEOFF statements to enable or disable transformation rules, respectively, and thereby, get additional insight into how the Query Optimizer works. However, before you do that, first be warned: because these undocumented statements impact the entire optimization process performed by the Query Optimizer, they should be used only in a test system for experimentation purposes.

To demonstrate the effects of these statements, let's continue with the same query, copied again here:

```
SELECT c.CustomerID, COUNT(*)
FROM Sales.Customer c JOIN Sales.SalesOrderHeader o
```

```
ON c.CustomerID = o.CustomerID
GROUP BY c.CustomerID
```

Run the following statement to temporarily disable the use of the GbAggBeforeJoin transformation rule for the current session:

```
DBCC RULEOFF('GbAggBeforeJoin')
```

After disabling this transformation rule and running the query again, the new plan, shown in *Figure 3.11*, will now show the aggregate after the join, which, according to the Query Optimizer, is a more expensive plan than the original. You can verify this by looking at their estimated costs: 0.285331 and 0.312394, for the original plan and the plan with GbAggBeforeJoin disabled, respectively. These costs are not shown in the figures, but you can see them by hovering the mouse over the **SELECT** icon and examining the Estimated Subtree Cost value, as explained before:

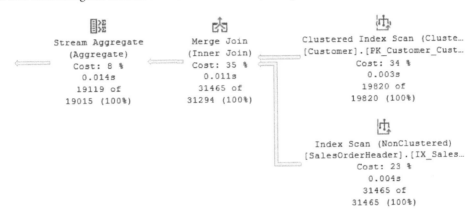

Figure 3.11 – Plan with the GbAggBeforeJoin rule disabled

Note that, for this exercise, an optimization may need to be forced to see the new plan, perhaps using the OPTION (RECOMPILE) hint or one of the methods we've discussed to remove the plan from the cache, such as DBCC FREEPROCCACHE.

What's more, there are a couple of additional undocumented statements to show which transformation rules are enabled and disabled; these are DBCC SHOWONRULES and DBCC SHOWOFFRULES, respectively. By default, DBCC SHOWONRULES will list all the 439 transformation rules listed by the sys.dm_exec_query_transformation_stats DMV. To test it, try running the following code:

```
DBCC TRACEON (3604)
DBCC SHOWONRULES
```

We start this exercise by enabling the 3604 trace flag, which, as explained earlier, instructs SQL Server to send the results to the client (in this case, your Management Studio session). After this, the output of DBCC SHOWONRULES (and later, DBCC SHOWOFFRULES), and the DBCC RULEON and DBCC RULEOFF statements will be conveniently available to us. The output is provided next (showing only a few of the possible rules, to preserve space). The previously disabled rule will not be shown in this output:

```
Rules that are on globally:
JNtoNL
LOJNtoNL
LSJNtoNL
LASJNtoNL
JNtoSM
FOJNtoSM
LOJNtoSM
ROJNtoSM
LSJNtoSM
RSJNtoSM
LASJNtoSM
RASJNtoSM
```

In the same way, the following code will show the rules that are disabled:

```
DBCC SHOWOFFRULES
```

In our case, it will show that only one rule has been disabled:

```
Rules that are off globally:
GbAggBeforeJoin
DBCC execution completed. If DBCC printed error messages,
contact your system administrator.
```

To continue with our example of the effects of the transformation rules, we can disable the use of a Merge Join by disabling the JNtoSM rule (*Join to Sort Merge Join*) by running the following code:

```
DBCC RULEOFF('JNtoSM')
```

If you have followed the example, this time, DBCC RULEOFF will show some output indicating that the rule is disabled for some specific SPID. For example, the output could be as follows:

```
DBCC RULEOFF GbAggBeforeJoin SPID 69
```

This also means that DBCC RULEON and DBCC RULEOFF work at the session level, but even in this case, your exercise may still impact the entire SQL Server instance because your created plans may be kept in the plan cache and potentially reused by other sessions. As a curious note, even when DBCC RULEOFF works at the session level, DBCC SHOWONRULES and DBCC SHOWOFFRULES show messages such as the following:

```
Rules that are off globally:
```

These are not exactly true (but after all, they are undocumented statements that users are not supposed to use anyway).

Running the sample query again will give us a new plan, using both a Hash Join and a Hash Aggregate, as shown in *Figure 3.12*:

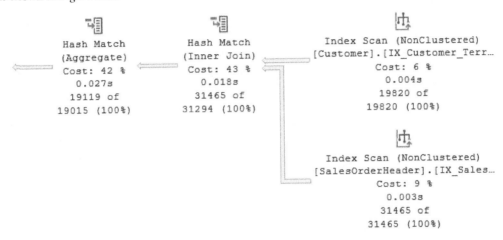

Figure 3.12 – Plan with the JNtoSM rule disabled

So far, we have disabled two optimizations or transformation rules, GbAggBeforeJoin and JNtoSM. This is the reason currently we have the aggregation after the join and we no longer have a Merge Join; instead, the Query Optimizer has selected a Hash Join. Let's try a couple more changes.

As we will cover in more detail in the next chapter, SQL Server provides two physical algorithms for aggregations, hash, and stream aggregations. Since the current plan in *Figure 3.11* is using a Hash Aggregation, let's disable that choice of algorithm to see what happens. This is performed by disabling the GbAggToHS (*Group by Aggregate to Hash*) rule, as shown next:

```
DBCC RULEOFF('GbAggToHS')
```

After this, we get the plan shown in *Figure 3.13*:

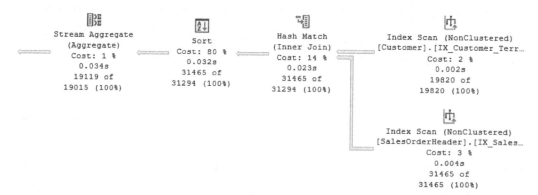

Figure 3.13 – Plan with the GbAggToHS rule disabled

The plan in *Figure 3.13* is very similar to the shape of the previous one, but now we have a stream aggregate instead of a hash aggregate. We know that using a stream aggregate is the only choice the Query Optimizer has left. So, what would happen if we also disable stream aggregates? To find out, run the following statement, which disables GbAggToStrm (*Group by Aggregate to Stream*), and run our test query again:

```
DBCC RULEOFF('GbAggToStrm')
```

As expected, the Query Optimizer is not able to get an execution plan and instead gives up returning the following error message:

```
Msg 8624, Level 16, State 1, Line 186
Internal Query Processor Error: The query processor could not
produce a query plan. For more information, contact Customer
Support Services.
```

In *Chapter 12,*Understanding Query Hints, you will learn how to obtain a similar behavior, disabling specific optimizations or physical operations in your queries, and using hints. Although the statements we covered in this section are undocumented and unsupported, hints are documented and supported but still need to be used very carefully and only when there is no other choice.

Finally, before we finish, don't forget to reenable the GbAggBeforeJoin and JNtoSM transformation rules by running the following commands:

```
DBCC RULEON('GbAggBeforeJoin')
DBCC RULEON('JNtoSM')
DBCC RULEON(GbAggToHS')
DBCC RULEON(GbAggToStrm')
```

Then, verify that no transformation rules are still disabled by running the following:

```
DBCC SHOWOFFRULES
```

You can also just close your current session since, as mentioned earlier, DBCC RULEON and DBCC RULEOFF work at the session level. You may also want to clear your plan cache (to make sure none of these experiment plans were left in memory) by once again running the following:

```
DBCC FREEPROCCACHE
```

A second choice to obtain the same behavior, disabling rules, is to use the also undocumented QUERYRULEOFF query hint, which will disable a rule at the query level. For example, the following code using the QUERYRULEOFF hint will disable the GbAggBeforeJoin rule only for the current optimization:

```
SELECT c.CustomerID, COUNT(*)
FROM Sales.Customer c JOIN Sales.SalesOrderHeader o
ON c.CustomerID = o.CustomerID
GROUP BY c.CustomerID
OPTION (RECOMPILE, QUERYRULEOFF GbAggBeforeJoin)
```

You can include more than one rule name while using the QUERYRULEOFF hint, like in the following example, to disable both the GbAggBeforeJoin and JNtoSM rules, as demonstrated before:

```
SELECT c.CustomerID, COUNT(*)
FROM Sales.Customer c JOIN Sales.SalesOrderHeader o
ON c.CustomerID = o.CustomerID
GROUP BY c.CustomerID
OPTION (RECOMPILE, QUERYRULEOFF GbAggBeforeJoin, QUERYRULEOFF
JNtoSM)
```

Also, the Query Optimizer will obey disabled rules both at the session level and at the query level. Because QUERYRULEOFF is a query hint, this effect lasts only for the optimization of the current query (therefore, no need for a QUERYRULEON hint).

In both cases, DBCC RULEOFF and QUERYRULEOFF, you can be at a point where enough rules have been disabled that the Query Optimizer is not able to produce an execution plan. For example, let's say you run the following query:

```
SELECT c.CustomerID, COUNT(*)
FROM Sales.Customer c JOIN Sales.SalesOrderHeader o
ON c.CustomerID = o.CustomerID
```

```
GROUP BY c.CustomerID
OPTION (RECOMPILE, QUERYRULEOFF GbAggToStrm, QUERYRULEOFF
GbAggToHS)
```

You would get the following error:

```
Msg 8622, Level 16, State 1, Line 1
Query processor could not produce a query plan because of
the hints defined in this query. Resubmit the query without
specifying any hints and without using SET FORCEPLAN
```

In this particular example, we are disabling both the GbAggToStrm (*Group by Aggregate to Stream*) and GbAggToHS (*Group by Aggregate to Hash*) rules. At least one of those rules is required to perform an aggregation; GbAggToStrm would allow me to use a Stream Aggregate and GbAggToHS would allow me to use a Hash Aggregate.

Although the Query Optimizer is, again, not able to produce a valid execution plan, the returned message is very different as this time, the query processor knows the query is using hints. It just simply asks you to resubmit the query without specifying any hints.

Finally, you can also obtain rules information using the undocumented 2373 trace flag. Although it is verbose and provides memory information, it can also be used to find out the transformation rules used during the optimization of a particular query. For example, let's say you run the following:

```
SELECT c.CustomerID, COUNT(*)
FROM Sales.Customer c JOIN Sales.SalesOrderHeader o
ON c.CustomerID = o.CustomerID
GROUP BY c.CustomerID
OPTION (RECOMPILE, QUERYTRACEON 2373)
```

This will show the following output (edited to fit the page):

```
Memory before rule NormalizeGbAgg: 27
Memory after rule NormalizeGbAgg: 27
Memory before rule IJtoIJSEL: 27
Memory after rule IJtoIJSEL: 28
Memory before rule MatchGet: 28
Memory after rule MatchGet: 28
Memory before rule MatchGet: 28
Memory after rule MatchGet: 28
Memory before rule JoinToIndexOnTheFly: 28
Memory after rule JoinToIndexOnTheFly: 28
```

```
Memory before rule JoinCommute: 28
Memory after rule JoinCommute: 28
Memory before rule JoinToIndexOnTheFly: 28
Memory after rule JoinToIndexOnTheFly: 28
Memory before rule GbAggBeforeJoin: 28
Memory after rule GbAggBeforeJoin: 28
Memory before rule GbAggBeforeJoin: 28
Memory after rule GbAggBeforeJoin: 30
Memory before rule IJtoIJSEL: 30
Memory after rule IJtoIJSEL: 30
Memory before rule NormalizeGbAgg: 30
Memory after rule NormalizeGbAgg: 30
Memory before rule GenLGAgg: 30
```

As covered in this section, applying transformation rules to existing logical and physical expressions will generate new logical and physical alternatives, which are stored in a memory structure called the Memo. Let's cover the Memo in the next section.

The Memo

The Memo structure was originally defined in *The Volcano Optimizer Generator* by *Goetz Graefe and William McKenna* in 1993. In the same way, the SQL Server Query Optimizer is based on the Cascades Framework, which was, in fact, a descendent of the Volcano Optimizer.

The Memo is a search data structure used to store the alternatives generated and analyzed by the Query Optimizer. These alternatives can be logical or physical operators and are organized into groups of equivalent alternatives, such that each alternative in the same group produces the same results. Alternatives in the same group also share the same logical properties, and in the same way that operators can reference other operators on a relational tree, groups can also reference other groups in the Memo structure.

A new Memo structure is created for each optimization. The Query Optimizer first copies the original query tree's logical expressions into the Memo structure, placing each operator from the query tree in its own group, and then triggers the entire optimization process. During this process, transformation rules are applied to generate all the alternatives, starting with these initial logical expressions.

As the transformation rules produce new alternatives, these are added to their equivalent groups. Transformation rules may also produce a new expression that is not equivalent to any existing group, and that causes a new group to be created. As mentioned before, each alternative in a group is a simple logical or physical expression, such as a join or a scan, and a plan will be built using a combination of these alternatives. The number of these alternatives (and even groups) in a Memo structure can be huge.

Although there is the possibility that different combinations of transformation rules may end up producing the same expressions, as indicated earlier, the Memo structure is designed to avoid both the duplication of these alternatives and redundant optimizations. By doing this, it saves memory and is more efficient because it does not have to search the same plan alternatives more than once.

Although both logical and physical alternatives are kept in the Memo structure, only the physical alternatives are costed. Therefore, at the end of the optimization process, the Memo contains all the alternatives considered by the Query Optimizer, but only one plan is selected, based on the cost of their operations.

Now, I will use some undocumented trace flags to show you how the Memo structure is populated and what its final state is after the optimization process has been completed. We can use the undocumented 8608 trace flag to show the initial content of the Memo structure. Also, notice that a very simple query may not show anything, like in the following example. Remember to enable the 3604 trace flag first:

```
SELECT ProductID, name FROM Production.Product
OPTION (RECOMPILE, QUERYTRACEON 8608)
```

The previous query uses a trivial optimization that requires no full optimization and no Memo structure, and therefore, creates a trivial plan. You can force a full optimization by using the undocumented 8757 trace flag and running something like this:

```
SELECT ProductID, name FROM Production.Product
OPTION (RECOMPILE, QUERYTRACEON 8608, QUERYTRACEON 8757)
```

In this case, we can see a simple Memo structure like the following:

```
--- Initial Memo Structure ---
Root Group 0: Card=504 (Max=10000, Min=0)
0 LogOp_Get
```

Let's try a simple query that does not qualify for a trivial plan and see its final logical tree using the undocumented 8606 trace flag:

```
SELECT ProductID, ListPrice FROM Production.Product
WHERE ListPrice > 90
OPTION (RECOMPILE, QUERYTRACEON 8606)
```

The final tree is as follows:

```
*** Tree After Project Normalization ***
LogOp_Select
LogOp_Get TBL: Production.Product Production.Product
```

```
TableID=1973582069 TableReferenceID=0 IsRow: COL: IsBaseRow1001
ScaOp_Comp x_cmpGt
ScaOp_Identifier QCOL: Production].[Product].ListPrice
ScaOp_Const TI(money,ML=8)
XVAR(money,Not Owned,Value=(10000units)=(900000))
```

Now, let's look at the initial Memo structure using the undocumented 8608 trace flag:

```
SELECT ProductID, ListPrice FROM Production.Product
WHERE ListPrice > 90
OPTION (RECOMPILE, QUERYTRACEON 8608)
```

We now have something like this:

```
--- Initial Memo Structure ---
Root Group 4: Card=216 (Max=10000, Min=0)
0 LogOp_Select 0 3
Group 3:
0 ScaOp_Comp 1 2
Group 2:
0 ScaOp_Const
Group 1:
0 ScaOp_Identifier
Group 0: Card=504 (Max=10000, Min=0)
0 LogOp_Get
```

As you can see, the operators on the final logical tree are copied to and used to initialize the Memo structure, and each operator is placed in its own group. We call group 4 the root group because it is the root operator of the initial plan (that is, the root node of the original query tree).

Finally, we can use the undocumented 8615 trace flag to see the Memo structure at the end of the optimization process:

```
SELECT ProductID, ListPrice FROM Production.Product
WHERE ListPrice > 90
OPTION (RECOMPILE, QUERYTRACEON 8615)
```

We would have a Memo structure with the following content:

```
--- Final Memo Structure ---
Root Group 4: Card=216 (Max=10000, Min=0)
```

```
1 PhyOp_Filter 0.2 3.0 Cost(RowGoal 0,ReW 0,ReB 0,Dist 0,Total
0)= 0.0129672
0 LogOp_Select 0 3
Group 3:
0 ScaOp_Comp 1.0 2.0 Cost(RowGoal 0,ReW 0,ReB 0,Dist 0,Total
0)= 3
Group 2:
0 ScaOp_Const Cost(RowGoal 0,ReW 0,ReB 0,Dist 0,Total 0)= 1
Group 1:
0 ScaOp_Identifier Cost(RowGoal 0,ReW 0,ReB 0,Dist 0,Total 0)=
1
Group 0: Card=504 (Max=10000, Min=0)
2 PhyOp_Range 1 ASC Cost(RowGoal 0,ReW 0,ReB 0,Dist 0,Total 0)=
0.0127253
0 LogOp_Get
```

Now, let's look at a complete example. Let's say you run the following query:

```
SELECT ProductID, COUNT(*)
FROM Sales.SalesOrderDetail
GROUP BY ProductID
OPTION (RECOMPILE, QUERYTRACEON 8608)
```

This will create the following initial Memo structure:

```
--- Initial Memo Structure ---
Root Group 18: Card=266 (Max=133449, Min=0)
0 LogOp_GbAgg 13 17
Group 17:
0 AncOp_PrjList 16
Group 16:
0 AncOp_PrjEl 15
Group 15:
0 ScaOp_AggFunc 14
Group 14:
0 ScaOp_Const
Group 13: Card=121317 (Max=133449, Min=0)
0 LogOp_Get
Group 12:
```

```
0 AncOp_PrjEl 11
Group 11:
0 ScaOp_Intrinsic 9 10
Group 10:
0 ScaOp_Const
Group 9:
0 ScaOp_Arithmetic 6 8
Group 8:
0 ScaOp_Convert 7
Group 7:
0 ScaOp_Identifier
Group 6:
0 ScaOp_Arithmetic 1 5
Group 5:
0 ScaOp_Arithmetic 2 4
Group 4:
0 ScaOp_Convert 3
Group 3:
0 ScaOp_Identifier
Group 2:
0 ScaOp_Const
Group 1:
0 ScaOp_Convert 0
Group 0:
0 ScaOp_Identifier
```

Now, run the following query to look at the final Memo structure:

```
SELECT ProductID, COUNT(*)
FROM Sales.SalesOrderDetail
GROUP BY ProductID
OPTION (RECOMPILE, QUERYTRACEON 8615)
```

This will show the following output:

```
--- Final Memo Structure ---
Group 32: Card=266 (Max=133449, Min=0)
0 LogOp_Project 30 31
```

```
Group 31:
0 AncOp_PrjList 21
Group 30: Card=266 (Max=133449, Min=0)
0 LogOp_GbAgg 25 29
Group 29:
0 AncOp_PrjList 28
Group 28:
0 AncOp_PrjEl 27
Group 27:
0 ScaOp_AggFunc 26
Group 26:
0 ScaOp_Identifier
Group 25: Card=532 (Max=133449, Min=0)
0 LogOp_GbAgg 13 24
Group 24:
0 AncOp_PrjList 23
…
2 PhyOp_Range 3 ASC Cost(RowGoal 0,ReW 0,ReB 0,Dist 0,Total 0)=
0.338953
0 LogOp_Get
Group 12:
0 AncOp_PrjEl 11
Group 11:
0 ScaOp_Intrinsic 9 10
Group 10:
0 ScaOp_Const
Group 9:
0 ScaOp_Arithmetic 6 8
Group 8:
0 ScaOp_Convert 7
Group 7:
0 ScaOp_Identifier
Group 6:
0 ScaOp_Arithmetic 1 5
Group 5:
0 ScaOp_Arithmetic 2 4
```

```
Group 4:
0 ScaOp_Convert 3
Group 3:
0 ScaOp_Identifier
Group 2:
0 ScaOp_Const
Group 1:
0 ScaOp_Convert 0
Group 0:
0 ScaOp_Identifier
```

The initial Memo structure had 18 groups, and the final went to 32, meaning that 14 new groups were added during the optimization process. As explained earlier, during the optimization process, several transformation rules will be executed that will create new alternatives. If the new alternatives are equivalent to an existing operator, they are placed in the same group as this operator. If not, additional groups will be created. You can also see that group 18 was the root group.

Toward the end of the process, after some implementation rules are applied, equivalent physical operators will be added to the available Memo groups. After the cost for each operator is estimated, the Query Optimizer will look for the cheapest way to assemble a plan using the alternatives available. In this example, the plan selected is shown in *Figure 3.14*:

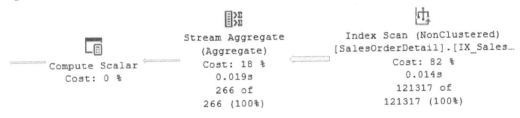

Figure 3.14 – Plan showing operators selected

As we saw earlier, a group by aggregation requires either the GbAggToStrm (*Group by Aggregate to Stream*) or the GbAggToHS (*Group by Aggregate to Hash*) transformation rule. In addition, applying any of the techniques explained earlier, you can see that both rules were used in the optimization process; however, only the GbAggToStrm rule was able to create an alternative in group 18, adding the PhyOp_StreamGbAgg physical operator as an equivalent to the original LogOp_GbAgg logical operator. The PhyOp_StreamGbAgg operator is the Stream Aggregate operator that you can see in the final plan, shown in *Figure 3.12*. Group 18 shows cardinality estimation 266, indicated as Card=266, and an accumulated cost of 0.411876, which you can also verify on the final execution plan. An Index Scan is also shown in the plan, which corresponds to the PhyOp_Range and LogOp_Get operators shown in group 13.

As an additional test, you can see the Memo contents when forcing a Hash Aggregate by running the following query with a hint:

```
SELECT ProductID, COUNT(*)
FROM Sales.SalesOrderDetail
GROUP BY ProductID
OPTION (RECOMPILE, HASH GROUP, QUERYTRACEON 8615)
```

Now that we have learned about the Memo, we will explore some optimizer statistics that are handy for gaining insights.

Statistics

To estimate the cost of an execution plan, the query optimizer needs to know, as precisely as possible, the number of records returned by a given query, and to help with this cardinality estimation, SQL Server uses and maintains optimizer statistics. Statistics contain information describing the distribution of values in one or more columns of a table, and will be explained in greater detail in *Chapter 6, Understanding Statistics*.

As covered in *Chapter 1, An Introduction to Query Tuning and Optimization*, you can use the OptimizerStatsUsage plan property to identify the statistics used by the Query Optimizer to produce an execution plan. The OptimizerStatsUsage property is available only starting with SQL Server 2017 and SQL Server 2016 SP2. Alternatively, you can use the undocumented 9292 and 9204 trace flags to show similar information about the statistics loaded during the optimization process. Although this method works with all the supported and some older versions of SQL Server, it works only with the legacy cardinality estimation model.

To test these trace flags, run the following exercise. Set the legacy cardinality estimator given as follows:

```
ALTER DATABASE SCOPED CONFIGURATION
SET LEGACY_CARDINALITY_ESTIMATION = ON
```

Enable the 3604 trace flag:

```
DBCC TRACEON(3604)
```

Run the following query:

```
SELECT ProductID, name FROM Production.Product
WHERE ProductID = 877
OPTION (RECOMPILE, QUERYTRACEON 9292, QUERYTRACEON 9204)
```

Once the legacy cardinality estimator is set, the preceding code block produces an output similar to the following:

```
Stats header loaded: DbName: AdventureWorks2012, ObjName:
Production.Product,
IndexId: 1, ColumnName: ProductID, EmptyTable: FALSE
Stats loaded: DbName: AdventureWorks2012, ObjName: Production.
Product,
IndexId: 1, ColumnName: ProductID, EmptyTable: FALSE
```

To better understand how it works, let's create additional statistics objects. You'll notice we are creating the same statistics four times.

The 9292 trace flag can be used to display the statistics objects that are considered interesting. Run the following query:

```
SELECT ProductID, name FROM Production.Product
WHERE ProductID = 877
OPTION (RECOMPILE, QUERYTRACEON 9292)
```

Here is the output. All the statistics are listed as shown in the following code block:

```
Stats header loaded: DbName: AdventureWorks2012, ObjName:
Production.Product,
IndexId: 1, ColumnName: ProductID, EmptyTable: FALSE
Stats header loaded: DbName: AdventureWorks2012, ObjName:
Production.Product,
IndexId: 10, ColumnName: ProductID, EmptyTable: FALSE
Stats header loaded: DbName: AdventureWorks2012, ObjName:
Production.Product,
IndexId: 11, ColumnName: ProductID, EmptyTable: FALSE
Stats header loaded: DbName: AdventureWorks2012, ObjName:
Production.Product,
IndexId: 12, ColumnName: ProductID, EmptyTable: FALSE
Stats header loaded: DbName: AdventureWorks2012, ObjName:
Production.Product,
IndexId: 13, ColumnName: ProductID, EmptyTable: FALSE
```

The 9204 trace flag can be used to display the statistics objects that were used to produce a cardinality estimate. Test the following code:

```
SELECT ProductID, name FROM Production.Product
WHERE ProductID = 877
OPTION (RECOMPILE, QUERYTRACEON 9204)
```

The output is just a single statistics object:

```
Stats loaded: DbName: AdventureWorks2012, ObjName: Production.
Product,
IndexId: 1, ColumnName: ProductID, EmptyTable: FALSE
```

To clean up, drop the statistics object you've just created:

```
DROP STATISTICS Production.Product.stat1
DROP STATISTICS Production.Product.stat2
DROP STATISTICS Production.Product.stat3
DROP STATISTICS Production.Product.stat4
```

Do not forget to disable the legacy cardinality estimator:

```
ALTER DATABASE SCOPED CONFIGURATION
SET LEGACY_CARDINALITY_ESTIMATION = OFF
```

Finally, as mentioned in *Chapter 1*, starting with SQL Server 2017 and SQL Server 2016 SP2, you can use the `OptimizerStatsUsage` XML plan element to identify the statistics used by the Query Optimizer to produce a query plan.

Full optimization

As shown in the processing steps in *Figure 3.15*, if a query does not qualify for a trivial plan, SQL Server will run the cost-based optimization process, which uses transformation rules to generate alternative plans, stores these alternatives in the Memo structure, and uses cost estimation to select the best plan. This optimization process can be executed in up to three stages or phases, with different transformation rules being applied at each stage.

Because some queries may have a huge number of possible query plans, it's sometimes not feasible to explore their entire search space—query optimization would take too long. So, in addition to applying transformation rules, several heuristics are used by the Query Optimizer to control the search strategy and to limit the number of alternatives generated to quickly find a good plan. The Query Optimizer needs to balance the optimization time and the quality of the selected plan. For example, as explained earlier, optimizing join orders can create a huge number of possible alternatives. So, a heuristic used by SQL Server creates an initial set of join orders based on their selectivity, as shown later in this section.

In addition, as introduced in *Chapter 1, An Introduction to Query Tuning and Optimization*, the optimization process can immediately finish if a good enough plan is found, relative to the Query Optimizer's internal thresholds, at the end of any of the three optimization phases (explained next). However, if at the end of any given phase the best plan is still very expensive, the Query Optimizer will run the next phase, which will run an additional set of (usually more complex) transformation rules. These phases are called `search 0`, `search 1`, and `search 2` on the `sys.dm_exec_query_optimizer_info` DMV and are shown in *Figure 3.15*:

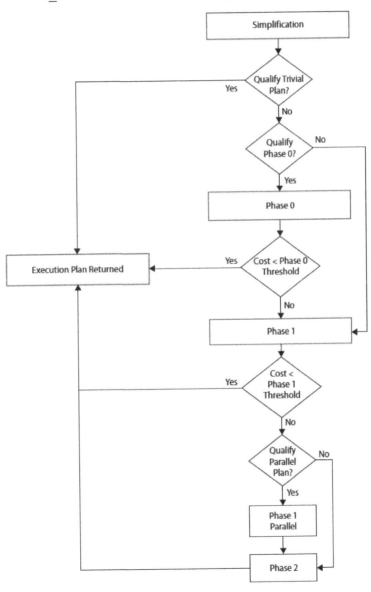

Figure 3.15 – The optimization process

Let's examine those three search phases in more detail.

Search 0

Similar to the concept of the trivial plan, the first phase, search 0, will aim to find a plan as quickly as possible without trying sophisticated transformations. Search 0, called the transaction processing phase, is ideal for the small queries typically found on transaction-processing systems and it is used for queries with at least three tables. Before the full optimization process is started, the Query Optimizer generates the initial set of join orders based on heuristics. These heuristics begin by first joining the smallest tables or the tables that achieve the largest filtering based on their selectivity. Those are the only join orders considered on search 0. At the end of this phase, the Query Optimizer compares the cost of the best-generated plan to an internal cost threshold. If the best plan is cheap enough compared to this threshold, the plan is selected and the query optimization process stops. If the plan is still very expensive, SQL Server will run the next phase.

Search 1

The next phase, search 1 (also called Quick Plan), uses additional transformation rules, and limited join reordering, and is appropriate for more complex queries. At the end of this phase, SQL Server compares the cost of the cheapest plan to a second internal cost threshold; if the best plan is cheap enough, it is selected. If the query is still expensive and the system can run parallel queries, this phase is executed again to find a good parallel plan, but no plan is selected for execution at this point. At the end of this phase, the costs of the best serial and parallel plans are compared, and the cheapest one is used in the following phase, search 2, which we'll come to in just a moment.

As an example, the following query does not qualify for search 0 and will go directly to search 1:

```
SELECT * FROM Sales.SalesOrderDetail
WHERE ProductID = 870
```

Using the sys.dm_exec_query_optimizer_info DMV, as explained earlier in this chapter, you can display its optimization information seen next, which shows that only the search 1 phase was executed:

Counter	Occurrence	Value
elapsed time	1	0.102
final cost	1	1.134781816
maximum DOP	1	0
optimizations	1	1
search 1	1	1
search 1 tasks	1	241
search 1 time	1	0.061
tables	1	1
tasks	1	241

The `sys.dm_exec_query_optimizer_info` DMV includes a counter named *gain stage 0 to stage 1*, which shows the number of times search 1 was executed after search 0, and includes the average decrease in cost from one stage to the other, as defined by the following formula:

(MinimumPlanCost(search 0) – MinimumPlanCost(search 1)) / MinimumPlanCost(search 0)

For example, run the following query:

```
SELECT soh.SalesOrderID, sod.SalesOrderDetailID, SalesReasonID
FROM Sales.SalesOrderHeader soh
JOIN Sales.SalesOrderDetail sod
ON soh.SalesOrderID = soh.SalesOrderID
JOIN Sales.SalesOrderHeaderSalesReason sohsr
ON sohsr.SalesOrderID = soh.SalesOrderID
WHERE soh.SalesOrderID = 43697
```

This will provide the optimization information shown next:

Counter	Occurrence	Value
elapsed time	1	0.002
final cost	1	1.413612922
gain stage 0 to stage 1	1	0.05339122
hints	1	1
maximum DOP	1	0
optimizations	1	1
search 0 tasks	1	158
search 0 time	1	0
search 1	1	1
search 1 tasks	1	101
search 1 time	1	0
tables	1	3
tasks	1	259

The output shows that the optimization process went through both the search 0 and search 1 stage and that a plan was found on the latter. It also shows a cost improvement of 5 percent by going from the search 0 stage to the search 1 stage.

Search 2

The last phase, search 2, is called full optimization and is used for queries ranging from complex to very complex. A larger set of the potential transformation rules, parallel operators, and other advanced optimization strategies are considered in this phase. Because this is the last phase, an execution plan must be found here (perhaps with the exception of the timeout event, as explained later).

The sys.dm_exec_query_optimizer_info DMV includes another useful counter, named *gain stage 1 to stage 2*, to show the number of times search 2 was executed after search 1, together with the average decrease in cost from one stage to the other, as defined by the following formula:

(MinimumPlanCost(search 1) – MinimumPlanCost(search 2)) / MinimumPlanCost(search 1)

We could also use the undocumented 8675 and 2372 trace flags to get additional information about these optimization phases. For example, run the following query using the 8675 trace flag:

```
SELECT DISTINCT pp.LastName, pp.FirstName
FROM Person.Person pp JOIN HumanResources.Employee e
ON e.BusinessEntityID = pp.BusinessEntityID
JOIN Sales.SalesOrderHeader soh
ON pp.BusinessEntityID = soh.SalesPersonID
JOIN Sales.SalesOrderDetail sod
```

```
ON soh.SalesOrderID = soh.SalesOrderID
JOIN Production.Product p
ON sod.ProductID = p.ProductID
WHERE ProductNumber = 'BK-M18B-44'
OPTION (RECOMPILE, QUERYTRACEON 8675)
```

It will create the optimization information shown next:

```
End of simplification, time: 0.003 net: 0.003 total: 0.003 net:
0.003
end exploration, tasks: 149 no total cost time: 0.005 net:
0.005 total: 0.009
end search(0), cost: 13.884 tasks: 332 time: 0.002 net: 0.002
total: 0.011
end exploration, tasks: 926 Cost = 13.884 time: 0.01 net: 0.01
total: 0.021
end search(1), cost: 3.46578 tasks: 1906 time: 0.009 net: 0.009
total: 0.031
end exploration, tasks: 3301 Cost = 3.46578 time: 0.008 net:
0.008 total: 0.04
*** Optimizer time out abort at task 4248 ***
end search(2), cost: 0.832242 tasks: 4248 time: 0.013 net:
0.013 total: 0.053
*** Optimizer time out abort at task 4248 ***
End of post optimization rewrite, time: 0 net: 0 total: 0.053
net: 0.053
End of query plan compilation, time: 0 net: 0 total: 0.054 net:
0.054
```

The optimization information shows that this query went throughout all the three stages of optimization and had optimization time out on search 2. The optimization timeout concept was briefly introduced in *Chapter 1, An Introduction to Query Tuning and Optimization*, and will be explained next.

Running the same query with the 2372 trace flag will show the following output, in which the search 0, 1, and 2 phases are named stage TP, QuickPlan, and Full, respectively:

```
Memory before NNFConvert: 25
Memory after NNFConvert: 25
Memory before project removal: 27
```

```
Memory after project removal: 29
Memory before simplification: 29
Memory after simplification: 58
Memory before heuristic join reordering: 58
Memory after heuristic join reordering: 65
Memory before project normalization: 65
Memory after project normalization: 65
Memory before stage TP: 68
Memory after stage TP: 84
Memory before stage QuickPlan: 84
Memory after stage QuickPlan: 126
Memory before stage Full: 126
Memory after stage Full: 172
Memory before copy out: 172
Memory after copy out: 173
```

As we've touched upon previously, the Query Optimizer has to find the best plan possible within the shortest amount of time. More to the point, it must eventually return a plan, even if that plan is not as efficient as it would like. To that end, the optimization process also includes the concept of an optimization cost budget. When this budget is exceeded, the search for the optimal plan is terminated, and the Query Optimizer will show an optimization timeout. This timeout is not a fixed amount of time but is instead calculated based on the number of transformations applied together with the elapsed time.

When a timeout is found, the Query Optimizer stops the optimization process and returns the least expensive plan it has found so far. The best plan found so far could be a plan found during the current optimization stage, but most likely, it would be the best plan found in the previous stage. This means that a timeout most likely will happen in the search 1 and search 2 stages. This timeout event is shown in the properties of a graphical plan as *Reason For Early Termination Of Statement Optimization* or in an XML plan as `StatementOptmEarlyAbortReason`. This event is also shown as the timeout counter on the `sys.dm_exec_query_optimizer_info` DMV. An example is shown in the following XML fragment, obtained by running the previous query in this section:

```
<StmtSimple StatementCompId="1"
    StatementEstRows="1"
    StatementId="1"
    StatementOptmLevel="FULL"
    StatementOptmEarlyAbortReason="TimeOut"
```

```
CardinalityEstimationModelVersion="140"

  ...

>
```

Finally, at the end of the optimization process, the chosen plan will be sent to the execution engine to be run, and the results will be sent back to the client.

Summary

This chapter showed how the Query Optimizer works, explaining how your query goes from a SQL statement submitted to SQL Server, all the way to the selected execution plan, including operations such as parsing, binding, simplification, trivial plan, and the full optimization stages. Important concepts that are part of the Query Optimizer architecture, such as transformation rules and the Memo structure, were also introduced.

The Query Optimizer generates a solution space and selects the best possible execution plan from it based on the plan cost. Transformation rules are used to generate these alternatives, which are stored in a memory structure called the Memo. Instead of exploring the search space exhaustively, heuristics are introduced to limit the number of possible solutions. Finally, the alternatives stored in the Memo are costed, and the best solution is returned for execution.

This chapter also showed that understanding how the Query Optimizer works can give you a great background to troubleshoot, optimize, and better tune your queries. But, you still need to learn more about the most-used query operators employed on the plans created by the Query Optimizer. We will cover that topic in the next chapter.

4

The Execution Engine

At its heart, the execution engine is a collection of physical operators that are software components performing the functions of the query processor. Their purpose is to execute your query efficiently. If we look at it from another perspective, the operations implemented by the execution engine define the choices available to the query optimizer when building execution plans. The execution engine and its operators were briefly covered in previous chapters. Now, we'll cover some of the most used operators, their algorithms, and their costs in greater detail. In this chapter, we will focus on operators related to data access, joins, aggregations, parallelism, and updates, as these are the ones most commonly used in queries, and also the ones that are used more in this book. Of course, many more operators are implemented by the execution engine, and you can find a complete list and description within the official SQL Server 2022 documentation. This chapter illustrates how the query optimizer decides between the various choices of operators provided by the execution engine. For example, we will see how the query processor chooses between a Nested Loops Join operator and a Hash Join operator and between a Stream Aggregate operator and a Hash Aggregate operator.

In this chapter, we will look at the data access operations, including the operators to perform scans, seeks, and bookmark lookups on database structures, such as heaps, clustered indexes, and nonclustered indexes. The concepts of sorting and hashing are also explained, along with how they impact some of the algorithms of both physical joins and aggregations, which are detailed later. In the same way, the section on joins presents the Nested Loops Join, Merge Join, and Hash Join physical operators. The next section focuses on aggregations and explains the Stream Aggregate and Hash Aggregate operators in detail. The chapter continues with parallelism and explains how it can help to reduce the response time of a query. Finally, the chapter concludes by explaining how the query processor handles update operations.

This chapter covers the following topics:

- Data access operators

- Aggregations

- Joins

- Parallelism

- Updates

Data access operators

In this section, we will learn about the operations that directly access the database, using either a base table or an index, examples of which include scans and seeks. A scan reads an entire structure, which could be a heap, a clustered index, or a nonclustered index. On the other hand, a seek does not scan an entire structure, but instead efficiently retrieves rows by navigating an index. Therefore, seeks can only be performed on a clustered index or a nonclustered index. Just to make the difference between these structures clear, a heap contains all the table columns, and its data is not stored and sorted in any particular order. Conversely, in a clustered index, the data is stored logically, sorted by the clustering key, and in addition to the clustering key, the clustered index also contains the remaining columns of the table. On the other hand, a nonclustered index can be created on a clustered index or a heap and, usually, contains only a subset of the columns of the table. The operations of these structures are summarized in *Table 4.1*:

Structure	Scan	Seek
Heap	Table Scan	
Clustered index	Clustered Index Scan	Clustered Index Seek
Nonclustered index	Index Scan	Index Seek

Table 4.1 – Data access operators

Scans

Let's start with the simplest example—by scanning a heap, which is performed by the Table Scan operator, as shown in *Table 4.1*. The following query on the AdventureWorks2019 database will use a Table Scan operator, as shown in *Figure 4.1*:

```
SELECT * FROM DatabaseLog
```

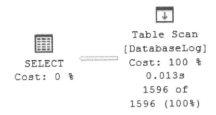

Figure 4.1 – A Table Scan operator

Similarly, the following query will show a Clustered Index Scan operator, as shown in the plan of *Figure 4.2*. The Table Scan and Clustered Index Scan operations are similar in that they both scan the entire base table, but the former is used for heaps and the latter for clustered indexes:

```
SELECT * FROM Person.Address
```

```
                                    Clustered Index Scan (Cluste…
                                    [Address].[PK_Address_Addres…
              SELECT                       Cost: 100 %
              Cost: 0 %                       0.011s
                                            19614 of
                                          19614 (100%)
```

Figure 4.2 – A Clustered Index Scan operator

Many SQL Server users assume that because a Clustered Index Scan operator was used, the data returned will be automatically sorted. The reality is that even when the data in a clustered index has been stored and sorted, using a Clustered Index Scan operator does not guarantee that the results will be sorted unless it has been explicitly requested.

By not automatically sorting the results, the storage engine has the option to find the most efficient way to access this data without worrying about returning it in an ordered set. Examples of these efficient methods used by the storage engine include using an allocation order scan based on **Index Allocation Map (IAM)** pages and using an index order scan based on the index-linked list. In addition, an advanced scanning mechanism called **merry-go-round scanning** (which is an Enterprise Edition-only feature) allows multiple query executions to share full table scans so that each execution might join the scan at a different location, thus saving the overhead of each query having to separately read the data.

If you want to know whether your data has been sorted, the Ordered property can show you if the data was returned in a manner ordered by the Clustered Index Scan operator. So, for example, the clustering key of the Person.Address table is AddressID, and if you run the following query and look at the tooltip of the Clustered Index Scan operator in a graphical plan, you could validate that the Ordered property is true:

```
SELECT * FROM Person.Address
ORDER BY AddressID
```

This is also shown in the following XML fragment plan:

```
<IndexScan Ordered="true" ScanDirection="FORWARD"
ForcedIndex="false" ForceSeek="false" … >
```

If you run the same query without the ORDER BY clause, the Ordered property will, unsurprisingly, show false. In some cases, SQL Server can benefit from reading the table in the order specified by the clustered index. Another example is shown in *Figure 4.13*, where a Stream Aggregate operator can benefit from the fact that a Clustered Index Scan operator can easily obtain the data that has already been sorted.

Next, we will see an example of an Index Scan operator. This example uses a nonclustered index to cover a query; that is, it can solve the entire query without accessing the base table (bearing in mind that a nonclustered index usually contains only a few of the columns of the table). Run the following query, which will show a plan that is similar to *Figure 4.3*:

```
SELECT AddressID, City, StateProvinceID
FROM Person.Address
```

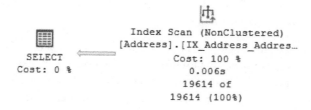

Figure 4.3 – An Index Scan operator

Note that the query optimizer was able to solve this query without even accessing the Person.Address base table, and instead decided to scan the IX_Address_AddressLine1_AddressLine2_City_StateProvinceID_PostalCode index, which comprises fewer pages when compared to the clustered index. The index definition includes AddressLine1, AddressLine2, City, StateProvinceID, and PostalCode, so it can clearly cover columns requested in the query. However, you might be wondering where the index is getting the AddressID column from. When a nonclustered index is created on a table with a clustered index, each nonclustered index row also includes the table clustering key. This clustering key is used to find which record from the clustered index is referred to by the nonclustered index row (a similar approach for nonclustered indexes on a heap will be explained later). In this case, as I mentioned earlier, `AddressID` is the clustering key of the table, and it is stored in every row of the nonclustered index, which is why the index was able to cover this column in the previous query.

Seeks

Now, let's look at Index Seeks. These can be performed by both Clustered Index Seek operators and Index Seek operators, which are used against clustered and nonclustered indexes, respectively. An Index Seek operator does not scan the entire index but instead navigates the B-tree index structure to quickly find one or more records. The next query, together with the plan in *Figure 4.4*, shows an example of a Clustered Index Seek operator. One benefit of a Clustered Index Seek operator, compared to a nonclustered Index Seek operator, is that the former can cover any column of the table. Of course, because the records of a clustered index are logically ordered by its clustering key, a table can only have one clustered index. If a clustered index was not defined, the table will, therefore, be a heap:

```
SELECT AddressID, City, StateProvinceID FROM Person.Address
WHERE AddressID = 12037
```

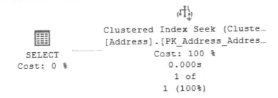

Figure 4.4 – A Clustered Index Seek operator

The next query and *Figure 4.5* both illustrate a nonclustered Index Seek operator. Here, it is interesting to note that the base table was not used at all, and it was not even necessary to scan the entire index: there is a nonclustered index on the `StateProvinceID` parameter, and as mentioned previously, it also contains the clustering key, `AddressID`:

```
SELECT AddressID, StateProvinceID FROM Person.Address
WHERE StateProvinceID = 32
```

Figure 4.5 – An Index Seek operator

Although both examples that are shown only return one row, an Index Seek operation can also be used to find multiple rows with either equality or nonequality operators, which is called a partially ordered scan. The previous query just returned one row, but you can change it to a new parameter, such as in the following example:

```
SELECT AddressID, StateProvinceID FROM Person.Address
WHERE StateProvinceID = 9
```

The query has been auto-parameterized, and the same plan will be used with any other parameter. You can try to force a new optimization and plan (for example, using OPTION (RECOMPILE)), but the same plan will be returned. In this case, the same plan that was shown in *Figure 4.5* will be used, and 4,564 rows will be returned without the need to access the base table at all. A partially ordered scan works by using the index to find the first row that qualifies and continues reading the remaining rows, which are all logically together on the same leaf pages of the index. More details about the index structure will be covered in *Chapter 5, Working with Indexes*. Parameterization is covered in greater detail in *Chapter 8, Understanding Plan Caching*.

A more complicated example of partially ordered scans involves using a nonequality operator or a BETWEEN clause, such as in the following example:

```
SELECT AddressID, City, StateProvinceID FROM Person.Address
WHERE AddressID BETWEEN 10000 and 20000
```

Because the clustered index is defined using AddressID, a plan similar to *Figure 4.4* will be used, where a Clustered Index Seek operation will be used to find the first row that qualifies for the filter predicate and will continue scanning the index—row by row—until the last row that qualifies is found. More accurately, the scan will stop on the first row that does not qualify.

Bookmark lookup

Now, the question that comes up is what happens if a nonclustered index is useful for quickly finding one or more records, but does not cover the query? In other words, what happens if the nonclustered index does not contain all the columns requested by the query? In this case, the query optimizer has to decide whether it is more efficient to use the nonclustered index to find these records quickly and then access the base table to obtain the additional fields. Alternatively, it can decide whether it is more optimal to just go straight to the base table and scan it, reading each row and testing to see whether it matches the predicates. For example, in our previous query, an existing nonclustered index covers both the AddressID and StateProvinceID columns. What if we also request the City and ModifiedDate columns in the same query? This is shown in the next query, which returns one record and produces the same plan as *Figure 4.6*:

```
SELECT AddressID, City, StateProvinceID, ModifiedDate
FROM Person.Address
WHERE StateProvinceID = 32
```

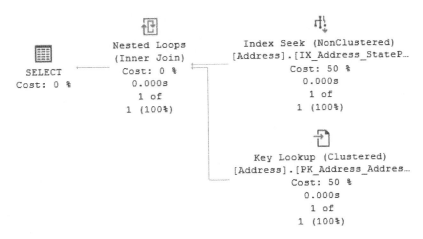

Figure 4.6 – A bookmark lookup example

As you can see in the previous example, the query optimizer is choosing the IX_Address_ StateProvinceID index to find the records quickly. However, because the index does not cover the additional columns, it also needs to use the base table (in this case, the clustered index) to get that additional information. This operation is called a bookmark lookup, and it is performed by the Key Lookup operator, which was introduced specifically to differentiate a bookmark lookup from a regular Clustered Index Seek operator. The Key Lookup operator only appears on a graphical plan (and then only from SQL Server 2005 Service Pack 2 and onward). Text and XML plans can show whether a Clustered Index Seek operator is performing a bookmark lookup by looking at the LOOKUP keyword and lookup attributes, as shown next. For example, let's run the following query:

```
SET SHOWPLAN_TEXT ON
GO
SELECT AddressID, City, StateProvinceID, ModifiedDate
FROM Person.Address
WHERE StateProvinceID = 32
GO
SET SHOWPLAN_TEXT OFF
GO
```

The output will show the following text plan, including a Clustered Index Seek operator with the LOOKUP keyword at the end:

```
|--Nested Loops(Inner Join, OUTER REFERENCES …)
|--Index Seek(OBJECT:([Address].[IX_Address_StateProvinceID]),
SEEK:([Address].[StateProvinceID]=(32)) ORDERED FORWARD)
```

```
|--Clustered Index Seek(OBJECT:([Address].[PK_Address_
AddressID]),
SEEK:([Address].[AddressID]=[Address].[AddressID]) LOOKUP
ORDERED FORWARD)
```

The XML plan shows the same information in the following way:

```
<RelOp LogicalOp="Clustered Index Seek" PhysicalOp="Clustered
Index Seek" …>

…

<IndexScan Lookup="true" Ordered="true" ScanDirection="FORWARD"
…>
```

Bear in mind that although SQL Server 2000 implemented a bookmark lookup using a dedicated operator (called Bookmark Lookup), essentially, the operation is the same.

Now run the same query, but this time, request StateProvinceID equal to 20. This will produce the plan that is shown in *Figure 4.7*:

```
SELECT AddressID, City, StateProvinceID, ModifiedDate
FROM Person.Address
WHERE StateProvinceID = 20
```

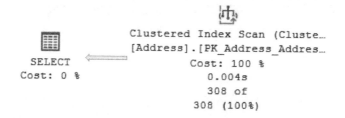

Figure 4.7 – A plan switching to a Clustered Index Scan operator

In the preceding execution, the query optimizer has selected a Clustered Index Scan operator and the query has returned 308 records, compared to just a single record for the StateProvinceID value: 32. So, the query optimizer is producing two different execution plans for the same query, with the only difference being the value of the StateProvinceID parameter. In this case, the query optimizer uses the value of the query's StateProvinceID parameter to estimate the cardinality of the predicate as it tries to produce an efficient plan for that parameter. We will learn more about this behavior, called parameter sniffing, in *Chapter 8*, Understanding *Plan Caching*, and *Chapter 9*, *The Query Store*. Additionally, we will learn how the estimation is performed in *Chapter 6*, Understanding *Statistics*.

This time, the query optimizer estimated that more records could be returned than when `StateProvinceID` was equal to 32, and it decided that it was cheaper to do a Table Scan than to perform many bookmark lookups. At this stage, you might be wondering what the tipping point is, in other words, at what point the query optimizer decides to change from one method to another. Because a bookmark lookup requires random I/Os, which is very expensive, it would not take many records for the query optimizer to switch from a bookmark lookup to a Clustered Index Scan (or a Table Scan) operator. We already know that when the query returned one record, for `StateProvinceID` 32, the query optimizer chose a bookmark lookup. Additionally, we saw that when we requested the records for `StateProvinceID` 20, which returned 308 records, it used a Clustered Index Scan operator. Logically, we can try requesting somewhere between 1 and 308 records to find this switchover point, right?

As you might already suspect, this is a cost-based decision that does not depend on the actual number of records returned by the query—rather, it is influenced by the estimated number of records. We can find these estimates by analyzing the histogram of the statistics object for the `IX_Address_StateProvinceID` index—something that will be covered in *Chapter 6*, Understanding *Statistics*.

We performed this exercise and found that the highest estimated number of records to get a bookmark lookup for this particular example was 62, and the first one to have a Clustered Index Scan operator was 106. Let's look at both examples here by running the query with the `StateProvinceID` values of 163 and 71. We will get the plans that are shown in *Figure 4.8* and *Figure 4.9*, respectively:

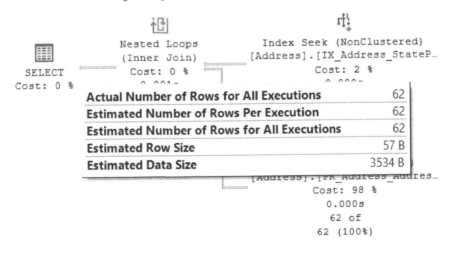

Figure 4.8 – The plan for the StateProvinceID = 163 predicate

The second plan is as follows:

Clustered Index Scan (Cluste...
[Address].[PK_Address_Addres...
Cost: 100 %

SELECT
Cost: 0 %

Actual Number of Rows for All Executions	106
Number of Rows Read	19614
Estimated Number of Rows Per Execution	106
Estimated Number of Rows for All Executions	106
Estimated Row Size	57 B
Estimated Data Size	6042 B

Figure 4.9 – The plan for the StateProvinceID = 71 predicate

Looking at the preceding plans, we can see that, for this specific example, the query optimizer selects a bookmark lookup for an estimated 62 records and changes to a Clustered Index Scan operator when that estimated number of records goes up to 106 (there are no estimated values between 62 and 106 for the histogram of this particular statistics object). Bear in mind that, although here, both the actual and estimated number of rows are the same, the query optimizer makes its decision based on the estimated number of rows. The actual number of rows is only known after the execution plan has been generated and executed, and the results are returned.

Finally, because nonclustered indexes can exist on both heaps and clustered indexes, we can also have a bookmark lookup on a heap. To follow the next example, create an index in the `DatabaseLog` table, which is a heap, by running the following statement:

```
CREATE INDEX IX_Object ON DatabaseLog(Object)
```

Then, run the following query, which will produce the plan shown in *Figure 4.10*:

```
SELECT * FROM DatabaseLog
WHERE Object = 'City'
```

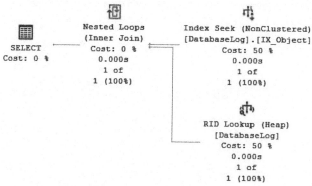

Figure 4.10 – A RID Lookup operator

Note that instead of the Key Lookup operator shown earlier, this plan displays a RID Lookup operator. This is because heaps do not have clustering keys in the same way that clustered indexes do, and instead, they use **row identifiers (RIDs)**. A RID is a row locator that includes information such as the database file, page, and slot numbers to allow a specific record to be easily located. Every row in a nonclustered index created on a heap contains the RID of the corresponding heap record.

To clean up and leave tables in their original state, remove the index you just created:

```
DROP INDEX DatabaseLog.IX_Object
```

In this section, we have seen how the execution engine accesses our tables and indexes. In the following sections, we will see the most common operations performed on such data.

Aggregations

Aggregations are operations used in databases to summarize information about some set of data. The result of aggregate operations can be a single value, such as the average salary for a company, or it can be a per-group value, such as the average salary by department. SQL Server has two operators to implement aggregations, Stream Aggregate and Hash Aggregate, and they can be used to solve queries with aggregation functions (such as SUM, AVG, and MAX), or when using the GROUP BY clause and the DISTINCT keyword.

Sorting and hashing

Before introducing the remaining operators of this chapter, let's discuss sorting and hashing, both of which play a very important role in some of the operators and algorithms of the execution engine. For example, two of the operators covered in this chapter, Stream Aggregate and Merge Join, require data to be already sorted. To provide sorted data, the query optimizer might employ an existing index, or it might explicitly introduce a Sort operator. On the other hand, hashing is used by the Hash Aggregate and Hash Join operators, both of which work by building a hash table in memory. The Hash Join operator only uses memory for the smaller of its two inputs, which is selected by the query optimizer.

Additionally, sorting uses memory and, similar to hashing operations, will also use the tempdb database if there is not enough available memory, which could become a performance problem. Both sorting and hashing are blocking operations (otherwise known as stop-and-go) meaning that they cannot produce any rows until they have consumed all of their input. In reality, this is only true for hashing operations during the time the build input is hashed, as explained later.

Stream Aggregate

Let's start with the Stream Aggregate operator by using a query with an aggregation function. Queries using an aggregate function (and no GROUP BY clause) are called scalar aggregates, as they return a single value and are always implemented by the Stream Aggregate operator. To demonstrate this, run the following query, which shows the plan from *Figure 4.11*:

```
SELECT AVG(ListPrice) FROM Production.Product
```

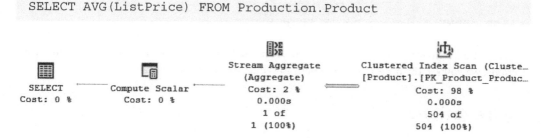

Figure 4.11 – A Stream Aggregate operator

A text plan can be useful to show more details about both the Stream Aggregate and Compute Scalar operators. Run the following query:

```
SET SHOWPLAN_TEXT ON
GO
SELECT AVG(ListPrice) FROM Production.Product
GO
SET SHOWPLAN_TEXT OFF
```

Here is the displayed text plan:

```
|--Compute Scalar(DEFINE:([Expr1002]=CASE WHEN [Expr1003]=(0)
THEN NULL ELSE
[Expr1004]/CONVERT_IMPLICIT(money,[Expr1003],0) END))
|--Stream Aggregate(DEFINE:([Expr1003]=Count(*),
[Expr1004]=SUM([Product].
[ListPrice])))
|--Clustered Index Scan(OBJECT:([Product].[PK_Product_
ProductID]))
```

The same information could be obtained from the graphical plan by selecting the *Properties* window (by pressing the *F4* key) of both the Stream Aggregate and Compute Scalar operators and then opening the Defined Values property.

In any case, note that to implement the AVG aggregation function, the Stream Aggregate operator is computing both a COUNT aggregate and a SUM aggregate, the results of which will be stored in the computed expressions of Expr1003 and Expr1004, respectively. The Compute Scalar operator verifies that there is no division by zero when using a CASE expression. As you can see in the text plan if Expr1003 (which is the value for the count) is zero, the Compute Scalar operator returns NULL; otherwise, it calculates and returns the average by dividing the sum by the count.

Now, let's see an example of a query—this time, using the GROUP BY clause. The following query produces the plan shown in *Figure 4.12*:

```
SELECT ProductLine, COUNT(*) FROM Production.Product
GROUP BY ProductLine
```

Figure 4.12 – Stream Aggregate using a Sort operator

A Stream Aggregate operator always requires its input to be sorted by the GROUP BY clause predicate. So, in this case, the Sort operator shown in the plan will provide the data sorted by the ProductLine column. After the sorted input has been received, the records for the same group will be next to each other, so the Stream Aggregate operator can now easily count the records for each group.

Note that although the first example in this section, using the AVG function, also used a Stream Aggregate operator, it did not require any sorted input. A query without a GROUP BY clause considers its entire input a single group.

A Stream Aggregate operator can also use an index to have its input sorted, as demonstrated in the following query, which produces the plan shown in *Figure 4.13*:

```
SELECT SalesOrderID, SUM(LineTotal) FROM Sales.SalesOrderDetail
GROUP BY SalesOrderID
```

Figure 4.13 – Stream Aggregate using an existing index

No Sort operator is needed in this plan because the Clustered Index Scan operator provides the data already sorted by `SalesOrderID`, which is part of the clustering key of the SalesOrderDetail table. As demonstrated in the previous example, the Stream Aggregate operator will consume the sorted data, but this time, it will calculate the sum of the `LineTotal` column for each group.

Because the purpose of the Stream Aggregate operator is to aggregate values based on groups, its algorithm relies on the fact that its input has already been sorted by the `GROUP BY` clause predicate; therefore, records from the same group are next to each other. Essentially, in this algorithm, the first record read will create the first group, and its aggregate value will be initialized. Any record read after that will be checked to see whether it matches the current group; if it does match, the record value will be aggregated to this group. On the other hand, if the record doesn't match the current group, a new group will be created, and its own aggregated value initialized. This process will continue until all the records have been processed.

Hash Aggregate

Now, let's take a look at the Hash Aggregate operator, shown as Hash Match (Aggregate) on the execution plans. This chapter describes two hash algorithms, Hash Aggregate and Hash Join, which work in a similar way and are, in fact, implemented by the same physical operator: Hash Match. In this section, we will cover the Hash Aggregate operator, while the *Joins* section will cover the Hash Join operator.

The query optimizer can select a Hash Aggregate operator for big tables where the data is not sorted, there is no need to sort it, and its cardinality estimates only a few groups. For example, the `SalesOrderHeader` table has no index on the `TerritoryID` column, so the following query will use a Hash Aggregate operator, as shown in *Figure 4.14*:

```
SELECT TerritoryID, COUNT(*)
FROM Sales.SalesOrderHeader
GROUP BY TerritoryID
```

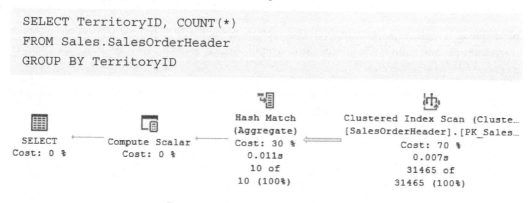

Figure 4.14 – A Hash Aggregate operator

As mentioned earlier, a hash operation builds a hash table in memory. The hash key used for this table is displayed in the **Properties** window of the **Hash Aggregate** operator as the **Hash Keys Build** property, which, in this case, is `TerritoryID`. Because this table is not sorted by the required column, `TerritoryID`, every row scanned can belong to any group.

The algorithm for the Hash Aggregate operator is similar to the Stream Aggregate operator, with the exception that, in this case, the input data does not have to be sorted, a hash table is created in memory, and a hash value is calculated for each row that has been processed. For each hash value calculated, the algorithm will check whether a corresponding group already exists in the hash table; if it does not exist, the algorithm will create a new entry for it. In this way, the values for each record are aggregated in this entry on the hash table, and only one row for each group is stored in memory.

Note, again, that a Hash Aggregate operator helps when the data has not been sorted. If you create an index that can provide sorted data, the query optimizer might select a Stream Aggregate operator instead. Run the following statement to create an index, and then execute the previous query again to verify that it uses a Stream Aggregate operator, as shown in *Figure 4.15*:

```
CREATE INDEX IX_TerritoryID ON Sales.
SalesOrderHeader(TerritoryID)
```

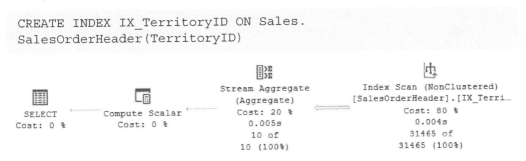

Figure 4.15 – A Stream Aggregate operator using an index

To clean up the changes on the table, drop the index using the following DROP INDEX statement:

```
DROP INDEX Sales.SalesOrderHeader.IX_TerritoryID
```

If the input is not sorted and order is explicitly requested in a query, the query optimizer might introduce a Sort operator and a Stream Aggregate operator, as shown earlier. Or it might decide to use a Hash Aggregate operator and then sort the results, as shown in the following query, which produces the plan shown in *Figure 4.16*. The query optimizer will estimate which operation is the least expensive: sorting the entire input and using a Stream Aggregate operator or using a Hash Aggregate operator and only sorting the aggregated results:

```
SELECT TerritoryID, COUNT(*)
FROM Sales.SalesOrderHeader
GROUP BY TerritoryID
ORDER BY TerritoryID
```

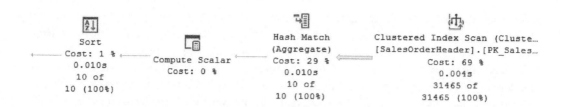

Figure 4.16 – A Hash Aggregate operator followed by a Sort operator

Distinct Sort

Finally, a query using the DISTINCT keyword can be implemented by a Stream Aggregate operator, a Hash Aggregate operator, or a Distinct Sort operator. The Distinct Sort operator is used to both remove duplicates and sort its input. In fact, a query using DISTINCT can be rewritten as a GROUP BY query, and both can generate the same execution plan. If an index to provide sorted data is available, the query optimizer can use a Stream Aggregate operator. If no index is available, SQL Server can introduce a Distinct Sort operator or a Hash Aggregate operator. Let's look at all three cases here. The following two queries return the same data and produce the same execution plan, as shown in *Figure 4.17*:

```
SELECT DISTINCT(JobTitle)
FROM HumanResources.Employee
GO
SELECT JobTitle
FROM HumanResources.Employee
GROUP BY JobTitle
```

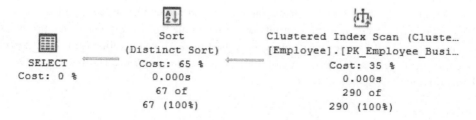

Figure 4.17 – A Distinct Sort operator

Note that the plan is using a Distinct Sort operator. This operator will sort the rows and eliminate any duplicates.

If we create an index, the query optimizer could instead use a Stream Aggregate operator because the plan can take advantage of the fact that the data is already sorted. To test it, run the following CREATE INDEX statement:

```
CREATE INDEX IX_JobTitle ON HumanResources.Employee(JobTitle)
```

Then, run the previous two queries again. Both queries will now produce a plan showing a Stream Aggregate operator. Drop the index before continuing by using a DROP INDEX statement:

```
DROP INDEX HumanResources.Employee.IX_JobTitle
```

Finally, for a bigger table without an index to provide order, a Hash Aggregate operator can be used, as shown in the two following examples:

```
SELECT DISTINCT(TerritoryID)
FROM Sales.SalesOrderHeader
GO
SELECT TerritoryID
FROM Sales.SalesOrderHeader
GROUP BY TerritoryID
```

Both queries produce the same results and will use the same execution plan using a Hash Aggregate operator. Now we will learn about the join operators used by SQL Server.

Joins

In this section, we will talk about the three physical join operators that SQL Server uses to implement logical joins: the Nested Loops Join, Merge Join, and Hash Join operators. It is important to understand that no join algorithm is better than any other and that the query optimizer will select the best join algorithm depending on the specific scenario, as we will explain next.

Nested Loops Join

Let's start with a query whose purpose is to list employees who are also salespersons. The following query creates the plan shown in *Figure 4.18*, which uses a Nested Loops Join operator:

```
SELECT e.BusinessEntityID, TerritoryID
FROM HumanResources.Employee AS e
JOIN Sales.SalesPerson AS s ON e.BusinessEntityID =
s.BusinessEntityID
```

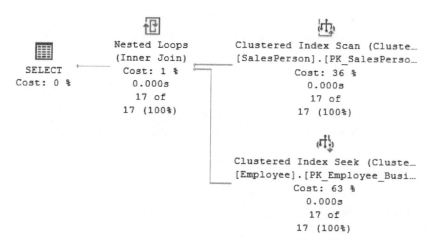

Figure 4.18 – A Nested Loops Join operator

The input shown at the top of the Nested Loops Join plan is known as the outer input, and the one at the bottom is the inner input. The algorithm for the Nested Loops Join operator is very simple: the operator used to access the outer input is executed only once, and the operator used to access the inner input is executed once for every record that qualifies on the outer input. Note that in this example, the plan is scanning the SalesPerson table for the outer input. Because there is no filter on the SalesPerson table, all of its 17 records are returned; therefore, as dictated by the algorithm, the inner input (the Clustered Index Seek operator) is also executed 17 times—once for each row from the outer table.

You can validate this information by looking at the Clustered Index Scan operator properties where you can find the actual number of executions (which, in this case, is 1) and the actual number of rows (which, in this case, is 17). A sample XML fragment is next:

```
<RelOp EstimateRows="17" PhysicalOp="Clustered Index Scan" … >
   <RunTimeInformation>
      <ActualRows="17" ActualRowsRead="17" ActualExecutions="1" …
/>
   </RunTimeInformation>
</RelOp>
```

In the same way, the following XML fragment demonstrates that both the actual number of rows and the number of executions are 17:

```
<RelOp EstimateRows="1" PhisicalOp="Clustered Index Seek" … >
   <RunTimeInformation>
```

```
    <ActualRows="17" ActualRowsRead="17" ActualExecutions="17"
... />
  </RunTimeInformation>
</RelOp>
```

Let's change the query to add a filter by TerritoryID:

```
SELECT e.BusinessEntityID, HireDate
FROM HumanResources.Employee AS e
JOIN Sales.SalesPerson AS s ON e.BusinessEntityID =
s.BusinessEntityID
WHERE TerritoryID = 1
```

This query produces a plan similar to the one shown previously using SalesPerson as the outer input and a Clustered Index Seek operator on the Employee table as the inner input. But this time, the filter on the SalesPerson table is asking for records with TerritoryID equal to 1, and only three records qualify. As a result, the Clustered Index Seek operator, which is the operator on the inner input, is only executed three times. You can verify this information by looking at the properties of each operator, as we did for the previous query.

So, in summary, in the Nested Loops Join algorithm, the operator for the outer input will be executed once and the operator for the inner input will be executed once for every row that qualifies on the outer input. The result of this is that the cost of this algorithm is proportional to the size of the outer input multiplied by the size of the inner input. As such, the query optimizer is more likely to choose a Nested Loops Join operator when the outer input is small, and the inner input has an index on the join key. This join type can be especially effective when the inner input is potentially large, as only a few rows, indicated by the outer input, will be searched.

Merge Join

Now, let's take a look at a Merge Join example. Run the following query, which produces the execution plan shown in *Figure 4.19*:

```
SELECT h.SalesOrderID, s.SalesOrderDetailID, OrderDate
FROM Sales.SalesOrderHeader h
JOIN Sales.SalesOrderDetail s ON h.SalesOrderID =
s.SalesOrderID
```

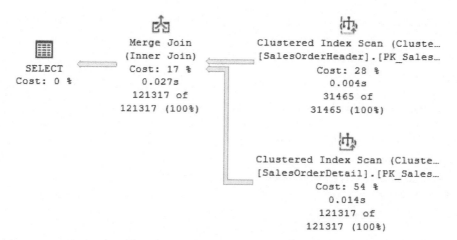

Figure 4.19 – A Merge Join example

One difference between this and Nested Loops Join is that, in Merge Join, both input operators are only executed once. You can verify this by looking at the properties of both operators, and you'll find that the number of executions is 1. Another difference is that a Merge Join operator requires an equality operator and its inputs sorted on the join predicate. In this example, the join predicate has an equality operator, which uses the `SalesOrderID` column, and both clustered indexes are ordered by `SalesOrderID`.

Benefitting from the fact that both of its inputs are sorted on the join predicate, a Merge Join operator simultaneously reads a row from each input and compares them. If the rows match, they are returned. If the rows do not match, the smaller value can be discarded—because both inputs are sorted, the discarded row will not match any other row on the other input table. This process continues until one of the tables has been completed. Even if there are still rows on the other table, they will clearly not match any rows on the fully scanned table, so there is no need to continue. Because both tables can potentially be scanned, the maximum cost of a Merge Join operator is the sum of scanning both inputs.

If the inputs have not already been sorted, the query optimizer is not likely to choose a Merge Join operator. However, it might decide to sort one or even both inputs if it deems the cost is cheaper than the other alternatives. Let's follow an exercise to see what happens if we force a Merge Join plan on, for example, a Nested Loops Join plan. If you run the following query, you will notice that it uses a Nested Loops Join operator, as shown in *Figure 4.20*:

```
SELECT * FROM Sales.SalesOrderDetail s
JOIN Production.Product p ON s.ProductID = p.ProductID
WHERE SalesOrderID = 43659
```

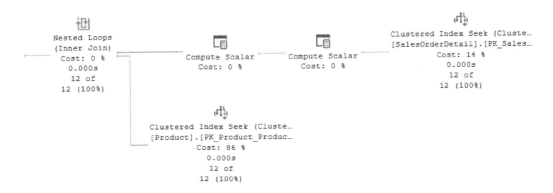

Figure 4.20 – A Nested Loops Join operator

In this case, a good plan is created using efficient Clustered Index Seek operators. If we force a Merge Join operator using a hint, as shown in the following query, the query optimizer has to introduce sorted sources such as Clustered Index Scan and Sort operators, both of which can be seen on the plan shown in *Figure 4.21*. Of course, these additional operations are more expensive than a Clustered Index Seek operator, and they are only introduced because we instructed the query optimizer to do so:

```
SELECT * FROM Sales.SalesOrderdetail s
JOIN Production.Product p ON s.ProductID = p.ProductID
WHERE SalesOrderID = 43659
OPTION (MERGE JOIN)
```

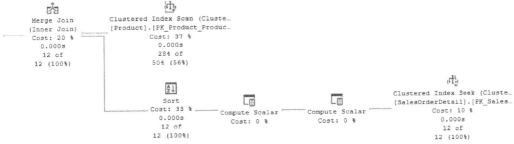

Figure 4.21 – A plan with a hint to use a Merge Join operator

In summary, given the nature of the Merge Join operator, the query optimizer is more likely to choose this algorithm when faced with medium to large inputs, where there is an equality operator on the join predicate, and when the inputs are sorted.

Hash Join

The third join algorithm used by SQL Server is Hash Join. Run the following query to produce the plan displayed in *Figure 4.22*, and then we'll take a closer look at the Hash Join operator:

```
SELECT h.SalesOrderID, s.SalesOrderDetailID FROM Sales.
SalesOrderHeader h
JOIN Sales.SalesOrderDetail s ON h.SalesOrderID =
s.SalesOrderID
```

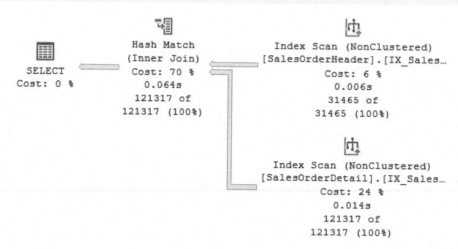

Figure 4.22 – A Hash Join example

In the same way as the Merge Join operator, the Hash Join operator requires an equality operator on the join predicate, but unlike Merge Join, it does not require its inputs to be sorted. In addition, the operations of both inputs are only executed once, which you can verify by looking at the operator properties, as shown earlier. However, a Hash Join operator works by creating a hash table in memory. The query optimizer will use cardinality estimation to detect the smaller of the two inputs, called the build input, and then use it to build a hash table in memory. If there is not enough memory to host the hash table, SQL Server can use a workfile in tempdb, which can impact the performance of the query. A Hash Join operator is a blocking operation, but only during the time the build input is hashed. After the build input has been hashed, the second table, called the probe input, will be read and compared to the hash table using the same mechanism described in the *Hash Aggregate* section. If the rows are matched, they will be returned, and the results will be streamed through. In the execution plan, the table at the top will be used as the build input and the table at the bottom as the probe input.

Finally, note that a behavior called "role reversal" might appear. If the query optimizer is not able to correctly estimate which of the two inputs is smaller, the build and probe roles may be reversed at execution time, and this will not be shown on the execution plan.

In summary, the query optimizer can choose a Hash Join operator for large inputs where there is an equality operator on the join predicate. Because both tables are scanned, the cost of a Hash Join operator is the sum of scanning both inputs, plus the cost of building the hash table. Now that we have learned about the main joins that we can use in SQL Server, we will explore parallelism, which will help us to run such queries quickly and efficiently.

Parallelism

SQL Server can use parallelism to help execute some expensive queries faster by using several processors simultaneously. However, even when a query might get better performance by using parallel plans, it could still use more resources than a similar serial plan.

For the query optimizer to consider parallel plans, the SQL Server installation must have access to at least two processors or cores or a hyper-threaded configuration. In addition, both the affinity mask and the maximum degree of parallelism advanced configuration options must allow the use of at least two processors, which they do by default. Finally, as explained later in this section, SQL Server will only consider parallelism for serial queries whose cost exceeds the configured cost threshold for parallelism, where the default value is 5.

The affinity mask configuration option specifies which processors are eligible to run SQL Server threads, and the default value of 0 means that all the processors can be used. The maximum degree of the parallelism configuration option is used to limit the number of processors that can be used in parallel plans, and similarly, its default value of 0 allows all available processors to be used. As you can see, if you have the proper hardware, SQL Server allows parallel plans by default, with no additional configuration.

Parallelism will be considered by the query processor when the estimated cost of a serial plan is higher than the value defined in the cost threshold for the parallelism configuration parameter. However, this doesn't guarantee that parallelism will actually be employed in the final execution plan, as the final decision to parallelize a query (or not) will be based on cost estimations. That is, there is no guarantee that the best parallel plan found will have a lower cost than the best serial plan, so the serial plan might still end up being the selected plan. Parallelism is implemented by the parallelism physical operator, also known as the exchange operator, which implements the Distribute Streams, Gather Streams, and Repartition Streams logical operations.

To create and test parallel plans, we will need to create a couple of large tables in the AdventureWorks2019 database. One of these tables will also be used in the next section. A simple way to do this is to copy the data from Sales.SalesOrderDetail a few times by running the following statements:

```
SELECT *
INTO #temp
FROM Sales.SalesOrderDetail
```

```
UNION ALL SELECT * FROM Sales.SalesOrderDetail
UNION ALL SELECT * FROM Sales.SalesOrderDetail
UNION ALL SELECT * FROM Sales.SalesOrderDetail
UNION ALL SELECT * FROM Sales.SalesOrderDetail
UNION ALL SELECT * FROM Sales.SalesOrderDetail
SELECT IDENTITY(int, 1, 1) AS ID, CarrierTrackingNumber,
OrderQty, ProductID,
UnitPrice, LineTotal, rowguid, ModifiedDate
INTO dbo.SalesOrderDetail FROM #temp
SELECT IDENTITY(int, 1, 1) AS ID, CarrierTrackingNumber,
OrderQty, ProductID,
UnitPrice, LineTotal, rowguid, ModifiedDate
INTO dbo.SalesOrderDetail2 FROM #temp
DROP TABLE #temp
```

The following query, using one of the tables we just created, will produce a parallel plan. Because this plan is too big to print in this book, only part of it is displayed in *Figure 4.23*:

Figure 4.23 – Part of a parallel plan

```
SELECT ProductID, COUNT(*)
FROM dbo.SalesOrderDetail
GROUP BY ProductID
```

One benefit of the graphical plans, compared to the text and XML plans, is that you can easily see which operators are being executed in parallel by looking at the parallelism symbol (a small yellow circle with arrows) included in the operator icon.

To see why a parallel plan was considered and selected, you can look at the cost of the serial plan. One way to do this is by using the MAXDOP hint to force a serial plan on the same query, as shown next:

```
SELECT ProductID, COUNT(*)
FROM dbo.SalesOrderDetail
```

```
GROUP BY ProductID
OPTION (MAXDOP 1)
```

The forced serial plan has a cost of 9.70746. Given that the default cost threshold for the parallelism configuration option is 5, this crosses that threshold. An interesting test you can perform in your test environment is to change the cost threshold for the parallelism option to 10 by running the following statements:

```
EXEC sp_configure 'cost threshold for parallelism', 10
GO
RECONFIGURE
GO
```

If you run the same query again, this time without the MAXDOP hint, you will get a serial plan with a cost of 9.70746. Because the cost threshold for parallelism is now 10, the query optimizer did not even try to find a parallel plan. If you have followed this exercise, do not forget to change the cost threshold for the parallelism configuration option back to the default value of 5 by running the following statement:

```
EXEC sp_configure 'cost threshold for parallelism', 5
GO
RECONFIGURE
GO
```

The exchange operator

As mentioned earlier, parallelism is implemented by the parallelism physical operator, which is also known as the exchange operator. Parallelism in SQL Server works by splitting a task among two or more copies of the same operator, each copy running in its own scheduler. For example, if you were to ask SQL Server to count the number of records on a small table, it might use a single Stream Aggregate operator to do that. But if you request it to count the number of records in a very large table, SQL Server might use two or more Stream Aggregate operators, with each counting the number of records of a part of the table. These Stream Aggregate operators would run in parallel, each one in a different scheduler and each performing part of the work. This is a simplified explanation, but this section will explain the details.

In most cases, the actual partitioning of data between these operators is handled by the parallelism or exchange operator. Interestingly, most of these operators do not need to be aware that they are being executed in parallel. For example, the Stream Aggregate operator we just mentioned only receives records, counts them, and then returns the results without knowing that other Stream Aggregate operators are also performing the same operation with distinct records of a table. Of course, there are also parallel-aware operators such as Parallel Scan, which we will cover next. To see how it works, run the next query, which creates the parallel plan shown in *Figure 4.24*:

```
SELECT * FROM dbo.SalesOrderDetail
WHERE LineTotal > 3234
```

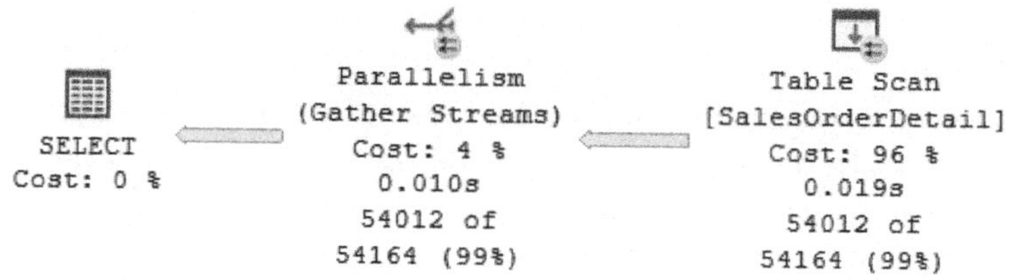

```
                                 Parallelism              Table Scan
                               (Gather Streams)       [SalesOrderDetail]
        SELECT                    Cost: 4 %               Cost: 96 %
       Cost: 0 %                    0.010s                  0.019s
                                   54012 of                54012 of
                                  54164 (99%)             54164 (99%)
```

Figure 4.24 – A Parallel Scan query

As mentioned earlier, Parallel Scan is one of the few parallel-aware operators in SQL Server and is based on the work performed by the parallel page supplier, a storage engine process that assigns sets of pages to operators in the plan. In the plan shown, SQL Server will assign two or more Table Scan operators, and the parallel page supplier will provide them with sets of pages. One great advantage of this method is that it does not need to assign an equal number of pages per thread. However, they are assigned on demand, which could help in cases where one CPU might be busy with some other system activities and might not be able to process many records; thus, it does not slow down the entire process. For example, in my test execution, I see two threads—one processing 27,477 and the other 26,535 rows, as shown in the following XML plan fragment (you can also see this information on the graphical plan by selecting the properties of the **Table Scan** operator and expanding the **Actual Number of Rows** section):

```
<RunTimeInformation>
<RunTimeCountersPerThread Thread="1" ActualRows="27477" … />
<RunTimeCountersPerThread Thread="2" ActualRows="26535" … />
<RunTimeCountersPerThread Thread="0" ActualRows="0" … />
</RunTimeInformation>
```

But of course, this depends on the activity of each CPU. To simulate this, we ran another test while one of the CPUs was busy, and the plan showed one thread processing only 11,746 rows, while the second was processing 42,266. Notice that the plan also shows thread 0, which is the coordinator or main thread, and does not process any rows.

Although the plan in *Figure 4.24* only shows a Gather Streams exchange operator, the exchange operator can take two additional functions or logical operations as Distribute Streams and Repartition Stream exchange operators.

A Gather Streams exchange is also called a start parallelism exchange, and it is always at the beginning of a parallel plan or region, considering that execution starts from the far left of the plan. This operator consumes several input streams, combines them, and produces a single output stream of records. For example, in the plan shown in *Figure 4.24*, the Gather Streams exchange operator consumes the data produced by the two Table Scan operators running in parallel and sends all of these records to its parent operator.

Opposite to a Gather Streams exchange, a Distribute Streams exchange is called a stop parallelism exchange. It takes a single input stream of records and produces multiple output streams. The third exchange logical operation is the Repartition Streams exchange, which can consume multiple streams and produce multiple streams of records.

In the previous example, we saw that Parallel Scan is a parallel-aware operator in which the parallel page supplier assigns sets of pages to operators in the plan. As indicated earlier, most of the time, operators are not aware they are running in parallel, and so it is the job of the exchange operator to send them rows using one of the partitioning types shown in *Table 4.2*:

Partitioning type	Description
Hash	Evaluates a hash function on one or more columns on the row to decide where to send each row.
Round robin	Each packet of rows is sent to the next consumer in the sequence.
Broadcast	All rows are sent to all consumer threads.
Demand	Each new row is sent to the consumer that asks for it. This is the only type of exchange that uses a pull rather than a push model for data flow.
Range	Evaluates a range function on one column on the row to decide where to send each row.

Table 4.2 – Types of partitioning

These types of partitioning are exposed to the user in the `Partitioning Type` property of execution plans, and they only make sense for Repartition Streams and Distribute Streams exchanges because, as shown in *Figure 4.24*, a Gather Streams exchange only routes the rows to a single consumer thread. A couple of examples of partitioning types will be shown later in this section.

Finally, another property of the exchange operators is that they preserve the order of the input rows. When they do this, they are called merging or order-preserving exchanges. Otherwise, they are called non-merging or non-order-preserving exchanges. Merging exchanges do not perform any sort operation; rows must be already in sorted order. Because of this, this order-preserving operation only makes sense for Gather Streams and Repartition Streams exchanges. With a Distribute Streams exchange, there is only one producer, so there is nothing to merge. However, it is also worth mentioning that merging exchanges might not scale as well as non-merging exchanges. For example, compare the execution plans of these two versions of the first example in this section, the second one using an ORDER BY clause:

```
SELECT ProductID, COUNT(*)
FROM dbo.SalesOrderDetail
GROUP BY ProductID
GO
SELECT ProductID, COUNT(*)
FROM dbo.SalesOrderDetail
GROUP BY ProductID
ORDER BY ProductID
```

Although both plans are almost the same, the second one returns results that have been sorted by using an order-preserving exchange operator. You can verify that by looking at the properties of the Gather Streams exchange operator in a graphical plan, which includes an Order By section. This is also shown in the following XML fragment:

```
<RelOp LogicalOp="Gather Streams" PhysicalOp="Parallelism" … >
  <Parallelism>
    <OrderBy>
      <OrderByColumn Ascending="true">
        <ColumnReference … Column="ProductID" />
      </OrderByColumn>
    </OrderBy>
```

Hash partitioning is the most common partitioning type and can be used to parallelize a Merge Join operator or a Hash Join operator, such as in the following example. Run the next query, which will get the plan shown in *Figure 4.25*:

```
SELECT * FROM dbo.SalesOrderDetail s1 JOIN dbo.
SalesOrderDetail2 s2
ON s1.id = s2.id
```

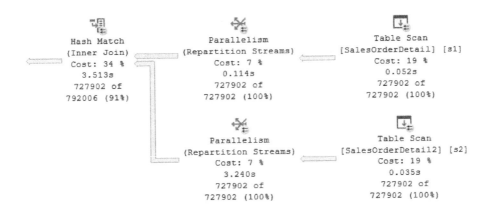

Figure 4.25 – A hash partitioning example

Although not shown here, you can validate that hash partitioning is being used by the Repartition Streams exchanges by looking at the `Partitioning Type` property of one of these operators in a graphical plan. This is shown in the following XML plan fragment. In this case, hash partitioning distributes the build and probe rows among the individual Hash Join threads:

```
<RelOp LogicalOp="Repartition Streams" PhysicalOp="Parallelism"
... >
    <Parallelism PartitioningType="Hash">
```

Finally, the following query, which includes a very selective predicate, produces the plan in *Figure 4.26* and shows both a start parallelism operator or a Gather Streams exchange and a stop parallelism operator or a Distribute Streams exchange:

```
SELECT * FROM dbo.SalesOrderDetail s1
JOIN dbo.SalesOrderDetail2 s2 ON s1.ProductID = s2.ProductID
WHERE s1.id = 123
```

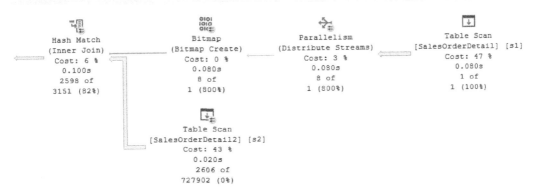

Figure 4.26 – A broadcast partitioning example

The Distribute Streams exchange operator uses broadcast partitioning, as you can verify from the properties of the operator in a graphical plan (look for the partitioning type of `Broadcast`) and also shown in the following XML fragment. Broadcast partitioning sends the only row that qualifies from `table1` to all the Hash Join threads. Additionally, a bitmap operator is used to eliminate most of the rows from `table2`, which greatly improves the performance of the query:

```
<RelOp LogicalOp="Distribute Streams" PhysicalOp="Parallelism"
... >
  <Parallelism PartitioningType="Broadcast">
```

We will cover bitmap operators in more detail in *Chapter 11*, An Introduction to *Data Warehouses*, where you will see how they are used to optimize the performance of data warehouse queries.

Limitations

You might see cases when you have an expensive query that is not parallelized. There are several SQL Server features that can inhibit a parallel plan from creating a serial plan instead:

- Scalar-valued user-defined functions
- CLR user-defined functions with data access
- Miscellaneous built-in functions such as `OBJECT_ID()`, `ERROR_NUMBER()`, and `@@TRANCOUNT`
- Dynamic cursors

Similarly, there are some other features that force a serial zone within a parallel plan, which can lead to performance problems. These features include the following:

- Multistatement, table-valued, and user-defined functions
- TOP clauses
- Global scalar aggregates
- Sequence functions
- Multiconsumer spools
- Backward scans
- System table scans
- Recursive queries

For example, the following code shows how the first parallel example in this section turns into a serial plan while using a simple user-defined function:

```
CREATE FUNCTION dbo.ufn_test(@ProductID int)
RETURNS int
AS
BEGIN
RETURN @ProductID
END
GO
SELECT dbo.ufn_test(ProductID), ProductID, COUNT(*)
FROM dbo.SalesOrderDetail
GROUP BY ProductID
```

As covered in *Chapter 1, An Introduction to Query Tuning and Optimization*, the NonParallelPlanReason optional attribute of the QueryPlan element contains a high-level description of why a parallel plan might not be chosen for the optimized query, which in this case is CouldNotGenerateValidParallelPlan, as shown in the following XML plan fragment:

```
<QueryPlan …
NonParallelPlanReason="CouldNotGenerateValidParallelPlan" … >
```

There is an undocumented and, therefore, unsupported trace flag that you could try to force a parallel plan. Trace flag 8649 can be used to set the cost overhead of parallelism to 0, encouraging a parallel plan, which could help in some cases (mostly cost-related). As mentioned earlier, an undocumented trace flag must not be used in a production environment. Just for demonstration purposes, see the following example using a small table (note it is the SalesOrderDetail table in the **Sales** schema, not the bigger table in the dbo schema that we created earlier):

```
SELECT ProductID, COUNT(*)
FROM Sales.SalesOrderDetail
GROUP BY ProductID
```

The previous query creates a serial plan with a cost of 0.429621. Using trace flag 8649, as shown next, we will create a parallel plan with a slightly lower cost of 0.386606 units:

```
SELECT ProductID, COUNT(*)
FROM Sales.SalesOrderDetail
GROUP BY ProductID
OPTION (QUERYTRACEON 8649)
```

So far, we have focused on how the query processor solves SELECT queries, so in the next and last section, we will talk about update operations.

Updates

Update operations are an intrinsic part of database operations, but they also need to be optimized so that they can be performed as quickly as possible. In this section, bear in mind that when we say "updates," in general, we are referring to any operation performed by the INSERT, DELETE, and UPDATE statements, as well as the MERGE statement, which was introduced in SQL Server 2008. In this chapter, I explain the basics of update operations and how they can quickly become complicated, as they need to update existing indexes, access multiple tables, and enforce existing constraints. We will see how the query optimizer can select per-row and per-index plans to optimize UPDATE statements. Additionally, we will describe the Halloween protection problem and how SQL Server avoids it.

Even when performing an update that involves some other areas of SQL Server, such as a transaction, concurrency control, or locking, update operations are still totally integrated within the SQL Server query processor framework. Also, update operations are optimized so that they can be performed as quickly as possible. So, in this section, I will talk about updates from a query-processing point of view. As mentioned earlier, for this section, we refer to any operations performed by the INSERT, DELETE, UPDATE, and MERGE statements as "updates."

Update plans can be complicated because they need to update existing indexes alongside data. Also, because of objects such as check constraints, referential integrity constraints, and triggers, those plans might have to access multiple tables and enforce existing constraints. Updates might also require the updating of multiple tables when cascading referential integrity constraints or triggers are defined. Some of these operations, such as updating indexes, can have a big impact on the performance of the entire update operation, and we will take a deeper look at that now.

Update operations are performed in two steps, which can be summarized as a read section followed by the update section. The first step provides the details of the changes to apply and which records will be updated. For INSERT operations, this includes the values to be inserted, and for DELETE operations, it includes obtaining the keys of the records to be deleted, which could be the clustering keys for clustered indexes or the RIDs for heaps. However, for update operations, a combination of both the keys of the records to be updated and the data to be inserted is needed. In this first step, SQL Server might read the table to be updated, just like in any other SELECT statement. In the second step, the update operations are performed, including updating indexes, validating constraints, and executing triggers. The entire update operation will fail and roll back if it violates any defined constraint.

Let's start with an example of a very simple update operation. Inserting a new record on the Person. CountryRegion table using the following query creates a very simple plan, as shown in *Figure 4.27*:

```
INSERT INTO Person.CountryRegion (CountryRegionCode, Name)
VALUES ('ZZ', 'New Country')
```

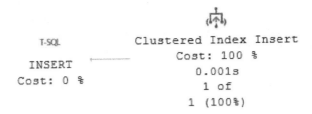

Figure 4.27 – An insert example

However, the operation gets complicated very quickly when you try to delete the same record by running the following statement, as shown in *Figure 4.28*:

```
DELETE FROM Person.CountryRegion
WHERE CountryRegionCode = 'ZZ'
```

Figure 4.28 – A delete example

As you can see in the preceding plan, in addition to CountryRegion, three additional tables (StateProvince, CountryRegionCurrency, and SalesTerritory) are accessed. The reason behind this is that these three tables have foreign keys referencing CountryRegion, so SQL Server needs to validate that no records exist on these tables for this specific value of CountryRegionCode. Therefore, the tables are accessed and an Assert operator is included at the end of the plan to perform this validation. If a record with the CountryRegionCode value to be deleted exists in any of these tables, the Assert operator will throw an exception and SQL Server will roll back the transaction, returning the following error message:

```
Msg 547, Level 16, State 0, Line 1
The DELETE statement conflicted with the REFERENCE constraint
"FK_CountryRegionCurrency_CountryRegion_CountryRegionCode".
The conflict occurred in database "AdventureWorks2019", table
"Sales.CountryRegionCurrency", column 'CountryRegionCode'.
The statement has been terminated.
```

As you can see, the preceding example shows how update operations can access some other tables not included in the original query—in this case, because of the definition of referential integrity constraints. The updating of nonclustered indexes is covered in the next section.

Per-row and per-index plans

An important operation performed by updates is the modifying and updating of existing nonclustered indexes, which is done by using per-row or per-index maintenance plans (also called narrow and wide plans, respectively). In a per-row maintenance plan, the updates to the base table and the existing indexes are performed by a single operator, one row at a time. On the other hand, in a per-index maintenance plan, the base table and each nonclustered index are updated in separate operations.

Except for a few cases where per-index plans are mandatory, the query optimizer can choose between a per-row plan and a per-index plan based on performance reasons, and an index-by-index basis. Although factors such as the structure and size of the table, along with the other operations performed by the update statement, are all considered, choosing between per-index and per-row plans will mostly depend on the number of records being updated. The query optimizer is more likely to choose a per-row plan when a small number of records is being updated, and a per-index plan when the number of records to be updated increases because this choice scales better. A drawback with the per-row approach is that the storage engine updates the nonclustered index rows using the clustered index key order, which is not efficient when a large number of records needs to be updated.

The following DELETE statement will create a per-row plan, which is shown in *Figure 4.29*. Some additional queries might be shown on the plan due to the execution of an existing trigger.

> **Note**
>
> In this section, two queries update data from the AdventureWorks2019 database, so perhaps you should request an estimated plan if you don't want the records to be updated. Also, the BEGIN TRANSACTION and ROLLBACK TRANSACTION statements can be used to create and roll back the transaction. Alternatively, you could perform the updates and later restore a fresh copy of the AdventureWorks2019 database.

```
DELETE FROM Sales.SalesOrderDetail
WHERE SalesOrderDetailID = 61130
```

Figure 4.29 – A per-row plan

In addition to updating the clustered index, this delete operation will update two existing nonclustered indexes, IX_SalesOrderDetail_ProductID and AK_SalesOrderDetail_rowguid, which you can verify by looking at the properties of the **Clustered Index Delete** operator.

To see a per-index plan, we need a table with a large number of rows, so we will be using the dbo.SalesOrderDetail table that we created in the *Parallelism* section. Let's add two nonclustered indexes to the table by running the following statements:

```
CREATE NONCLUSTERED INDEX AK_SalesOrderDetail_rowguid
ON dbo.SalesOrderDetail (rowguid)
CREATE NONCLUSTERED INDEX IX_SalesOrderDetail_ProductID
ON dbo.SalesOrderDetail (ProductID)
```

As indicated earlier, when a large number of records is being updated, the query optimizer might choose a per-index plan, which the following query will demonstrate, by creating the per-index plan shown in *Figure 4.30*:

```
DELETE FROM dbo.SalesOrderDetail WHERE ProductID < 953
```

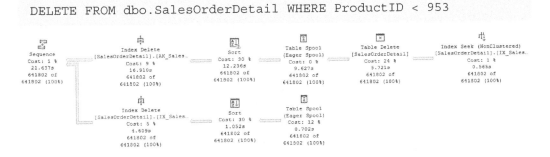

Figure 4.30 – A per-index plan

In this per-index update plan, the base table is updated using a **Table Delete** operator, while a **Table Spool** operator is used to read the data of the key values of the indexes to be updated and a **Sort** operator sorts the data in the order of the index. In addition, an **Index Delete** operator updates a specific nonclustered index in one operation (the name of which you can see in the properties of each operator). Although the table spool is listed twice in the plan, it is the same operator being reused. Finally, the **Sequence** operator makes sure that each **Index Delete** operation is performed in sequence, as shown from top to bottom.

You can now delete the tables you have created for these exercises by using the following DROP TABLE statements:

```
DROP TABLE dbo.SalesOrderDetail
DROP TABLE dbo.SalesOrderDetail2
```

For demonstration purposes only, you could use the undocumented and unsupported trace flag, 8790, to force a per-index plan on a query, where the number of records being updated is not large enough to produce this kind of plan. For example, the following query on `Sales.SalesOrderDetail` requires this trace flag to produce a per-index plan; otherwise, a per-row plan will be returned instead:

```
DELETE FROM Sales.SalesOrderDetail
WHERE SalesOrderDetailID < 43740
OPTION (QUERYTRACEON 8790)
```

In summary, bear in mind that, except for a few cases where per-index plans are mandatory, the query optimizer can choose between a per-row plan and a per-index plan on an index-by-index basis, so it is even possible to have both maintenance choices in the same execution plan.

Finally, we close this chapter by covering an interesting behavior of update operations, called Halloween protection.

Halloween protection

Halloween protection refers to a problem that appears in certain update operations and was discovered more than 30 years ago by researchers working on the System R project at the IBM Almaden Research Center. The System R team was testing a query optimizer when they ran a query to update the salary column on an `Employee` table. The UPDATE statement was supposed to give a 10 percent raise to every employee with a salary of less than $25,000.

Even when there were salaries considerably lower than $25,000, to their surprise, no employee had a salary under $25,000 after the update query was completed. They noticed that the query optimizer had selected an index based on the salary column and had updated some records multiple times until they reached the $25,000 salary value. Because the salary index was used to scan the records, when the salary column was updated, some records were moved within the index and were then scanned again later, so those records were updated more than once. The problem was called the Halloween problem because it was discovered on Halloween day, probably in 1976 or 1977.

As I mentioned at the beginning of this section, update operations have a read section followed by an update section, and that is a crucial distinction to bear in mind at this stage. To avoid the Halloween problem, the read and update sections must be completely separated; the read section must be completed in its entirety before the write section is run. In the next example, we will show you how SQL Server avoids the Halloween problem. Run the following statement to create a new table:

```
SELECT * INTO dbo.Product FROM Production.Product
```

Run the following UPDATE statement, which produces the execution plan shown in *Figure 4.31*:

```
UPDATE dbo.Product SET ListPrice = ListPrice * 1.2
```

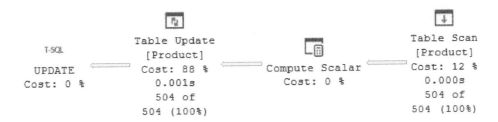

Figure 4.31 – An update without Halloween protection

In this case, no Halloween protection is needed because the statement updates the ListPrice column, which is not part of any index, so updating the data does not move any rows around. Now, to demonstrate the problem, let's create a clustered index on the ListPrice column, by running the following statement:

```
CREATE CLUSTERED INDEX CIX_ListPrice ON dbo.Product(ListPrice)
```

Run the preceding UPDATE statement again. The query will show a similar plan, but this time including a **Table Spool** operator, which is a blocking operator, separating the read section from the write section. A blocking operator has to read all of the relevant rows before producing any output rows for the next operator. In this example, the table spool separates the **Clustered Index Scan** operator from the **Clustered Index Update operator**, as shown in *Figure 4.32*:

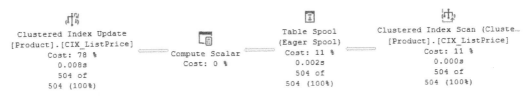

Figure 4.32 – An update with Halloween protection

The spool operator scans the original data and saves a copy of it in a hidden spool table in tempdb before it is updated. Generally, a **Table Spool** operator is used to avoid the Halloween problem because it is a cheap operator. However, if the plan already includes another operator that can be used, such as **Sort**, then the **Table Spool** operator is not needed, and the **Sort** operator can perform the same blocking job instead.

Finally, drop the table you have just created:

```
DROP TABLE dbo.Product
```

Summary

In this chapter, we described the execution engine as a collection of physical operators, which also defines the choices that are available for the query optimizer to build execution plans with. Some of the most commonly used operators of the execution engine were introduced, including their algorithms, relative costs, and the scenarios in which the query optimizer is more likely to choose them. In particular, we looked at operators for data access, aggregations, joins, parallelism, and update operations.

Also, the concepts of sorting and hashing were introduced as a mechanism used by the execution engine to match and process data. Data access operations included the scanning of tables and indexes, the index seeks, and bookmark lookup operations. Aggregation algorithms such as Stream Aggregate and Hash Aggregate were discussed, along with join algorithms such as the Nested Loops Join, Merge Join, and Hash Join operators. Additionally, an introduction to parallelism was presented, closing the chapter with update topics such as per-row and per-index plans and Halloween protection.

Understanding how these operators work, along with what they are likely to cost, will give you a much stronger sense of what is happening under the hood when you investigate how your queries are being executed. In turn, this will help you to find potential problems in your execution plans and to understand when to resort to any of the techniques we describe later in the book..

5
Working
with Indexes

Indexing is one of the most important techniques used in query tuning and optimization. By using the right indexes, SQL Server can speed up your queries and drastically improve the performance of your applications. In this chapter, we will introduce indexes and show you how SQL Server uses them, how you can provide better indexes, and how you can verify that your execution plans are using these indexes correctly. There are several kinds of indexes in SQL Server. This chapter focuses on clustered and nonclustered indexes and discusses several topics, including covering indexes, filtered indexes, how to choose a clustered index key, and index fragmentation. *Chapter 11, An Introduction to Data Warehouses*, covers columnstore indexes in detail. Memory-optimized nonclustered indexes and hash indexes are covered in *Chapter 7, In-Memory OLTP*. Other types of indexes, such as XML, spatial, and full-text indexes, are outside the scope of this book.

This chapter also includes sections about the **Database Engine Tuning Advisor** (**DTA**) and the Missing Indexes feature, which will show you how you can use the query optimizer itself to provide index-tuning recommendations. However, it is important to emphasize that, no matter what index recommendations these tools give, it is ultimately up to the database administrator or developer to do their own index analysis, test these recommendations thoroughly, and finally decide which of these recommendations to implement.

Finally, the sys.dm_db_index_usage_stats DMV is introduced as a tool to identify existing indexes that are not being used by your queries. Indexes that are not being used will provide no benefit to your databases, use valuable disk space, and slow down your update operations, so they should be considered for removal.

This chapter covers the following topics:

- Introduction to indexes
- Creating indexes

- Understanding index operations

- The Database Engine Tuning Advisor

- Missing indexes

- Index fragmentation

- Unused indexes

Introduction to indexes

As mentioned in *Chapter 4, The Execution Engine*, SQL Server can use indexes to perform seek and scan operations. Indexes can be used to speed up the execution of a query by quickly finding records, without performing table scans, by delivering all of the columns requested by the query without accessing the base table (that is, covering the query, which we will return to later), or by providing a sorted order, which will benefit queries with GROUP BY, DISTINCT, or ORDER BY clauses.

Part of the query optimizer's job is to determine whether an index can be used to resolve a predicate in a query. This is basically a comparison between an index key and a constant or variable. In addition, the query optimizer needs to determine whether the index covers the query—that is, whether the index contains all of the columns required by the query (in which case it is referred to as a **covering index**). The query optimizer needs to confirm this because a nonclustered index usually contains only a subset of the columns in the table.

SQL Server can also consider using more than one index and joining them to cover all of the columns required by the query. This operation is called "index intersection." If it's not possible to cover all of the columns required by the query, SQL Server may need to access the base table, which could be a clustered index or a heap, to obtain the remaining columns. This is called a **bookmark lookup operation** (which could be a key lookup or an RID lookup operation, as explained in *Chapter 4, The Execution Engine*). However, because a bookmark lookup requires random I/O, which is a very expensive operation, its usage can be effective only for a relatively small number of records.

Also, keep in mind that although one or more indexes could be used, that does not mean that they will finally be selected in an execution plan, as this is always a cost-based decision. So, after creating an index, make sure you verify that the index is in fact used in a plan and, of course, that your query is performing better, which is probably the primary reason why you are defining an index. An index that is not being used by any query will just take up valuable disk space and may negatively affect the performance of update operations without providing any benefit. It is also possible that an index that was useful when it was originally created is no longer used by any query now; this could be a result of changes in the database, the data, or even the query itself. To help you avoid this situation, the last section in this chapter shows you how you can identify which indexes are no longer being used by any of your queries. Let's get started with creating indexes in the next section.

Creating indexes

Let's start this section with a summary of some basic terminology used in indexes, some of which may already have been mentioned in previous chapters of the book, as follows:

- **Heap**: A heap is a data structure where rows are stored without a specified order. In other words, it is a table without a clustered index.

- **Clustered index**: In SQL Server, you can have the entire table logically sorted by a specific key in which the bottom, or leaf level, of the index contains the actual data rows of the table. Because of this, only one clustered index per table is possible. The data pages in the leaf level are linked in a doubly linked list (that is, each page has a pointer to the previous and next pages). Both clustered and nonclustered indexes are organized as B-trees.

- **Nonclustered index**: A nonclustered index row contains the index key values and a pointer to the data row on the base table. Nonclustered indexes can be created on both heaps and clustered indexes. Each table can have up to 999 nonclustered indexes, but usually, you should keep this number to a minimum. A nonclustered index can optionally contain non-key columns when using the INCLUDE clause, which is particularly useful when covering a query.

- **Unique index**: As the name suggests, a unique index does not allow two rows of data to have identical key values. A table can have one or more unique indexes, although it should not be very common. By default, unique indexes are created as nonclustered indexes unless you specify otherwise.

- **Primary key**: A primary key is a key that uniquely identifies each record in the table and creates a unique index, which, by default, will also be a clustered index. In addition to the uniqueness property required for the unique index, its key columns are required to be defined as NOT NULL. By definition, only one primary key can be defined on a table.

Although creating a primary key is straightforward, something not everyone is aware of is that when a primary key is created, by default, it is created using a clustered index. This can be the case, for example, when using **Table Designer** in SQL Server Management Studio (**Table Designer** is accessed when you right-click **Tables** and select **New Table...**) or when using the CREATE TABLE and ALTER TABLE statements, as shown next. If you run the following code to create a primary key, where the CLUSTERED or NONCLUSTERED keywords are not specified, the primary key will be created using a clustered index as follows:

```
CREATE TABLE table1 (
col1 int NOT NULL,
col2 nchar(10) NULL,
CONSTRAINT PK_table1 PRIMARY KEY(col1)
)
```

Or it can be created using the following code:

```
CREATE TABLE table1
(
col1 int NOT NULL,
col2 nchar(10) NULL
)
GO
ALTER TABLE table1 ADD CONSTRAINT
PK_table1 PRIMARY KEY
(
col1
)
```

The code generated by Table Designer will explicitly request a clustered index for the primary key, as in the following code (but this is usually hidden and not visible to you):

```
ALTER TABLE table1 ADD CONSTRAINT
PK_table1 PRIMARY KEY CLUSTERED
(
col1
)
```

Creating a clustered index along with a primary key can have some performance consequences, as we will see later on in this chapter, so it is important to understand that this is the default behavior. Obviously, it is also possible to have a primary key that is a nonclustered index, but this needs to be explicitly specified. Changing the preceding code to create a nonclustered index will look like the following code, where the CLUSTERED clause was changed to NONCLUSTERED:

```
ALTER TABLE table1 ADD CONSTRAINT
PK_table1 PRIMARY KEY NONCLUSTERED
(
col1
)
```

After the preceding code is executed, PK_table1 will be created as a unique nonclustered index.

Although the preceding code created an index as part of a constraint definition (in this case, a primary key), most likely, you will be using the CREATE INDEX statement to define indexes. The following is a simplified version of the CREATE INDEX statement:

```
CREATE [UNIQUE ] [ CLUSTERED | NONCLUSTERED ] INDEX index_name
ON <object> ( column [ ASC | DESC ] [ ,...n ] )
[ INCLUDE ( column_name [ ,...n ] ) ]
[ WHERE <filter_predicate> ]
[ WITH ( <relational_index_option> [ ,...n ] ) ]
```

The UNIQUE clause creates a unique index in which no two rows are permitted to have the same index key value. CLUSTERED and NONCLUSTERED define clustered and nonclustered indexes, respectively. The INCLUDE clause allows you to specify non-key columns to be added to the leaf level of the nonclustered index. The WHERE <filter_predicate> clause allows you to create a filtered index that will also create filtered statistics. Filtered indexes and the INCLUDE clause will be explained in more detail later on in this section. The WITH <relational_index_option> clause specifies the options to use when the index is created, such as FILLFACTOR, SORT_IN_TEMPDB, DROP_EXISTING, or ONLINE.

In addition, the ALTER INDEX statement can be used to modify an index and perform operations such as disabling, rebuilding, and reorganizing indexes. The DROP INDEX statement will remove the specified index from the database. Using DROP INDEX with a nonclustered index will remove the index data pages from the database. Dropping a clustered index will not delete the index data but keep it stored as a heap instead.

Let's do a quick exercise to show some of the concepts and T-SQL statements mentioned in this section. Create a new table by running the following statement:

```
SELECT * INTO dbo.SalesOrderDetail
FROM Sales.SalesOrderDetail
```

Let's use the sys.indexes catalog view to inspect the table properties as follows:

```
SELECT * FROM sys.indexes
WHERE object_id = OBJECT_ID('dbo.SalesOrderDetail')
```

As shown in the following results (not all the columns are listed), a heap will be created as described in the type and type_desc columns. A heap always has an index_id value of 0:

object_id	Name	index_id	type	type_desc	is_unique
1287675635	NULL	0	0	HEAP	0

Let's create a nonclustered index as follows:

```
CREATE INDEX IX_ProductID ON dbo.SalesOrderDetail(ProductID)
```

The `sys.indexes` catalog now shows the following, where you can see that in addition to the heap, we now have a nonclustered index with `index_id` as 2. Nonclustered indexes can have `index_id` values between 2 and 250 and between 256 and 1,005. This range covers the maximum of 999 nonclustered indexes mentioned earlier. The values between 251 and 255 are reserved as follows:

object_id	Name	index_id	type	type_desc	is_unique
1287675635	NULL	0	0	HEAP	0
1287675635	IX_ProductID	2	2	NONCLUSTERED	0

Now create a clustered index as follows:

```
CREATE CLUSTERED INDEX IX_SalesOrderID_SalesOrderDetailID
  ON dbo.SalesOrderDetail(SalesOrderID, SalesOrderDetailID)
```

Note that instead of a heap, now we have a clustered index and the `index_id` value is now 1. A clustered index always has an `index_id` value of 1. Internally, the nonclustered index has been rebuilt to now use a cluster key pointer rather than a **row identifier (RID)**.

object_id	Name	index_id	type	type_desc	is_unique
1287675635	IX_SalesOrderID_SalesOrderDetailID	1	1	CLUSTERED	0
1287675635	IX_ProductID	2	2	NONCLUSTERED	0

Dropping the nonclustered index will remove the index pages entirely, leaving only the clustered index as follows:

```
DROP INDEX dbo.SalesOrderDetail.IX_ProductID
```

object_id	Name	index_id	type	type_desc	is_unique
1287675635	IX_SalesOrderID_SalesOrderDetailID	1	1	CLUSTERED	0

But notice that deleting the clustered index, which is considered the entire table, does not delete the underlying data; it simply changes the table structure to be a heap as follows:

```
DROP INDEX dbo.SalesOrderDetail.IX_SalesOrderID_
SalesOrderDetailID
```

object_id	name	index_id	type	type_desc	is_unique
1287675635	NULL	0	0	HEAP	0

For more details about the CREATE INDEX, ALTER INDEX, and DROP INDEX statements, refer to the SQL Server documentation.

As shown in *Figure 5.1*, a clustered index is organized as a B-tree, which consists of a root node (the top node of the B-tree), leaf nodes (the bottom-level nodes, which contain the data pages of the table), and intermediate levels (the nodes between the root and leaf nodes). To find a specific record on a clustered index B-tree, SQL Server uses the root- and intermediate-level nodes to navigate to the leaf node, as the root and intermediate nodes contain index pages and a pointer to either an intermediate-level page or a leaf node page. To put this in perspective, and based on the example in *Figure 5.1*, with only one intermediate level, SQL Server is required to read three pages to find a specific row. A table with a larger number of records could have more than one intermediate level, requiring SQL Server to read four or more pages to find a row. This is the operation performed by an Index Seek operator, and it is very effective when only one row is required or when a partial scan can be used to satisfy the query.

However, this operation can be very expensive when it needs to be performed for many records, each one requiring access to at least three pages. This is the problem we usually face when we have a nonclustered index that does not cover the query and needs to look at the clustered index for the remaining columns required by the table. In this case, SQL Server has to navigate on both the B-tree of the nonclustered index and the clustered index. The query optimizer places a high cost on these operations, and this is why sometimes when a large number of records is required by the query, SQL Server decides to perform a clustered index scan instead. More details about these operations are provided in *Chapter 4, The Execution Engine*.

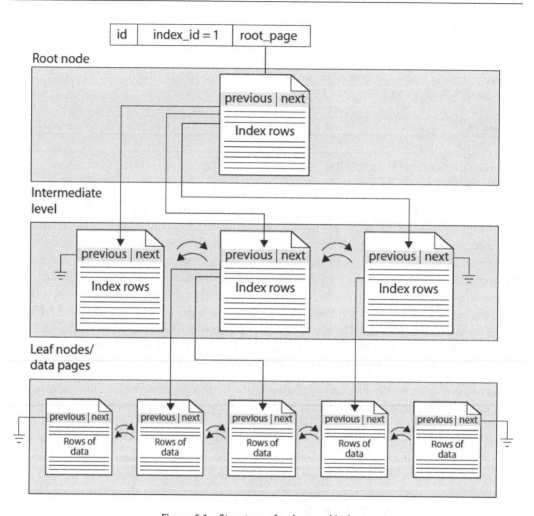

Figure 5.1 – Structure of a clustered index

Clustered indexes versus heaps

One of the main decisions you have to make when creating a table is whether to use a clustered index or a heap. Although the best solution may depend on your table definition and workload, it is usually recommended that each table be defined with a clustered index, and this section will show you why. Let's start with a summary of the advantages and disadvantages of organizing tables as clustered indexes or heaps. Some of the good reasons to leave a table as a heap are the following:

- When the heap is a very small table. Although, a clustered index could work fine for a small table, too.

- When an RID is smaller than a candidate clustered index key. As introduced in *Chapter 4*, individual rows in a heap are identified by an RID, which is a row locator that includes information such as the database file, page, and slot numbers to allow a specific record to be easily located. An RID uses 8 bytes and, in many cases, could be smaller than a clustered index key. Because every row in every nonclustered index contains the RID or the clustered index key to point to the corresponding record on the base table, a smaller size could greatly benefit the number of resources used.

You definitely want to use a clustered index in the following cases:

- You frequently need to return data in a sorted order or query ranges of data. In this case, you would need to create the clustered index key in the column's desired order. You may need the entire table in a sorted order or only a range of the data. Examples of the last operation, called a partial ordered scan, were provided in *Chapter 4*.

- You frequently need to return data grouped together. In this case, you would need to create the clustered index key on the columns used by the GROUP BY clause. As you learned in *Chapter 4*, to perform aggregate operations, SQL Server requires sorted data, and if it is not already sorted, a likely expensive sort operation may need to be added.

In the white paper *SQL Server Best Practices Article*, available at http://technet.microsoft.com/en-us/library/cc917672.aspx, the authors performed a series of tests to show the difference in performance while using heaps and clustered indexes. Although these tests may or may not resemble your own schema, workload, or application, you could use them as a guideline to estimate the impact on your application.

The test used a clustered index with three columns as the clustered index key and no other nonclustered index and compared it with a heap with only one nonclustered index defined using the same three columns. You can look at the paper for more details about the test, including the test scenarios. The interesting results shown by the six tests in the research are as follows:

- The performance of INSERT operations on a table with a clustered index was about 3 percent faster than performing the same operation on a heap with a corresponding nonclustered index. The reason for this difference is that even though inserting data into the heap had 62.8 percent fewer page splits/second, writing into the clustered index required a single write operation, whereas inserting the data on the heap required two—one for the heap and another for the nonclustered index.

- The performance of UPDATE operations on a nonindexed column in a clustered index was 8.2 percent better than performing the same operation on a heap with a corresponding nonclustered index. The reason for this difference is that updating a row on the clustered index only required an Index Seek operation, followed by an update of the data row; however, for the heap, it required an Index Seek operation using the nonclustered index, followed by an RID lookup to find the corresponding row on the heap, and finally an update of the data row.

- The performance of DELETE operations on a clustered index was 18.25 percent faster than performing the same operation on a heap with a corresponding nonclustered index. The reason for this difference is that, similar to the preceding UPDATE case, deleting a row on the clustered index only required an Index Seek operation, followed by a delete of the data row; however, for the heap, it required an Index Seek operation using the nonclustered index, followed by an RID lookup to find the corresponding row on the heap, and finally a delete. In addition, the row on the nonclustered index had to be deleted as well.

- The performance of a single-row SELECT operation on a clustered index was 13.8 percent faster than performing the same operation on a heap with a corresponding nonclustered index. This test assumes that the search predicate is based on the index keys. Again, finding a row in a clustered index only required a seek operation, and once the row was found, it contained all of the required columns. In the case of the heap, once again, it required an Index Seek operation using the nonclustered index, followed by an RID lookup to find the corresponding row on the heap.

- The performance of a SELECT operation on a range of rows on a clustered index was 29.41 percent faster than performing the same operation on a heap with a corresponding nonclustered index. The specific query selected 228 rows. Once again, a Clustered Index Seek operation helped to find the first record quickly, and, because the rows are stored in the order of the indexed columns, the remaining rows would be on the same pages or contiguous pages. As mentioned earlier, selecting a range of rows, called a partial ordered scan, is one of the cases where using a clustered index is definitely a superior choice to using a heap, because fewer pages must be read. Also, keep in mind that in this scenario, the cost of performing multiple lookups may be so high in some cases that the query optimizer may decide to scan the entire heap instead. That is not the case for the clustered index, even if the specified range is large.

- For the disk utilization test following INSERT operations, the test showed little difference between the clustered index and a heap with a corresponding nonclustered index. However, for the disk utilization test following DELETE operations, the clustered index test showed a significant difference between the clustered index and a heap with a corresponding nonclustered index. The clustered index shrunk almost the same amount as the amount of data deleted, whereas the heap shrunk only a fraction of it. The reason for this difference is that empty extents are automatically deallocated in a clustered index, which is not the case for heaps where the extents are held onto for later reuse. Recovering this unused disk space on a heap usually requires additional tasks, such as performing a table rebuild operation (using the ALTER TABLE REBUILD statement).

- For the concurrent INSERT operations, the test showed that as the number of processes that are concurrently inserting data increases, the amount of time per insert also increases. This increase is more significant in the case of the clustered index compared with the heap. One of the main reasons for this was the contention found while inserting data in a particular location. The test showed that the page latch waits per second were 12 percent higher for the clustered index compared with the heap when 20 processes were concurrently inserting data, and this value grew to 61 percent when 50 concurrent processes inserted data. However, the test found that for the case of the 50 concurrent sessions, the overhead per insert was only an average of 1.2 milliseconds per insert operation and was not considered significant.

- Finally, because the heap required a nonclustered index to provide the same seek benefits as the clustered index, the disk space used by the clustered index was almost 35 percent smaller than the table organized as a heap.

The research paper concluded that, in general, the performance benefits of using a clustered index outweigh the negatives according to the tests performed. Finally, it is worth remembering that although clustered indexes are generally recommended, your performance may vary depending on your own table schema, workload, and specific configuration, so you may want to test both choices carefully.

Clustered index key

Deciding which column or columns will be part of the clustered index key is also a very important design consideration because they need to be chosen carefully. As a best practice, indexes should be unique, narrow, static, and ever-increasing. But remember that, as with other general recommendations, this may not apply to all cases, so you should also test thoroughly for your database and workload. Let's explain why these may be important and how they may affect the performance of your database as follows:

- **Unique**: If a clustered index is not defined using the UNIQUE clause, SQL Server will add a 4-byte uniquifier to each record, increasing the size of the clustered index key. As a comparison, an RID used by nonclustered indexes on heaps is only 8 bytes long.

- **Narrow**: As mentioned earlier in this chapter, because every row in every nonclustered index contains, in addition to the columns defining the index, the clustered index key to point to the corresponding row on the base table, a small-sized key could greatly benefit the number of resources used. A small key size will require less storage and memory, which will also benefit performance. Again, as a comparison, an RID used by nonclustered indexes on heaps is only 8 bytes long.

- **Static or nonvolatile**: Updating a clustered index key can have some performance consequences, such as page splits and fragmentation created by the row relocation within the clustered index. In addition, because every nonclustered index contains the clustered index key, the changing rows in the nonclustered index will have to be updated as well to reflect the new clustered key value.

- **Ever-increasing**: A clustered index key would benefit from having ever-increasing values instead of having more random values, such as in the last name column, for example. Having to insert new rows based on random entry points creates page splits and therefore fragmentation. However, you need to be aware that, in some cases, having ever-increasing values can also cause contention, as multiple processes could be written on the last page of a table.

Covering indexes

A covering index is a very simple but very important concept in query optimization where an index can solve or is able to return all of the columns requested by a query without accessing the base table at all. For example, the following query is already covered by an existing index, IX_SalesOrderHeader_CustomerID, as you can see in the plan in *Figure 5.2*:

```
SELECT SalesOrderID, CustomerID FROM Sales.SalesOrderHeader
WHERE CustomerID = 16448
```

```
                                          ⛁
                              Index Seek (NonClustered)
              ⊞               [SalesOrderHeader].[IX_Sales…
            SELECT                    Cost: 100 %
           Cost: 0 %                    0.000s
                                          3 of
                                        2 (150%)
```

Figure 5.2 – A covering index

In the plan, we can see that there is no need to access the base table at all. If we slightly change the query to also request the SalesPersonID column, this time there is no index that covers the query, and the plan in *Figure 5.3* is produced instead, as follows:

```
SELECT SalesOrderID, CustomerID, SalesPersonID FROM Sales.
SalesOrderHeader
WHERE CustomerID = 16448
```

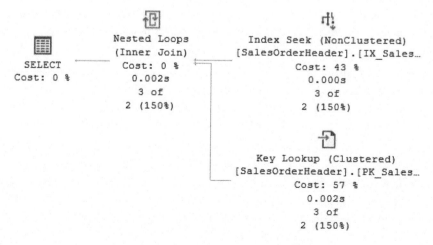

Figure 5.3 – A plan with a key lookup operation

The plan shows that IX_SalesOrderHeader_CustomerID was used to quickly locate the required record, but because the index didn't include SalesPersonID, a lookup operation to the clustered index was required as well. Keep in mind that trying to cover the query does not mean that you need to add another column to the index key unless you must also perform search operations using that column. Instead, you could use the INCLUDE clause of the CREATE or ALTER INDEX statements to add the additional column. At this point, you may decide to just update an existing index to include the required column, but in the following example, we will create another one:

```
CREATE INDEX IX_SalesOrderHeader_CustomerID_SalesPersonID
ON Sales.SalesOrderHeader(CustomerID)
INCLUDE (SalesPersonID)
```

If you run the query again, the query optimizer will use a plan similar to the one shown previously in *Figure 5.2* with just an Index Seek operation, this time with the new IX_SalesOrderHeader_CustomerID_SalesPersonID index and no need to access the base table at all. However, notice that creating many indexes on a table can also be a performance problem because multiple indexes need to be updated on each update operation, not to mention the additional disk space required.

Finally, to clean up, drop the temporarily created index as follows:

```
DROP INDEX Sales.SalesOrderHeader.IX_SalesOrderHeader_
CustomerID_SalesPersonID
```

Filtered indexes

You can use filtered indexes in queries where a column only has a small number of relevant values. This can be the case, for example, when you want to focus your query on some specific values in a table where a column has mostly NULL values and you need to query the non-NULL values. Handily, filtered indexes can also enforce uniqueness within the filtered data. Filtered indexes have the benefit of requiring less storage than regular indexes, and maintenance operations on them will be faster as well. In addition, a filtered index will also create filtered statistics, which may have a better quality than a statistics object created for the entire table, as a histogram will be created just for the specified range of values. As covered in more detail in *Chapter 6, Understanding Statistics*, a histogram can have up to a maximum of 200 steps, which can be a limitation with a large number of distinct values. To create a filtered index, you need to specify a filter using the WHERE clause of the CREATE INDEX statement.

For example, if you look at the plan for the following query, you will see that it uses both IX_
SalesOrderHeader_CustomerID to filter on the CustomerID = 13917 predicate plus
a key lookup operation to find the records on the clustered index and filter for TerritoryID =
4 (remember from *Chapter 4* that in this case, a key lookup is really a Clustered Index Seek operator,
which you can directly see if you use the SET SHOWPLAN_TEXT statement):

```
SELECT CustomerID, OrderDate, AccountNumber FROM Sales.
SalesOrderHeader
WHERE CustomerID = 13917 AND TerritoryID = 4
```

Create the following filtered index:

```
CREATE INDEX IX_CustomerID ON Sales.
SalesOrderHeader(CustomerID)
WHERE TerritoryID = 4
```

If you run the previous SELECT statement again, you will see a similar plan as shown in *Figure 5.4*, but
in this case, using the just-created filtered index. Index Seek is doing a seek operation on CustomerID,
but the key lookup no longer has to filter on TerritoryID because IX_CustomerID already
filtered that out:

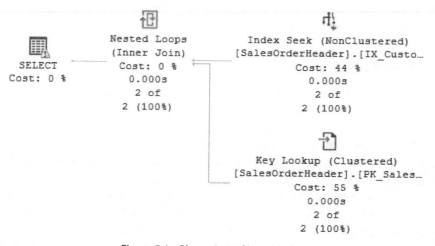

Figure 5.4 – Plan using a filtered index

Keep in mind that although the filtered index may not seem to provide more query performance
benefits than a regular nonclustered index defined with the same properties, it will use less storage,
will be easier to maintain, and can potentially provide better optimizer statistics because the filtered
statistics will be more accurate since they cover only the rows in the filtered index.

However, a filtered index may not be used to solve a query when a value is not known, for example, when using variables or parameters. Because the query optimizer has to create a plan that can work for every possible value in a variable or parameter, the filtered index may not be selected. As introduced in *Chapter 1, An Introduction to Query Tuning and Optimization*, you may see the `UnmatchedIndexes` warning in an execution plan in these cases. Using our current example, the following query will show an `UnmatchedIndexes` warning, indicating that the plan was not able to use the `IX_CustomerID` index, even when the value requested for `TerritoryID` was 4, the same used in the filtered index:

```
DECLARE @territory int
SET @territory = 4
SELECT CustomerID, OrderDate, AccountNumber FROM Sales.
SalesOrderHeader
WHERE CustomerID = 13917 AND TerritoryID = @territory
```

Drop the index before continuing, as follows:

```
DROP INDEX Sales.SalesOrderHeader.IX_CustomerID
```

Now that we have learned how to create and use indexes, we will explore some basic operations that can be performed on them.

Understanding index operations

In a seek operation, SQL Server navigates throughout the B-tree index to quickly find the required records without the need for an index or table scan. This is similar to using an index at the end of a book to find a topic quickly, instead of reading the entire book. Once the first record has been found, SQL Server can then scan the index leaf level forward or backward to find additional records. Both equality and inequality operators can be used in a predicate, including =, <, >, <=, >=, <>, !=, !<, !>, BETWEEN, and IN. For example, the following predicates can be matched to an Index Seek operation if there is an index on the specified column or a multicolumn index with that column as a leading index key:

- `ProductID = 771`
- `UnitPrice` < 3.975
- `LastName` = 'Allen'
- `LastName` LIKE 'Brown%'

As an example, look at the following query, which uses an Index Seek operator and produces the plan in *Figure 5.5*:

```
SELECT ProductID, SalesOrderID, SalesOrderDetailID
FROM Sales.SalesOrderDetail
WHERE ProductID = 771
```

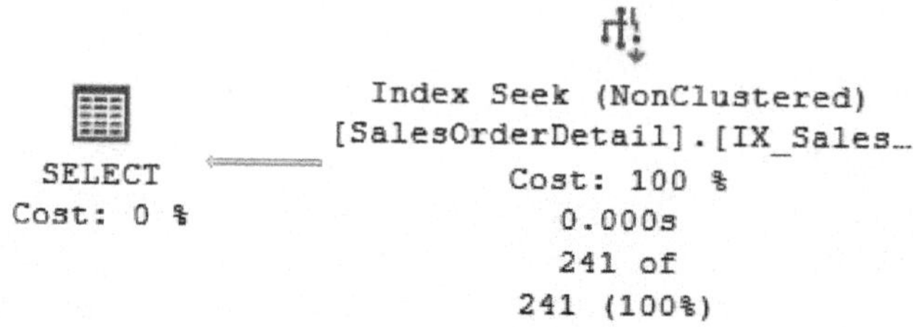

```
                                              ┌┴┐
                                               ↓

              ▦              Index Seek (NonClustered)
                            [SalesOrderDetail].[IX_Sales…
           SELECT    ⇐          Cost: 100 %
          Cost: 0 %                0.000s
                                    241 of
                                 241 (100%)
```

Figure 5.5 – Plan using an Index Seek

The `SalesOrderDetail` table has a multicolumn index with `ProductID` as the leading column. The Index Seek operator properties, which you can inspect in a graphical plan, include the following `Seek` predicate on the `ProductID` column, which shows that SQL Server was effectively able to use the index to seek on this column:

```
Seek Keys[1]: Prefix: [AdventureWorks2019].[Sales].
[SalesOrderDetail].ProductID = Scalar Operator (CONVERT_
IMPLICIT(int,[@1],0))
```

An index cannot be used to seek on some complex expressions, expressions using functions, or strings with a leading wildcard character, as in the following predicates:

- `ABS(ProductID) = 771`
- `UnitPrice + 1 < 3.975`
- `LastName LIKE '%Allen'`
- `UPPER(LastName) = 'Allen'`

Compare the following query to the preceding example; by adding an `ABS` function to the predicate, SQL Server is no longer able to use an Index Seek operator and instead chooses to do an Index Scan, as shown in the plan in *Figure 5.6*:

```
SELECT ProductID, SalesOrderID, SalesOrderDetailID
FROM Sales.SalesOrderDetail
WHERE ABS(ProductID) = 771
```

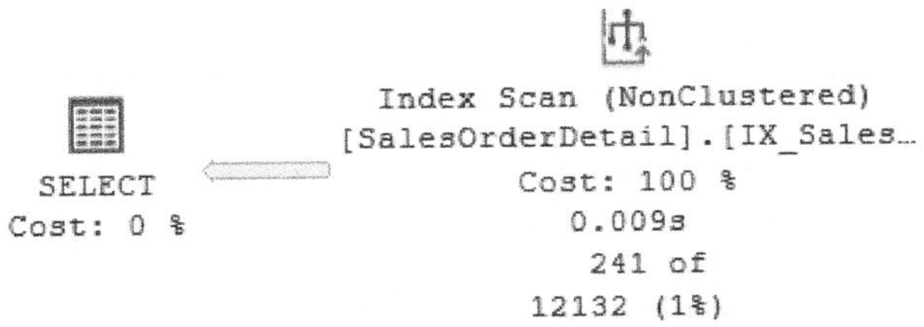

Figure 5.6 – Plan using an Index Scan

If you look at the properties of the Index Scan operator, for example, in a graphical plan, you could verify that the following predicate is used:

```
abs([AdventureWorks2019].[Sales].[SalesOrderDetail].
[ProductID])=CONVERT_IMPLICIT(int,[@1],0)
```

In the case of a multicolumn index, SQL Server can only use the index to seek on the second column if there is an equality predicate on the first column. So, SQL Server can use a multicolumn index to seek on both columns in the following cases, supposing that a multicolumn index exists on both columns in the order presented:

- `ProductID = 771 AND SalesOrderID > 34000`

- `LastName = 'Smith' AND FirstName = 'Ian'`

That being said, if there is no equality predicate on the first column, or if the predicate cannot be evaluated on the second column, as is the case in a complex expression, then SQL Server may still only be able to use a multicolumn index to seek on just the first column, as in the following examples:

- `ProductID < 771 AND SalesOrderID = 34000`

- `LastName > 'Smith' AND FirstName = 'Ian'`

- `ProductID = 771 AND ABS(SalesOrderID) = 34000`

However, SQL Server is not able to use a multicolumn index for an Index Seek in the following examples because it is not even able to search on the first column:

- `ABS(ProductID) = 771 AND SalesOrderID = 34000`

- `LastName LIKE '%Smith' AND FirstName = 'Ian'`

Finally, run the following query and take a look at the Index Seek operator properties:

```
SELECT ProductID, SalesOrderID, SalesOrderDetailID
FROM Sales.SalesOrderDetail
WHERE ProductID = 771 AND ABS(SalesOrderID) = 45233
```

The `Seek` predicate is using only the `ProductID` column as follows:

```
Seek Keys[1]: Prefix: [AdventureWorks2019].[Sales].
[SalesOrderDetail].ProductID =
Scalar Operator (CONVERT_IMPLICIT(int,[@1],0)
```

An additional predicate on the `SalesOrderID` column is evaluated like any other scan predicate as follows:

```
abs([AdventureWorks2019].[Sales].[SalesOrderDetail].
[SalesOrderID])=[@2]
```

In summary, this shows that, as we expected, SQL Server was able to perform a seek operation on the `ProductID` column, but, because of the use of the `ABS` function, it was not able to do the same for `SalesOrderID`. The index was used to navigate directly to find the rows that satisfy the first predicate but then had to continue scanning to validate the second predicate.

The Database Engine Tuning Advisor

Currently, all major commercial database vendors include a physical database design tool to help with the creation of indexes. However, when these tools were first developed, there were just two main architectural approaches considered for how the tools should recommend indexes. The first approach was to build a stand-alone tool with its own cost model and design rules. The second approach was to build a tool that could use the query optimizer cost model.

A problem with building a stand-alone tool is the requirement for duplicating the cost module. On top of that, having a tool with its own cost model, even if it's better than the query optimizer's cost model, may not be a good idea because the optimizer still chooses its plan based on its own model.

The second approach, using the query optimizer to help with physical database design, was proposed in the database research community as far back as 1988. Because it is the query optimizer that chooses the indexes for an execution plan, it makes sense to use the query optimizer itself to help find which missing indexes would benefit existing queries. In this scenario, the physical design tool would use the optimizer to evaluate the cost of queries given a set of candidate indexes. An additional benefit of this approach is that, as the optimizer cost model evolves, any tool using its cost model can automatically benefit from it.

SQL Server was the first commercial database product to include a physical design tool, in the shape of the Index Tuning Wizard, which was shipped with SQL Server 7.0 and was later replaced by the **DTA** in SQL Server 2005. Both tools use the query optimizer cost model approach and were created as part of the AutoAdmin project at Microsoft, the goal of which was to reduce the **total cost of ownership** (**TCO**) of databases by making them self-tuning and self-managing. In addition to indexes, the DTA can help with the creation of indexed views and table partitioning.

However, creating real indexes in a DTA tuning session is not feasible; its overhead could affect operational queries and degrade the performance of your database. So how does the DTA estimate the cost of using an index that does not yet exist? Actually, even during regular query optimization, the query optimizer does not use indexes to estimate the cost of a query. The decision on whether to use an index or not relies only on some metadata and statistical information regarding the columns of the index. Index data itself is not needed during query optimization, but will, of course, be required during query execution if the index is chosen.

So, to avoid creating real indexes during a DTA session, SQL Server uses a special kind of index called hypothetical indexes, which were also used by the Index Tuning Wizard. As the name implies, hypothetical indexes are not real indexes; they only contain statistics and can be created with the undocumented WITH STATISTICS_ONLY option of the CREATE INDEX statement. You may not be able to see these indexes during a DTA session because they are dropped automatically when they are no longer needed. However, you could see the CREATE INDEX WITH STATISTICS_ONLY and DROP INDEX statements if you run a SQL Server Profiler session to see what the DTA is doing.

Let's take a quick tour of some of these concepts. To get started, create a new table on the AdventureWorks2019 database as follows:

```
SELECT * INTO dbo.SalesOrderDetail
FROM Sales.SalesOrderDetail
```

Then copy the following query and save it to a file:

```
SELECT * FROM dbo.SalesOrderDetail
WHERE ProductID = 897
```

Open a new DTA session. The DTA is found in the **Tools** menu in SQL Server Management Studio with the full name **Database Engine Tuning Advisor**. You can optionally run a SQL Server Profiler session if you want to inspect what the DTA is doing. On the **Workload File** option, select the file containing the SQL statement that you just created and then specify **AdventureWorks2019** as both the database to tune and the database for workload analysis. Click the **Start Analysis** button and, when the DTA analysis finishes, run the following query to inspect the contents of the msdb.. DTA_reports_query table:

```
SELECT * FROM msdb..DTA_reports_query
```

Running the preceding query shows the following output (edited for space):

StatementString	CurrentCost	RecommendedCost
SELECT * FROM dbo.SalesOrderDetail WHERE ProductID = 897	1.2471	0.00333395

Notice that the query returns information such as the query that was tuned as well as the current and recommended cost. The current cost, 1.2471, is easy to obtain by directly requesting an estimated execution plan for the query, as shown in *Figure 5.7*:

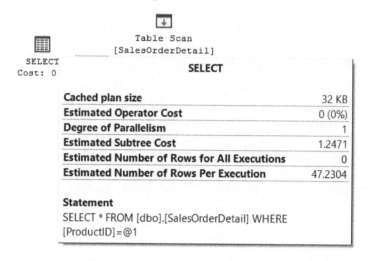

Cached plan size	32 KB
Estimated Operator Cost	0 (0%)
Degree of Parallelism	1
Estimated Subtree Cost	1.2471
Estimated Number of Rows for All Executions	0
Estimated Number of Rows Per Execution	47.2304

Statement
SELECT * FROM [dbo].[SalesOrderDetail] WHERE [ProductID]=@1

Figure 5.7 – Plan showing the total cost

Since the DTA analysis was completed, the required hypothetical indexes were already dropped. To obtain the indexes recommended by the DTA, click the **Recommendations** tab and look at the **Index Recommendations** section, where you can find the code to create any recommended index by clicking the **Definition** column. In our example, it will show the following code:

```
CREATE CLUSTERED INDEX [_dta_index_
SalesOrderDetail_c_5_1440724185__K5]
ON [dbo].[SalesOrderDetail]
(
[ProductID] ASC
)WITH (SORT_IN_TEMPDB = OFF, DROP_EXISTING = OFF, ONLINE = OFF)
ON [PRIMARY]
```

In the following statement, and for demonstration purposes only, we will go ahead and create the index recommended by the DTA. However, instead of a regular index, we will create it as a hypothetical index by adding the WITH STATISTICS_ONLY clause. Keep in mind that hypothetical indexes cannot be used by your queries and are only useful for the DTA:

```
CREATE CLUSTERED INDEX cix_ProductID ON dbo.
SalesOrderDetail(ProductID)
WITH STATISTICS_ONLY
```

You can validate that a hypothetical index was created by running the following query:

```
SELECT * FROM sys.indexes
WHERE object_id = OBJECT_ID('dbo.SalesOrderDetail')
AND name = 'cix_ProductID'
```

The output is as follows (note that the `is_hypothetical` field shows that this is, in fact, just a hypothetical index):

object_id	name	index_id	type	type_desc	is_hypothetical
1607676775	cix_ProductID	3	1	CLUSTERED	1

Remove the hypothetical index by running the following statement:

```
DROP INDEX dbo.SalesOrderDetail.cix_ProductID
```

Finally, implement the DTA recommendation, creating the `_dta_index_SalesOrderDetail_c_5_1440724185__K5` index, as previously indicated. After implementing the recommendation and running the query again, the clustered index is, in fact, now being used by the query optimizer. This time, the plan shows a Clustered Index Seek operator and an estimated cost of 0.0033652, which is very close to the recommended cost listed when querying the `msdb..DTA_reports_query` table.

Tuning a workload using the plan cache

In addition to the traditional options for tuning a workload using the **File or Table** choices, which allow you to specify a script or a table containing the T-SQL statements to tune, starting with SQL Server 2012, you can also specify the plan cache as a workload to tune. In this case, the DTA will select the top 1,000 events from the plan cache based on the total elapsed time of the query (that is, based on the `total_elapsed_time` column of the `sys.dm_exec_query_stats` DMV, as explained in *Chapter 2*). Let's try an example, and to make it easy to see the results, let's clear the plan cache and run only one query in SQL Server Management Studio as follows:

```
DBCC FREEPROCCACHE
GO
SELECT SalesOrderID, OrderQty, ProductID
FROM dbo.SalesOrderDetail
WHERE CarrierTrackingNumber = 'D609-4F2A-9B'
```

After the query is executed, most likely, it will be kept in the plan cache. Open a new DTA session. In the **Workload** option, select **Plan Cache** and specify `AdventureWorks2019` as both the database to tune and the database for workload analysis. Click the **Start Analysis** button. After the analysis is completed, you can select the **Recommendations** tab and select **Index Recommendations**, which will include the following recommendations (which you can see by looking at the **Definition** column):

```
CREATE NONCLUSTERED INDEX [_dta_index_
SalesOrderDetail_5_807673925__K3_1_4_5]
ON [dbo].[SalesOrderDetail]
(
[CarrierTrackingNumber] ASC
)
INCLUDE ([SalesOrderID],
[OrderQty],
[ProductID]) WITH (SORT_IN_TEMPDB = OFF, DROP_EXISTING = OFF,
ONLINE = OFF)
ON [PRIMARY]
```

Finally, drop the table you just created by running the following statement:

```
DROP TABLE dbo.SalesOrderDetail
```

Offload of tuning overhead to test server

One of the most interesting and perhaps lesser-known features of the DTA is that you can use it with a test server to tune the workload of a production server. As mentioned earlier, the DTA relies on the query optimizer to make its tuning recommendations, and you can use it to make these optimizer calls to a test server instance without affecting the performance of the production server.

To better understand how this works, let's first review what kind of information the query optimizer needs to optimize a query. Basically, the most important information it needs to perform an optimization is the following:

- The database metadata (that is, table and column definitions, indexes, constraints, and so on)
- Optimizer statistics (index and column statistics)
- Table size (number of rows and pages)
- Available memory and number of processors

The DTA can gather the database metadata and statistics from the production server and use them to create a similar database, with no data, on a different server. This database is called a shell database. The DTA can also obtain the available memory and number of processors on the production server by using the `xp_msver` extended stored procedure and use this information for the optimization process. It is important to remember that no data is needed for the optimization process. This process is summarized in *Figure 5.8*:

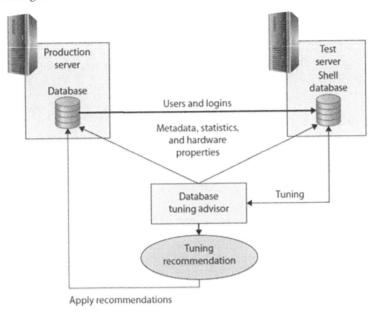

Figure 5.8 – Using a test server and a shell database with the DTA

This process provides the following benefits:

- There is no need to do an expensive optimization on the production server, which can affect its resource usage. The production server is only used to gather initial metadata and the required statistics.

- There is no need to copy the entire database to a test server either (which is especially important for big databases), thus saving disk space and time to copy the database.

- There are no problems where test servers are not as powerful as production servers because the DTA tuning session will consider the available memory and number of processors on the production server.

Let's now see an example of how to run a tuning session. First of all, the use of a test server is not supported by the DTA graphical user interface, so the use of the dta utility (the command-prompt version of DTA) is required. Configuring a test server also requires an XML input file containing the dta input information. We will be using the following input file (saved as input.xml) for this example. You will need to change production_instance and test_instance where appropriate. These must also be different SQL Server instances, as follows:

```
<?xml version="1.0" encoding="utf-16" ?>
<DTAXML xmlns:xsi="http://www.w3.org/2001/XMLSchema-instance"
xmlns="http://schemas.microsoft.com/sqlserver/2004/07/dta">
<DTAInput>
<Server>
<Name>production_instance</Name>
<Database>
<Name>AdventureWorks2019</Name>
</Database>
</Server>
<Workload>
<File>workload.sql</File>
</Workload>
<TuningOptions>
<TestServer>test_instance</TestServer>
<FeatureSet>IDX</FeatureSet>
<Partitioning>NONE</Partitioning>
<KeepExisting>NONE</KeepExisting>
</TuningOptions>
</DTAInput>
</DTAXML>
```

The Server and Database elements of the XML file include the production SQL Server instance and database. The Workload element includes the definition of a script containing the workload to tune. TuningOptions includes the TestServer sub-element, which is used to include the name of the test SQL Server instance.

Create the workload.sql file containing a simple query as follows:

```
SELECT * FROM AdventureWorks2019.Sales.SalesOrderDetail
WHERE ProductID = 898
```

Run the following command (note the difference in − S and − s because case is important here):

```
dta -ix input.xml -S production_instance -s session1
```

If the dta utility is not reachable with your current PATH environment variable, you can find it either on your SQL Server or your SQL Server Management Studio installation. For example, older versions of SQL Server may have it at C:\Program Files\Microsoft SQL Server\ nnn\Tools\Binn, assuming you installed the software on the C: volume. Our current installation points to C:\Program Files (x86)\Microsoft SQL Server Management Studio 19\Common7.

A successful execution will show the following output:

```
Microsoft (R) SQL Server Microsoft SQL Server Database Engine
Tuning Advisor command line utility
Version 16.0.19056.0 ((SSMS_Rel_19).220520-2253)
Copyright (c) Microsoft. All rights reserved.
Tuning session successfully created. Session ID is 3.
Total time used: 00:00:49
Workload consumed: 100%, Estimated improvement: 88%
Tuning process finished.
```

This example creates an entire copy of AdventureWorks2019 (with no data) and performs the requested optimization. The shell database is automatically deleted after the tuning session is completed. Optionally, you can keep the shell database (for example, if you want to use it again on another tuning exercise) by using RetainShellDB in the TuningOptions element, as in the following XML fragment:

```
<TuningOptions>
<TestServer>test_instance</TestServer>
<FeatureSet>IDX</FeatureSet>
<Partitioning>NONE</Partitioning>
<KeepExisting>NONE</KeepExisting>
<RetainShellDB>1</RetainShellDB>
</TuningOptions>
```

If the shell database already exists when you request a tuning session, the database creation process will be skipped. However, you will have to manually delete this database when it is no longer needed.

Once the tuning session is completed, you can use the DTA graphical user interface as usual to see the recommendations. To do this, open the DTA, open the session you used by double-clicking its session name (`session1` in our example), and choose the **Recommendations** tab if it is not already selected.

Although the DTA automatically gathers the metadata and statistics to build the shell database, we will see how to script the required objects and statistics to tune a simple query. This can be helpful in cases where you don't want to script the entire database. Scripting database objects is a fairly simple process well known by SQL Server professionals. Something that may be new for many, though, is how to script the statistics. Created scripts make use of the undocumented `STATS_STREAM`, `ROWCOUNT`, and `PAGECOUNT` options of the `CREATE/UPDATE STATISTICS` statement.

As an example, to optimize the simple query shown earlier, try the following steps in SQL Server Management Studio:

1. Expand **Databases** in **Object Explorer**.

2. Right-click the AdventureWorks2019 database, select **Tasks | Generate Scripts**, and then click **Next**.

3. Select **Select specific database objects**.

4. Expand **Tables**.

5. Select **Sales.SalesOrderDetail** and click **Next**.

6. Click **Advanced**.

7. Look for the **Script Statistics** choice and select **Script statistics and histograms**.

8. Choose **True** on **Script Indexes**.

   Your **Advanced Scripting Options** window should look similar to *Figure 5.9*:

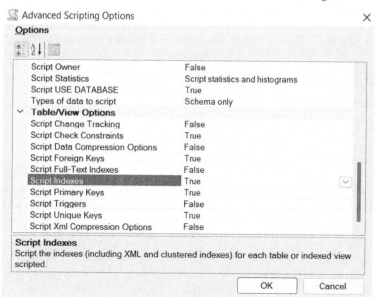

Figure 5.9 – Advanced Scripting Options window

Click **OK** to finish the wizard and generate the scripts. You will get a script with a few UPDATE STATISTICS statements similar to the following (with the STAT_STREAM value shortened to fit on this page):

```
UPDATE STATISTICS [Sales].[SalesOrderDetail]([IX_
SalesOrderDetail_ProductID])
WITH STATS_STREAM = 0x01000000030000000000000000000000041858B290
0000000141A00 …,
ROWCOUNT = 121317, PAGECOUNT = 274
```

These UPDATE STATISTICS statements are used to update the statistics of existing indexes (obviously, the related CREATE INDEX statements were scripted as well). If the table also has column statistics, it will include CREATE STATISTICS statements instead.

Finally, we will see an example of how to use scripted statistics to obtain plans and cost estimates on an empty table. Running the following query on the regular AdventureWorks2019 database creates the following plan with an estimated number of rows of 9 and a cost of 0.0296836:

```
SELECT * FROM Sales.SalesOrderDetail
WHERE ProductID = 898
```

Let's produce the same plan on a new and empty database. First, create the Sales schema as follows:

```
CREATE SCHEMA Sales
```

Following the procedure described earlier, you can script the Sales.SalesOrderDetail table. You will end up with multiple statements, including the following statements (again shortened to fit in this space). Although the script created many statements, the following are the minimum statements required for this exercise:

```
CREATE TABLE [Sales].[SalesOrderDetail](
[SalesOrderID] [int] NOT NULL,
...
) ON [PRIMARY]
GO
CREATE NONCLUSTERED INDEX [IX_SalesOrderDetail_ProductID] ON
[Sales].[SalesOrderDetail]
(
[ProductID] ASC
)
GO
```

```
UPDATE STATISTICS [Sales].[SalesOrderDetail]([IX_
SalesOrderDetail_ProductID])
WITH STATS_STREAM = 0x010000000300000000000000000000041858B290
0000000141A00 …,
ROWCOUNT = 121317, PAGECOUNT = 274
GO
UPDATE STATISTICS [Sales].[SalesOrderDetail]([PK_
SalesOrderDetail_SalesOrderID_SalesOrderDetailID])
WITH STATS_STREAM = 0x010000000200000000000000000000005175
2A6300000000431500 …,
ROWCOUNT = 121317, PAGECOUNT = 1237
```

Run at least the preceding four statements using the scripts you got in the previous step (note that this text does not include the entire statement—it is only shown for reference). After implementing the script on an empty database and running the sample query, you will again get the plan with a cost of 0.0296836 and an estimated number of rows of 9.

Missing indexes

SQL Server provides a second approach that can help you find useful indexes for your existing queries. Although not as powerful as the DTA, this option, called the missing indexes feature, does not require the database administrator to decide when tuning is needed, to explicitly identify what workload represents the load to tune, or to run any tool. This is a lightweight feature that is always on and, like the DTA, was also introduced with SQL Server 2005. Let's take a look at what it does.

During optimization, the query optimizer defines what the best indexes for a query are and, if these indexes don't exist, it will make this index information available in the query XML plan (which is also available in a graphical plan in SQL Server Management Studio 2008 or later). Alternatively, it will aggregate this information for optimized queries since the instance was started, and make it all available on the sys.dm_db_missing_index DMVs. Note that just by displaying this information, the query optimizer is not only warning you that it might not be selecting an efficient plan, but it is also showing you which indexes may help to improve the performance of your query. In addition, database administrators and developers should be aware of the limitations of this feature, as described in *"Limitations of the Missing Indexes Feature,"* at http://msdn.microsoft.com/en-us/library/ms345485(v=sql.105).aspx.

So, with all that in mind, let's take a quick look to see how this feature works. Create the dbo.SalesOrderDetail table on the AdventureWorks2019 database by running the following statement:

```
SELECT * INTO dbo.SalesOrderDetail
FROM Sales.SalesOrderDetail
```

Run the following query and request a graphical or XML execution plan:

```
SELECT * FROM dbo.SalesOrderDetail
WHERE SalesOrderID = 43670 AND SalesOrderDetailID > 112
```

This query could benefit from an index on the `SalesOrderID` and `SalesOrderDetailID` columns, but no missing indexes information is shown this time. One limitation of the missing indexes feature that this example has revealed is that it does not work with a trivial plan optimization. You can verify that this is a trivial plan by looking at the graphical plan properties, shown as `Optimization Level TRIVIAL`, or by looking at the XML plan, where `StatementOptmLevel` is shown as `TRIVIAL`. You can avoid trivial plan optimization in several ways, as explained in *Chapter 3, The Query Optimizer*. In our case, we're just going to create a non-related index by running the following statement:

```
CREATE INDEX IX_ProductID ON dbo.SalesOrderDetail(ProductID)
```

What is significant about this is that, although the index created will not be used by our previous query, the query no longer qualifies for a trivial plan. Run the query again, and this time the XML plan will contain the following entry:

```
<MissingIndexes>
<MissingIndexGroup Impact="99.7142">
<MissingIndex Database="[AdventureWorks2019]" Schema="[dbo]"
Table="[SalesOrderDetail]">
<ColumnGroup Usage="EQUALITY">
<Column Name="[SalesOrderID]" ColumnId="1" />
</ColumnGroup>
<ColumnGroup Usage="INEQUALITY">
<Column Name="[SalesOrderDetailID]" ColumnId="2" />
</ColumnGroup>
</MissingIndex>
</MissingIndexGroup>
</MissingIndexes>
```

The `MissingIndexes` entry in the XML plan can show up to three groups—equality, inequality, and included—and the first two are shown in this example using the `ColumnGroup` attribute. The information contained in these groups can be used to create the missing index; the key of the index can be built by using the `equality` columns, followed by the `inequality` columns, and the `included` columns can be added using the `INCLUDE` clause of the `CREATE INDEX` statement. Management Studio (versions SQL Server 2008 and later) can build the `CREATE INDEX` statement for you. In fact, if you look at the graphical plan, you can see a `Missing Index` warning at the top, including a `CREATE INDEX` command, as shown in *Figure 5.10*:

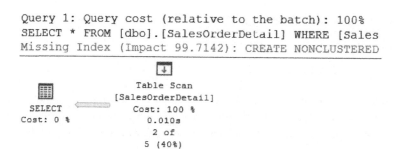

```
Query 1: Query cost (relative to the batch): 100%
SELECT * FROM [dbo].[SalesOrderDetail] WHERE [Sales
Missing Index (Impact 99.7142): CREATE NONCLUSTERED
```

Figure 5.10 – Plan with a Missing Index warning

Notice the impact value of 99.7142. Impact is a number between 0 and 100 that gives you an estimate of the average percentage benefit that the query could obtain if the proposed index were available. You can right-click the graphical plan and select **Missing Index Details** to see the CREATE INDEX command that can be used to create this desired index as follows:

```
/*
Missing Index Details from SQLQuery1.sql - (local).
AdventureWorks2019
The Query Processor estimates that implementing the following
index could
improve the query cost by 99.7142%.
*/
/*
USE [AdventureWorks2019]
GO
CREATE NONCLUSTERED INDEX [<Name of Missing Index, sysname,>]
ON [dbo].[SalesOrderDetail]
([SalesOrderID],[SalesOrderDetailID])
GO
*/
```

Create the recommended index, after you provide a name for it, by running the following statement:

```
CREATE NONCLUSTERED INDEX IX_SalesOrderID_SalesOrderDetailID
ON [dbo].[SalesOrderDetail]([SalesOrderID],
[SalesOrderDetailID])
```

If you run our previous SELECT statement again and look at the execution plan, this time you'll see an Index Seek operator using the index you've just created, and both the Missing Index warning and the MissingIndex element of the XML plan are gone.

Finally, remove the dbo.SalesOrderDetail table you've just created by running the following statement:

```
DROP TABLE dbo.SalesOrderDetail
```

So far, we have discussed how to use indexes to optimize query performance. Let's end the chapter with a couple of sections about the maintenance of indexes.

Index fragmentation

Although SQL Server automatically maintains indexes after any INSERT, UPDATE, DELETE, or MERGE operation, some index maintenance activities on your databases may still be required, mostly due to index fragmentation. Fragmentation happens when the logical order of pages in an index does not match the physical order in the data file. Because fragmentation can affect the performance of some queries, you need to monitor the fragmentation level of your indexes and, if required, perform reorganize or rebuild operations on them.

It is also worth clarifying that fragmentation may affect only queries performing scans or range scans; queries performing Index Seeks may not be affected at all. The query optimizer does not consider fragmentation either, so the plans it produces will be the same whether you have high fragmentation or no fragmentation at all. The query optimizer does not consider whether the pages in an index are in a physical order or not. However, one of the inputs for the query optimizer is the number of pages used by a table or index, and this number of pages may increase when there is a lot of unused space.

You can use the sys.dm_db_index_physical_stats DMF to analyze the fragmentation level of your indexes; you can query this information for a specific partition or index, or look at all of the indexes on a table, database, or even the entire SQL Server instance. The following example will return fragmentation information for the Sales.SalesOrderDetail of the AdventureWorks2019 database:

```
SELECT a.index_id, name, avg_fragmentation_in_percent,
fragment_count,
avg_fragment_size_in_pages
FROM sys.dm_db_index_physical_stats (DB_
ID('AdventureWorks2019'),
OBJECT_ID('Sales.SalesOrderDetail'), NULL, NULL, NULL) AS a
JOIN sys.indexes AS b ON a.object_id = b.object_id AND a.index_
id = b.index_id
```

In our copy of AdventureWorks2019, we got the following output (not all the columns are shown to fit the page):

index_id	name	avg_fragmentation_in_percent
1	PK_SalesOrderDetail_SalesOrderID_SalesOrderDetailID	36.13581245
2	AK_SalesOrderDetail_rowguid	2.643171806
3	IX_SalesOrderDetail_ProductID	25.83892617

Although the level of fragmentation considered a problem may vary and depend on your database and application, a best practice is to reorganize indexes with more than 10 percent and up to 30 percent fragmentation. An index rebuild operation could be more appropriate if you have fragmentation greater than 30 percent. A fragmentation of 10 percent or less should not be considered a problem.

An index reorganization operation defragments the leaf level of clustered and nonclustered indexes and is always an online operation. When rebuilding an index, you can optionally use the ONLINE = ON clause to perform an online operation for most of the index rebuild operation (a very short phase at the beginning and the end of the operation will not allow concurrent user activity). Rebuilding an index drops and re-creates the index and removes fragmentation by compacting the index pages based on the specified or existing fill factor configuration. The fill factor is a value from 1 to 100 that specifies a percentage that indicates how full the leaf level of each index page must be during index creation or alteration.

To rebuild all of the indexes on the SalesOrderDetail table, use the following statement:

```
ALTER INDEX ALL ON Sales.SalesOrderDetail REBUILD
```

Here is the fragmentation in our copy of AdventureWorks2019 after running the preceding statement:

index_id	Name	avg_fragmentation_in_percent
1	PK_SalesOrderDetail_SalesOrderID_SalesOrderDetailID	0.24291498
2	AK_SalesOrderDetail_rowguid	0
3	IX_SalesOrderDetail_ProductID	0

If you need to reorganize the index, which is not the case here, you can use a command such as the following:

```
ALTER INDEX ALL ON Sales.SalesOrderDetail REORGANIZE
```

As mentioned earlier, fragmentation can also be removed from a heap by using the ALTER TABLE REBUILD statement. However, this could be an expensive operation because it causes all nonclustered indexes to be rebuilt as the heap RIDs obviously change. Rebuilding an index also has an impact on statistics maintenance. For more details about index and statistics maintenance, see *Chapter 6, Understanding Statistics.*

Unused indexes

We will end this chapter on indexes by introducing the functionality of the sys.dm_db_index_usage_stats DMV, which you can use to learn about the operations performed by your indexes. It is especially helpful in discovering indexes that are not used by any query or are only minimally used. As we've already discussed, indexes that are not being used will provide no benefit to your databases but will use valuable disk space and slow your update operations, so they should be considered for removal.

The sys.dm_db_index_usage_stats DMV stores the number of seek, scan, lookup, and update operations performed by both user and system queries, including the last time each type of operation was performed, and its counters are reset when the SQL Server service starts. Keep in mind that this DMV, in addition to nonclustered indexes, will also include heaps, listed as index_id equal to 0, and clustered indexes, listed as index_id equal to 1. For this section, you may want to just focus on nonclustered indexes, which include index_id values of 2 or greater. Because heaps and clustered indexes contain the table's data, they may not even be candidates for removal in the first place.

By inspecting the user_seeks, user_scans, and user_lookup values of your nonclustered indexes, you can see how your indexes are being used, and you can also look at the user_updates values to see the number of updates performed on the index. All of this information will help give you a sense of how useful an index actually is. Bear in mind that all we will be demonstrating is how to look up information from this DMV and what sort of situations will trigger different updates to the information it returns.

As an example, run the following code to create a new table with a nonclustered index:

```
SELECT * INTO dbo.SalesOrderDetail
FROM Sales.SalesOrderDetail
CREATE NONCLUSTERED INDEX IX_ProductID ON dbo.
SalesOrderDetail(ProductID)
```

If you want to keep track of the values for this example, follow these steps carefully, because every query execution may change the index usage statistics. When you run the following query, it will initially contain only one record, which was created because of table access performed when the IX_ProductID index was created:

```
SELECT DB_NAME(database_id) AS database_name,
    OBJECT_NAME(s.object_id) AS object_name, i.name, s.*
```

```
FROM sys.dm_db_index_usage_stats s JOIN sys.indexes i
ON s.object_id = i.object_id AND s.index_id = i.index_id
AND OBJECT_ID('dbo.SalesOrderDetail') = s.object_id
```

However, the values that we will be inspecting in this exercise—user_seeks, user_scans, user_lookups, and user_updates—are all set to 0. Now run the following query, let's say, three times:

```
SELECT * FROM dbo.SalesOrderDetail
```

This query is using a **Table Scan** operator, so, if you rerun our preceding query using the sys.dm_db_index_usage_stats DMV, it will show the value 3 on the user_scans column. Note that the index_id column is 0, denoting a heap, and the name of the table is also listed (as a heap is just a table with no clustered index). Run the following query, which uses an Index Seek, twice:

```
SELECT ProductID FROM dbo.SalesOrderDetail
WHERE ProductID = 773
```

After the query is executed, a new record will be added for the nonclustered index, and the user_seeks counter will show a value of 2.

Now, run the following query four times, and it will use both Index Seek and RID lookup operators:

```
SELECT * FROM dbo.SalesOrderDetail
WHERE ProductID = 773
```

Because user_seeks for the nonclustered index had a value of 2, it will be updated to 6, and the user_lookups value for the heap will be updated to 4.

Finally, run the following query once:

```
UPDATE dbo.SalesOrderDetail
SET ProductID = 666
WHERE ProductID = 927
```

Note that the UPDATE statement is doing an Index Seek and a Table Update, so user_seek will be updated for the index, and user_updates will be updated once for both the nonclustered index and the heap. The following is the final output of our query using the sys.dm_db_index_usage_stats DMV (edited for space):

name	index_id	user_seeks	user_scans	user_lookups	user_updates
NULL	0	0	3	4	1
IX_ProductID	2	7	0	0	1

Finally, drop the table you just created as follows:

```
DROP TABLE dbo.SalesOrderDetail
```

Summary

In this chapter, we introduced indexing as one of the most important techniques used in query tuning and optimization and covered clustered and nonclustered indexes. In addition, we discussed related topics such as how SQL Server uses indexes, how to choose a clustered index key, and how to fix index fragmentation.

We also explained how you can define the key of your indexes so that they are likely to be considered for seek operations, which can improve the performance of your queries by finding records more quickly. Predicates were analyzed in the contexts of both single and multicolumn indexes, and we also covered how to verify an execution plan to validate that indexes were selected and properly used by SQL Server.

The Database Engine Tuning Advisor and the missing indexes feature, both introduced with SQL Server 2005, were presented to show you how the query optimizer itself can indirectly be used to provide index-tuning recommendations.

Finally, we introduced the `sys.dm_db_index_usage_stats` DMV and its ability to provide valuable information regarding your nonclustered indexes usage. Although we didn't discuss all the practicalities of using this DMV, we covered enough for you to be able to easily find nonclustered indexes that are not being used by your SQL Server instance.

6

Understanding Statistics

The SQL Server Query Optimizer is cost-based, so the quality of the execution plans it generates is directly related to the accuracy of its cost estimations. In the same way, the estimated cost of a plan is based on the algorithms or operators used, as well as their cardinality estimations. For this reason, to correctly estimate the cost of an execution plan, the Query Optimizer needs to estimate, as precisely as possible, the number of records returned by a given query.

During query optimization, SQL Server explores many candidate plans, estimates their relative costs, and selects the most efficient one. As such, incorrect cardinality and cost estimation may cause the Query Optimizer to choose inefficient plans, which can harm the performance of your database.

In this chapter, we will discuss the statistics that are used by the Query Optimizer, how to make sure you are providing it with the best possible quality of statistics, and what to do in cases where bad cardinality estimations are inevitable. Query Optimizer statistics contain three major pieces of information: the histogram, the density information, and the string statistics, all of which help with different parts of the cardinality estimation process. We will show you how statistics are created and maintained, and how they are used by the Query Optimizer. We will also show you how to detect cardinality estimation errors that can negatively impact the quality of your execution plans, as well as recommendations on how to fix them.

We will also cover cardinality estimation, including details and the differences between the old and new cardinality estimators. Finally, we will provide an overview of the costing module, which estimates the I/O and CPU cost for each operator, to obtain the total cost of the query plan.

This chapter covers the following topics:

- Exploring statistics
- Histograms in SQL Server
- A new cardinality estimator
- Cardinality estimation errors
- Incremental statistics

- Statistics on computed columns

- Filtered statistics

- Statistics on ascending keys

- UPDATE STATISTICS with ROWCOUNT and PAGECOUNT

- Statistics maintenance

- Cost estimation

Exploring statistics

SQL Server creates and maintains statistics to allow the Query Optimizer to calculate cardinality estimation. A cardinality estimate is the estimated number of rows that will be returned by a query or by a specific query operation, such as a join or a filter. Selectivity is a concept similar to cardinality estimation, which can be described as the fraction of rows in a set that satisfies a predicate, and it is always a value between 0 and 1, inclusive. A highly selective predicate returns a small number of rows. Rather than say any more on the subject here, we'll dive into more detail about these concepts later in this chapter.

Creating and updating statistics

To get started, let's take a look at the various ways statistics can be created and updated. Statistics are created in several ways: automatically by the Query Optimizer (if the default option to automatically create statistics, AUTO_CREATE_STATISTICS, is on), when an index is created, and explicitly (for example, the CREATE STATISTICS statement). Statistics can be created on one or more columns, and both the index and explicit creation methods support single- and multicolumn statistics. However, the statistics that are automatically generated by the Query Optimizer are always single-column statistics. As we briefly mentioned, the components of statistics objects are the histogram, the density information, and the string statistics. Both histograms and string statistics are only created for the first column of a statistics object, the latter only if the column is of a string data type.

Density information, which we will discuss in more detail later in this chapter, is calculated for each set of columns, forming a prefix in the statistics object. Filtered statistics, on the other hand, are not created automatically by the Query Optimizer, but only when a filtered index is created or when a CREATE STATISTICS statement with a WHERE clause is issued. Both filtered indexes and statistics are a feature introduced in SQL Server 2008. Filtered indexes were covered in *Chapter 5, Working with Indexes*, and we will touch on filtered statistics later in this chapter.

With the default configuration (if AUTO_UPDATE_STATISTICS is on), the Query Optimizer automatically updates statistics when they are out of date. As indicated earlier, the Query Optimizer does not automatically create multicolumn or filtered statistics, but once they are created, by using any of the methods described earlier, they can be automatically updated. Alternatively, index rebuild operations and statements such as UPDATE STATISTICS can be used to update statistics. Because both the auto-create and auto-update default choices will give you good quality statistics most of the time, it is strongly recommended that you keep these defaults. Naturally, you also have the choice to use some other statements if you need more control over the quality of the statistics.

So, by default, statistics may be automatically created (if nonexistent) and automatically updated (if out of date) as necessary during query optimization. By out of date, we refer to the data being changed and therefore the statistics not being representative of the underlying data (more on the exact mechanism later). If an execution plan for a specific query exists in the plan cache and the statistics that were used to build the plan are now out of date, then the plan is discarded, the statistics are updated, and a new plan is created. Similarly, updating statistics, either manually or automatically, invalidates any existing execution plan that used those statistics and will cause a new optimization the next time the query is executed.

When it comes to determining the quality of your statistics, you must consider the size of the sample of the target table that will be used to calculate said statistics. The Query Optimizer determines a statistically significant sample by default when it creates or updates statistics, and the minimum sample size is 8 MB (1,024 pages) or the size of the table if it's smaller than 8 MB. The sample size will increase for bigger tables, but it may still only be a small percentage of the table.

If needed, you can use the CREATE STATISTICS and UPDATE STATISTICS statements to explicitly request a bigger sample or scan the entire table to have better quality statistics. To do that, you need to specify a sample size or use the WITH FULLSCAN option to scan the entire table. This sample size can be specified as the number of rows or a percentage and, since the Query Optimizer must scan all the rows on a data page, these values are approximate. Using WITH FULLSCAN or a larger sample can be of benefit, especially with data that is not randomly distributed throughout the table. Scanning the entire table will give you the most accurate statistics possible. Consider that if statistics are built after scanning 50% of a table, then SQL Server will assume that the 50% of the data that it has not seen is statistically the same as the 50% it has seen. In fact, given that statistics are always created alongside a new index, and given that this operation scans the entire table anyway, index statistics are initially created with the equivalent of the WITH FULLSCAN option. However, if the Query Optimizer needs to automatically update these index statistics, it must go back to a default small sample because it may take too long to scan the entire table again.

By default, SQL Server needs to wait for the update statistics operation to complete before optimizing and executing the query; that is, statistics are updated synchronously. A database configuration option that was introduced with SQL Server 2005, AUTO_UPDATE_STATISTICS_ASYNC, can be used to change this default and let the statistics be updated asynchronously. As you may have guessed, with asynchronous statistics updates, the Query Optimizer does not wait for the update statistics operation to complete, and instead just uses the current statistics for the optimization process. This can help in situations where applications experience timeouts caused by delays related to the statistics being automatically updated. Although the current optimization will use the out-of-date statistics, they will be updated in the background and will be used by any later query optimization. However, asynchronous statistics updates usually only benefit OLTP workloads and may not be a good solution for more expensive queries, where getting a better plan is more important than an infrequent delay in statistics updates.

SQL Server defines when statistics are out of date by using column modification counters, or colmodctrs, which count the total number of modifications for the leading statistics column since the last time statistics were updated. Traditionally, this means for versions older than SQL Server 2016, tables bigger than 500 rows, or a statistics object that was considered out of date if the colmodctr value of the leading column has changed by more than 500, plus 20% of the number of rows in the table. The same formula was used by filtered statistics, but because they are only built from a subset of the records of the table, the colmodctr value is first multiplied by the selectivity of the filter. colmodctrs are exposed in the modification_counter column of the sys.dm_db_stats_properties DMF, which is available starting with SQL Server 2008 R2 Service Pack 2 and SQL Server 2012 Service Pack 1. Previously, colmodctrs were only available if you used a dedicated administrator connection and looked at the rcmodified column of the sys.sysrscols base system table in SQL Server 2008 or the sysrowset columns for SQL Server 2005.

> **Note**
>
> SQL Server 2000 used rowmodctrs, or row modification counters, to keep track of the number of changes in a table or index. The main difference with colmodctrs is that rowmodctr tracks any change to the row, whereas colmodctrs only track changes to the leading column of the statistics object. At the time of writing, the sp_updatestats statement, which is another way to update statistics, is still based on rowmodctrs, whose values are available as the rowmodctr column of the sys.sysindexes compatibility view.

Trace flag 2371 was introduced with SQL Server 2008 R2 Service Pack 1 as a way to automatically update statistics at a lower and dynamic percentage rate, instead of the aforementioned 20% threshold. With this dynamic percentage rate, the higher the number of rows in a table, the lower this threshold will become to trigger an automatic update of statistics. Tables with less than 25,000 records will still use the 20% threshold, but as the number of records in the table increase, this threshold will be lower and lower.

Starting with SQL Server 2016, and for databases and databases with database compatibility level 130 or higher, SQL Server implements the behavior of trace flag 2371 by default, so there is no need to use this trace flag anymore. You should be aware that you can still have the old behavior on recent versions of SQL Server if your database compatibility level is lower than 130. Currently supported versions of SQL Server and SQL Server 2022 CTP 2.0 allow a database to go back to a compatibility level of 100 or SQL Server 2008.

The new and default algorithm that was introduced with trace flag 2371 will use whatever number of changes is smaller between the new formula, defined as SQRT (1,000 * number of rows), and the old one, using 20% of the table. If you do the math using both formulas, you will find that the new threshold changes with tables that contain around 25,000 rows, which in both cases return the same value, will be 5,000 changes. For example, with the old algorithm requiring 20% of changes, a table with a billion rows would require 200 million changes to trigger a statistics update. The new algorithm would require a smaller threshold – in this case, SQRT (1,000 * 1,000,000,000) or 1 million.

Finally, the density information on multicolumn statistics may improve the quality of execution plans in the case of correlated columns or statistical correlations between columns. As mentioned previously, density information is kept for all the columns in a statistics object, in the order that they appear in the statistics definition. By default, SQL Server assumes columns are independent; therefore, if a relationship or dependency exists between columns, multicolumn statistics can help with cardinality estimation problems in queries that use these columns. Density information also helps with filters and GROUP BY operations, as we'll see in the *The density vector* section later. Filtered statistics, which are also explained later in this chapter, can be used for cardinality estimation problems with correlated columns. More details about the independency assumption will be covered in the *The new cardinality estimator* section.

Inspecting statistics objects

Let's look at an example of a statistics object and inspect the data it stores. Existing statistics for a specific object can be displayed using the sys.stats catalog view, as used in the following query:

```
SELECT * FROM sys.stats
WHERE object_id = OBJECT_ID('Sales.SalesOrderDetail')
```

An output similar to the following (edited to fit the page) will be shown:

object_id	name	stats_id
1154103152	PK_SalesOrderDetail_SalesOrderID_SalesOrderDetailID	1
1154103152	AK_SalesOrderDetail_rowguid	2
1154103152	IX_SalesOrderDetail_ProductID	3

One record for each statistics object is shown. Traditionally, you can use the DBCC SHOW_STATISTICS statement to display the details of a statistics object by specifying the column name or the name of the statistics object. In addition, as mentioned previously, starting with SQL Server 2012 Service Pack 1, you can use the sys.dm_db_stats_properties DMV to programmatically retrieve header information contained in the statistics object for non-incremental statistics. If you need to see the header information for incremental statistics, you can use sys.dm_db_incremental_stats_properties, which was introduced with SQL Server 2012 Service Pack 1 and SQL Server 2014 Service Pack 2. Finally, if you want to display the histogram information of a statistics object, you can use sys.dm_db_stats_histogram, which is available starting with SQL Server 2016 Service Pack 1 Cumulative Update 2.

DBCC SHOW_STATISTICS is available on any version of SQL Server and there are no plans for this statement to be deprecated. To show you an example of using this statement, run the following statement to verify that there are no statistics on the UnitPrice column of the Sales.SalesOrderDetail table:

```
DBCC SHOW_STATISTICS ('Sales.SalesOrderDetail', UnitPrice)
```

If no statistics object exists, which is the case for a fresh installation of the AdventureWorks2019 database, you will receive the following error message:

```
Msg 2767, Level 16, State 1, Line 1
Could not locate statistics 'UnitPrice' in the system catalogs.
```

By running the following query, the Query Optimizer will automatically create statistics on the UnitPrice column, which is used in the query predicate:

```
SELECT * FROM Sales.SalesOrderDetail
WHERE UnitPrice = 35
```

Running the previous DBCC SHOW_STATISTICS statement again will now show a statistics object similar to the following output (displayed as text and edited to fit the page):

Name	Updated Rows	Rows	Rows Sampled	Steps
_WA_Sys_00000007_44CA3770	Jun 3 2022 11:55PM	121317	110388	200

All density	Average Length	Columns
0.003205128	8	UnitPrice

RANGE_HI_KEY	RANGE_ROWS	EQ_ROWS	DISTINCT_RANGE_ROWS	AVG_RANGE_ROWS
1.3282	0	1	0	1
1.374	35.19722	142.3062	0	370.2226
2.29	35.19722	2747.751	0	370.2226
2.994	417.5509	341.9168	3	123.5255
3.975	35.19722	1	0	370.2226
3.99	35.19722	2061.052	0	370.2226

If you want to see the same information while using the new DMVs, you would have to run the following statements, both requiring the object ID and the statistics ID. In addition, you would have to inspect the sys.stats catalog view to find out the statistics stats_id value. I am using stats_id value 4, but since this is system-generated, your value may be different:

```
SELECT * FROM sys.dm_db_stats_properties(OBJECT_ID('Sales.
SalesOrderDetail'), 4)
SELECT * FROM sys.dm_db_stats_histogram(OBJECT_ID('Sales.
SalesOrderDetail'), 4)
```

Something else you may notice is that the new DMVs do not display any density information. The DBCC SHOW_STATISTICS statement's output is separated into three result sets called the header, the density vector, and the histogram, although the header information has been truncated to fit onto the page, and only a few rows of the histogram are shown. Let's look at the columns of the header while using the previous statistics object example, bearing in mind that some of the columns we will describe are not visible in the previous output:

- **Name**: _WA_Sys_00000007_44CA3770. This is the name of the statistics object and will probably be different in your SQL Server instance. All automatically generated statistics have a name that starts with _WA_Sys. The 00000007 value is the column_id value of the column that these statistics are based on, as can be seen on the sys.columns catalog, while 44CA3770 is the hexadecimal equivalent of the object_id value of the table (which can easily be verified using the calculator program available in Windows). WA stands for Washington, the state in the United States where the SQL Server development team is located.

- **Updated**: Jun 3 2022 11:55PM. This is the date and time when the statistics object was created or last updated.

- **Rows**: 121317. This is the number of rows that existed in the table when the statistics object was created or last updated.

- **Rows Sampled**: 110388. This is the number of rows that were sampled when the statistics object was created or last updated.

- **Steps**: 200. This is the number of steps of the histogram, which will be explained in the next section.

- **Density**: 0.06236244. The density of all the values sampled, except the RANGE_HI_KEY values (RANGE_HI_KEY will be explained later in the *Histogram* section). This density value is no longer used by the Query Optimizer, and it is only included for backward compatibility.

- **Average Key Length**: 8. This is the average number of bytes for the columns of the statistics object.

- **String Index**: NO. This value indicates if the statistics object contains string statistics, and the only choices are YES or NO. String statistics contain the data distribution of substrings in a string column and can be used to estimate the cardinality of queries with LIKE conditions. As mentioned previously, string statistics are only created for the first column, and only when the column is of a string data type.

- **Filter Expression and Unfiltered Rows**: These columns will be explained in the *Filtered statistics* section, later in this chapter.

Below the header, you'll find the density vector, which includes a wealth of potentially useful density information. We will look at this in the next section.

The density vector

To better explain the density vector, run the following statement to inspect the statistics of the existing index, IX_SalesOrderDetail_ProductID:

```
DBCC SHOW_STATISTICS ('Sales.SalesOrderDetail', IX_
SalesOrderDetail_ProductID)
```

This will display the following density vector, which shows the densities for the ProductID column, as well as a combination of ProductID and SalesOrderID, and then ProductID, SalesOrderID, and SalesOrderDetailID columns:

```
All density   Average Length Columns
------------  -------------- --------------------------------------------

0.003759399   4              ProductID
8.242868E-06  8              ProductID, SalesOrderID
8.242868E-06  12             ProductID, SalesOrderID, SalesOrderDetailID
```

Density, which is defined as 1 / "number of distinct values," is listed in the `All density` field, and it is calculated for each set of columns, forming a prefix for the columns in the statistics object. For example, the statistics object that was listed was created for the `ProductID`, `SalesOrderID`, and `SalesOrderDetailID` columns, so the density vector will show three different density values: one for `ProductID`, another for `ProductID` and `SalesOrderID` combined, and a third for `ProductID`, `SalesOrderID`, and `SalesOrderDetailID` combined. The names of the analyzed columns will be displayed in the **Columns** field, and the `Average Length` column will show the average number of bytes for each density value. In the previous example, all the columns were defined using the `int` data type, so the average lengths for each of the density values will be 4, 8, and 12 bytes, respectively. Now that we've seen how density information is structured, let's take a look at how it is used.

Density information can be used to improve the Query Optimizer's estimates for GROUP BY operations, and on equality predicates where a value is unknown, as in the case of a query that uses local variables. To see how this is done, let's consider, for example, the number of distinct values for `ProductID` on the `Sales.SalesOrderDetail` table, which is 266. Density can be calculated, as mentioned earlier, as 1 / "number of distinct values," which in this case would be 1 / 266, which is 0.003759399, as shown by the first density value in the previous `DBCC SHOW_STATISTICS` example at the beginning of this section.

So, the Query Optimizer can use this density information to estimate the cardinality of GROUP BY queries. GROUP BY queries can benefit from the estimated number of distinct values, and this information is already available in the density value. If you have this density information, then all you have to do is find the estimated number of distinct values by calculating the reciprocal of the density value. For example, to estimate the cardinality of the following query using GROUP BY `ProductID`, we can calculate the reciprocal of the `ProductID` density shown in the following statement. In this case, we have 1 / 0.003759399, which gives us 266, which is the estimated number of rows shown in the plan in *Figure 6.1*:

```
SELECT ProductID FROM Sales.SalesOrderDetail
GROUP BY ProductID
```

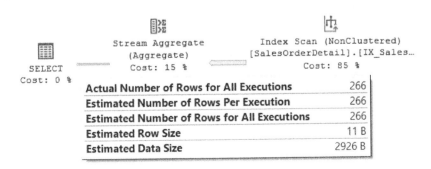

Figure 6.1 – Cardinality estimation example using a GROUP BY clause

Similarly, to test GROUP BY ProductID and SalesOrderID, we would need 1 / 8.242868E-06, which gives us an answer of 121,317. That is to say that in the sampled data, there are 121,317 unique combinations of ProductID and SalesOrderID. You can also verify this by obtaining that query's graphical plan.

The following example shows how the density can be used to estimate the cardinality of a query using local variables:

```
DECLARE @ProductID int
SET @ProductID = 921
SELECT ProductID FROM Sales.SalesOrderDetail
WHERE ProductID = @ProductID
```

In this case, the Query Optimizer does not know the value of the @ProductID local variable at optimization time, so it can't use the histogram (which we'll discuss shortly). This means it will use the density information instead. The estimated number of rows is obtained using the density multiplied by the number of records in the table, which in our example is 0.003759399 * 121317, or 456.079, as shown here:

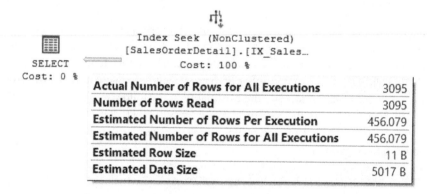

Figure 6.2 – Cardinality estimation example using a local variable

Because the Query Optimizer does not know the value of @ProductID at optimization time, the value 921 in the previous listing does not matter; any other value will give the same estimated number of rows and execution plan since it is the average number of rows per value. Finally, run this query with an inequality operator:

```
DECLARE @pid int = 897
SELECT * FROM Sales.SalesOrderDetail
WHERE ProductID < @pid
```

As mentioned previously, the value 897 does not matter; any other value will give you the same estimated number of rows and execution plan. However, this time, the Query Optimizer can't use the density information and instead uses the standard guess of 30% selectivity for inequality comparisons. This means that the estimated number of rows is always 30% of the total number of records for an inequality operator; in this case, 30% of 121,317 is 36,395.1, as shown here:

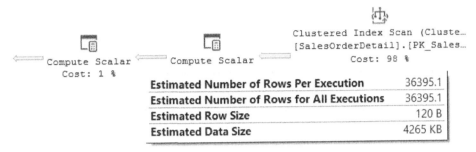

Estimated Number of Rows Per Execution	36395.1
Estimated Number of Rows for All Executions	36395.1
Estimated Row Size	120 B
Estimated Data Size	4265 KB

Figure 6.3 – Cardinality estimation example using a 30% guess

However, the use of local variables in a query limits the quality of the cardinality estimate when using the density information with equality operators. Worse, local variables result in no estimate at all when used with an inequality operator, which results in a guessed percentage. For this reason, local variables should be avoided in queries, and parameters or literals should be used instead. When parameters or literals are used, the Query Optimizer can use the histogram, which will provide better-quality estimates than the density information on its own.

As it happens, the last section of the DBCC SHOW_STATISTICS output is the histogram, which we will learn about in the next section.

Histograms

In SQL Server, histograms are only created for the first column of a statistics object, and they compress the information of the distribution of values in that column by partitioning that information into subsets called buckets or steps. The maximum number of steps in a histogram is 200, but even if the input contains 200 or more unique values, a histogram may still have fewer than 200 steps. To build the histogram, SQL Server finds the unique values in the column and tries to capture the most frequent ones using a variation of the maxdiff algorithm, so that the most statistically significant information is preserved. Maxdiff is one of the available histograms whose purpose is to accurately represent the distribution of data values in relational databases.

> **Note**
>
> You can find a simplified version of the algorithm that was used to build the histogram in the Microsoft white paper *Statistics Used by the Query Optimizer in Microsoft SQL Server 2008*, by Eric Hanson and Yavor Angelov.

To see how the histogram is used, run the following statement to display the current statistics of the IX_SalesOrderDetail_ProductID index on the Sales.SalesOrderDetail table:

```
DBCC SHOW_STATISTICS ('Sales.SalesOrderDetail', IX_
SalesOrderDetail_ProductID)
```

Both the multicolumn index and statistics objects include the ProductID, SalesOrderID, and SalesOrderDetailID columns, but because the histogram is only for the first column, this data is only available for the ProductID column.

Next, we will see some examples of how the histogram may be used to estimate the cardinality of some simple predicates. Let's look at a section of the histogram, as shown in the following output:

RANGE_HI_KEY	RANGE_ROWS	EQ_ROWS	DISTINCT_RANGE_ROWS	AVG_RANGE_ROWS
826	0	305	0	1
831	110	198	3	36.66667
832	0	256	0	1

RANGE_HI_KEY is the upper boundary of a histogram step; the value 826 is the upper boundary for the first step shown, while 831 is the upper boundary for the second step shown. This means that the second step may only contain values from 827 to 831. The RANGE_HI_KEY values are usually the more frequent values in the distribution.

With that in mind, and to understand the rest of the histogram structure and how the histogram information was aggregated, run the following query to obtain the real number of records for ProductIDs 827 to 831. We'll compare them against the histogram:

```
SELECT ProductID, COUNT(*) AS Total
FROM Sales.SalesOrderDetail
WHERE ProductID BETWEEN 827 AND 831
GROUP BY ProductID
```

This produces the following output:

ProductID	Total
827	31
828	46
830	33
831	198

Going back to the histogram, EQ_ROWS is the estimated number of rows whose column value equals RANGE_HI_KEY. So, in our example, for the RANGE_HI_KEY value of 831, EQ_ROWS shows 198, which we know is also the actual number of existing records for ProductID 831.

RANGE_ROWS is the estimated number of rows whose column value falls inside the range of the step, excluding the upper boundary. In our example, this is the number of records with values from 827 to 830 (831, the upper boundary or RANGE_HI_KEY, is excluded). The histogram shows 110 records, and we could obtain the same value by getting the sum of 31 records for ProductID 827, 46 records for ProductID 828, 0 records for ProductID 829, and 33 records for ProductID 830.

DISTINCT_RANGE_ROWS is the estimated number of rows with a distinct column value inside this range, once again excluding the upper boundary. In our example, we have records for three distinct values (827, 828, and 830), so DISTINCT_RANGE_ROWS is 3. There are no records for ProductIDs 829 and 831, which is the upper boundary, which is again excluded.

Finally, AVG_RANGE_ROWS is the average number of rows per distinct value, excluding the upper boundary, and it is simply calculated as RANGE_ROWS / DISTINCT_RANGE_ROWS. In our example, we have a total of 110 records for 3 DISTINCT_RANGE_ROWS, which gives us 110 / 3 = 36.6667, also shown in the second step of the histogram shown previously. The histogram assumes the value 110 is evenly split between all three ProductIDs.

Now let's see how the histogram is used to estimate the selectivity of some queries. Let's look at the first query:

```
SELECT * FROM Sales.SalesOrderDetail
WHERE ProductID = 831
```

Because 831 is RANGE_HI_KEY on the second step of the histogram shown previously, the Query Optimizer will use the EQ_ROWS value (the estimated number of rows whose column value equals RANGE_HI_KEY) directly, and the estimated number of rows will be 198, as shown here:

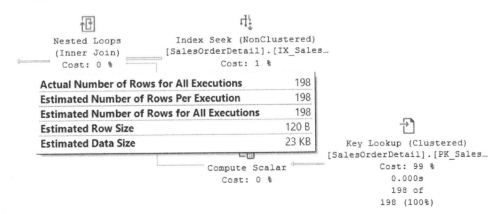

Figure 6.4 – Cardinality estimation example using a RANGE_HI_KEY value

Now, run the same query with the value set to 828. This time, the value is inside the range of the second step but is not a RANGE_HI_KEY value inside the histogram, so the Query Optimizer uses the value calculated for AVG_RANGE_ROWS (the average number of rows per distinct value), which is 36.6667, as shown in the histogram. The plan for this query is shown in *Figure 6.5* and, unsurprisingly, we get the same estimated number of rows for any of the other values within the range (except for RANGE_HI_KEY). This even includes the value 829, for which there are no rows inside the table:

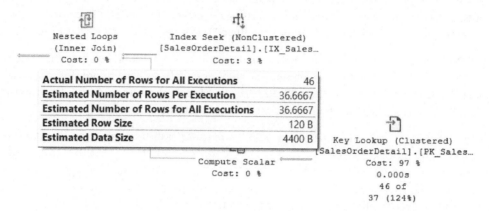

Figure 6.5 – Cardinality estimation example using an AVG_RANGE_ROWS value

Now, let's use an inequality operator and try to find the records with a ProductID less than 714. Because this requires all the records, both inside the range of a step and the upper boundary, we need to calculate the sum of the values of both the RANGE_ROWS and EQ_ROWS columns for steps 1 through 7, as shown in the following histogram, which gives us a total of 13,223 rows:

RANGE_HI_KEY	RANGE_ROWS	EQ_ROWS	DISTINCT_RANGE_ROWS	AVG_RANGE_ROWS
707	0	3083	0	1
708	0	3007	0	1
709	0	188	0	1
710	0	44	0	1
711	0	3090	0	1
712	0	3382	0	1
713	0	429	0	1
714	0	1218	0	1
715	0	1635	0	1

The following is the query in question:

```
SELECT * FROM Sales.SalesOrderDetail
WHERE ProductID < 714
```

The estimated number of rows can be seen in the following execution plan:

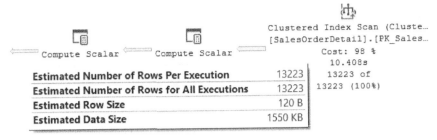

Figure 6.6 – Cardinality estimation example using an inequality operator

Histograms are also used for cardinality estimations on multiple predicates; however, as of SQL Server 2022, this estimation depends on the version of the cardinality estimation used. We will cover this in the next section.

A new cardinality estimator

As mentioned in the introduction, SQL Server 2014 introduced a new cardinality estimator, and in this and later versions, the old cardinality estimator is still available. This section explains what a cardinality estimator is, why a new cardinality estimator was built, and how to enable the new and the old cardinality estimators.

The cardinality estimator is the component of the query processor whose job is to estimate the number of rows returned by relational operations in a query. This information, along with some other data, is used by the Query Optimizer to select an efficient execution plan. Cardinality estimation is inherently inexact because it is a mathematical model that relies on statistical information. It is also based on several assumptions that, although not documented, have been known over the years – some of them include the uniformity, independence, containment, and inclusion assumptions. The following is a brief description of these assumptions:

- **Uniformity**: This is used when the distribution for an attribute is unknown – for example, inside range rows in a histogram step or when a histogram is not available.

- **Independence**: This is used when the attributes in a relationship are independent unless a correlation between them is known.

- **Containment**: This is used when two attributes might be the same; in this case, they are assumed to be the same.

- **Inclusion**: This is used when comparing an attribute with a constant; it is assumed there is always a match.

The current cardinality estimator was written along with the entire query processor for SQL Server 7.0, which was released back in December 1998. This component has faced multiple changes over several years and multiple releases of SQL Server, including fixes, adjustments, and extensions to accommodate cardinality estimation for new T-SQL features. So, you may be thinking, why replace a component that has been successfully used for about the last 15 years?

In the paper *Testing Cardinality Estimation Models in SQL Server*, by Campbell Fraser et al., the authors explain some of the reasons for the cardinality estimator being redesigned, including the following:

- To accommodate the cardinality estimator to new workload patterns.

- Changes made to the cardinality estimator over the years made the component difficult to *debug, predict, and understand.*

- Trying to improve on the current model was difficult using the current architecture, so a new design was created that focused on the separation of tasks of (a) deciding how to compute a particular estimate and (b) performing the computation.

It is surprising to read in the paper that the authors admit that, according to their experience in practice, the previously listed assumptions are frequently incorrect.

A major concern that comes to mind with such a huge change inside the Query Optimizer is plan regressions. The fear of plan regressions has been considered the biggest obstacle to Query Optimizer improvements. Regressions are problems that are introduced after a fix has been applied to the Query Optimizer and are sometimes referred to as the classic *two wrongs make a right*. This can happen when two bad estimations – for example, the first overestimating a value and the second underestimating it – cancel each other out, luckily giving a good estimate. Correcting only one of these values may now lead to a bad estimation, which may negatively impact the choice of plan selection, thus causing a regression.

To help avoid regressions related to the new cardinality estimator, SQL Server provides a way to enable or disable it, depending on the database's compatibility level. This can be changed using the `ALTER DATABASE` statement, as indicated earlier. Setting a database to compatibility level 120 will use the new cardinality estimator, whereas a compatibility level less than 120 will use the old cardinality estimator. In addition, once you are using a specific cardinality estimator, there are two trace flags you can use to change to the other. Trace flag 2312 can be used to enable the new cardinality estimator, whereas trace flag 9481 can be used to disable it. You can even use the trace flags for a specific query by using the `QUERYTRACEON` hint. Both trace flags and their use with the `QUERYTRACEON` hint are documented and supported.

> **Note**
> The compatibility level of a database will be changed several times in this chapter for demonstration purposes to show the behaviors of the old and new cardinality estimators. In a production environment, a database compatibility level should be static and never or rarely changed.

Finally, SQL Server includes several new extended events we can use to troubleshoot problems with cardinality estimation, or just to explore how it works. These events include `query_optimizer_estimate_cardinality`, `inaccurate_cardinality_estimate`, `query_optimizer_force_both_cardinality_estimation_behaviors`, and `query_rpc_set_cardinality`.

The remainder of this section will show the difference in estimations between the new and old cardinality estimators regarding AND'ed and OR'ed predicates, known as conjunctions and disjunctions, respectively. Some other sections in the chapter explain the difference in other topics (for example, when using statistics on ascending keys).

First, let's look at the traditional behavior. For that, make sure you are using the old cardinality estimator by running the following statement on the AdventureWorks2019 database:

```
ALTER DATABASE AdventureWorks2019 SET COMPATIBILITY_LEVEL = 110
```

Then, run the following statement:

```
SELECT * FROM Person.Address WHERE City = 'Burbank'
```

By looking at the execution plan, you will see an estimate of 196 records. Similarly, the following statement will get an estimate of 194:

```
SELECT * FROM Person.Address WHERE PostalCode = '91502'
```

Both estimations of single predicates use the histogram, as explained earlier. Now, let's use both predicates, as in the following query, which will have an estimated 1.93862 rows:

```
SELECT * FROM Person.Address
WHERE City = 'Burbank' AND PostalCode = '91502'
```

Because SQL Server doesn't know anything about any data correlation between both predicates, it assumes they are independent and, again, uses the histograms, as we saw previously, to find the intersection between both sets of records, multiplying the selectivity of both clauses. The selectivity of the `City = 'Burbank'` predicate is calculated as 196 / 19,614 (where 19,614 is the total number of rows in the table), or 0.009992862. The selectivity of the `PostalCode = '91502'` predicate is calculated as 194 / 19,614, or 0.009890894. To get the intersection of these sets, we need to multiply the selectivity values of both predicate clauses, 0.009992862 and 0.009890894, to get 9.88383E-05. Finally, the calculated selectivity is multiplied by the total number of records to obtain the estimate, 9.88383E-05 * 19614, obtaining 1.93862. A more direct formula could be to simply use (196 * 194) / 19614.0 to get the same result.

Let's see the same estimations while using the new cardinality estimator. To achieve this, you can use a database compatibility level newer than SQL Server 2012, which can be 120, 130, 140, 150, or 160:

```
ALTER DATABASE AdventureWorks2019 SET COMPATIBILITY_LEVEL = 160
GO

SELECT * FROM Person.Address WHERE City = 'Burbank' AND
PostalCode = '91502'
```

> **Note**
>
> As suggested earlier, SQL Server 2022 CTP 2.0 and all SQL Server supported versions allow you to change a database to any compatibility level starting with 100, which corresponds to the SQL Server 2008 release. Trying a different value will get you error message 15048, which states **Valid values of the database compatibility level are 100, 110, 120, 130, 140, 150, or 160.**

Running the same statement again will give an estimate of 19.3931 rows, as shown in the following screenshot. You may need to clear the plan cache or force a new optimization if you are still getting the previous estimation:

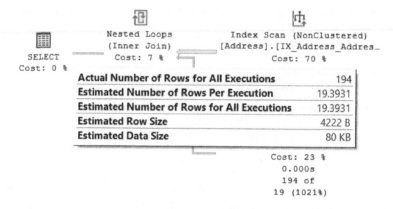

Figure 6.7 – AND'ed predicates with the new cardinality estimator

The new formula that's used in this case is as follows:

*selectivity of most selective filter * SQRT(selectivity of next most selective filter)*

This is the equivalent of (194/19614) * SQRT(196/19614) * 19614, which gives 19.393. If there were a third (or more) predicate, the formula would be extended by adding an SQRT operation for each predicate, such as in the following formula:

*selectivity of most selective filter * SQRT(selectivity of next most selective filter) * SQRT(SQRT(selectivity of next most selective filter))*

Now, keep in mind that the old cardinality estimator is using the original independence assumption. The new cardinality estimator is using a new formula, relaxing this assumption, which is now called the exponential backoff. This new formula does not assume total correlation either, but at least the new estimation is better than the original. Finally, note that the Query Optimizer is unable to know if the data is correlated, so it will be using these formulas, regardless of whether or not the data is correlated. In our example, the data is correlated; ZIP code 91502 corresponds to the city of Burbank, California.

Now, let's test the same example using OR'ed predicates, first using the old cardinality estimator:

```
ALTER DATABASE AdventureWorks2019 SET COMPATIBILITY_LEVEL = 110
GO
SELECT * FROM Person.Address WHERE City = 'Burbank' OR
PostalCode = '91502'
```

By definition, an OR'ed predicate is the union of the sets of rows of both clauses, without duplicates. That is, this should be the rows estimated for the `City = 'Burbank'` predicate, plus the rows estimated for `PostalCode = '91502'`, but if there are any rows that may belong to both sets, then they should only be included once. As indicated in the previous example, the estimated number of rows for the `City = 'Burbank'` predicate alone is 196 rows, and the estimated number of rows for the `PostalCode = '91502'` predicate alone is 194 rows. As we saw previously, the estimated number of records that belong to both sets in the AND'ed predicate is 1.93862 rows. Therefore, the estimated number of rows for the OR'ed predicate is 196 + 194 – 1.93862, or 388.061.

Testing the same example for the new cardinality estimator would return an estimate of 292.269 rows, as shown in the following screenshot. Once again, you may need to clear the plan cache or force a new optimization if you are still getting the previous estimation:

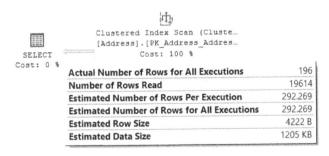

Figure 6.8 – OR'ed predicates with the new cardinality estimator

Try the following code to see such plans:

```
ALTER DATABASE AdventureWorks2019 SET COMPATIBILITY_LEVEL = 160
GO
SELECT * FROM Person.Address WHERE City = 'Burbank' OR
PostalCode = '91502'
```

The formula to obtain this estimation was suggested in the white paper *Optimizing Your Query Plans with the SQL Server 2014 Cardinality Estimator*, which indicates that SQL Server calculates this value by first transforming disjunctions into a negation of conjunctions. In this case, we can update our previous formula to (1-(1-(196/19614)) * SQRT(1-(194/19614))) * 19614, which returns 292.269.

If you have enabled the new cardinality estimator at the database level but want to disable it for a specific query to avoid a plan regression, you can use trace flag 9481, as explained earlier:

```
ALTER DATABASE AdventureWorks2019 SET COMPATIBILITY_LEVEL = 160
GO

SELECT * FROM Person.Address WHERE City = 'Burbank' AND
PostalCode = '91502'
OPTION (QUERYTRACEON 9481)
```

> **Note**
>
> As indicated in *Chapter 1, An Introduction to Query Optimization*, the QUERYTRACEON query hint is used to apply a trace flag at the query level, and currently, it is only supported in a limited number of scenarios, including trace flags 2312 and 9481, which were mentioned in this section.

Finally, starting with SQL Server 2014, two cardinality estimators are available, so we must figure out which one was used by a specific optimization, especially for troubleshooting purposes. You can find this information on execution plans by looking at the `CardinalityEstimationModelVersion` property of a graphical plan or the `CardinalityEstimationModelVersion` attribute of the `StmtSimple` element in an XML plan, as shown in the following XML fragment:

```
<StmtSimple … CardinalityEstimationModelVersion="160" …>
```

A value of 70 means that the old cardinality estimator is being used. A `CardinalityEstimationModelVersion` value of 120 or greater means that the new cardinality estimator is being used and will match the database compatibility level.

Trace flag 4137

Finally, trace flag 4137 can be used as another choice to help with correlated AND predicates. Trace flag 4137 (which was originally released as a fix for SQL Server 2008 Service Pack 2, SQL Server 2008 R2 Service Pack 1, and SQL Server 2012 RTM) will select the lowest cardinality estimation of a list of AND'ed predicates. For example, the following code will show an estimated number of rows of 194, because 194 is the smallest of both cardinality estimations for the `City = 'Burbank'` and `PostalCode = '91502'` predicates, as explained earlier:

```
ALTER DATABASE AdventureWorks2019 SET COMPATIBILITY_LEVEL = 110
GO
```

```
SELECT * FROM Person.Address
WHERE City = 'Burbank' AND PostalCode = '91502'
OPTION (QUERYTRACEON 4137)
```

> **Note**
>
> Using trace flag 4137 with QUERYTRACEON is documented and supported.

To make things a little bit more confusing, trace flag 4137 does not work with the new cardinality estimator, so trace flag 9471 needs to be used instead. Another difference with trace flag 9471 is that it impacts both conjunctive and disjunctive predicates, whereas trace flag 4137 only works with conjunctive predicates.

In addition, filtered statistics, which will be covered later in this chapter, may be helpful in some cases when data is correlated.

Finally, cardinality estimation feedback, a new feature with SQL Server 2022, was designed to find if an estimation model assumption is producing a suboptimal plan and instead try a different model assumption that fits a given query and data distribution better. Cardinality estimation feedback is based on the query store and covered in more detail in *Chapter 10, Intelligent Query Processing*.

Cardinality estimation errors

Cardinality estimation errors can lead to the Query Optimizer making poor choices as to how best to execute a query and, therefore, to badly performing execution plans. Fortunately, you can easily check whether you have cardinality estimation errors by comparing the estimated against the actual number of rows, as shown in graphical or XML execution plans, or by using the SET STATISTICS PROFILE statement. In the following query, we will show you how to use the SET STATISTICS PROFILE statement with one of our previous examples, where SQL Server is making a blind guess regarding the selectivity of certain columns:

```
SET STATISTICS PROFILE ON
GO
SELECT * FROM Sales.SalesOrderDetail
WHERE OrderQty * UnitPrice > 10000
GO
SET STATISTICS PROFILE OFF
GO
```

This is the resulting output, with the `EstimateRows` column manually moved just after the `Rows` column, and edited to fit the page:

Rows   EstimateRows StmtText

```
Rows     EstimateRows StmtText

------   ------------ -----------------------------------------------------
772      36395.1 SELECT * FROM [Sales].[SalesOrderDetail] WHERE [OrderQty]
772      36395.1 |--Filter(WHERE:([Expr1003]>($10000.0000)))
0        121317  |--Compute Scalar(DEFINE:([AdventureWorks2019].[Sales]
0        121317  |--Compute Scalar(DEFINE:([AdventureWorks2019].[S
121317   121317  |--Clustered Index Scan(OBJECT:([AdventureWo
```

Using this output, you can easily compare the actual number of rows, shown on the `Rows` column, against the estimated number of records, shown on the `EstimateRows` column, for each operator in the plan. Introduced with SQL Server 2012, the `inaccurate_cardinality_estimate` extended event can also be used to detect inaccurate cardinality estimations by identifying which query operators output significantly more rows than those estimated by the Query Optimizer.

Because each operator relies on previous operations for its input, cardinality estimation errors can propagate exponentially throughout the query plan. For example, a cardinality estimation error on a `Filter` operator can impact the cardinality estimation of all the other operators in the plan that consume the data produced by that operator. If your query is not performing well and you find cardinality estimation errors, check for problems such as missing or out-of-date statistics, very small samples being used, correlation between columns, use of scalar expressions, guessing selectivity issues, and so on.

Recommendations to help with these issues have been provided throughout this chapter and include topics such as using the auto-create and auto-update statistics default configurations, updating statistics using `WITH FULLSCAN`, avoiding local variables in queries, avoiding non-constant-foldable or complex expressions on predicates, using computed columns, and considering multicolumn or filtered statistics, among other things. In addition, parameter sniffing and parameter-sensitive queries will be covered in more detail in *Chapter 8*, Understanding *Plan Caching*. That's a fairly long list, but it should help convince you that you are already armed with pragmatically useful information.

Some SQL Server features, such as table variables, have no statistics, so you may want to consider using a temporary table or a standard table instead if you're having performance problems related to cardinality estimation errors. Multistatement table-valued user-defined functions have no statistics either. In this case, you can consider using a temporary table or a standard table as a temporary holding place for their results. In both these cases (table variables and multistatement table-valued user-defined functions), the Query Optimizer will guess at one row (which has been updated to 100 rows for multistatement table-valued user-defined functions in SQL Server 2014). In addition, for complex queries that are not performing well because of cardinality estimation errors, you may want to consider breaking down the query into two or more steps while storing the intermediate results in temporary tables. This will allow SQL Server to create statistics on the intermediate results, which will help the Query Optimizer produce a better execution plan. More details about breaking down complex queries will be covered in *Chapter 12, Understanding Query Hints*.

> **Note**
>
> A new trace flag, 2453, was introduced with SQL Server 2012 Service Pack 2 and SQL Server 2014, which provides better cardinality estimation while using table variables. For more details, see `http://support.microsoft.com/kb/2952444`.

Now that we have learned about cardinality estimation, we will explore another key feature in SQL Server: incremental statistics.

Incremental statistics

A major problem with updating statistics in large tables in SQL Server was that the entire table always had to be sampled, even if only recent data had changed. This was also true when partitioning was being used: even if only the newest partition had changed since the last time statistics were updated, updating statistics again required sampling the entire table, including all the partitions that hadn't changed. Incremental statistics, a feature introduced with SQL Server 2014, can help with this problem.

Using incremental statistics, you can only update the statistics on the partition or partitions that have been modified, and the information on these partitions will be merged with the existing information to create the final statistics object. Another advantage of incremental statistics is that the percentage of data changes required to trigger an automatic update of the statistics now works at the partition level, instead of the table level. Unfortunately, the histogram is still limited to 200 steps for the entire statistics object in this version of SQL Server.

Let's look at an example of how to update statistics at the partition level to explore its behavior. First, we need to create a partitioned table using the AdventureWorks2019 database:

```
CREATE PARTITION FUNCTION TransactionRangePF1 (datetime)
AS RANGE RIGHT FOR VALUES
(
'20130901', '20131001', '20131101', '20131201',
'20140101', '20140201', '20140301', '20140401',
'20140501', '20140601', '20140701'
)
GO
CREATE PARTITION SCHEME TransactionsPS1 AS PARTITION
TransactionRangePF1 TO
(
```

```
    [PRIMARY], [PRIMARY], [PRIMARY], [PRIMARY], [PRIMARY],
    [PRIMARY], [PRIMARY], [PRIMARY], [PRIMARY], [PRIMARY],
    [PRIMARY], [PRIMARY], [PRIMARY]
)
GO
CREATE TABLE dbo.TransactionHistory
(
TransactionID int NOT NULL,
ProductID int NOT NULL,
ReferenceOrderID int NOT NULL,
ReferenceOrderLineID int NOT NULL DEFAULT (0),
TransactionDate datetime NOT NULL DEFAULT (GETDATE()),
TransactionType nchar(1) NOT NULL,
Quantity int NOT NULL,
ActualCost money NOT NULL,
ModifiedDate datetime NOT NULL DEFAULT (GETDATE()),
CONSTRAINT CK_TransactionType
CHECK (UPPER(TransactionType) IN (N'W', N'S', N'P'))
)
ON TransactionsPS1 (TransactionDate)
GO
```

> **Note**
>
> For details about partitioning and the CREATE PARTITION FUNCTION/SCHEME statements, please refer to *Partitioned Tables and Indexes* in the SQL Server documentation.

We currently have data to populate 12 partitions. Let's start by populating only 11:

```
INSERT INTO dbo.TransactionHistory
SELECT * FROM Production.TransactionHistory
WHERE TransactionDate < '2014-07-01'
```

If required, you can use the following query to inspect the contents of the partitions, where you will see that all the partitions except the last one are now populated:

```
SELECT * FROM sys.partitions
WHERE object_id = OBJECT_ID('dbo.TransactionHistory')
```

Let's create an incremental statistics object using the CREATE STATISTICS statement with the new INCREMENTAL clause set to ON (OFF is the default):

```
CREATE STATISTICS incrstats ON dbo.
TransactionHistory(TransactionDate)
WITH FULLSCAN, INCREMENTAL = ON
```

You can also create incremental statistics while creating an index using the new STATISTICS_ INCREMENTAL clause of the CREATE INDEX statement. You can inspect the created statistics object using the following query:

```
DBCC SHOW_STATISTICS('dbo.TransactionHistory', incrstats)
```

Among other things, you will notice that the created histogram has 200 steps (only the last three are shown here):

	RANGE_HI_KEY	RANGE_ROWS	EQ_ROWS	DISTINCT_RANGE_ROWS
198	2014-06-24 00:00:00.000	187	100	2
199	2014-06-27 00:00:00.000	204	131	2
200	2014-06-30 00:00:00.000	150	131	2

So, we already have the maximum number of steps in a statistics object. What would happen if we added data to a new partition? Let's add data to partition 12:

```
INSERT INTO dbo.TransactionHistory
SELECT * FROM Production.TransactionHistory
WHERE TransactionDate >= '2014-07-01'
```

Now, we must update the statistics object using the following statement:

```
UPDATE STATISTICS dbo.TransactionHistory(incrstats)
WITH RESAMPLE ON PARTITIONS(12)
```

Note the new syntax specifying the partition, where you can specify multiple partitions, separated by commas. The UPDATE STATISTICS statement reads the specified partitions and then merges their results with the existing statistics object to build the global statistics. Note the RESAMPLE clause; this is required because partition statistics objects need to have the same sample rates to be merged to build the global statistics objects. Although only the specified partition was scanned, you can see that SQL Server has rearranged the histogram. The last three steps now show data for the added partition. You can also compare the original histogram with the new one for other minor differences:

	RANGE_HI_KEY	RANGE_ROWS	EQ_ROWS	DISTINCT_RANGE_ROWS
197	2014-06-30 00:00:00.000	150	131	2
198	2014-07-12 00:00:00.000	300	36	9
199	2014-07-22 00:00:00.000	229	43	7
200	2014-08-03 00:00:00.000	363	37	11

If you want to disable the incremental statistics object for any reason, you can use the following statement to go back to the original behavior (or optionally just drop the statistics object and create a new one):

```
UPDATE STATISTICS dbo.TransactionHistory(incrstats)
WITH FULLSCAN, INCREMENTAL = OFF
```

After disabling the incremental statistics, trying to update a partition, as shown previously, will return the following error message:

```
Msg 9111, Level 16, State 1, Line 1
UPDATE STATISTICS ON PARTITIONS syntax is not supported for
non-incremental statistics.
```

Finally, you can also enable incremental statistics for your automatic statistics at the database level, if needed. This requires the INCREMENTAL = ON clause in the ALTER DATABASE statement and also requires AUTO_CREATE_STATISTICS to be set to ON.

To clean up the objects that were created for this exercise, run the following statements:

```
DROP TABLE dbo.TransactionHistory
DROP PARTITION SCHEME TransactionsPS1
DROP PARTITION FUNCTION TransactionRangePF1
```

With this, we have learned all about incremental statistics and how to use it. In the next section, we will learn how to apply statistics to computed columns.

Statistics on computed columns

Another interesting step that's performed during query optimization is automatically matching computed columns. Although computed columns have been available in previous versions of SQL Server, the automatic matching feature was only introduced with SQL Server 2005. In this section, we will show you how this feature works and explain how computed columns can help improve the performance of your queries.

A problem that's faced by some queries that use scalar expressions is that they usually cannot benefit from statistics, and without statistics, the Query Optimizer will use the 30% selectivity guess on inequality comparisons, which may produce inefficient execution plans. A solution to this problem is using computed columns since SQL Server can automatically create and update statistics on these columns. A great benefit of this solution is that you do not need to specify the name of the computed column in your queries for SQL Server to use its statistics. The Query Optimizer automatically matches the computed column definition to an existing scalar expression in a query, so your applications do not need to be changed.

To see an example, run the following query:

```
SELECT * FROM Sales.SalesOrderDetail
WHERE OrderQty * UnitPrice > 10000
```

This creates the following plan:

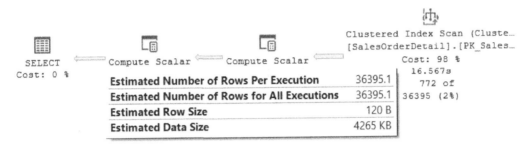

Figure 6.9 – Cardinality estimation example using a 30% guess

The estimated number of rows is 36,395.1, which is 30% of the total number of rows (121,317), although the query returns only 772 records. SQL Server is using a selectivity guess because it cannot estimate the selectivity of the OrderQty * UnitPrice > 10000 expression.

Now, create a computed column:

```
ALTER TABLE Sales.SalesOrderDetail
ADD cc AS OrderQty * UnitPrice
```

Run the previous SELECT statement again and note that, this time, the estimated number of rows has changed and is close to the actual number of rows returned by the query, as shown in the following screenshot. Optionally, you can test replacing 10,000 with some other value, such as 10, 100, 1,000, or 5,000, and compare the actual and the estimated number of rows returned:

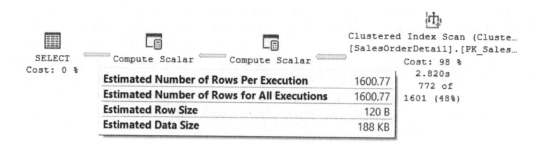

Figure 6.10 – Cardinality estimation example using computed columns

Note that creating the computed column does not create statistics; these statistics are created the first time the query is optimized. You can run the following query to display the information about the statistics objects for the `Sales.SalesOrderDetail` table:

```
SELECT * FROM sys.stats
WHERE object_id = OBJECT_ID('Sales.SalesOrderDetail')
```

The newly created statistics object will most likely be at the end of the list. Copy the name of the object and use the following command to display the details about the statistics object (we have used the name of my local object here, but you should replace that as appropriate):

```
DBCC SHOW_STATISTICS ('Sales.SalesOrderDetail', _WA_
Sys_0000000E_44CA3770)
```

You can also use `cc` as the name of the object to get the same results. The `cc` column should be shown on the `Columns` field in the density section. In any case, the number of rows is estimated using the histogram of the created statistics object, as explained earlier for inequality comparisons:

```
DBCC SHOW_STATISTICS ('Sales.SalesOrderDetail', cc)
```

Unfortunately, and still true for SQL Server 2022, for automatic matching to work, the expression must be the same as the computed column definition. So, if we change the query to `UnitPrice * OrderQty` instead of `OrderQty * UnitPrice`, the execution plan will show an estimated number of rows of 30% again, as shown by the following query:

```
SELECT * FROM Sales.SalesOrderDetail
WHERE UnitPrice * OrderQty > 10000
```

Finally, drop the created computed column:

```
ALTER TABLE Sales.SalesOrderDetail
DROP COLUMN cc
```

Now, let's check out some filtered statistics.

Filtered statistics

Filtered statistics are statistics created on a subset of records in a table. Filtered statistics are automatically created when filtered indexes are created, but they can also be created manually by specifying a WHERE clause on the CREATE STATISTICS statement, in which case a filtered index is not required. As you may imagine, filtered statistics can help with queries accessing specific subsets of data. They can also be useful in situations such as correlated columns, especially when one of these columns has a small number of unique values, and you can create multiple filtered statistics for each of these distinct values. As shown in the *Histogram* section, when using multiple predicates, SQL Server assumes that each clause in a query is independent. If the columns used in this query were correlated, then the cardinality estimation would be incorrect. Even with the exponential backoff behavior of the new cardinality estimator, you can still get better cardinality estimation with filter statistics because each statistics object has its own histogram. Filtered statistics may also help with huge tables where a large number of unique values are not accurately represented in the 200-step limitation currently enforced on histograms.

Next, we learn how to use filtered statistics to help in a problem with correlated columns. Running the following query will correctly estimate the number of rows to be 93:

```
SELECT * FROM Person.Address
WHERE City = 'Los Angeles'
```

In the same way, running the following query will correctly estimate 4,564 rows:

```
SELECT * FROM Person.Address
WHERE StateProvinceID = 9
```

However, because StateProvinceID 9 corresponds to the state of California (which you can verify by looking at the Person.StateProvince table), somebody can run this query, which in this case will show a less precise estimate of 44.8614 rows (this is using the new cardinality estimator, or 21.6403 using the old one):

```
SELECT * FROM Person.Address
WHERE City = 'Los Angeles' AND StateProvinceID = 9
```

This can be seen in the following plan:

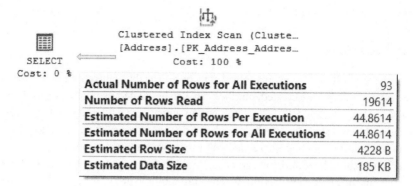

Figure 6.11 – Cardinality estimate with exponential backoff

Because of the assumption of independence, SQL Server will multiply the cardinality of both predicates, as explained earlier in this chapter. The calculation, abbreviated as (93 * 4,564) / 19,614, will give us a value of 21.6403 for the old cardinality estimator (19,614 is the total number of rows in the table). In the case of the exponential backoff used by the new cardinality estimator, the calculation would be (93 / 19,614) * SQRT(4,564 / 19,614) * 19,614, which will be roughly 44.861 rows.

However, both the independence assumption and the exponential backoff are incorrect in this example because the columns are statistically correlated. To help with this problem, you can create a filtered statistics object for the state of California, as shown in the following statement:

```
CREATE STATISTICS california
ON Person.Address(City)
WHERE StateProvinceID = 9
```

Clearing the cache and running the previous query again will now give a better estimate:

```
DBCC FREEPROCCACHE
GO
SELECT * FROM Person.Address
WHERE City = 'Los Angeles' AND StateProvinceID = 9
```

This can be seen in the following plan:

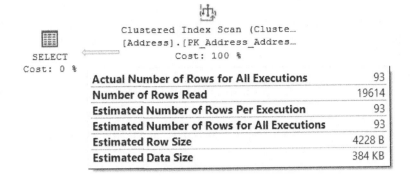

Figure 6.12 – Cardinality estimate with filtered statistics

Now, let's inspect the filtered statistics object by running the following statement:

```
DBCC SHOW_STATISTICS('Person.Address', california)
```

This will produce the following output (edited here to fit the page), showing the estimate of 93 rows for Los Angeles on the EQ_ROWS column:

Name	Rows	Rows Sampled	Filter Expression	Unfiltered Rows
california	4564	4564	([StateProvinceID]=(9))	19614

RANGE_HI_KEY	RANGE_ROWS	EQ_ROWS	DISTINCT_RANGE_ROWS	AVG_RANGE_ROWS
Alhambra	0	1	0	1
Alpine	0	1	0	1
Altadena	0	2	0	1
Auburn	0	1	0	1
Baldwin Park	0	1	0	1
Barstow	0	2	0	1
...				
Los Angeles	0	93	0	1

Notice that the filter definition is shown on the `Filter Expression` field and that the `Unfiltered Rows` field shows the total number of records in the table when the filtered statistics were created. Also, note that this time, the `Rows` column number is less than the total number of rows in the table and corresponds to the number of records that satisfied the `filter` predicate when the statistics object was created. The filter definition can also be seen on the `filter_definition` column of the `sys.stats` catalog view. Also, notice that the histogram only shows cities for California, according to the filter definition (only a few steps are shown).

Finally, drop the statistics object you have just created by running the following statement:

```
DROP STATISTICS Person.Address.california
```

Now, let's explore more functions for statistics.

Statistics on ascending keys

Statistics on ascending keys presents a cardinality estimation problem that has been present in all versions of SQL Server since version 7. Using trace flags 2389 and 2390 has been the best solution to this problem. Starting with SQL Server 2014, you can also use the new cardinality estimator to obtain the same estimation, but without having to use these trace flags.

But first, let's explain what the problem is. As we saw earlier, SQL Server builds a histogram on the first column of each statistics object. With statistics on ascending or descending key columns, such as `IDENTITY` and real-time timestamp columns, newly inserted values usually fall outside the range of values covered by the histogram. In addition, the number of records added might be too small to trigger an automatic update of statistics. Because recently added rows are not covered in the histogram when a significant number of rows should be included, running a query using those values may result in inaccurate cardinality estimates, which may also result in poorly performing plans.

The traditional recommendation from Microsoft to fix this problem has been to manually update statistics after loading data, but unfortunately, this may also require more frequent statistics updates, which may not always be feasible. Trace flags 2389 and 2390, which were first published by Ian Jose from Microsoft in his article *Ascending Keys and Auto Quick Corrected Statistics*, were also introduced with SQL Server 2005 Service Pack 1 to help with this problem.

To show you what the problem is and how these trace flags work, let's start by creating a table in AdventureWorks2019. But first, make sure you are using the old cardinality estimator:

```
ALTER DATABASE AdventureWorks2019 SET COMPATIBILITY_LEVEL = 110
GO
CREATE TABLE dbo.SalesOrderHeader (
SalesOrderID int NOT NULL,
```

```
RevisionNumber tinyint NOT NULL,
OrderDate datetime NOT NULL,
DueDate datetime NOT NULL,
ShipDate datetime NULL,
Status tinyint NOT NULL,
OnlineOrderFlag dbo.Flag NOT NULL,
SalesOrderNumber nvarchar(25) NOT NULL,
PurchaseOrderNumber dbo.OrderNumber NULL,
AccountNumber dbo.AccountNumber NULL,
CustomerID int NOT NULL,
SalesPersonID int NULL,
TerritoryID int NULL,
BillToAddressID int NOT NULL,
ShipToAddressID int NOT NULL,
ShipMethodID int NOT NULL,
CreditCardID int NULL,
CreditCardApprovalCode varchar(15) NULL,
CurrencyRateID int NULL,
SubTotal money NOT NULL,
TaxAmt money NOT NULL,
Freight money NOT NULL,
TotalDue money NOT NULL,
Comment nvarchar(128) NULL,
rowguid uniqueidentifier NOT NULL,
ModifiedDate datetime NOT NULL
)
```

Populate the table with some initial data and create an index on it (notice that both tables have the same name, but in the dbo and Sales schemas, respectively):

```
INSERT INTO dbo.SalesOrderHeader SELECT * FROM Sales.
SalesOrderHeader
WHERE OrderDate < '2014-06-19 00:00:00.000'
CREATE INDEX IX_OrderDate ON SalesOrderHeader(OrderDate)
```

After creating the index, SQL Server will also create a statistics object for it, so a query like this will have a good cardinality estimate of 35 rows (as there is data for July 19, and it is captured on the last step of the statistics histogram object, which you can verify by using the DBCC SHOW_ STATISTICS statement):

```
SELECT * FROM dbo.SalesOrderHeader WHERE OrderDate = '2014-06-
18 00:00:00.000'
```

Now, let's suppose we add new data for June 19:

```
INSERT INTO dbo.SalesOrderHeader SELECT * FROM Sales.
SalesOrderHeader
WHERE OrderDate = '2014-06-19 00:00:00.000'
```

So, let's change the query to look for records for June 19:

```
SELECT * FROM dbo.SalesOrderHeader WHERE OrderDate = '2014-06-
19 00:00:00.000'
```

Because the number of rows added is not enough to trigger an automatic update of statistics, June 19 is not represented on the existing histogram. This anomaly means that SQL Server will use an estimate of 1, as shown here:

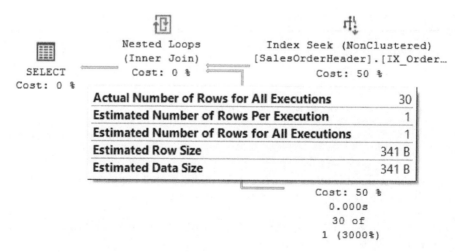

Figure 6.13 – Bad cardinality estimate after new records are added

Although the plans for both queries in this example are very similar, a bad cardinality estimate may produce bad plans in some more realistic scenarios and queries.

Trace flag 2389

Now, let's see how trace flag 2389 helps with this problem. Run the following statements (notice that trace flag 2388 has not been mentioned before and will be explained shortly):

```
DBCC TRACEON (2388)
DBCC TRACEON (2389)
```

Trace flag 2389, which was introduced with SQL Server 2005 Service Pack 1, begins to track the nature of columns via subsequent operations of updating statistics. When the statistics are seen to increase three times in a row, the column is branded Ascending. Trace flag 2388 is not required to enable the behavior described in this article but enables previously hidden metadata to be displayed. This is useful to show how trace flags 2389 and 2390 work and determine if a column has been branded as Ascending. The trace flag changes the output of the DBCC SHOW_STATISTICS statement to show you a historical view of the most recent statistics update operations.

Trace flag 2390 enables a similar behavior to 2389, even if the ascending nature of the column is not known, but we will not cover that here. Run DBCC SHOW_STATISTICS:

```
DBCC SHOW_STATISTICS ('dbo.SalesOrderHeader', 'IX_OrderDate')
```

The statement shows the following output (condensed to fit the page):

Updated	Rows Above	Rows Below	Inserts Since Last Update	Deletes Since Last Update	Leading column Type
Jun 7 2022	NULL	NULL	NULL	NULL	Unknown

There's not much data for now. However, we will show you this output after three consecutive batches of inserting data and updating statistics. Run the following statement to update the statistics, including the data you just added for June 19:

```
UPDATE STATISTICS dbo.SalesOrderHeader WITH FULLSCAN
```

DBCC SHOW_STATISTICS now shows the following:

Updated	Rows Above	Rows Below	Inserts Since Last Update	Deletes Since Last Update	Leading column Type
Jun 7 2022	30	0	30	0	Unknown
Jun 7 2022	NULL	NULL	NULL	NULL	NULL

Here, Rows Above and Inserts Since Last Update account for the 30 rows that were added previously (you may need to scroll to the right). Now, run the second batch for June 20:

```
INSERT INTO dbo.SalesOrderHeader SELECT * FROM Sales.
SalesOrderHeader
WHERE OrderDate = '2014-06-20 00:00:00.000'
```

Again, running this query will verify the one-row estimate in the plan:

```
SELECT * FROM dbo.SalesOrderHeader WHERE OrderDate = '2014-06-
20 00:00:00.000'
```

Now, update the statistics again:

```
UPDATE STATISTICS dbo.SalesOrderHeader WITH FULLSCAN
```

DBCC SHOW_STATISTICS now shows the following. Notice a new record with Inserts Since Last Update and Rows Above, with a value of 27. Leading column Type still shows Unknown:

Updated	Rows Above	Rows Below	Inserts Since Last Update	Deletes Since Last Update	Leading column Type
Jun 7 2022	27	0	27	0	Unknown
Jun 7 2022	30	0	30	0	NULL
Jun 7 2022	NULL	NULL	NULL	NULL	NULL

Now, it's time for a third batch:

```
INSERT INTO dbo.SalesOrderHeader SELECT * FROM Sales.
SalesOrderHeader
WHERE OrderDate = '2014-06-21 00:00:00.000'
```

Update the statistics one last time:

```
UPDATE STATISTICS dbo.SalesOrderHeader WITH FULLSCAN
DBCC SHOW_STATISTICS now shows this:
```

Updated	Rows Above	Rows Below	Inserts Since Last Update	Deletes Since Last Update	Leading column Type
Jun 7 2022	32	0	32	0	Ascending
Jun 7 2022	27	0	27	0	NULL
Jun 7 2022	30	0	30	0	NULL
Jun 7 2022	NULL	NULL	NULL	NULL	NULL

In addition to the new record accounting for the 32 rows that were added, you will notice that the branding was changed to `Ascending`. Once the column is branded as `Ascending`, SQL Server will be able to give you a better cardinality estimate, without having to manually update the statistics. To test it, try this batch:

```
INSERT INTO dbo.SalesOrderHeader SELECT * FROM Sales.
SalesOrderHeader
WHERE OrderDate = '2014-06-22 00:00:00.000'
```

Now, run the following query:

```
SELECT * FROM dbo.SalesOrderHeader WHERE OrderDate = '2014-06-
22 00:00:00.000'
```

This time, we get a better cardinality estimate. Notice that UPDATE STATISTICS wasn't required this time. Instead of the estimate of one row, now, we get 27.9677. But where is this value coming from? The Query Optimizer is now using the density information of the statistics object. As explained earlier, the definition of density is 1 / "number of distinct values," and the estimated number of rows is obtained using the density multiplied by the number of records in the table, which in this case is 0.000896861 * 31184, or 27.967713424, as shown in the plan. Also, notice that density information is only used for values not covered in the histogram (you can see the density information using the same DBCC SHOW_STATISTICS statement, but in another session where trace flag 2388 is not enabled).

In addition, if we look for data that does not exist, we still get the one-row estimate, which is always adequate because it will return 0 records:

```
SELECT * FROM dbo.SalesOrderHeader WHERE OrderDate = '2014-06-
23 00:00:00.000'
```

Notice that branding a column as `Ascending` requires statistics to increase three times in a row. If we insert older data later, breaking the ascending sequence, the `Leading column Type` column will show as `Stationary` and the query processor will be back to the original cardinality estimate behavior. Making three new additional updates to a row with increasing values can brand it as `Ascending` again.

Finally, you could use the trace flags on a query without defining them at the session or global level using the QUERYTRACEON hint, as shown here:

```
SELECT * FROM dbo.SalesOrderHeader WHERE OrderDate = '2014-06-
22 00:00:00.000'
OPTION (QUERYTRACEON 2389, QUERYTRACEON 2390)
```

Trace flags 2389 and 2390 are no longer needed if you are using the new cardinality estimator, and you will get the same behavior and estimation. To see how it works, drop the `dbo.SalesOrderHeader` table:

```
DROP TABLE dbo.SalesOrderHeader
```

Disable trace flags 2388 and 2389, as shown here, or open a new session:

```
DBCC TRACEOFF (2388)
DBCC TRACEOFF (2389)
```

> **Note**
>
> You can also make sure that the trace flags are not enabled by running DBCC TRACESTATUS.

Create `dbo.SalesOrderHeader`, as indicated at the beginning of this section. Insert some data again and create an index, as shown here:

```
INSERT INTO dbo.SalesOrderHeader SELECT * FROM Sales.
SalesOrderHeader
WHERE OrderDate < '2014-06-19 00:00:00.000'
CREATE INDEX IX_OrderDate ON SalesOrderHeader(OrderDate)
```

Now, add new data for June 19:

```
INSERT INTO dbo.SalesOrderHeader SELECT * FROM Sales.
SalesOrderHeader
WHERE OrderDate = '2014-06-19 00:00:00.000'
```

This is the same as we got previously because the number of rows that we've added is too small – it is not enough to trigger an automatic update of statistics. Running the following query with the old cardinality estimator will estimate one row, as we saw earlier:

```
ALTER DATABASE AdventureWorks2019 SET COMPATIBILITY_LEVEL = 110
GO
SELECT * FROM dbo.SalesOrderHeader WHERE OrderDate = '2014-06-
19 00:00:00.000'
```

Running the same query with the new cardinality estimator will give a better estimate of 27.9631, without the need to use trace flags 2390 and 2390:

```
ALTER DATABASE AdventureWorks2019 SET COMPATIBILITY_LEVEL = 160
GO
```

```
SELECT * FROM dbo.SalesOrderHeader WHERE OrderDate = '2014-06-
19 00:00:00.000'
```

27.9631 is estimated the same way as explained earlier – that is, using the density multiplied by the number of records in the table, which in this case is 0.0008992806 * 31095, or 27.9631302570. But remember to use DBCC SHOW_STATISTICS against this new version of the table to obtain the new density.

Now that we have covered various statistics functions, we will explore some unique options that are part of the UPDATE STATISTICS statement.

UPDATE STATISTICS with ROWCOUNT and PAGECOUNT

The undocumented ROWCOUNT and PAGECOUNT options of the UPDATE STATISTICS statement are used by the **Data Engine Tuning Advisor (DTA)** to script and copy statistics when you want to configure a test server to tune the workload of a production server. You can also see these statements in action if you script a statistics object. As an example, try the following in Management Studio: select **Databases**, right-click the **AdventureWorks2019** database, select **Tasks**, **Generate Scripts…**, click **Next**, select **Select specific database objects**, expand **Tables**, select **Sales.SalesOrderDetail**, click **Next**, click **Advanced**, look for the **Script Statistics** choice, and select **Script statistics and histograms**. Finally, choose **True** for **Script Indexes**. Click **OK** and finish the wizard to generate the scripts. You will get a script with a few UPDATE STATISTICS statements, similar to what's shown here (with the STATS_STREAM value shortened to fit this page):

```
UPDATE STATISTICS [Sales].[SalesOrderDetail]([IX_
SalesOrderDetail_ProductID])
WITH STATS_STREAM = 0x0100000003000000000000000 ..., ROWCOUNT =
121317,
PAGECOUNT = 274
```

In this section, you will learn how to use the ROWCOUNT and PAGECOUNT options of the UPDATE STATISTICS statement in cases where you want to see which execution plans would be generated for huge tables (for example, with millions of records), but then test those plans in small or even empty tables. As you can imagine, these options can be helpful for testing in some scenarios where you may not want to spend time or disk space creating big tables.

By using this method, you are asking the Query Optimizer to generate execution plans using cardinality estimations as if the table contained millions of records, even if your table is tiny or empty. Note that this option, available since SQL Server 2005, only helps in creating the execution plan for your queries. Running the query will use the real data in your test table, which will, of course, execute faster than a table with millions of records.

Using these UPDATE STATISTICS options does not change the table statistics – it only changes the counters for the numbers of rows and pages of a table. As we will see shortly, the Query Optimizer uses this information to estimate the cardinality of queries. Finally, before we look at examples, keep in mind that these are undocumented and unsupported options and should not be used in a production environment.

So, let's look at an example. Run the following query to create a new table on the Adventure Works2019 database:

```
SELECT * INTO dbo.Address
FROM Person.Address
```

Inspect the number of rows by running the following query; the row_count column should show 19,614 rows:

```
SELECT * FROM sys.dm_db_partition_stats
WHERE object_id = OBJECT_ID('dbo.Address')
```

Now, run the following query and inspect the graphical execution plan:

```
SELECT * FROM dbo.Address
WHERE City = 'London'
```

Running this query will create a new statistics object for the City column and will show the following plan. Note that the estimated number of rows is 434 and that it's using a simple **Table Scan** operator:

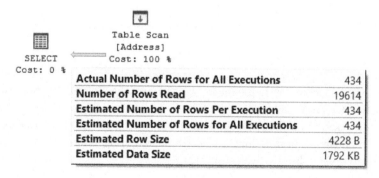

Actual Number of Rows for All Executions	434
Number of Rows Read	19614
Estimated Number of Rows Per Execution	434
Estimated Number of Rows for All Executions	434
Estimated Row Size	4228 B
Estimated Data Size	1792 KB

Figure 6.14 – Cardinality estimation example using a small table

We can discover where the Query Optimizer is getting the estimated number of rows by inspecting the statistics object. Using the methodology shown in the *Histogram* section, you can find out the name of the statistics object and then use DBCC SHOW_STATISTICS to show its histogram. By looking at the histogram, you can find a value of 434 on EQ_ROWS for the RANGE_HI_KEY value 'London'.

Now, run the following UPDATE STATISTICS WITH ROWCOUNT, PAGECOUNT statement (you can specify any other value for ROWCOUNT and PAGECOUNT):

```
UPDATE STATISTICS dbo.Address WITH ROWCOUNT = 1000000,
PAGECOUNT = 100000
```

If you inspect the number of rows from sys.dm_db_partition_stats again, as shown previously, it will now show 1,000,000 rows (the new number of pages is also shown by the in_row_data_page_count column). Clear the plan cache and run the query again:

```
DBCC FREEPROCCACHE
GO
SELECT * FROM dbo.Address WHERE City = 'London'
```

Note that the estimated number of rows has changed from 434 to 22,127.1, as shown here:

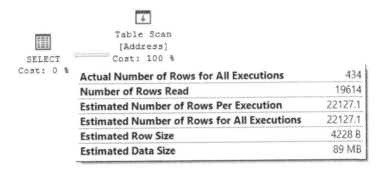

Actual Number of Rows for All Executions	434
Number of Rows Read	19614
Estimated Number of Rows Per Execution	22127.1
Estimated Number of Rows for All Executions	22127.1
Estimated Row Size	4228 B
Estimated Data Size	89 MB

Figure 6.15 – Cardinality estimation using ROWCOUNT and PAGECOUNT

However, if you look at the statistics object again while using DBCC SHOW_STATISTICS, as shown previously, you'll see that the histogram has not changed. One way to obtain the estimated number of rows shown in the new execution plan is by calculating the percentage (or fraction) of rows for London from the statistics sample, which in this case is 19,614. So, the fraction is 434 / 19,614, or 0.022127052. Next, we apply the same percentage to the new "current" number of rows, which results in 1,000,000 * 0.022127052, and we get 22,127.1, which is the estimated number of rows displayed in the preceding plan.

Finally, if you want to restore the real values for rows and pages, perhaps to perform additional testing, you can use the DBCC UPDATEUSAGE statement. DBCC UPDATEUSAGE can be used to correct pages and row count inaccuracies in the catalog views. Run the following statement:

```
DBCC UPDATEUSAGE(AdventureWorks2019, 'dbo.Address') WITH COUNT_
ROWS
```

However, after you finish your testing, it is recommended that you drop this table to avoid any page and row count inaccuracies left by mistake:

```
DROP TABLE dbo.Address
```

Now that we know how to work with various statistics options, we will learn how to maintain and update them.

Statistics maintenance

As mentioned previously, the Query Optimizer will, by default, automatically update statistics when they are out of date. Statistics can also be updated with the UPDATE STATISTICS statement, which you can schedule to run as a maintenance job. Another statement that's commonly used, sp_updatestats, also runs UPDATE STATISTICS behind the scenes.

There are two important benefits of updating statistics in a maintenance job. The first is that your queries will use updated statistics without having to wait for the statistics to be automatically updated, thus avoiding delays in the optimization of your queries (although asynchronous statistics updates can also be used to partially help with this problem). The second benefit is that you can use a bigger sample than the Query Optimizer will use, or you can even scan the entire table. This can give you better-quality statistics for big tables, especially for those where data is not randomly distributed in their data pages. Manually updating statistics can also be a benefit after operations such as batch data loads, which update large amounts of data, are performed.

On the other hand, note that updating the statistics will cause plans already in the plan cache that are using these statistics to be compiled, so you may not want to update statistics too frequently either.

An additional consideration for manually updating statistics in a maintenance job is how they relate to index rebuild maintenance jobs, which also update the index statistics. Keep the following items in mind when combining maintenance jobs for both indexes and statistics, remembering that there are both index and non-index column statistics, and that index operations may only impact the first of these:

- Rebuilding an index (for example, by using the ALTER INDEX ... REBUILD statement) will also update index statistics by scanning all the rows in the table, which is the equivalent of using UPDATE STATISTICS WITH FULLSCAN. Rebuilding indexes does not update any column statistics.

- Reorganizing an index (for example, using the ALTER INDEX ... REORGANIZE statement) does not update any statistics, not even index statistics.

- By default, the UPDATE STATISTICS statement updates both index and column statistics. Using the INDEX option will only update index statistics while using the COLUMNS option will only update nonindexed column statistics.

Therefore, depending on your maintenance jobs and scripts, several scenarios can exist. The simplest maintenance plan is if you want to rebuild all the indexes and update all the statistics. As mentioned previously, if you rebuild all your indexes, then all the index statistics will also be automatically updated by scanning all the rows in the table. Then, you just need to update your non-indexed column statistics by running UPDATE STATISTICS WITH FULLSCAN, COLUMNS. Because the index rebuild job only updates index statistics, and the second one only updates column statistics, it does not matter which one is executed first.

Of course, more complicated maintenance plans exist – for example, when indexes are rebuilt or reorganized depending on their fragmentation level, a topic that was covered in more detail in *Chapter 5, Working with Indexes.* You should keep the items mentioned previously in mind so that you can avoid problems such as updating the index statistics twice, which could occur when both the index rebuild and update statistics operations are performed. You should also avoid discarding previously performed work – for example, when you rebuild the indexes of a table, which also updates statistics by scanning the entire table – and later running a job that updates the statistics with the default or smaller sample. In this case, previously updated statistics are replaced with statistics that have potentially less quality.

Let me show you how these commands work with some examples. Create a new table called dbo.SalesOrderDetail:

```
SELECT * INTO dbo.SalesOrderDetail FROM Sales.SalesOrderDetail
```

The following query uses the sys.stats catalog view to show that there are no statistics objects for the new table:

```
SELECT name, auto_created, STATS_DATE(object_id, stats_id) AS
update_date
FROM sys.stats
WHERE object_id = OBJECT_ID('dbo.SalesOrderDetail')
```

Now, run the following query:

```
SELECT * FROM dbo.SalesOrderDetail
WHERE SalesOrderID = 43670 AND OrderQty = 1
```

Use the previous query using sys.stats to verify that two statistics objects were created – one for the SalesOrderID column and a second for the OrderQty column. Now, create the following index and run the sys.stats query again to verify that a new statistics object for the ProductID column has been created:

```
CREATE INDEX IX_ProductID ON dbo.SalesOrderDetail(ProductID)
```

The following table shows the output of the `sys.stats` query so far:

name	auto_created	update_date
_WA_Sys_00000004_4DD47EBD	1	1/11/2014 8:11:34 PM
_WA_Sys_00000001_4DD47EBD	1	1/11/2014 8:11:34 PM
IX_ProductID	0	1/11/2014 8:14:31 PM

Notice how the value of the `auto_created` column, which indicates whether the statistics were created by the Query Optimizer, is 0 for the `IX_ProductID` statistics object. Run the following command to update just the column statistics:

```
UPDATE STATISTICS dbo.SalesOrderDetail WITH FULLSCAN, COLUMNS
```

You can validate that only the column statistics were updated by comparing the `update_date` column with the previous output. The `update_date` column uses the `STATS_DATE` function to display the last point in time when the statistics were updated, as shown in the following output:

Name	auto_created	update_date
_WA_Sys_00000004_4DD47EBD	1	1/11/2014 8:16:54 PM
_WA_Sys_00000001_4DD47EBD	1	1/11/2014 8:16:55 PM
IX_ProductID	0	1/11/2014 8:14:31 PM

This command will do the same for just the index statistics:

```
UPDATE STATISTICS dbo.SalesOrderDetail WITH FULLSCAN, INDEX
```

The following commands will update both the index and column statistics:

```
UPDATE STATISTICS dbo.SalesOrderDetail WITH FULLSCAN
UPDATE STATISTICS dbo.SalesOrderDetail WITH FULLSCAN, ALL
```

As mentioned earlier, if you run the `sys.stats` query after each of the following two queries, you'll see how an `ALTER INDEX REBUILD` statement only updates index statistics:

```
ALTER INDEX ix_ProductID ON dbo.SalesOrderDetail REBUILD
```

You can verify that reorganizing an index does not update any statistics like so:

```
ALTER INDEX ix_ProductID on dbo.SalesOrderDetail REORGANIZE
```

Finally, for good housekeeping, remove the table you have just created:

```
DROP TABLE dbo.SalesOrderDetail
```

Finally, we strongly recommend using Ola Hallengren's SQL Server maintenance solution for SQL Server backup, integrity check, and index and statistics maintenance jobs. Ola Hallengren's SQL Server maintenance solution is free and you can find it at `https://ola.hallengren.com`.

Cost estimation

As we have established, the quality of the execution plans the Query Optimizer generates is directly related to the accuracy of its costing estimates. Even when the Query Optimizer can enumerate low-cost plans, an incorrect cost estimation may result in the Query Optimizer choosing inefficient plans, which can negatively impact the performance of your database. During query optimization, the Query Optimizer explores many candidate plans, estimates their cost, and then selects the most efficient one.

Costs are estimated for any partial or complete plan, as shown in *Chapter 3, The Query Optimizer*, when we explored the content of the Memo structure. Cost computation is done per operator, and the total plan cost is the sum of the costs of all the operators in that plan. The cost of each operator depends on its algorithm and the estimated number of records it returns.

Some operators, such as Sort and Hash Join, also consider the available memory in the system. A high-level overview of the cost of the algorithms for some of the most used operators was provided in *Chapter 4, The Execution Engine*.

So, each operator has an associated CPU cost; some of them will also have some I/O cost, and the cost of the operator as a whole is the sum of these costs. An operator such as a Clustered Index Scan has both CPU and I/O costs, whereas some other operators, such as Stream Aggregate, will only have a CPU cost. Because it is not documented how these costs are calculated, I will show you a basic example of how the cost of a plan is estimated.

To demonstrate this in an example, let's look at the largest table in the AdventureWorks database. Run the following query and look at the estimated CPU and I/O costs for the Clustered Index Scan operator:

```
SELECT * FROM Sales.SalesOrderDetail
WHERE LineTotal = 35
```

Note that in an older version of SQL Server, when the current Query Optimizer was built, the cost used to mean the estimated time in seconds that a query would take to execute on a specific hardware configuration. However, at the time of writing, this value is meaningless as an objective unit of measurement and should not be interpreted as one. Its purpose is to solely be used internally to pick between different candidate plans.

For a Clustered Index Scan operator, it has been observed that the CPU cost is 0.0001581 for the first record, plus 0.0000011 for any additional record after that. Because we have an estimated 121,317 records here, we can calculate 0.0001581 + 0.0000011 * (121317 – 1), which comes to 0.133606, which is the value shown as Estimated CPU Cost in *Figure 6.17*. Similarly, we noticed that the minimum I/O cost is 0.003125 for the first database page, and then it grows in increments of 0.00074074 for every additional page. Because this operator scans the entire table, we can use the following query to find the number of database pages (which turns out to be 1,239):

```
SELECT in_row_data_page_count, row_count
FROM sys.dm_db_partition_stats
WHERE object_id = OBJECT_ID('Sales.SalesOrderDetail')
AND index_id = 1
```

In this case, we have 0.003125 + 0.00074074 * (1238), which comes to roughly 0.920162, which is the value shown as Estimated I/O Cost.

Finally, we add both costs, 0.133606 + 0. 920162, to get 1.05377, which is the total estimated cost of the operator. Notice that this formula is for the Clustered Index Scan operator. Other operations may have similar or different formulas. In the same way, adding the cost of all the operators will give us the total cost of the plan. In this case, the cost of the Clustered Index Scan (1. 05377) plus the cost of the first Compute Scalar operator (0.01213), the second Compute Scalar operator (0.01213), and the Filter operator (0.05823) will give the total cost of the plan as 1.13626.

Summary

In this chapter, we learned how SQL Server uses statistics to estimate the cardinality as well as the cost of operators and execution plans. The most important elements of a statistics object – namely the histogram, the density information, and string statistics – were introduced and explained. Examples of how to use histograms were shown, including queries with equality and inequality operators and both AND'ed and OR'ed predicates. The use of density information was shown in GROUP BY operations, as well as in cases when the Query Optimizer can't use a histogram, such as in the case of local variables.

Statistics maintenance was also explained, with some emphasis on how to proactively update statistics to avoid delays during query optimization, and how to improve the quality of statistics by scanning the entire table instead of a default sample. We also discussed how to detect cardinality estimation errors, which can negatively impact the quality of your execution plans, and we looked at recommendations on how to fix them.

7
In-Memory OLTP

Relational database management systems (RDBMSs) were originally architected in the late 1970s. Since the hardware was vastly different in those days, recently, there has been extensive research in the database community indicating that a new design and architectural approach should be required for the hardware available today.

RDBMSs were originally designed under the assumption that computer memory was limited and expensive and that databases were many times larger than the main memory. Because of that, it was decided that data should reside on disk. With current hardware having memory sizes and disk volumes thousands of times larger, and processors thousands of times faster, these assumptions are no longer true. In addition, disk access has been subject to physical limits since its introduction; it has not increased at a similar pace and continues to be the slowest part of the system. Although memory capacity has grown dramatically – which is not the case for the size of OLTP databases – one of the new design considerations is that an OLTP engine should be memory-based instead of disk-oriented since most OLTP databases can now fit into the main memory.

In addition, research performed early on for the Hekaton project at Microsoft showed that even with the current hardware available today, a 10 to 100 times performance improvement could not be achieved using current SQL Server mechanisms; instead, it would require dramatically changing the way data management systems are designed. SQL Server is already highly optimized, so using existing techniques could not deliver dramatic performance gains or orders of magnitude speedup. Even after the main memory engine was built, there was still significant time spent in query processing, so they realized they needed to drastically reduce the number of instructions executed. Taking advantage of available memory is not just a matter of reading more of the existing disk pages to memory – it involves redesigning data management systems using a different approach to gain the most benefit from this new hardware. Finally, standard concurrency control mechanisms available today do not scale up to the high transaction rates achievable by an in-memory-optimized database, so locking becomes the next bottleneck.

Specialized in-memory database engines have appeared on the market in the last two decades, including **Oracle TimesTen** and **IBM solidDB**. Microsoft also started shipping in-memory technologies with the xVelocity in-memory analytics engine as part of SQL Server Analysis Services and the xVelocity memory-optimized columnstore indexes integrated into the SQL Server database engine. In-memory OLTP, code-named Hekaton, was introduced in SQL Server 2014 as a new OLTP in-memory database engine. Hekaton's performance improvement is based on three major architecture areas: optimization for main memory access, compiling procedures to native code, and lock and latches elimination. We will look at these three major areas in this chapter.

In this chapter, we cover Hekaton. xVelocity memory-optimized columnstore indexes will be covered in *Chapter 11, An Introduction to Data Warehouses*. To differentiate the Hekaton engine terminology from the standard SQL Server engine covered in the rest of this book, this chapter will call Hekaton tables and stored procedures memory-optimized tables and natively compiled stored procedures, respectively. Standard tables and procedures will be called disk-based tables and regular or interpreted stored procedures, respectively.

This chapter covers the following topics:

- In-memory OLTP architecture
- Tables and indexes
- Natively compiled stored procedures
- Limitations and later enhancements

In-memory OLTP architecture

One of the main strategic decisions made during the Hekaton project was to build a new database engine fully integrated into SQL Server instead of creating a new, separate product as other vendors did. This gave users several advantages, such as enabling existing applications to run without code changes, and not needing to buy and learn about a separate product. As mentioned earlier, Hekaton can provide a several orders of magnitude performance increase based on the following:

- **Optimized tables and indexes for main memory data access**: Hekaton tables and indexes are designed and optimized for memory. They are not stored as database pages, and they do not use a memory buffer pool either.

- **T-SQL modules compiled to native code**: Stored procedures can be optimized by the SQL Server query optimizer, like any regular stored procedure, and then compiled into highly efficient machine code. When this happens, trigger and scalar user-defined functions can also be natively compiled.

- **Locks and latches elimination**: Hekaton implements a new optimistic **multiversion concurrency control** (MVCC) mechanism, which uses new data structures to eliminate traditional locks and latches, so there is no waiting because of blocking.

Note

In-memory OLTP was mostly known as Hekaton in its first few years and the name was used extensively in many texts and documents, including the first edition of this book. We will try to use in-memory OLTP as much as possible in the rest of this chapter.

The lack of a locking and latching mechanism does not mean that chaos will ensue as in-memory OLTP uses MVCC to provide snapshots, repeatable read, and serializable transaction isolation, as covered later. The Hekaton database engine has three major components, as shown in the following diagram:

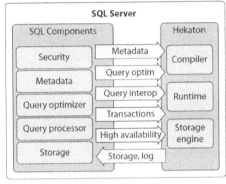

Figure 7.1 – The Hekaton database engine

The three major components are as follows:

- **Hekaton storage engine**: This component manages tables and indexes while providing support for storage, transactions, recoverability, high availability, and so on.

- **Hekaton compiler**: This component compiles procedures and tables into native code, which are loaded as DLLs into the SQL Server process.

- **Hekaton runtime system**: This component provides integration with other SQL Server resources.

Hekaton memory-optimized tables are stored in memory using new data structures that are completely different from traditional disk-based tables. They are also kept on disk but only for durability purposes, so they are only read from disk during database recovery, such as when the SQL Server instance starts. In-memory OLTP tables are fully ACID – that is, they guarantee the Atomicity, Consistency, Isolation, and Durability properties – although a nondurable version of the tables is available as well, in which data is not persisted on disk. Memory-optimized tables must have at least one index, and there is no data structure equivalent to a heap. SQL Server uses the same transaction log as the normal engine to log operations for both disk-based and memory-optimized tables, but in-memory transaction log records are optimized and consume less overall log space. In-memory OLTP indexes are only maintained in memory, so they are never persisted on disk. Consequently, their operations are never logged. Indexes are rebuilt when data is loaded into memory at SQL Server restart.

Although natively compiled stored procedures can only access memory-optimized tables, SQL Server provides operators for accessing and updating Hekaton tables, which can be used by interpreted T-SQL. This functionality is provided by a new component called the query interop, which also allows you to access and update both memory-optimized and regular tables in the same transaction.

In-memory OLTP can help in applications experiencing CPU, I/O, and locking bottlenecks. By using natively compiled stored procedures, fewer instructions are executed than with a traditional stored procedure, thus helping in cases where the execution time is dominated by the stored procedure code. Except for logging, no I/O is required during normal database operations, and Hekaton even requires less logging than operations with regular disk-based tables. Applications with concurrency issues, such as contention in locks, latches, and spinlocks, can also greatly benefit from Hekaton because it does not use locks and latches when accessing data.

> **Note**
>
> A particular scenario where in-memory OLTP can greatly improve performance is in the so-called last-page insert problem on traditional tables. This problem happens when latch contention is caused. This is when many threads continually attempt to update the last page of an index due to the use of incremental keys. By eliminating latches and locks, Hekaton can make these operations extremely fast.

However, in-memory OLTP cannot be used to improve performance if your application has memory or network bottlenecks. Hekaton requires that all the tables defined as memory-optimized actually fit in memory, so your installation must have enough RAM to fit them all.

Finally, Hekaton was originally only available in the 64-bit version of SQL Server 2014 and was an Enterprise Edition-only feature. However, starting with SQL Server 2016 Service Pack 1, in-memory OLTP, along with all the application and programmability features of SQL Server, has been available on all the editions of the product, including Express and Standard. Also, starting with the 2016 release, SQL Server is only available for the 64-bit architecture.

Now that we have a better understanding of the in-memory OLTP architecture, let's start looking at the technology.

Tables and indexes

As explained earlier, Hekaton tables can be accessed either by natively compiled stored procedures or by standard T-SQL, such as ad hoc queries or standard stored procedures. Tables are stored in memory, and each row can potentially have multiple versions. Versions are kept in memory instead of `tempdb`, which is what the versioning mechanism of the standard database engine uses. Versions that are no longer needed – that is, that are no longer visible to any transaction – are deleted to avoid filling up the available memory. This process is known as garbage collection.

Chapter 5, Working with Indexes, introduced indexes for traditional tables. Memory-optimized tables also benefit from indexes, and in this section, we will talk about these indexes and how they are different from their disk-based counterparts. As explained earlier, Hekaton indexes are never persisted to disk; they only exist in memory, and because of that, their operations are not logged in the transaction log. Only index metadata is persisted, and indexes are rebuilt when data is loaded into memory at SQL Server restart.

Two different kinds of indexes exist on Hekaton: hash and range indexes, both of which are lock-free implementations. Hash indexes support index seeks on equality predicates, but they cannot be used with inequality predicates or to return sorted data. Range indexes can be used for range scans, ordered scans, and operations with inequality predicates. Range indexes can also be used for index seeks on equality predicates, but hash indexes offer far better performance and are the recommended choice for this kind of operation.

> **Note**
> Range indexes are called *nonclustered indexes* or *memory-optimized nonclustered indexes* in the latest updates of the SQL Server documentation. Keep that in mind in case *range indexes* is no longer used in future documentation.

Hash indexes are not ordered indexes; scanning them would return records in random order. Both kinds of indexes are covering indexes; the index contains memory pointers to the table rows where all the columns can be retrieved. You cannot directly access a record without using an index, so at least one index is required to locate the data in memory.

Although the concepts of fragmentation and fill factor, as explained in *Chapter 5, Working with Indexes*, do not apply to Hekaton indexes, we may see that we can get similar but new behavior with the bucket count configuration: a hash index can have empty buckets, resulting in wasted space that impacts the performance of index scans, or there might be a large number of records in a single bucket, which may impact the performance of search operations. In addition, updating and deleting records can create a new kind of fragmentation on the underlying data disk storage.

Creating in-memory OLTP tables

Creating a memory-optimized table requires a memory-optimized filegroup. The following error is returned if you try to create a table and you do not have one:

```
Msg 41337, Level 16, State 0, Line 1
Cannot create memory optimized tables. To create memory
optimized tables, the database must have a MEMORY_OPTIMIZED_
FILEGROUP that is online and has at least  one container.
```

You can either create a new database with a memory-optimized filegroup or add one to an existing database. The following statement shows the first scenario:

```
CREATE DATABASE Test
ON PRIMARY (NAME = Test_data,
FILENAME = 'C:\DATA\Test_data.mdf', SIZE=500MB),
FILEGROUP Test_fg CONTAINS MEMORY_OPTIMIZED_DATA
(NAME = Test_fg, FILENAME = 'C:\DATA\Test_fg')
LOG ON (NAME = Test_log, Filename='C:\DATA\Test_log.ldf',
SIZE=500MB)
COLLATE Latin1_General_100_BIN2
```

Note that in the preceding code, a `C:\Data` folder is being used; change this as appropriate for your installation. The following code shows how to add a memory-optimized data filegroup to an existing database:

```
CREATE DATABASE Test
ON PRIMARY (NAME = Test_data,
FILENAME = 'C:\DATA\Test_data.mdf', SIZE=500MB)
LOG ON (NAME = Test_log, Filename='C:\DATA\Test_log.ldf',
SIZE=500MB)
GO
ALTER DATABASE Test ADD FILEGROUP Test_fg CONTAINS MEMORY_
OPTIMIZED_DATA
GO
ALTER DATABASE Test ADD FILE (NAME = Test_fg, FILENAME = N'C:\
DATA\Test_fg')
TO FILEGROUP Test_fg
GO
```

> **Note**
>
> You may have noticed that the first `CREATE DATABASE` statement has a `COLLATE` clause but the second does not. There were some collation restrictions on the original release that were lifted on SQL Server 2016. More details on this can be found at the end of this chapter.

Once you have a database with a memory-optimized filegroup, you are ready to create your first memory-optimized table. For this exercise, you will copy data from AdventureWorks2019 to the newly created Test database. You may notice that scripting any of the AdventureWorks2019 tables and using the resulting code to create a new memory-optimized table will immediately show the first limitation of Hekaton: not all table properties were supported on the initial release, as we will see later. You could also use Memory Optimization Advisor to help you migrate disk-based tables to memory-optimized tables.

> **Note**
> You can run Memory Optimization Advisor by right-clicking a table in SQL Server Management Studio and selecting it from the available menu choices. In the same way, you can run Native Compilation Advisor by right-clicking any stored procedure you want to convert into native code.

Creating a memory-optimized table requires the MEMORY_OPTIMIZED clause, which needs to be set to ON. Explicitly defining DURABILITY as SCHEMA_AND_DATA is also recommended, although this is its default value if the DURABILITY clause is not specified.

Using our new Test database, you can try to create a table that only defines MEMORY_OPTIMIZED, as shown here:

```
CREATE TABLE TransactionHistoryArchive (
TransactionID int NOT NULL,
ProductID int NOT NULL,
ReferenceOrderID int NOT NULL,
ReferenceOrderLineID int NOT NULL,
TransactionDate datetime NOT NULL,
TransactionType nchar(1) NOT NULL,
Quantity int NOT NULL,
ActualCost money NOT NULL,
ModifiedDate datetime NOT NULL
) WITH (MEMORY_OPTIMIZED = ON)
```

However, you will get the following error:

```
Msg 41321, Level 16, State 7, Line 1
The memory optimized table 'TransactionHistoryArchive' with
DURABILITY=SCHEMA_AND_DATA must have a primary key.
Msg 1750, Level 16, State 0, Line 1
Could not create constraint or index. See previous errors.
```

Because this error indicates that a memory-optimized table must have a primary, you could define one by changing the following line:

```
TransactionID int NOT NULL PRIMARY KEY,
```

However, you will still get the following message:

```
Msg 12317, Level 16, State 76, Line 17
Clustered indexes, which are the default for primary keys, are
not supported with memory optimized tables.
```

Change the previous line so that it specifies a nonclustered index:

```
TransactionID int NOT NULL PRIMARY KEY NONCLUSTERED,
```

The statement will finally succeed and create a table with a range or nonclustered index.

A hash index can also be created for the primary key if you explicitly use the HASH clause, as specified in the following example, which also requires the BUCKET_COUNT option. First, let's drop the new table by using DROP TABLE in the same way as with a disk-based table:

```
DROP TABLE TransactionHistoryArchive
```

Then, we can create the table:

```
CREATE TABLE TransactionHistoryArchive (
TransactionID int NOT NULL PRIMARY KEY NONCLUSTERED HASH WITH
(BUCKET_COUNT = 100000),
ProductID int NOT NULL,
ReferenceOrderID int NOT NULL,
ReferenceOrderLineID int NOT NULL,
TransactionDate datetime NOT NULL,
TransactionType nchar(1) NOT NULL,
Quantity int NOT NULL,
ActualCost money NOT NULL,
ModifiedDate datetime NOT NULL
) WITH (MEMORY_OPTIMIZED = ON)
```

> **Note**
> The initial release of in-memory OLTP did not allow a table to be changed. You would need to drop the table and create it again to implement any changes. Starting with SQL Server 2016, you can use the ALTER TABLE statement to achieve that. More details can be found at the end of this chapter.

So, a memory-optimized table must also have a primary key, which could be a hash or a range index. The maximum number of indexes was originally limited to eight, but starting with SQL Server 2017, Microsoft has removed this limitation. But the same as with disk-based indexes, you should keep the number of indexes to a minimum. We can have both hash and range indexes on the same table, as shown in the following example (again, dropping the previous table if needed):

```
CREATE TABLE TransactionHistoryArchive (
TransactionID int NOT NULL PRIMARY KEY NONCLUSTERED HASH WITH
(BUCKET_COUNT = 100000),
ProductID int NOT NULL,
ReferenceOrderID int NOT NULL,
ReferenceOrderLineID int NOT NULL,
TransactionDate datetime NOT NULL,
TransactionType nchar(1) NOT NULL,
Quantity int NOT NULL,
ActualCost money NOT NULL,
ModifiedDate datetime NOT NULL,
INDEX IX_ProductID NONCLUSTERED (ProductID)
) WITH (MEMORY_OPTIMIZED = ON)
```

The preceding code creates a hash index on the TransactionID column, which is also the table's primary key, and a range index on the ProductID column. The NONCLUSTERED keyword is optional for range indexes in this example. Now that the table has been created, we are ready to populate it by copying data from AdventureWorks2019. However, the following will not work:

```
INSERT INTO TransactionHistoryArchive
SELECT * FROM AdventureWorks2019.Production.
TransactionHistoryArchive
```

We will get the following error message:

```
Msg 41317, Level 16, State 3, Line 1
A user transaction that accesses memory optimized tables or
natively compiled procedures cannot access more than one user
```

```
database or databases model and msdb, and it cannot write to
master.
```

As indicated in the error message, a user transaction that accesses memory-optimized tables cannot access more than one user database. For the same reason, the following code for joining two tables from two user databases will not work either:

```
SELECT * FROM TransactionHistoryArchive tha
JOIN AdventureWorks2019.Production.TransactionHistory ta
ON tha.TransactionID = ta.TransactionID
```

However, you can copy this data in some other ways, such as using the Import and Export Wizard or using a temporary table, as shown in the following code:

```
SELECT * INTO #temp
FROM AdventureWorks2019.Production.TransactionHistoryArchive
GO
INSERT INTO TransactionHistoryArchive
SELECT * FROM #temp
```

However, as explained earlier, a user transaction that's accessing memory-optimized tables and disk-based tables on the same database is supported (except in the case of natively compiled stored procedures). The following example will create a disk-based table and join both a memory-optimized and a disk-based table:

```
CREATE TABLE TransactionHistory (
TransactionID int,
ProductID int)
GO
SELECT * FROM TransactionHistoryArchive tha
JOIN TransactionHistory ta ON tha.TransactionID =
ta.TransactionID
```

As shown earlier, the minimum requirement to create a memory-optimized table is to use the MEMORY_OPTIMIZED clause and define a primary key, which itself requires an index. A second and optional clause, DURABILITY, is also commonly used and supports the SCHEMA_AND_DATA and SCHEMA_ONLY options. SCHEMA_AND_DATA, which is the default, allows both schema and data to be persisted on disk. SCHEMA_ONLY means that the table data will not be persisted on disk upon instance restart; only the table schema will be persisted. SCHEMA_ONLY creates nondurable tables, which can improve the performance of transactions by significantly reducing the I/O impact of the workload. This can be used in scenarios such as session state management and staging tables that are used in ETL processing.

The following diagram shows the structure of a record in a memory-optimized table in which we can identify two main parts: a row header and a row body or payload. The row header starts with a begin and end timestamp, which is used to identify where the record is valid for a transaction, as explained later in this section:

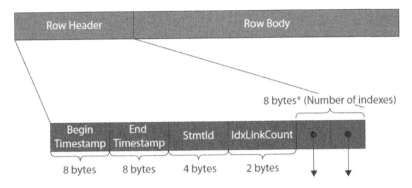

Figure 7.2 – Structure of a Hekaton row

Next is `StmtId`, which is the statement ID value of the statement that created the row. The last section of the header consists of index pointers, one per index available on the table. The row body is the record itself and contains the index key columns, along with the remaining columns of the row. Because the row body contains all the columns of the record, we could say that, in Hekaton, there is no need to define covering indexes as with traditional indexes: a memory-optimized index is a covering index, meaning that all the columns are included in the index. An index contains a memory pointer to the actual row in the table.

Now, let's review hash and nonclustered (range) indexes in more detail.

Hash indexes

Hash indexes were introduced previously. Now, let's look at them in more detail. The following diagram shows an example of hash indexes containing three records: the *Susan* row, the *Jane* row, and the *John* row. Notice that *John* has two versions, the complexities and relationships of which will be explained shortly. Two hash indexes are defined: the first on the `Name` column and the second on the `City` column, so a hash table is allocated for each index, with each box representing a different hash bucket. The first part of the record (for example, 90, 150) is the begin and end timestamp shown previously in *Figure 7.2*. The infinity symbol (∞) at the end timestamp means that this is the currently valid version of the row. For simplicity, this example assumes that each hash bucket contains records based on the first letter of the key, either `Name` or `City`, although this is not how the hash function works, as explained later:

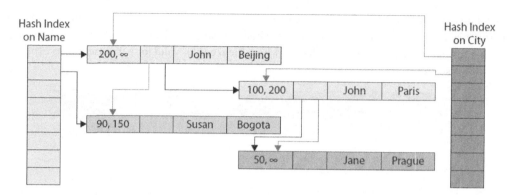

Figure 7.3 – Example of Hekaton rows and indexes

Because the table has two indexes, each record has two pointers, one for each index, as shown in *Figure 7.2*. The first hash bucket for the **Name** index has a chain of three records: two versions for John and one version for Jane. The links between these records are shown with gray arrows. The second hash bucket for the **Name** index only has a chain of one record – the Susan record – so no links are shown. In the same way, the preceding diagram shows two buckets for the **City** index – the first with two records for Beijing and Bogota, and the second for Paris and Prague. The links are shown in black arrows. The *John, Beijing* record has a valid time from 200 to infinity, which means it was created by a transaction that was committed at time 200 and the record is still valid. The other version (*John, Paris*) was valid from time 100 to 200, when it was updated to *John, Beijing*. In the MVCC system, UPDATEs are treated as INSERTs and DELETEs. Rows are only visible from the begin timestamp and up until (but not including) the end timestamp, so in this case, the existing version was expired by setting the end timestamp, and a new version with an infinity end timestamp was created.

A transaction that was started at time 150 would then see the *John, Paris* version, while one started at 220 would find the latest version of *John, Beijing*. But how does SQL Server find the records using the index? This is where the hash function comes into play.

For the statement, we will use the following code:

```
SELECT * FROM Table WHERE City = 'Beijing'
```

SQL Server will apply the hash function to the predicate. Remember that for simplicity, our hash function example was based on the first letter of the string, so in this case, the result is *B*. SQL Server will then look directly into the hash bucket and pull the pointer to the first row. Looking at the first row, it will now compare the strings; if they are the same, it will return the required row details. Then, it will walk the chain of index pointers, comparing the values and returning rows where appropriate.

Finally, notice that the example uses two hash indexes, but the same example would work if we had used, for example, a hash index on **Name** and a range index on **City**, or both range indexes.

BUCKET_COUNT controls the size of the hash table, so this value should be chosen carefully. The recommendation is to have it twice the maximum expected number of distinct values in the index key, rounded up to the nearest power of two, although Hekaton will round up for you if needed. An inadequate BUCKET_COUNT value can lead to performance problems: a value too large can lead to many empty buckets in the hash table. This can cause higher memory usage as each bucket uses 8 bytes. Also, scanning the index will be more expensive because it has to scan those empty buckets. However, a large BUCKET_COUNT value does not affect the performance of index seeks. On the other hand, a BUCKET_COUNT value that's too small can lead to long chains of records that will cause searching for a specific record to be more expensive. This is because the engine has to traverse multiple values to find a specific row.

Let's see some examples of how BUCKET_COUNT works, starting with an empty table. Drop the existing TransactionHistoryArchive table:

```
DROP TABLE TransactionHistoryArchive
```

Now, create the table again with a BUCKET_COUNT of 100,000:

```
CREATE TABLE TransactionHistoryArchive (
TransactionID int NOT NULL PRIMARY KEY NONCLUSTERED HASH WITH
(BUCKET_COUNT = 100000),
ProductID int NOT NULL,
ReferenceOrderID int NOT NULL,
ReferenceOrderLineID int NOT NULL,
TransactionDate datetime NOT NULL,
TransactionType nchar(1) NOT NULL,
Quantity int NOT NULL,
ActualCost money NOT NULL,
ModifiedDate datetime NOT NULL
) WITH (MEMORY_OPTIMIZED = ON)
```

You can use the sys.dm_db_xtp_hash_index_stats DMV to show statistics about hash indexes. Run the following code:

```
SELECT * FROM sys.dm_db_xtp_hash_index_stats
```

You will get the following output:

total_bucket_count	empty_bucket_count	avg_chain_length	max_chain_length
131072	131072	0	0

Here, we can see that instead of 100,000 buckets, SQL Server rounded up to the nearest power of two (in this case, 2 ^ 17, or 131,072), as shown in the `total_bucket_count` column.

Insert the same data again by running the following statements:

```
DROP TABLE #temp
GO
SELECT * INTO #temp
FROM AdventureWorks2019.Production.TransactionHistoryArchive
GO
INSERT INTO TransactionHistoryArchive
SELECT * FROM #temp
```

This time, 89,253 records have been inserted. Run the `sys.dm_db_xtp_hash_index_stats` DMV again. This time, you will get data similar to the following:

total_bucket_count	empty_bucket_count	avg_chain_length	max_chain_length
131072	66316	1	7

We can note several things here. The total number of buckets (131,072) minus the empty buckets (66,316), shown as `empty_bucket_count`, gives us the number of buckets used (64,756). Because we inserted 89,253 records in 39,191 buckets, this gives us 1.37 records per bucket on average, which is represented by the `avg_chain_len` value of 1, documented as the average length of the row chains over all the hash buckets in the index. `max_chain_len` is the maximum length of the row chains in the hash buckets.

Just to show an extreme case where performance may be impaired, run the same exercise, but request only 1,024 as BUCKET_COUNT. After inserting the 89,253 records, we will get the following output:

total_bucket_count	empty_bucket_count	avg_chain_length	max_chain_length
1024	0	87	129

In this case, we have 89,253 records divided by 1,024 (or 87.16 records per bucket). Hash collisions occur when two or more index keys are mapped to the same hash bucket, as in this example, and a large number of hash collisions can impact the performance of lookup operations.

The other extreme case is having too many buckets compared to the number of records. Running the same example for 1,000,000 buckets and inserting the same number of records would give us this:

total_bucket_count	empty_bucket_count	avg_chain_length	max_chain_length
1048576	962523	1	3

This example has 91.79% unused buckets, which will both use more memory and impact the performance of scan operations because of it having to read many unused buckets.

Are you wondering what the behavior will be if we have the same number of buckets as records? Change the previous code to create 65,536 buckets. Then, run the following code:

```
DROP TABLE #temp
GO
SELECT TOP 65536 * INTO #temp
FROM AdventureWorks2019.Production.TransactionHistoryArchive
GO
INSERT INTO TransactionHistoryArchive
SELECT * FROM #temp
```

You will get the following output:

total_bucket_count	empty_bucket_count	avg_chain_length	max_chain_length
65536	24284	1	7

So, after looking at these extreme cases, it is worth reminding ourselves that the recommendation is to configure BUCKET_COUNT as twice the maximum expected number of distinct values in the index key, keeping in mind that changing BUCKET_COUNT is not a trivial matter and requires the table to be dropped and recreated.

SQL Server uses the same hashing function for all the hash indexes. It is deterministic, which means that the same index key will always be mapped to the same bucket in the index. Finally, as we were able to see in the examples, multiple index keys can also be mapped to the same hash bucket, and because key values are not evenly distributed in the buckets, there can be several empty buckets, and used buckets may contain one or more records.

Nonclustered or range indexes

Although hash indexes support index seeks on equality predicates and are the best choice for point lookups, the index seeks on inequality predicates, like the ones that use the >, <, <=, and >= operators, are not supported on this kind of index. So, an inequality predicate will skip a hash index and use a table scan instead. In addition, because all the index key columns are used to compute the hash value, index seeks on a hash index cannot be used when only a subset of these index key columns are used in an equality predicate. For example, if the hash index is defined as lastname, firstname, you cannot use it in an equality predicate using only lastname or only firstname. Hash indexes cannot be used to retrieve the records sorted by the index definition either.

Range indexes can be used to help in all these scenarios and have the additional benefit that they do not require you to define several buckets. However, although range indexes have several advantages over hash indexes, keep in mind that range indexes could lead to suboptimal performance for index seek operations, where hash indexes are recommended instead.

Range indexes are a new form of B-tree, called a Bw-tree, and are designed for new hardware to take advantage of the cache of modern multicore processors. They are in-memory structures that achieve outstanding performance via latch-free techniques and were originally described by Microsoft Research in the paper *The Bw-Tree: A B-tree for New Hardware Platforms*, by Justin Levandoski and others. The following diagram shows the general structure of a Bw-tree:

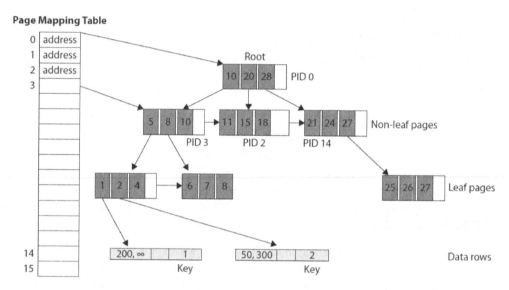

Figure 7.4 – Structure of a Bw-tree

Similar to a regular B-tree, as explained in *Chapter 5, Working with Indexes*, in a Bw-tree, the root and non-leaf pages point to index pages at the next level of the tree, and the leaf pages contain a set of ordered key values with pointers that point to the data rows. Each non-leaf page has a logical **page ID (PID)**, and a page mapping table contains the mapping of these PIDs to their physical memory address. For example, in the preceding diagram, the top entry of the page mapping table specifies the number 0 and points to the page with PID 0. Keys on non-leaf pages contain the highest value possible that this page references. Leaf pages do not have a PID, only memory addresses pointing to the data rows. So, to find the row with a key equal to 2, SQL Server would start with the root page (PID 0), follow the link for key = 10 (because 10 is greater than 2), which points to the page with PID 3, and then follow the link for key = 5 (which again is greater than 2). The pointed leaf page contains key 2, which contains the memory address that points to the required record. For more details about the internals of these new memory structures, you may want to refer to the research paper listed previously.

Now, let's run some queries to get a basic understanding of how these indexes work and what kind of execution plans they create. In this section, we will use ad hoc T-SQL, which in Hekaton is said to use query interop capabilities. The examples in this section use the following table with both a hash and a range index. Also, you must load data into this table, as explained previously:

```
CREATE TABLE TransactionHistoryArchive (
TransactionID int NOT NULL PRIMARY KEY NONCLUSTERED HASH WITH
(BUCKET_COUNT = 100000),
ProductID int NOT NULL,
ReferenceOrderID int NOT NULL,
ReferenceOrderLineID int NOT NULL,
TransactionDate datetime NOT NULL,
TransactionType nchar(1) NOT NULL,
Quantity int NOT NULL,
ActualCost money NOT NULL,
ModifiedDate datetime NOT NULL,
INDEX IX_ProductID NONCLUSTERED (ProductID)
) WITH (MEMORY_OPTIMIZED = ON)
```

First, run the following query:

```
SELECT * FROM TransactionHistoryArchive
WHERE TransactionID = 8209
```

Because we defined a hash index on the `TransactionID` column, we get the plan shown here, which uses an **Index Seek** operator:

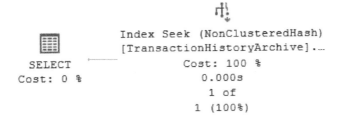

Figure 7.5 – Index Seek operation on a hash index

The index is named PK__Transact__55433A4A7EB94404. This name was given automatically but it is also possible to specify a name, if required, as you'll see later. As mentioned previously, hash indexes are efficient for point lookups, but they do not support index seeks on inequality predicates. If you change the previous query so that it uses an inequality predicate, as shown here, it will create a plan with a **Table Scan**, as shown in the following plan:

```
SELECT * FROM TransactionHistoryArchive
WHERE TransactionID > 8209
```

Figure 7.6 – Index Scan operation on a hash index

Now, let's try a different query:

```
SELECT * FROM TransactionHistoryArchive
WHERE ProductID = 780
```

Because we have a range nonclustered index defined on ProductID, an **Index Seek** operation will be used on that index, IX_ProductID, as shown here:

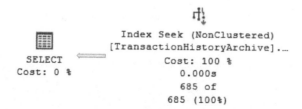

Figure 7.7 – Index Seek operation on a range index

Now, let's try an inequality operation on the same column:

```
SELECT * FROM TransactionHistoryArchive
WHERE ProductID < 10
```

This time, the range index can be used to access the data, without the need for an **Index Scan** operation. The resulting plan can be seen here:

Figure 7.8 – Index Seek operation on a range index with an inequality predicate

Hash indexes cannot be used to return data that's been sorted because their rows are stored in a random order. The following query will use a **Sort** operation to sort the requested data, as shown in the following plan:

```
SELECT * FROM TransactionHistoryArchive
ORDER BY TransactionID
```

Figure 7.9 – Plan with a Sort operation

However, a range index can be used to return sorted data. Running the following query will simply scan the range index without the need for it to sort its data, as shown in the following plan. You could even verify that the **Ordered** property is True via the operator properties:

```
SELECT * FROM TransactionHistoryArchive
ORDER BY ProductID
```

Figure 7.10 – Using a range index to return sorted data

However, unlike disk-based indexes, range indexes are unidirectional, which is something that may surprise you. Therefore, when requesting the same query using ORDER BY ProductID DESC, it will not be able to use the index-sorted data. Instead, it will use a plan with an expensive **Sort** operator, similar to the one shown in *Figure 7.9*.

Finally, let's look at an example of a hash index with two columns. Let's assume you have the following version of the TransactionHistoryArchive table, which uses a hash index with both TransactionID and ProductID columns. Once again, load some data into this table, as explained earlier:

```
CREATE TABLE TransactionHistoryArchive (
TransactionID int NOT NULL,
ProductID int NOT NULL,
ReferenceOrderID int NOT NULL,
ReferenceOrderLineID int NOT NULL,
TransactionDate datetime NOT NULL,
TransactionType nchar(1) NOT NULL,
Quantity int NOT NULL,
ActualCost money NOT NULL,
ModifiedDate datetime NOT NULL,
CONSTRAINT PK_TransactionID_ProductID PRIMARY KEY NONCLUSTERED
HASH (TransactionID, ProductID) WITH (BUCKET_COUNT = 100000)
) WITH (MEMORY_OPTIMIZED = ON)
```

Because all the index key columns are required to compute the hash value, as explained earlier, SQL Server will be able to use a very effective **Index Seek** on the PK_TransactionID_ProductID hash index in the following query:

```
SELECT * FROM TransactionHistoryArchive
WHERE TransactionID = 7173 AND ProductID = 398
```

However, it will not be able to use the same index in the following query, which will resort to a **Table Scan**:

```
SELECT * FROM TransactionHistoryArchive
WHERE TransactionID = 7173
```

Although the execution plans shown in this section use the familiar **Index Scan and Index Seek** operations, keep in mind that these indexes and the data are in memory and there is no disk access at all. In this case, the table and indexes are in memory and use different structures. So, how do you identify them when you see them in execution plans, especially when you query both memory-optimized and disk-based tables? You can look at the `Storage` property in the operator details and see a value of `MemoryOptimized`. Although you will see `NonClusteredHash` after the name of the operator for hash indexes, range indexes just show `NonClustered`, which is the same that's shown for regular disk-based nonclustered indexes.

Natively compiled stored procedures

As mentioned previously, to create natively compiled stored procedures, Hekaton leverages the SQL Server query optimizer to produce an efficient query plan, which is later compiled into native code and loaded as DLLs into the SQL Server process. You may want to use natively compiled stored procedures mostly in performance-critical parts of an application or in procedures that are frequently executed. However, you need to be aware of the limitations of the T-SQL-supported features on natively compiled stored procedures. These will be covered later in this chapter.

Creating natively compiled stored procedures

Now, let's create a natively compiled stored procedure that, as shown in the following example, requires the `NATIVE_COMPILATION` clause:

```
CREATE PROCEDURE test
WITH NATIVE_COMPILATION, SCHEMABINDING, EXECUTE AS OWNER
AS
BEGIN ATOMIC WITH (TRANSACTION ISOLATION LEVEL = SNAPSHOT,
LANGUAGE = 'us_english')
SELECT TransactionID, ProductID, ReferenceOrderID
FROM dbo.TransactionHistoryArchive
WHERE ProductID = 780
END
```

After creating the procedure, you can execute it by using the following command:

```
EXEC test
```

You can display the execution plan that's being used by clicking **Display Estimated Execution Plan** or using the `SET SHOWPLAN_XML ON` statement. If you run this against the first table that was created in the *Nonclustered or range indexes* section, you will get the following plan:

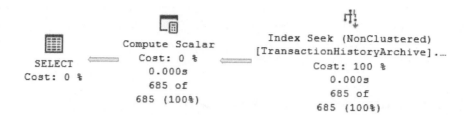

Figure 7.11 – Execution plan of a natively compiled stored procedure

In addition to NATIVE_COMPILATION, the code shows other required clauses: SCHEMABINDING, EXECUTE AS, and BEGIN ATOMIC. Leaving any of these out will produce an error. These choices must be set at compile time and aim to minimize the number of runtime checks and operations that must be performed at execution time, thus helping with the performance of the execution.

SCHEMABINDING refers to the fact that natively compiled stored procedures must be schema bound, which means that tables referenced by the procedure cannot be dropped. This helps to avoid costly schema stability locks before execution. Trying to delete the dbo.TransactionHistoryArchive table we created earlier would produce the following error:

```
Msg 3729, Level 16, State 1, Line 1
Cannot DROP TABLE 'dbo.TransactionHistoryArchive' because it is
being referenced by object 'test'.
```

The EXECUTE AS requirement focuses on avoiding permission checks at execution time. In natively compiled stored procedures, the default of EXECUTE AS CALLER is not supported, so you must use any of the other three choices available: EXECUTE AS SELF, EXECUTE AS OWNER, or EXECUTE AS user_name.

BEGIN ATOMIC is part of the ANSI SQL standard, and in SQL Server, it's used to define an atomic block in which either the entire block succeeds or all the statements in the block are rolled back. If the procedure is invoked outside the context of an active transaction, BEGIN ATOMIC will start a new transaction and the atomic block will define the beginning and end of the transaction. However, if a transaction has already been started when the atomic block begins, the transaction borders will be defined by the BEGIN TRANSACTION, COMMIT TRANSACTION, and ROLLBACK TRANSACTION statements. BEGIN ATOMIC supports five options: TRANSACTION ISOLATION LEVEL and LANGUAGE, which are required, and DELAYED_DURABILITY, DATEFORMAT, and DATEFIRST, which are optional.

TRANSACTION ISOLATION LEVEL defines the transaction isolation level to be used by the natively compiled stored procedure, and the supported values are SNAPSHOT, REPEATABLEREAD, and SERIALIZABLE. LANGUAGE defines the language used by the stored procedure and determines the date and time formats and system messages. Languages are defined in sys.syslanguages. DELAYED_DURABILITY is used to specify the durability of the transaction and, by default, is OFF, meaning that transactions are fully durable. When DELAYED_DURABILITY is enabled, transaction commits are asynchronous and can improve the performance of transactions if log records are written to the transaction log in batches. However, this can lead to data loss if a system failure occurs.

> **Note**
>
> Delayed transaction durability is a feature that was introduced with SQL Server 2014. It can also be used outside Hekaton and is useful in cases where you have performance issues due to latency in transaction log writes and you can tolerate some data loss. For more details about delayed durability, see http://msdn.microsoft.com/en-us/library/dn449490(v=sql.120).aspx.

As mentioned earlier, Hekaton tables support the SNAPSHOT, REPEATABLE READ, and SERIALIZABLE isolation levels and utilize an MVCC mechanism. The isolation level can be specified in the ATOMIC clause, as was done earlier, or directly in interpreted T-SQL using the SET TRANSACTION ISOLATION LEVEL statement. It is interesting to note that although multiversioning is also supported on disk-based tables, they only use the SNAPSHOT and READ_COMMITTED_SNAPSHOT isolation levels. In addition, versions in Hekaton are not maintained in tempdb, as is the case with disk-based tables, but rather in memory as part of the memory-optimized data structures. Finally, there is no blocking on memory-optimized tables. It is an optimistic assumption that there will be no conflicts, so if two transactions try to update the same row, a write-write conflict is generated. Because Hekaton does not use locks, locking hints are not supported with memory-optimized tables either.

Finally, although query optimizer statistics are automatically created in memory-optimized tables, they were not automatically updated in the original SQL Server 2014 release, so it was strongly recommended that you manually updated your table statistics before creating your natively compiled stored procedures. Starting with SQL Server 2016, statistics are automatically updated, but you can still benefit from updating statistics manually so that you can use a bigger sample, for example. However, natively compiled stored procedures are not recompiled when statistics are updated. Native code can manually be recompiled using the sp_recompile system stored procedure. As mentioned earlier, native code is also recompiled when the SQL Server instance starts, when there is a database failover, or if a database is taken offline and brought back online.

Inspecting DLLs

The Hekaton engine uses some SQL Server engine components for compiling native procedures – namely, the query-processing stack we discussed in *Chapter 3, The Query Optimizer*, for parsing, binding, and query optimization. But because the final purpose is to produce native code, other operations must be added to create a DLL.

Translating the plan that's been created by the query optimizer into C code is not a trivial task, and additional steps are required to perform this operation. Keep in mind that native code is also produced when a memory-optimized table is created, not only for native procedures. Table operations such as computing a hash function on a key, comparing two records, or serializing a record into a log buffer are compiled into native code.

First, the created plan is used to create a data structure called the **Mixed Abstract Tree** (**MAT**), which is later transformed into a structure that can be more easily converted into C code, called the **Pure Imperative Tree** (**PIT**). Later, the required C code is generated using the PIT, and in the final step, a C/C++ compiler and linker are used to produce a DLL. The Microsoft C/C++ Optimizing Compiler and Microsoft Incremental Linker are used in this process and can be found as `cl.exe` and `link.exe` as part of the SQL Server installation, respectively.

Several of the files that are created here will be available in the filesystem, as shown later, including the C code. All these steps are performed automatically, and the process is transparent to the user – you only have to create the memory-optimized table or natively compiled stored procedure. Once the DLL has been created, it is loaded into the SQL Server address space, where it can be executed. These steps and the architecture of the Hekaton compiler are shown in the following diagram:

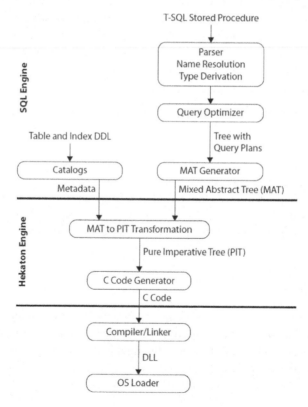

Figure 7.12 – Architecture of the Hekaton compiler

DLLs for both memory-optimized tables and natively compiled stored procedures are recompiled during recovery every time the SQL Server instance is started. SQL Server maintains the information that's required to recreate these DLLs in each database metadata.

It is interesting to note that the generated DLLs are not kept in the database but in the filesystem. You can find them, along with some other intermediate files, by looking at the location that's returned by the following query:

```
SELECT name, description FROM sys.dm_os_loaded_modules
where description = 'XTP Native DLL'
```

The following is a sample output:

Name	description
C:\Program Files\Microsoft SQL Server\MSSQL16MSSQLSERVER\MSSQL\DATA\xtp\7\ xtp_t_7_277576027.dll	XTP Native DLL
C:\Program Files\Microsoft SQL Server\MSSQL16.MSSQLSERVER\MSSQL\DATA\xtp\7\ xtp_p_7_309576141.dll	XTP Native DLL

A directory is created in the xtp directory that's named after the database ID – in this case, 7. Next, the names of the DLL files start with xtp, followed by t for tables and p for stored procedures. Again, we have the database ID on the name (in this case, 7), followed by the object ID, which is 885578193 for the TransactionHistoryArchive table and 917578307 for the test natively compiled stored procedure.

> **Note**
>
> You may have noticed the name xtp several times in this chapter already. xtp stands for eXtreme Transaction Processing and was reportedly the original name of the feature before it was changed to in-memory OLTP.

You can inspect the listed directories and find the DLL file, the C source code, and several other files, as shown in the following screenshot:

Name ▲	Date modified	Type	Size
xtp_p_7_917578307.c	4/9/2014 11:45 PM	C File	12 KB
xtp_p_7_917578307.dll	4/9/2014 11:45 PM	Application extension	76 KB
xtp_p_7_917578307.obj	4/9/2014 11:45 PM	OBJ File	97 KB
xtp_p_7_917578307.out	4/9/2014 11:45 PM	OUT File	1 KB
xtp_p_7_917578307.pdb	4/9/2014 11:45 PM	PDB File	587 KB
xtp_p_7_917578307.xml	4/9/2014 11:45 PM	XML Document	9 KB
xtp_t_7_885578193.c	4/9/2014 11:45 PM	C File	8 KB
xtp_t_7_885578193.dll	4/9/2014 11:45 PM	Application extension	75 KB
xtp_t_7_885578193.obj	4/9/2014 11:45 PM	OBJ File	84 KB
xtp_t_7_885578193.out	4/9/2014 11:45 PM	OUT File	1 KB
xtp_t_7_885578193.pdb	4/9/2014 11:45 PM	PDB File	595 KB
xtp_t_7_885578193.xml	4/9/2014 11:45 PM	XML Document	3 KB

Figure 7.13 – DLL and other files created during the compilation process

There is no need to maintain these files because SQL Server automatically removes them when they are no longer needed. If you drop both the table and procedure we just created, all these files will be automatically deleted by the garbage collector, although it may not happen immediately, especially for tables. Run the following statements to test this:

```
DROP PROCEDURE test
DROP TABLE TransactionHistoryArchive
```

Also, notice that you would need to delete the procedure first to avoid error 3729, as explained earlier.

Having those files on the filesystem does not represent a security risk (for example, in the case that they could be manually altered). Every time Hekaton has to load the DLLs again, such as when an instance is restarted or a database is put offline and then back online, SQL Server will compile the DLLs again, and those existing files are never used. That being said, let's check out some of the limitations and enhancements that OLTP has.

Limitations and later enhancements

Without a doubt, the main limitation of the original release of Hekaton, SQL Server 2014, was that tables couldn't be changed after being created: a new table with the required changes would have to be created instead. This was the case for any change you wanted to make to a table, such as adding a new column or index or changing the bucket count of a hash index. Creating a new table would require several other operations as well, such as copying its data to another location, dropping the table, creating the new table with the needed changes, and copying the data back, which would require some downtime for a production application. This limitation was probably the biggest challenge for deployed applications, which, of course, demanded serious thinking and architecture design to avoid or minimize changes once the required memory-optimized tables were in production.

In addition, dropping and creating a table would usually imply some other operations, such as scripting all its permissions. And because natively compiled stored procedures are schema bound, this also means that they need to be dropped first before the table can be dropped. That is, you need to script these procedures, drop them, and create them again once the new table is created. Similar to tables, you may need to script the permissions of the procedures as well. Updating statistics with the FULLSCAN option was also highly recommended after the table was created and all the data was loaded to help the query optimizer get the best possible execution plan.

You also weren't able to alter natively compiled stored procedures on the original release, or even recompile them (except in a few limited cases, such as when the SQL Server instance was restarted or when a database was put offline and back online). As mentioned previously, to alter a native stored procedure, you would need to script the permissions, drop the procedure, create the new version of the procedure, and apply for the permissions again. This means that the procedure would not be available while you were performing those steps.

Starting with SQL Server 2016, the second in-memory OLTP release, the feature now includes the ability to change tables and native procedures by using the ALTER TABLE and ALTER PROCEDURE statements, respectively. This is a remarkable improvement after the initial release. However, some of the previously listed limitations remain. For example, although you can just use ALTER TABLE to change a table structure, SQL Server will still need to perform some operations in the background, such as copying its data to another location, dropping the table, creating the new table with the needed changes, and copying the data back, which would still require some downtime in the case of a production application. Because of this, you still need to carefully work on your original database design. There is no longer the need to script permissions for either tables or native store procedures when you use the ALTER TABLE and ALTER PROCEDURE statements.

Finally, there were some differences regarding statistics and recompiles in Hekaton compared to disk-based tables and traditional stored procedures on the original release. As the data in Hekaton tables changed, statistics were never automatically updated and you needed to manually update them by running the UPDATE STATISTICS statement with the FULLSCAN and NORECOMPUTE options. Also, even after your statistics are updated, existing natively compiled stored procedures cannot benefit from them automatically, and, as mentioned earlier, you cannot force a recompile either. You have to manually drop and recreate the native stored procedures.

Starting with SQL Server 2016, statistics used by the query optimizer are now automatically updated, as is the case for disk-based tables. You can also specify a sample when manually updating statistics as `UPDATE STATISTICS` with the `FULLSCAN` option was the only choice available in SQL Server 2014. However, updated statistics still do not immediately benefit native stored procedures in the same way as with traditional stored procedures. This means that a change in the `statistics` object will never trigger a new procedure optimization. So, you will still have to manually recompile a specific native stored procedure using `sp_recompile`, available only on SQL Server 2016 and later.

The original release of in-memory OLTP had serious limitations regarding memory as the total size for all the tables in a database could not exceed 256 GB. After the release of SQL Server 2016, this limit was originally extended to 2 TB, which was not a hard limit, just a supported limit. A few weeks after SQL Server 2016 was released, this new limit was also removed and Microsoft announced that memory-optimized tables could use any amount of memory available to the operating system.

> **Note**
>
> The documentation at `https://docs.microsoft.com/en-us/sql/sql-server/what-s-new-in-sql-server-2016` still shows a supported limit of up to 2 TB, but `https://techcommunity.microsoft.com/t5/sql-server-blog/increased-memory-size-for-in-memory-oltp-in-sql-server-2016/ba-p/384750` indicates that you can grow your memory-optimized tables as large as you like, so long as you have enough memory available.

The `FOREIGN KEY`, `UNIQUE`, and `CHECK` constraints were not supported in the initial release. They were supported starting with SQL Server 2016. Computed columns in memory-optimized tables and the `CROSS APPLY` operator on natively compiled modules are supported starting with SQL Server 2019.

The original release of in-memory OLTP required you to use a BIN2 collation when creating indexes on string columns, such as `char`, `nchar`, `varchar`, or `nvarchar`. In addition, comparing, sorting, and manipulating character strings that did not use a BIN2 collation was not supported with natively compiled stored procedures. Both restrictions have been lifted with SQL Server 2016 and now you can use any collation you wish.

Finally, you can use the following document to review all the SQL Server features that are not supported on a database that contains memory-optimized objects: `https://docs.microsoft.com/en-us/sql/relational-databases/in-memory-oltp/unsupported-sql-server-features-for-in-memory-oltp`. Hekaton tables and stored procedures do not support the full T-SQL surface area that is supported by disk-based tables and regular stored procedures. For an entire list of unsupported T-SQL constructs on Hekaton tables and stored procedures, see `http://msdn.microsoft.com/en-us/library/dn246937(v=sql.120).aspx`.

Summary

This chapter covered in-memory OLTP, originally known as Hekaton, which without a doubt was the most important new feature of SQL Server 2014. The Hekaton OLTP database engine is a response to a new design and architectural approach looking to achieve the most benefit of the new hardware available today. Although optimization for main memory access is its main feature and is even part of its name, Hekaton's performance improvement is also complemented by other major architecture areas, such as compiling procedures to native code, as well as latches and lock elimination.

This chapter covered the Hekaton architecture and its main components – memory-optimized tables, hash, and range indexes, and natively compiled stored procedures were explained in great detail. Although Hekaton had several limitations in its first release in SQL Server 2014, multiple limitations have been lifted after four new releases, including SQL Server 2022.

xVelocity memory-optimized columnstore indexes, another in-memory technology, will be covered in *Chapter 11, An Introduction to Data Warehouses*. In the next chapter, we will learn more about plan caching.

8

Understanding Plan Caching

In the previous chapter, we learned how the query optimization process produces an execution plan. In this chapter, we will focus on what happens to those plans. Understanding how the plan cache works is extremely important for the performance of your queries and SQL Server in general. Query optimization is a relatively expensive operation, so if plans can be cached and reused, this optimization cost can be avoided. Trying to minimize this cost saves on optimization time and server resources such as CPU. Plan caching also needs to be balanced with keeping the plan cache size to a minimum so that memory resources can be used by your queries.

However, there might be cases when reusing a plan is not appropriate and would instead create a performance problem, for example, with parameter-sensitive queries. This chapter will show you how to identify those performance problems and what the available solutions are. Although parameter sniffing is sometimes seen as something bad, it is, in fact, a performance optimization that allows SQL Server to optimize a query for the parameter values that were initially passed into a stored procedure. The fact that it does not work fine in all cases is what has given it somewhat of a bad reputation and is usually referred to as the parameter-sniffing problem.

Finally, this chapter will cover parameter-sensitive query optimization, which was introduced with SQL Server 2022 and is part of the intelligent query processing family of features. Parameter-sensitive query optimization intends to help with performance problems related to parameter-sensitive queries.

This chapter covers the following topics:

- Batch compilation and recompilation
- Exploring the plan cache

- Understanding parameterization
- Parameter sniffing
- Parameter sensitivity plan optimization

Batch compilation and recompilation

As mentioned in *Chapter 1, An Introduction to Query Tuning and Optimization*, every time a batch is submitted to SQL Server for execution, SQL Server checks the plan cache to see whether an execution plan for that batch already exists. Query optimization is a relatively expensive operation, so if a valid plan is available in the plan cache and can be used, the optimization process can be skipped and the associated cost, in terms of optimization time, CPU resources, and so on, can be avoided. If a plan is not found, the batch is compiled to generate an execution plan for all the queries in the stored procedure, trigger, or dynamic SQL batch.

The query optimizer begins by loading all the interesting statistics and also validating whether any of these statistics are outdated. Then, it updates any outdated statistics, except in cases where the `AUTO_UPDATE_STATISTICS_ASYNC` configuration option is used, in which case the query optimizer will use the existing statistics, even if they are out of date. In this case, the statistics are updated asynchronously, ready for the next query optimization that may require them. The query optimizer then proceeds with the optimization process, which was explained in detail in *Chapter 3, The Query Optimizer*.

If a plan is found in the plan cache or a new one is created, it can now be executed. Query execution technically begins at this point, as shown in the following diagram, but the plan is still validated for correctness-related reasons, which include schema changes. If the schema is not valid, the plan is discarded and the batch or individual query is compiled again. If the schema is valid, the query optimizer then checks for data statistics changes, looking for new applicable statistics or outdated statistics. If newer statistics are available, the plan is discarded and the batch or individual query is compiled again. Such compilations are known as **recompilations**. As you may have noticed, recompilations are performed for good reasons – both to ensure plan correctness and plan optimality (that is, to obtain potentially faster query execution plans). Recompilations may also need to be monitored to make sure they are not occurring too frequently and causing performance issues. The entire compilation and recompilation process is summarized in the following diagram:

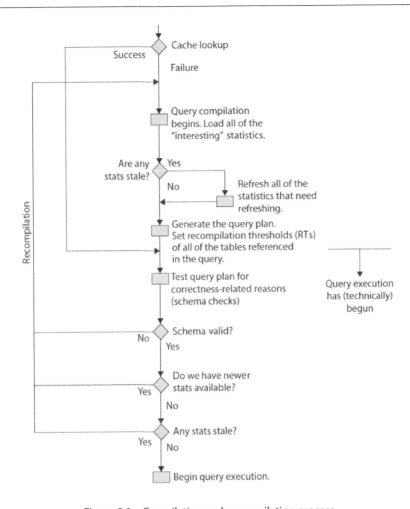

Figure 8.1 – Compilation and recompilation process

You can look for excessive compiles and recompiles using the SQL Compilations/sec and SQL Re-Compilations/sec counters of the `SQLServer:SQL Statistics` object in **Windows System Monitor**. SQL Compilations/sec allows you to see the number of compilations per second. Because plans are cached and reused, after SQL Server user activity is stable, this value should reach a steady state. SQL Re-Compilations/sec allows you to see the number of recompiles per second. As shown earlier, recompilations are performed for good reasons, but generally, you want the number of recompiles to be low.

Once you know you have a high number of recompiles, you can use the SP:Recompile and SQL:StmtRecompile trace events or the sql_statement_recompile extended event to troubleshoot and get additional information. As an example, let's look at the following exercise. Start a **Profiler** session on your test instance and select the following trace events (some of which were covered in *Chapter 2, Troubleshooting Queries*). These are located in the **Stored Procedures** event class and the **TSQL** event class:

- SP:Recompile
- SQL:StmtRecompile
- SP:Starting
- SP:StmtStarting
- SP:Completed
- SP:StmtCompleted

Run the following code to do so:

```
DBCC FREEPROCCACHE
GO
CREATE OR ALTER PROCEDURE test
AS
CREATE TABLE #table1 (name varchar(40))
SELECT * FROM #table1
GO
EXEC test
```

You should see the following sequence of events, which includes **3 – Deferred compile** in the EventSubClass column in **Profiler** for both the **SP:Recompile** and **SQL:StmtRecompile** events:

EventClass	TextData	EventSubClass
SP:Starting	EXEC test	
SP:StmtStarting	CREATE TABLE #table1 (name varchar(40))	
SP:StmtCompleted	CREATE TABLE #table1 (name varchar(40))	
SP:StmtStarting	SELECT * FROM #table1	
SP:Recompile	SELECT * FROM #table1	3 – Deferred compile
SQL:StmtRecompile	SELECT * FROM #table1	3 – Deferred compile
SP:StmtStarting	SELECT * FROM #table1	
SP:StmtCompleted	SELECT * FROM #table1	
SP:Completed	EXEC test	

The captured events show a deferred compile caused by the SELECT statement as the reason for the recompiles. Remember that when a stored procedure is executed for the first time, it is also optimized, and an execution plan is created as a result. A plan can be created for the CREATE TABLE statement inside the stored procedure. However, the SELECT statement cannot be optimized at this moment because it references the #table1 table, which does not exist yet. Remember that this is still the optimization process, and to create the #table1 object, the resulting plan should be executed first. Only after the #table1 table is created during the execution of the stored procedure will SQL Server finally be able to optimize the SELECT statement, but this time, it will show as a recompile.

Deferred compile is one of the possible values for EventSubClass. You can find the other documented values by running the following query:

```
SELECT map_key, map_value FROM sys.dm_xe_map_values
WHERE name = 'statement_recompile_cause'
```

Running the previous query shows the following output:

SubclassName	SubclassValue	Detailed Reason for Recompilation
Schema changed	1	Schema, bindings, or permissions changed between compile and execute.
Statistics changed	2	Statistics changed.
Deferred compile	3	Recompile because of **Deferred Name Resolution** (**DNR**). Object not found at compile time, deferred check to runtime.
Set option change	4	Set option changed in batch.
Temp table changed	5	Temp table schema, binding, or permission changed.
Remote rowset changed	6	Remote rowset schema, binding, or permission changed.
FOR BROWSE permissions changed	7	Permissions changed in FOR BROWSE (deprecated DBLIB option).
Query notification environment changed	8	Query notification environment changed.
Partition view changed	9	SQL Server sometimes adds data-dependent implied predicates to the WHERE clauses of queries in some indexed views. If the underlying data changes, such implied predicates become invalid, and the associated cached query plan needs to be recompiled.
Cursor options changed	10	Change in cursor options.
Option (recompile) requested	11	A recompile was requested.
Parameterized plan flushed	12	The parameterized plan was flushed from the cache (SQL Server 2008 and later).
Test plan linearization	13	For internal tests only (SQL Server 2008 and later).
Plan affecting database version changed	14	For internal tests only (SQL Server 2008 and later).
QDS plan forcing policy changed	15	For internal tests only (SQL Server 2014).
QDS plan forcing failed	16	For internal tests only (SQL Server 2014).

Now that you know the methods for performing batch compilation and recompilation, let's learn how to use queries to explore the plan cache.

Exploring the plan cache

As you saw in *Chapter 2, Troubleshooting Queries*, you can use the sys.dm_exec_query_stats DMV to return aggregate performance statistics for cached query plans in SQL Server, where each entry represents a query statement within the cached plan. You saw examples of how to find the most expensive queries using different criteria such as CPU, logical reads, physical reads, logical writes, CLR time, and elapsed time. We also indicated that to get the same information in the past, you would have to capture a usually expensive server trace and analyze the collected data using third-party tools or your own created methods, which was a very time-consuming process. However, although the information of the sys.dm_exec_query_stats DMV is available automatically without any required configuration, it also has a few limitations – mainly that not every query gets cached or that a cached plan can be removed at any time. Despite these limitations, using this DMV is still a huge improvement over running server traces manually.

> **Note**
> Starting with SQL Server 2016, you can use the query store to capture performance and plan information about all the queries running in your databases. The query store is now, by far, the recommended method to get query performance information.

In addition, as covered in *Chapter 5, Working with Indexes*, the **Database Engine Tuning Advisor (DTA)** can use the information on this DMV when you specify the plan cache as a workload to tune, which uses the most expensive queries based on the query's elapsed time. This means that you don't even have to search for the most expensive queries and input them on the DTA – everything is available directly with only a few mouse clicks.

Regardless of the method you are using to capture the most expensive queries in your system, you should always take into account cases where a query alone may not use many resources (for example, CPU cycles), but the cumulative cost could be very high because it is so frequently executed.

Another DMV that's useful for looking at the plan cache is sys.dm_exec_cached_plans, which returns a row for each query plan that is cached by SQL Server. We will use this DMV to explore the plan cache in the remaining sections of this chapter, where we will focus mostly on the following three columns:

- usecounts: The number of times the cache object has been looked up
- cacheobjtype: The type of object in the plan cache, which can be one of the following:
  - Compiled Plan.
  - Compiled Plan Stub.

- **Parse Tree**: As mentioned in *Chapter 3, The Query Optimizer*, a query processor component called the algebrizer produces a tree that represents the logical structure of a query. This structure is called an algebrizer tree, although it may sometimes be referred to as a parse tree or a normalized tree, and is later handed off to the query optimizer, which uses it to produce an execution plan. Because the produced execution plan is cached, there is no need to cache these algebrizer trees – the only exception being the trees for views, defaults, and constraints – because they can be referenced by many different queries.

- **Extended Proc**: Cached objects that track metadata for an extended stored procedure.

- CLR Compiled Func.

- CLR Compiled Proc.

- Objtype: The type of object, which can be one of the following:

  - **Proc** (stored procedure)

  - Prepared (prepared statement)

  - Adhoc (ad hoc query)

  - ReplProc (replication-filter procedure)

  - Trigger

  - View

  - Default

  - UsrTab (user table)

  - SysTab (system table)

  - Check (check constraint)

  - Rule

You can use the sys.dm_os_memory_cache_counters DMV to provide runtime information about the number of entries in the plan cache, along with the amount of memory allocated and in use. The following query provides a quick summary of what you can see in detail on the sys.dm_exec_cached_plans DMV:

```
SELECT * FROM sys.dm_os_memory_cache_counters
WHERE type IN ('CACHESTORE_OBJCP', 'CACHESTORE_SQLCP',
'CACHESTORE_PHDR',
'CACHESTORE_XPROC')
```

Notice that we are filtering the query to the following four cache stores:

- CACHESTORE_OBJCP: Used for stored procedures, functions, and triggers
- CACHESTORE_SQLCP: Used for ad hoc and prepared queries
- CACHESTORE_PHDR: Used for algebrizer trees of views, defaults, and constraints
- CACHESTORE_XPROC: Used for extended procedures

Finally, although not directly related to the plan cache, introduced with the SQL Server 2014 release (and only on the Enterprise edition), SQL Server allows you to use nonvolatile storage, usually **solid-state drives (SSDs)**, as an extension to the memory subsystem rather than the disk subsystem. This feature is known as the **buffer pool extension** and is configured using the new BUFFER POOL EXTENSION clause of the ALTER SERVER CONFIGURATION statement. In addition, you can use the is_in_bpool_extension column of the sys.dm_os_buffer_descriptors DMV to return information about all the data pages currently in the SQL Server buffer pool that are also being used by the buffer pool extension feature. For more details about this new feature, refer to the SQL Server documentation.

How to remove plans from memory

So far in this book, we have made extensive use of the DBCC FREEPROCCACHE statement because it makes it very easy to clean the entire plan cache for testing purposes, and by this point, you should be aware that you need to be extremely careful about not using it in a production environment. Along with this, some other statements can allow you to be more selective when cleaning the plan cache, which is an instance-wide resource. You may clean the plans for a specific database, a resource governor pool, or even an individual plan. Here is a summary of these statements:

```
DBCC FREEPROCCACHE [ ( { plan_handle | sql_handle | pool_name }
) ]
```

The following statement can be used to remove all the cache entries from the plan cache, a specific plan by specifying a plan handle or SQL handle, or all the plans associated with a specified resource pool:

```
DBCC FREESYSTEMCACHE ( 'ALL' [, pool_name ] )
```

The following statement releases all unused cache entries from all caches, in addition to the plan cache. ALL can be used to specify all supported caches, while pool_name can be used to specify a resource governor pool cache:

```
DBCC FLUSHPROCINDB( db_id )
```

This statement can be used to remove all the cache entries for a specific database.

In addition, you need to be aware that many other statements that you run in a SQL Server instance can remove the plans for the entire instance or a specific database. For example, detaching or restoring a database or changing some SQL Server configuration options can remove all the plans for the entire cache. Some ALTER DATABASE choices may remove all the plans for a specific database. For an entire list, please refer to the SQL Server documentation.

Finally, you can also remove all the plans for a specific database. You can either use DBCC FLUSHPROCINDB or, new with SQL Server 2016, ALTER DATABASE SCOPED CONFIGURATION CLEAR PROCEDURE_CACHE. DBCC FLUSHPROCINDB requires the database ID.

Understanding parameterization

We briefly introduced autoparameterization in *Chapter 2, Troubleshooting Queries*, while covering the query_hash and plan_hash values. To understand how SQL Server caches a plan, along with the different mechanisms by which a plan can be reused, you need to understand parameterization in more detail. Parameterization allows an execution plan to be reused by automatically replacing literal values in statements with parameters. Let's examine those queries again, but this time using the sys.dm_exec_cached_plans DMV, which you can use to return each query plan currently cached by SQL Server. One particular column, usecounts, will be useful because it returns the number of times a specific cache object has been looked up in the plan cache, basically indicating the number of times the plan has been reused. The cacheobjtype and objtype columns, which were introduced in the previous section, will be used as well.

Let's look at the following query:

```
DBCC FREEPROCCACHE
GO
SELECT * FROM Person.Address
WHERE StateProvinceID = 79
GO
SELECT * FROM Person.Address
WHERE StateProvinceID = 59
GO
SELECT * FROM sys.dm_exec_cached_plans
CROSS APPLY sys.dm_exec_sql_text(plan_handle)
WHERE text like '%Person%'
```

We get the following output, abbreviated to fit the page. You can ignore the first two result sets showing the data from the Person.Address table and the query using sys.dm_exec_cached_plans itself, which appears in the third result set:

usecounts	cacheobjtype	objtype	text
1	Compiled Plan	Adhoc	SELECT * FROM Person.Address WHERE StateProvinceID = 59
1	Compiled Plan	Adhoc	SELECT * FROM Person.Address WHERE StateProvinceID = 79

In this case, we can see that each sentence or batch was compiled into an execution plan, even when they only differ on the value for `StateProvinceID`. SQL Server is, by default, very conservative about deciding when to autoparameterize a query, so in this case, no plan was reused because it is not safe to do so ("not safe" meaning that by doing so, there is the potential for performance degradation). If you take a look at the plan (for example, by using the `sys.dm_exec_query_plan` DMF, which was introduced in *Chapter 1, An Introduction to Query Tuning and Optimization*) and the `plan_handle` column of `sys.dm_exec_cached_plans`, as shown in the following query, you will see that they are different execution plans – one uses an Index Seek/Key Lookup combination and the second one uses Clustered Index Scan. The query will return the query text, along with a link that you can click to show the graphical plan:

```
SELECT text, query_plan FROM sys.dm_exec_cached_plans
CROSS APPLY sys.dm_exec_sql_text(plan_handle)
CROSS APPLY sys.dm_exec_query_plan(plan_handle)
WHERE text like '%Person%'
```

As mentioned in *Chapter 2, Troubleshooting Queries*, because a filter with an equality comparison on `StateProvinceID` could return zero, one, or more rows, it is not considered safe for SQL Server to autoparameterize the query. That is, if the query optimizer decides that, for different parameters, different execution plans may be produced, then it is not safe to parameterize.

Autoparameterization

However, let's say we use the second version of the queries, as shown in the following code:

```
DBCC FREEPROCCACHE
GO
SELECT * FROM Person.Address
WHERE AddressID = 12
GO
SELECT * FROM Person.Address
WHERE AddressID = 37
GO
SELECT * FROM sys.dm_exec_cached_plans
CROSS APPLY sys.dm_exec_sql_text(plan_handle)
WHERE text like '%Person%'
```

We get the following output, again abbreviated to fit the page:

usecounts	cacheobjtype	objtype	text
1	Compiled Plan	Adhoc	SELECT * FROM Person.Address WHERE AddressID = 37
1	Compiled Plan	Adhoc	SELECT * FROM Person.Address WHERE AddressID = 12
2	Compiled Plan	Prepared	(@1 tinyint)SELECT * FROM [Person].[Address] WHERE [AddressID]=@1

Because AddressID is part of a unique index here, an equality predicate on AddressID will always return a maximum of one record, so it is safe for the query optimizer to autoparameterize the query and reuse the same plan, as shown in the last row, with a usecounts value of 2 and an objtype value of Prepared. Autoparameterization is also called "simple parameterization" and is usually applied to those queries whose parameterized form would result in a trivial plan. The first two rows in this example are considered shell queries and do not contain a full execution plan, which you can verify by using the sys.dm_exec_query_plan DMF, as shown earlier.

The Optimize for Ad Hoc Workloads option

Optimize for Ad Hoc Workloads is a configuration option introduced with SQL Server 2008 that can be very helpful in cases where you have a large number of ad hoc queries with a low or no possibility of being reused. When this option is used, SQL Server will store a small, compiled plan stub in the plan cache when a query is optimized for the first time instead of the full execution plan. Only after a second optimization will the plan stub be replaced with the full execution plan. Avoiding plans that are never reused can help minimize the size of the plan cache and therefore free up system memory. There is no downside to using this option, so you may consider enabling it for every SQL Server installation.

Let's look at an example of using sp_configure to enable this option. Execute the following statements:

```
EXEC sp_configure 'optimize for ad hoc workloads', 1
RECONFIGURE
DBCC FREEPROCCACHE
GO
SELECT * FROM Person.Address
WHERE StateProvinceID = 79
GO
SELECT * FROM sys.dm_exec_cached_plans
CROSS APPLY sys.dm_exec_sql_text(plan_handle)
WHERE text like '%Person%'
```

Here, we have enabled the **Optimize for Ad Hoc Workloads** configuration option at the instance level. After executing the first SELECT statement, we will see the following output:

usecounts	size_in_bytes	cacheobjtype	objtype	Text
1	352	Compiled Plan Stub	Adhoc	SELECT * FROM Person.Address WHERE StateProvinceID = 79

As you can see, the compiled plan stub is a small object that uses a small number of bytes (in this case, 352). The usecounts column is always 1 for a compiled plan stub because it is never reused. It is also worth clarifying that a plan stub is not the same as the shell query mentioned earlier in this section.

Now, execute the following statements:

```
SELECT * FROM Person.Address
WHERE StateProvinceID = 79
GO
SELECT * FROM sys.dm_exec_cached_plans
CROSS APPLY sys.dm_exec_sql_text(plan_handle)
WHERE text like '%Person%'
```

This time, we get the following output:

usecounts	size_in_bytes	cacheobjtype	Objtype	text
1	16384	Compiled Plan	Adhoc	SELECT * FROM Person.Address WHERE StateProvinceID = 79

After the query is optimized the second time, the compiled plan stub is replaced with a full execution plan, as shown in the cacheobjtype column. Also, notice that the size of the plan is considerably larger than the plan stub (in this case, 16,384 bytes).

However, keep in mind that although this configuration option can be useful in scenarios where you may not have control over the queries submitted to SQL Server, it does not mean that writing a large number of ad hoc queries is recommended or encouraged. Using explicit parameterization (for example, with stored procedures) is recommended instead. Finally, although it is recommended to keep this configuration option enabled in your environments, don't forget to disable it to continue testing the remaining code in this book using the default configuration:

```
EXEC sp_configure 'optimize for ad hoc workloads', 0
RECONFIGURE
```

Forced parameterization

Remember the first example in this section, where we used the `StateProvinceID = 79` predicate and it wasn't safe for SQL Server to parameterize? There might be some special cases where you want to parameterize similar queries if you know that using the same plan can provide better performance. Although you could create stored procedures to do just that, if your application generates ad hoc SQL calls, there is an option that was introduced with SQL Server 2008 that can help you do that – and without changing a single line of application source code. This option is forced parameterization, which can be set at the database level or for a specific query. Forced parameterization applies to the `SELECT`, `INSERT`, `UPDATE`, and `DELETE` statements, and it is subject to certain limitations, which are defined in the SQL Server documentation.

To enable this feature and test how it works, enable forced parameterization at the database level by running the following statement:

```
ALTER DATABASE AdventureWorks2019 SET PARAMETERIZATION FORCED
```

To test it, run the following queries again:

```
DBCC FREEPROCCACHE
GO
SELECT * FROM Person.Address
WHERE StateProvinceID = 79
GO
SELECT * FROM Person.Address
WHERE StateProvinceID = 59
GO
SELECT * FROM sys.dm_exec_cached_plans
CROSS APPLY sys.dm_exec_sql_text(plan_handle)
WHERE text like '%Person%'
```

Different from our first example, where we got two distinct plans, with one customized for each query, this time, we only get one, as shown in the following output:

usecounts	cacheobjtype	objtype	text
1	Compiled Plan	Adhoc	SELECT * FROM Person.Address WHERE StateProvinceID = 59
1	Compiled Plan	Adhoc	SELECT * FROM Person.Address WHERE StateProvinceID = 79
2	Compiled Plan	Prepared	(@0 int)select * from Person.Address where StateProvinceID = @0

In this case, we have only one query plan, as shown in the third row. The first two rows are not execution plans but rather shell queries, as indicated earlier in this section.

You may remember that the original plans that were created in the first example of this section included one with Clustered Index Scan and the other with an Index/Key Lookup combination. You may be wondering which plan was chosen to be shared for both executions. If you have made it this far in this book, you may easily guess that this plan is defined in the first optimization. If you use the query with the StateProvinceID = 79 predicate first, you will get a plan with Clustered Index Scan for both executions, whereas if you use the query with StateProvinceID = 59, you will get the Index/Key Lookup combination, again for both executions. Using some other values of StateProvinceID may even produce different execution plans.

However, because all the similar queries will be using the same plan, this may not be adequate in all scenarios and should be tested thoroughly in your application to verify that it is producing better query performance. The next section talks about problems with queries sensitive to parameters, or what many SQL Server users call the **parameter-sniffing problem**.

Finally, there are also the PARAMETERIZATION SIMPLE and PARAMETERIZATION FORCED query hints, which can be used to override the current database-level parameterization setting and can only be used inside a plan guide. For example, if you define the use of ALTER DATABASE AdventureWorks2019 SET PARAMETERIZATION FORCED, as shown earlier, you can define a plan guide that includes OPTION (PARAMETERIZATION SIMPLE) to override this behavior for a particular query.

Again, don't forget to disable forced parameterization by running the following statement to return to the default parameterization setting:

```
ALTER DATABASE AdventureWorks2019 SET PARAMETERIZATION SIMPLE
```

> **Note**
> Forced parameterization should be used carefully and your database queries should be tested thoroughly.

Stored procedures

Finally, if you want to explicitly take advantage of parameterization and plan reuse, you have a few choices, which include using stored procedures, user-defined scalar functions, and multistatement table-valued functions. All these objects are designed to promote plan reuse and will show a value of Proc on the objtype column of the sys.dm_exec_cached_plans DMV. Therefore, let's see what happens if you use a query that, by itself, was not automatically parameterized and see the behavior in a stored procedure using a parameter. Create the following stored procedure:

```
CREATE OR ALTER PROCEDURE test (@stateid int)
AS
```

```
SELECT * FROM Person.Address
WHERE StateProvinceID = @stateid
```

Run the following code:

```
DBCC FREEPROCCACHE
GO
exec test @stateid = 79
GO
exec test @stateid = 59
GO
SELECT * FROM sys.dm_exec_cached_plans
CROSS APPLY sys.dm_exec_sql_text(plan_handle)
WHERE text like '%Person%'
```

We get the following output:

usecounts	cacheobjtype	objtype	text
2	Compiled Plan	Proc	CREATE PROCEDURE test (@stateid int) AS …

Similar to the case with forced parameterization, where it was important to know which query was optimized first, in the case of a stored procedure, it is also critical to understand that the first optimization will use the parameter provided at that moment to produce the execution plan. In this case, where the 79 parameter is first used, you will notice that both plans are the same and use a Clustered Index Scan operator. You can run the following code, where the 59 parameter is used first, in which case the created plan will use an Index Seek/Key Lookup combination:

```
DBCC FREEPROCCACHE
GO
exec test @stateid = 59
GO
exec test @stateid = 79
GO
SELECT * FROM sys.dm_exec_cached_plans
CROSS APPLY sys.dm_exec_sql_text(plan_handle)
WHERE text like '%Person%'
```

Now that we've learned about parameterization, let's learn what parameter sniffing is.

> **Note**
>
> If you are using SQL Server 2022 and especially for large amounts of data, SQL Server may trigger a parameter-sensitive plan optimization and you will get two different plans. Parameter-sensitive plan optimization will be covered at the end of this chapter.

Parameter sniffing

In this section, we will cover the cases in which reusing a plan can create performance problems. As you saw in *Chapter 6, Understanding Statistics*, SQL Server can use the histogram of statistics objects to estimate the cardinality of a query and then use this information to try and produce an optimal execution plan. The query optimizer accomplishes this by inspecting the values of the query parameters. This behavior is called **parameter sniffing**, and it is a very good thing: getting an execution plan tailored to the current parameters of a query improves the performance of your applications. This chapter has explained that the plan cache can store these execution plans so that they can be reused the next time the same query needs to be executed. This saves optimization time and CPU resources because the query does not need to be optimized again.

However, although the query optimizer and the plan cache work well together most of the time, some performance problems can occasionally appear. Given that the query optimizer can produce different execution plans for syntactically identical queries, depending on their parameters, caching and reusing only one of these plans may create a performance issue for alternative instances of this query that would benefit from a better plan. This is a known problem with T-SQL code using explicit parameterization, such as stored procedures. In this section, we will learn more about this problem, along with a few recommendations on how to fix it.

To see an example, let's write a simple stored procedure using the `Sales.SalesOrderDetail` table on the `AdventureWorks2019` database. As usual, you may have to use `ALTER PROCEDURE` if the procedure already exists:

```
CREATE OR ALTER PROCEDURE test (@pid int)
AS
SELECT * FROM Sales.SalesOrderDetail
WHERE ProductID = @pid
```

Run the following statement to execute the stored procedure:

```
EXEC test @pid = 897
```

The query optimizer estimates that only a few records will be returned by this query and produces the execution plan shown in *Figure 8.2*, which uses an Index Seek operator to quickly find the records on an existing nonclustered index, and a Key Lookup operator to search on the base table for the remaining columns requested by the query:

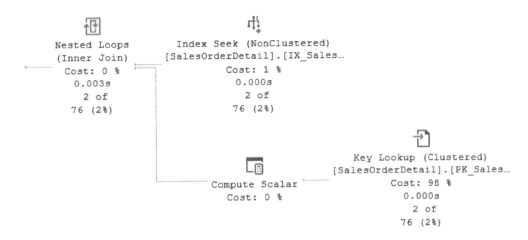

Figure 8.2 – A plan using the Index Seek and Key Lookup operators

This combination of the Index Seek and Key Lookup operators was a good choice because, although it's a relatively expensive combination, the query was highly selective. However, what if a different parameter is used, producing a less selective predicate? For example, try the following code, which includes a SET STATISTICS IO ON statement to display the amount of disk activity generated by the query's execution:

```
SET STATISTICS IO ON
GO
EXEC test @pid = 870
GO
```

The **Messages** tab will show the following output:

```
Table 'SalesOrderDetail'. Scan count 1, logical reads 18038,
physical reads 57, read-ahead reads 447, lob logical reads 0,
lob physical reads 0, lob read-ahead reads 0.
```

As you can see, on this execution alone, SQL Server is performing 18,038 logical reads when the base table only has 1,246 pages; therefore, it's using over 14 times more I/O operations than just simply scanning the entire table. As you saw in *Chapter 4, The Execution Engine*, performing Index Seeks plus Key Lookups on the base table, which uses random I/Os, is a very expensive operation.

Now, clear the plan cache to remove the execution plan currently held in memory and run the stored procedure again, using the same parameter, as shown here:

```
DBCC FREEPROCCACHE
GO
```

```
EXEC test @pid = 870
GO
```

This time, you'll get a different execution plan. The I/O information will now show that only 1,246 pages were read, and the execution plan will include Clustered Index Scan, as shown in *Figure 8.3*. Because there was no optimized version of the stored procedure in the plan cache, SQL Server optimized it from scratch using the new parameter and created a new optimal execution plan:

Figure 8.3 – A plan using Clustered Index Scan

Of course, this doesn't mean you're not supposed to trust your stored procedures anymore or that maybe all your code is incorrect. This is just a problem that you need to be aware of and research, especially if you have queries where performance changes dramatically when different parameters are introduced. If you happen to have this problem, you have a few choices available, which we'll explore next.

Another related problem is that you don't have control over the lifetime of a plan in the cache, so every time a plan is removed from the cache, the newly created execution plan may depend on whichever parameter happens to be passed next. Some of the following choices allow you to have a certain degree of plan stability by asking the query optimizer to produce a plan based on a typical parameter or the average column density.

Finally, as mentioned earlier, new with SQL Server 2022, a new feature of the intelligent query processing family, parameter-sensitive plan optimization, was introduced to help with this problem. This will be covered at the end of this chapter. Next, we will cover some other traditional solutions that you can use if you are still on an older version of SQL Server or have to use an older database compatibility level.

Optimizing for a typical parameter

There might be cases where most of the executions of a query use the same execution plan and you want to avoid an ongoing optimization cost by reusing that plan. In these cases, you can use a hint that was introduced with SQL Server 2005 called OPTIMIZE FOR, which is useful when an optimal plan can be generated for the majority of values that are used in a specific parameter. In addition, it can provide more plan stability. As a result, only a few executions that use an atypical parameter may not have an optimal plan.

Suppose that almost all the executions of our stored procedure would benefit from the previous plan using Index Seek and a Key Lookup operator. To take advantage of this, you could write the following stored procedure:

```
ALTER PROCEDURE test (@pid int)
AS
SELECT * FROM Sales.SalesOrderDetail
WHERE ProductID = @pid
OPTION (OPTIMIZE FOR (@pid = 897))
```

When you run the stored procedure for the first time, it will be optimized for a value of 897, no matter what parameter value was specified for the execution. If you want to check this, test the case by running the following command:

```
EXEC test @pid = 870
```

You can find the following entry close to the end of the XML plan (or the **Parameter List** property in a graphical plan):

```
<ParameterList>
<ColumnReference Column="@pid" ParameterCompiledValue="(897)"
ParameterRuntimeValue="(870)" />
</ParameterList>
```

This entry clearly shows which parameter value was used during optimization and which one was used during execution. In this case, the stored procedure is optimized only once, and the plan is stored in the plan cache and reused as many times as needed. The benefit of using this hint, in addition to avoiding optimization costs, is that you have total control over which plan is produced during the query optimization process and stored in the plan cache. The OPTIMIZE FOR query hint can also allow you to use more than one parameter, separated by commas.

Optimizing on every execution

If using different parameters produces different execution plans and you want the best performance for every query, the solution might be to optimize for every execution. You will get the best possible plan on every execution but will end up paying for the optimization cost, so you'll need to decide whether that's a worthwhile trade-off. To do this, use the RECOMPILE hint, as shown here:

```
ALTER PROCEDURE test (@pid int)
AS
SELECT * FROM Sales.SalesOrderDetail
```

```
WHERE ProductID = @pid
 OPTION (RECOMPILE)
```

Using `OPTION (RECOMPILE)` can also allow the values of local variables to be sniffed, as shown in the next section. Not surprisingly, this option will return **Option (Recompile) requested** in the `EventSubClass` column in SQL Trace for both the **SP:Recompile** and **SQL:StmtRecompile** events, as you saw earlier in this chapter.

Local variables and the OPTIMIZE FOR UNKNOWN hint

Another solution that has been traditionally implemented in the past is the use of local variables in queries instead of parameters. As mentioned in *Chapter 6, Understanding Statistics*, the query optimizer can't see the values of local variables at optimization time because these values are usually only known at execution time. However, by using local variables, you are disabling parameter sniffing, which means that the query optimizer will not be able to access the statistics histogram to find an optimal plan for the query. Instead, it will rely on just the density information of the statistics object, a subject also covered in *Chapter 6, Understanding Statistics*.

This solution will simply ignore the parameter values and use the same execution plan for all the executions, but at least you're getting a consistent plan every time. A variation of the `OPTIMIZE FOR` hint shown previously is the `OPTIMIZE FOR UNKNOWN` hint. This hint was introduced with SQL Server 2008 and has the same effect as using local variables. A benefit of the `OPTIMIZE FOR UNKNOWN` hint compared to `OPTIMIZE FOR` is that it does not require you to specify a value for a parameter. Also, you don't have to worry if a specified value becomes atypical over time.

Running the following two versions of our stored procedure will have equivalent outcomes and will produce the same execution plan. The first version uses local variables, while the second one uses the `OPTIMIZE FOR UNKNOWN` hint:

```
ALTER PROCEDURE test (@pid int)
AS
DECLARE @p int = @pid
SELECT * FROM Sales.SalesOrderDetail
WHERE ProductID = @p
ALTER PROCEDURE test (@pid int)
AS
SELECT * FROM Sales.SalesOrderDetail
WHERE ProductID = @pid
OPTION (OPTIMIZE FOR UNKNOWN)
```

In this case, the query optimizer will create the plan using the Clustered Index Scan shown previously, no matter which parameter you use to execute the stored procedure. Note that the OPTIMIZE FOR UNKNOWN query hint will apply to all the parameters used in a query unless you use the following syntax to target only a specific parameter:

```
ALTER PROCEDURE test (@pid int)
AS
SELECT * FROM Sales.SalesOrderDetail
WHERE ProductID = @pid
OPTION (OPTIMIZE FOR (@pid UNKNOWN))
```

Finally, keep in mind that parameter sniffing is a desired optimization, and you would only want to disable it when you have any of the problems mentioned in this section and if it improves the general performance of your query.

It is interesting to note that as of SQL Server 2005, where statement-level compilation was introduced to allow you to optimize an individual statement, it was technically possible to sniff the values of local variables in the same way as with a parameter. However, this behavior was not implemented because there was already a lot of code using local variables to explicitly disable parameter sniffing. Local variables, however, can be sniffed while using the RECOMPILE query hint, which was explained earlier. For example, let's use the following code with both local variables and the OPTION (RECOMPILE) hint:

```
ALTER PROCEDURE test (@pid int)
AS
DECLARE @p int = @pid
SELECT * FROM Sales.SalesOrderDetail
WHERE ProductID = @p
OPTION (RECOMPILE)
```

Then, run the following:

```
EXEC test @pid = 897
```

The query optimizer will be able to see the value of the local variable (in this case, 897) and get a plan optimized for that specific value (in this case, the plan with the Index Seek/Key Lookup operations, instead of the plan with Clustered Index Scan, which was shown earlier when no value could be sniffed).

Although *Chapter 6, Understanding Statistics*, explained how to use the histogram and the density vector of the statistics object to estimate the cardinality of a query, let's review this again here from the point of view of disabling parameter sniffing. Any of the stored procedures at the beginning of this section – either using local variables or the OPTIMIZE FOR UNKNOWN hint – will return the following plan, with an estimated cardinality of 456.079:

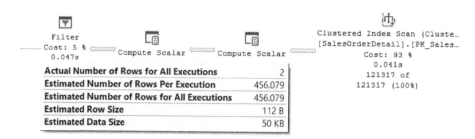

Figure 8.4 – Cardinality estimate with parameter sniffing disabled

Let's see how SQL Server is obtaining a value of 456.079 and what the reasoning behind this is. As explained in *Chapter 6, Understanding Statistics*, density is defined as follows:

1 / number of distinct values

The SalesOrderDetail table has 266 distinct values for ProductID, so the density is calculated as 1 / 266, or 0.003759399, which you can verify by looking at the statistics object (for example, using the DBCC SHOW_STATISTICS statement). One assumption in the statistics mathematical model that's used by SQL Server is the uniformity assumption and because in this case, SQL Server cannot use the histogram, the uniformity assumption tells us that for any given value, the data distribution is the same. To obtain the estimated number of records, SQL Server will multiply the density by the current total number of records (0.003759399 * 121,317, or 456.079), as shown in the plan. This is also the same as dividing the total number of records by the number of distinct values (121,317 / 266, which also equals 456.079).

Finally, the benefit of using the OPTIMIZE FOR UNKNOWN hint is that you only need to optimize the query once and can reuse the produced plan many times. Also, there is no need to specify a value like in the OPTIMIZE FOR hint.

Disabling parameter sniffing

As mentioned in the previous section, when you use local variables in a query to avoid using a stored procedure parameter or when you use the OPTIMIZE FOR UNKNOWN query hint, you are disabling parameter sniffing. Microsoft has also published trace flag 4136 to disable parameter sniffing at the instance level. As described in Microsoft Knowledge Base article 980653, this trace flag was first introduced as a cumulative update for older versions of SQL Server such as SQL Server 2005 SP3, SQL Server 2008 SP1, and SQL Server 2008 R2, and it is available on the latest versions as well, including SQL Server 2014. There are still three cases where this trace flag has no effect:

- Queries that use the OPTIMIZE FOR query hint
- Queries that use the OPTION (RECOMPILE) hint
- Queries in a stored procedure that use the WITH RECOMPILE option

As with using forced parameterization at the database level, this should be considered an extreme option that can only be used in some limited cases and should be used with caution. You should make sure you test your application thoroughly to validate that it improves performance. In addition, you could use this trace flag if the majority of your queries benefit from disabling parameter sniffing and still use any of the three exceptions listed previously for queries that may not. At least, Microsoft has recommended that users of their Dynamics AX application consider using this trace flag, as documented at `http://blogs.msdn.com/b/axperf/archive/2010/05/07/important-sql-server-change-parameter-sniffing-and-plan-caching.aspx`.

Finally, starting with SQL Server 2016, you can disable parameter sniffing at the database level or the query level by using `ALTER DATABASE SCOPED CONFIGURATION SET PARAMETER_SNIFFING = OFF` or the `DISABLE_PARAMETER_SNIFFING` hint, respectively.

Parameter sniffing and SET options affecting plan reuse

One interesting problem that we have sometimes been asked to troubleshoot is when a stored procedure is taking too long to execute or is timing out on a web application but returning immediately when executed directly in SQL Server Management Studio – even for the same parameters. Although there could be a few reasons for a performance problem like this, including blocking, the most frequent reason for this happening is related to a behavior where two different plans were created with different `SET` options, and at least one of those plans was optimized using a combination of parameters that produced a "bad" plan for some other executions of the same stored procedure with different parameters. Although you may be tempted to just run `sp_recompile` to force a new optimization and allow the application to continue working, this does not fix the problem, and it may eventually come back. You may also encounter a similar scenario where you have updated statistics, rebuilt an index, or changed something else to find out that, suddenly, the problem seems to be fixed. It is not. Those changes probably just forced a new optimization with the "good" parameter you were just testing. The best thing to do for this kind of problem is to capture the "bad" plan for further analysis to provide a permanent solution. In this section, we will learn how to do that.

Remember that, in general, query optimization is an expensive operation, and to avoid this optimization cost, the plan cache will try to keep the generated execution plans in memory so that they can be reused. However, if a new connection running the same stored procedure has different `SET` options, it may generate a new plan instead of reusing one already in the plan cache. This new plan can then be reused by later executions of the same stored procedure, but only if the same connection settings are used. A new plan will be needed because some of these `SET` options may impact the choice of an execution plan. This is because they affect the results of evaluating constant expressions during the optimization process. Another connection setting, `FORCEPLAN`, acts similarly to a hint, requesting that the query optimizer preserves the join order, as specified on the query syntax, and uses nested loop joins only. The following `SET` options will affect the reuse of execution plans:

- `ANSI_NULL_DFLT_OFF`
- `ANSI_NULL_DFLT_ON`

- ANSI_NULLS

- ANSI_PADDING

- ANSI_WARNINGS

- ARITHABORT

- CONCAT_NULL_YIELDS_NULL

- DATEFIRST

- DATEFORMAT

- FORCEPLAN

- LANGUAGE

- NO_BROWSETABLE

- NUMERIC_ROUNDABORT

- QUOTED_IDENTIFIER

> **Note**
>
> The ANSI_NULLS OFF, ANSI_PADDING OFF, and CONCAT_NULL_YIELDS_NULL OFF SET statements and database options have been deprecated. In future versions of SQL Server, these SET statements and database options will always be set to ON.

Unfortunately, management and development tools such as SQL Server Management Studio, the ADO.NET framework, and even the sqlcmd utility have different SET options in their default configuration. You will find that often, the problem is that one of the options, ARITHABORT, is OFF by default in ADO.NET and ON by default in Management Studio. Therefore, it may be possible that, in our example, Management Studio and the web application are using distinct cached plans, but the plan that was created for the web application was not good for some other executions of the same stored procedure with different parameters.

Now, let's learn how to prove that optimizing with different parameters is, in fact, the problem for your specific instance of the issue. We'll look at how to extract the plans to inspect both the parameters and the SET options that are used during optimization. Because AdventureWorks2019 does not have the default SET options of a new database, we'll create our own database, copy some data from AdventureWorks2019, and create a new stored procedure. Run the following code to do so:

```
CREATE DATABASE Test
GO
USE Test
```

```
GO
SELECT * INTO dbo.SalesOrderDetail
FROM AdventureWorks2019.Sales.SalesOrderDetail
GO
CREATE NONCLUSTERED INDEX IX_SalesOrderDetail_ProductID
ON dbo.SalesOrderDetail(ProductID)
GO
CREATE OR ALTER PROCEDURE test (@pid int)
AS
SELECT * FROM dbo.SalesOrderDetail
WHERE ProductID = @pid
```

Let's test two different applications by executing the stored procedure from both SQL Server Management Studio and a .NET application (the C# code for this application is included at the end of this section). For this test, we want to assume that a plan with a table scan is a bad plan and that a plan that uses an Index Seek/RID Lookup is the optimal one.

Start with a clean plan cache by running the following command:

```
DBCC FREEPROCCACHE
```

Run the .NET application from a command prompt window and provide a value of 870 as a parameter. Note that the only purpose of this .NET application is to run the test stored procedure we created earlier:

```
C:\TestApp\test
Enter ProductID: 870
```

Now, we can start inspecting the plan cache to see the plans that are available in memory. Run the following script from the Test database (we will be running this script again later in this exercise):

```
SELECT plan_handle, usecounts, pvt.set_options
FROM (
SELECT plan_handle, usecounts, epa.attribute, epa.value
FROM sys.dm_exec_cached_plans
OUTER APPLY sys.dm_exec_plan_attributes(plan_handle) AS epa
WHERE cacheobjtype = 'Compiled Plan') AS ecpa
PIVOT (MAX(ecpa.value) FOR ecpa.attribute IN ("set_options",
"objectid")) AS pvt
WHERE pvt.objectid = OBJECT_ID('dbo.test')
```

You should get an output similar to the following:

plan_handle	usecounts	set_options
0x050007002255970F9042B8F80100000001000000000000000 ...	1	251

The preceding output shows that we have one execution plan in the plan cache, it has been used once (as indicated by the usecounts value), and that the set_options value (taken from the sys. dm_exec_plan_attributes DMF) is 251. Because this was the first execution of the stored procedure, it was optimized using the 870 parameter, which in this case created a plan using a table scan (here, this is considered a "bad" plan). Now, run the application again using a parameter that returns only a few records and that should benefit from an Index Seek/RID Lookup plan:

```
C:\TestApp\test
Enter ProductID: 898
```

If you inspect the plan cache again, you will notice that the plan has been used twice, as noted by the usecounts column; unfortunately, this time, it was not good for the second parameter that was used. In a real production database, this second execution may not perform as expected, taking too long to execute, and it may cause the developer to try to troubleshoot the problem by running the stored procedure in Management Studio using something like this:

```
EXEC test @pid = 898
```

Now, the developer may be confused by the fact that SQL Server is returning a good execution plan and the query is returning its results immediately. Inspecting the plan cache again will show something similar to the following:

plan_handle	usecounts	set_options
0x050007002255970FB049B8F80100000001000000000000000 ...	1	4347
0x050007002255970F9042B8F80100000001000000000000000 ...	2	251

As you can see, a new plan was added for the Management Studio execution with a different value for set_options (in this case, 4347).

What should we do next? It is time to inspect the plans and look at the SET options and parameters that were used during the optimization. Select plan_handle of the first plan that was created (the one with a set_options value of 251 in your example) and use it to run the following query:

```
SELECT * FROM sys.dm_exec_query_
plan(0x050007002255970F9042B8F80100000001000000000000000 ...)
```

You can find the SET options at the beginning of the XML plan (also available using the **Properties** window of a graphical execution plan):

```
<StatementSetOptions QUOTED_IDENTIFIER="true"
ARITHABORT="false"
CONCAT_NULL_YIELDS_NULL="true" ANSI_NULLS="true" ANSI_
PADDING="true"
ANSI_WARNINGS="true" NUMERIC_ROUNDABORT="false" />
```

You will find the used parameters at the end (also available in the graphical execution plan):

```
<ParameterList>
<ColumnReference Column="@pid" ParameterCompiledValue="(870)"
/>
</ParameterList>
```

Do the same for the second plan. You will get the following information for the SET options:

```
<StatementSetOptions QUOTED_IDENTIFIER="true" ARITHABORT="true"
CONCAT_NULL_YIELDS_NULL="true" ANSI_NULLS="true" ANSI_
PADDING="true"
ANSI_WARNINGS="true" NUMERIC_ROUNDABORT="false" />
```

You will get the following parameter information:

```
<ParameterList>
<ColumnReference Column="@pid" ParameterCompiledValue="(898)"
/>
</ParameterList>
```

This information shows that the ARITHABORT SET option has a different value on these plans and that the parameter that was used to optimize the query on the web application was 870. You can also verify the operators that were used in the plan – the first one used a table scan, while the second one used an Index Seek/RID Lookup combination. Now that you have captured the plans, you can force a new optimization so that the application can use a better plan immediately (keeping in mind that this is not a permanent solution). Try this:

```
sp_recompile test
```

Optionally, you could use the following script to display the configured `SET` options for a specific `set_options` value:

```
DECLARE @set_options int = 4347
IF ((1 & @set_options) = 1) PRINT 'ANSI_PADDING'
IF ((4 & @set_options) = 4) PRINT 'FORCEPLAN'
IF ((8 & @set_options) = 8) PRINT 'CONCAT_NULL_YIELDS_NULL'
IF ((16 & @set_options) = 16) PRINT 'ANSI_WARNINGS'
IF ((32 & @set_options) = 32) PRINT 'ANSI_NULLS'
IF ((64 & @set_options) = 64) PRINT 'QUOTED_IDENTIFIER'
IF ((128 & @set_options) = 128) PRINT 'ANSI_NULL_DFLT_ON'
IF ((256 & @set_options) = 256) PRINT 'ANSI_NULL_DFLT_OFF'
IF ((512 & @set_options) = 512) PRINT 'NoBrowseTable'
IF ((4096 & @set_options) = 4096) PRINT 'ARITH_ABORT'
IF ((8192 & @set_options) = 8192) PRINT 'NUMERIC_ROUNDABORT'
IF ((16384 & @set_options) = 16384) PRINT 'DATEFIRST'
IF ((32768 & @set_options) = 32768) PRINT 'DATEFORMAT'
IF ((65536 & @set_options) = 65536) PRINT 'LanguageID'
```

This will return the following output for the `set_options` value of `4347`:

```
ANSI_PADDING
CONCAT_NULL_YIELDS_NULL
ANSI_WARNINGS
ANSI_NULLS
QUOTED_IDENTIFIER
ANSI_NULL_DFLT_ON
ARITH_ABORT
```

Now that you have identified that this is a problem related to parameter sniffing, you can apply any of the techniques shown earlier in this section.

Finally, the following C# code can be used for the .NET application that was used in this section. You may need to reformat and keep the connection string in a single line to avoid any compilation errors:

```
using System;
using System.Data;
using System.Data.SqlClient;
class Test
```

```
{
    static void Main()
    {
        SqlConnection cnn = null;
        SqlDataReader reader = null;
        try
        {
            Console.Write("Enter ProductID: ");
            string pid = Console.ReadLine();
            cnn = new SqlConnection("Data
                Source=(local);Initial Catalog=Test;
                Integrated Security=SSPI");
            SqlCommand cmd = new SqlCommand();
            cmd.Connection = cnn;
            cmd.CommandText = "dbo.test";
            cmd.CommandType = CommandType.StoredProcedure;
            cmd.Parameters.Add
                ("@pid", SqlDbType.Int).Value = pid;
            cnn.Open();
            reader = cmd.ExecuteReader();
            while (reader.Read())
            {
                Console.WriteLine(reader[0]);
            }
            return;
        }
        catch (Exception e)
        {
            throw e;
        }
        finally
        {
            if (cnn != null)
            {
                if (cnn.State != ConnectionState.Closed)
                    cnn.Close();
```

```
            }
        }
    }
}
```

Same as with the C# code shown in *Chapter 2, Troubleshooting Queries*, to compile this code, you need to run the following in a command prompt window, assuming the code was saved in a file named `test.cs`:

```
csc test.cs
```

Visual Studio is not required to compile this code, just the Microsoft .NET Framework, which is needed to install SQL Server. Therefore, it will already be installed on your system. You may need to find the location of the `.csc` executable, though, if it is not included on the system PATH (although it is usually inside the `C:\Windows\Microsoft.NET` directory). The connection string in the code assumes you are connecting to a default instance of SQL Server using Windows authentication, so you may need to change these values if they are different in your installation. In the next section, we will learn about one of the most interesting features in SQL Server 2022 – that is, parameter-sensitive plan optimization.

Parameter-sensitive plan optimization

One of the most exciting features of SQL Server 2022 is, without a doubt, parameter-sensitive plan optimization, which is part of the intelligent query processing family of features. Parameter-sensitive query optimization intends to help with performance problems related to parameter-sensitive queries. So, in this section, we will cover how it works and how to use it.

Let's explore and learn how the technology works; we will explain the details along the way. If you have followed all the examples in this book so far, after many changes, perhaps this could be a good moment to restore a fresh copy of `AdventureWorks2019`. You may notice that the database has a compatibility level of 140 or SQL Server 2017 (even when the database was given a 2019 name). As mentioned previously, this is a new SQL Server feature and it is only available under database compatibility level 160, so you need to run the following statement:

```
ALTER DATABASE AdventureWorks2019 SET COMPATIBILITY_LEVEL = 160
```

Although not required, it is highly recommended that you also enable the query store so that you can get additional insights into the parameter-sensitive plan optimization feature and the available execution plans. Run the following statements:

```
ALTER DATABASE AdventureWorks2019 SET QUERY_STORE = ON
ALTER DATABASE AdventureWorks2019 SET QUERY_STORE (OPERATION_
MODE = READ_WRITE)
ALTER DATABASE AdventureWorks2019 SET QUERY_STORE CLEAR ALL
```

Create our test procedure once again:

```
CREATE OR ALTER PROCEDURE test (@pid int)
AS
SELECT * FROM Sales.SalesOrderDetail
WHERE ProductID = @pid
```

Run the following statement, which we know must return only two rows:

```
EXEC test @pid = 897
```

Now, run the following statement:

```
EXEC test @pid = 870
```

Parameter-sensitive plan optimization does not seem to work so far. SQL Server seems to have the same behavior that we saw previously and has reused the same plan. In addition, by inspecting the XML plan, we can't see some new elements that we will cover soon.

SQL Server 2022 brings a new extended event, `parameter_sensitive_plan_optimization_skipped_reason`, which triggers when the parameter-sensitive plan optimization feature is skipped. As such, we can use this event to find out why parameter-sensitive plan optimization was skipped in our test. Create the following extended events session:

```
CREATE EVENT SESSION psp ON SERVER
ADD EVENT sqlserver.parameter_sensitive_plan_optimization_
skipped_reason
WITH (STARTUP_STATE = ON)
```

Start the session you just created:

```
ALTER EVENT SESSION psp
ON SERVER
STATE=START
```

Run the example again:

```
EXEC test @pid = 897
```

An easy way to see captured events is to use Watch Live Data, as explained in *Chapter 2, Troubleshooting Queries*. In our case, the reason that was returned was `SkewnessThresholdNotMet`, so if a specified skewness threshold was not met, perhaps we need more data to test this feature.

> **Note**
>
> Other reasons returned for some other queries in my test included `LoadStatsFailed`, `UnsupportedComparisonType`, `UnsupportedObject`, `SystemDB`, `OutputOrModifiedParam`, `DatatypesIncompat`, `ConjunctThresholdNotMet`, `UnsupportedStatementType`, `NonCacheable`, and `QueryTextTooLarge`. Although these names suggest the reason without additional explanation, at the time of writing, they are undocumented. You can get the entire list by running the following code:
>
> SELECT name, map_value
>
> FROM sys.dm_xe_map_values
>
> WHERE name = 'psp_skipped_reason_enum'

So, let's try a new data setup instead. Drop the `dbo.SalesOrderDetail` table if you still have it and create the following in `AdventureWorks2019`:

```
CREATE TABLE dbo.SalesOrderDetail (
    SalesOrderID int NOT NULL,
    SalesOrderDetailID int NOT NULL,
    CarrierTrackingNumber nvarchar(25) NULL,
    OrderQty smallint NOT NULL,
    ProductID int NOT NULL,
    SpecialOfferID int NOT NULL,
    UnitPrice money NOT NULL,
    UnitPriceDiscount money NOT NULL,
    LineTotal money,
    rowguid uniqueidentifier ROWGUIDCOL NOT NULL,
    ModifiedDate datetime NOT NULL)
```

Run the following code:

```
INSERT INTO dbo.SalesOrderDetail (
    SalesOrderID,
    SalesOrderDetailID,
    CarrierTrackingNumber,
    OrderQty,
    ProductID,
    SpecialOfferID,
    UnitPrice,
    UnitPriceDiscount,
```

```
    LineTotal,
    rowguid,
    ModifiedDate)
SELECT * FROM Sales.SalesOrderDetail
WHERE ProductID = 897
-- WHERE ProductID = 870
-- GO 50
```

First, execute the code as is. This will insert two records for ProductID 897. Execute the code a second time with the following changes, changing the comments in the last three lines:

```
-- WHERE ProductID = 897
WHERE ProductID = 870
GO 50
```

This second version of the code will insert 4,688 records for ProductID 897 and will run it 50 times for a total of 234,400 records. Now, create an index:

```
CREATE INDEX IX_ProductID ON dbo.SalesOrderDetail(ProductID)
```

We need this index to easily find the records with high selectivity. We will also use it to easily identify the query optimizer statistics later in this exercise. Change the test procedure so that it accesses the new table instead:

```
ALTER PROCEDURE test (@pid int)
AS
SELECT * FROM dbo.SalesOrderDetail
WHERE ProductID = @pid
```

Run our queries, as shown here, and inspect the resulting execution plans:

```
DBCC FREEPROCCACHE
GO
EXEC test @pid = 897
GO
EXEC test @pid = 870
```

Parameter-sensitive plan optimization seems to be working now. We got two different plans, each tailored for the submitted parameters. The first one uses Index Seek, while the second one uses Table Scan, as we saw earlier in this chapter. The first plan is shown here:

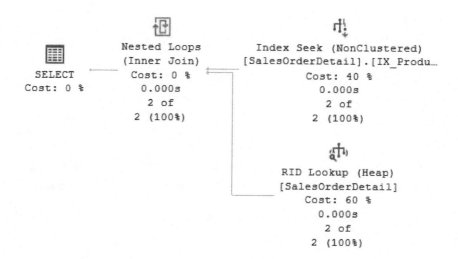

Figure 8.5 – A plan using parameter-sensitive plan optimization

Now, let's see how the feature works. Run the following code:

```
DBCC FREEPROCCACHE
GO
EXEC test @pid = 897
GO
EXEC test @pid = 870
GO 4
EXEC test @pid = 897
GO 2
SELECT * FROM sys.dm_exec_cached_plans CROSS APPLY
sys.dm_exec_sql_text(plan_handle)
```

You can find our original test procedure information by looking at the row with the objtype = 'Proc' column and the text column corresponding to the procedure definition. It has a usecount value of 7, which corresponds to the total number of executions. More interesting is to look at the two rows with objtype = 'Prepared' with usecounts values of 3 and 4, which correspond to each procedure and parameter number of executions. The text column on these two rows looks like this:

```
(@pid int)SELECT * FROM dbo.SalesOrderDetail  WHERE ProductID
= @pid option (PLAN PER VALUE(QueryVariantID = 3, predicate_
range([AdventureWorks2019].[dbo].[SalesOrderDetail].[ProductID]
= @pid, 100.0, 100000.0)))
```

Here, we have a few new concepts such as QueryVariantID and predicate_range, which we will cover next. We have the following two entries on the XML plan, which are also new. You will notice the Dispatcher element from one of the plans:

```
<Dispatcher>
    <ParameterSensitivePredicate LowBoundary="100"
HighBoundary="100000">
        <StatisticsInfo … Statistics="[IX_ProductID]"
ModificationCount="0" SamplingPercent="100" />
        <Predicate>
            <ScalarOperator ScalarString="[AdventureWorks2019].
[dbo].[SalesOrderDetail].[ProductID]=[@pid]">
                <Compare CompareOp="EQ">
...
</Dispatcher>
```

There's also the QueryVariantID attribute of the QueryPlan element:

```
<QueryPlan … QueryVariantID="3">
```

So, how does parameter-sensitive plan optimization work? When you run the query for the first time, the query optimizer will inspect the statistics histogram to identify non-uniform distributions and evaluate up to three out of all available predicates. Let's see the histogram of our trivial example:

```
DBCC SHOW_STATISTICS('dbo.SalesOrderDetail', IX_ProductID)
```

We will get the following trivial histogram:

RANGE_HI_KEY	RANGE_ROWS	EQ_ROWS	DISTINCT_RANGE_ROWS	AVG_RANGE_ROWS
870	0	234400	0	1
897	0	2	0	1

The initial optimization produces a dispatcher plan, which contains the optimization logic in what is called a dispatcher expression. A dispatcher maps to query variants based on the cardinality of the predicate boundaries. As shown in the XML fragment earlier, the Dispatcher element includes details about the predicate boundaries, which are based on the histogram. This can be found in the ParameterSensitivePredicate entry. It also includes the query variants as QueryVariantID in the QueryPlan element. In our case, it showed QueryVariantID values 1 and 3 for our two execution plans.

Also, notice the **equality operator (EQ)**. On this first release, only predicates with EQs are supported. According to data collected by Microsoft, these cases represent 90% of parameter-sensitive problems.

Finally, you can disable this feature if needed, such as in the typical case of performance regressions. You can use the ALTER DATABASE SCOPED CONFIGURATION SET PARAMETER_SENSITIVE_ PLAN_OPTIMIZATION = OFF statement or the DISABLE_PARAMETER_SENSITIVE_PLAN_ OPTIMIZATION hint to disable parameter-sensitive plan optimization at the database or query level, respectively. As usual, to clean up after finishing this exercise, drop the SalesOrderDetail table and stop and delete the extended events session.

Summary

This chapter covered plan caching and focused on what you need to know to efficiently reuse query plans. Query optimization is a relatively expensive operation, so if a query can be optimized once and the created plan can be reused many times, it can greatly improve the performance of your applications. We covered the batch compilation and recompilation process in detail and showed you how to identify problems with excessive compilations and recompilations.

Plan reuse is based on query parameterization, so this topic was also covered in detail. We looked at cases where SQL Server decides to automatically parameterize your queries, as well as cases when it has to be explicitly defined by either using the forced parameterization configuration option or objects such as stored procedures, user-defined scalar functions, and multistatement table-valued functions.

Although looking at the parameters of a query helps the query optimizer produce better execution plans, occasionally reusing some of these plans can also be a performance problem because they may not be optimal for the same query being executed with different parameters. We showed that parameter sniffing is, in fact, a performance optimization, but we also covered solutions to the cases when reusing such plans may not be adequate, especially in the case of parameter-sensitive queries.

Finally, we covered parameter-sensitive query optimization, which was introduced with SQL Server 2022 and is part of the intelligent query processing family of features. It intends to help with performance problems related to parameter-sensitive queries. In the next chapter, we will learn more about various intelligent query processing features that came with SQL Server.

9

The Query Store

This chapter covers the Query Store, a feature introduced with SQL Server 2016 that allows you to troubleshoot queries and execution plan-related issues and monitor performance history. The Query Store collects information about queries, plans, and runtime statistics, helping you pinpoint performance differences due to changes in execution plans.

The Query Store has been improved with every release since then and, new with SQL Server 2022, allows you to enable some of the new intelligent query processing features. For example, features such as memory grant feedback, cardinality estimation feedback, and degree of parallelism feedback use the Query Store to persist their information on queries and plans.

New with SQL Server 2022, the Query Store can also be enabled on secondary replicas used by Always On availability groups. This can help in scenarios where you want to troubleshoot query performance on read-only workloads running on secondary replicas.

In addition, this version introduced Query Store hints. Traditional query hints, which will be covered in the last chapter of this book, allow you to affect the query execution behavior, but they require you to rewrite the query text, something that may not always be possible in your production environment. As will be covered in *Chapter 12*, plan guides are a way to achieve the same as Query Store hints, although they are very complex to use.

This chapter provides an introduction to the Query Store and will show you the basics, such as how to configure and use the Query Store using both SQL Server Management Studio and T-SQL, as well as how to query the Query Store catalog views. Query store hints will be briefly covered in the next chapter since they are used by the cardinality estimation feedback feature. For more details about the Query Store, you can read the SQL Server documentation or my book *High-Performance SQL Server*.

This chapter covers the following topics:

- Using the Query Store
- Querying the Query Store

Using the Query Store

Configuring the Query Store is straightforward – we will enable it a few times in *Chapter 10*, so that we can work with some of the new intelligent query processing features. In this section, we will configure it. You may want to start with a fresh copy of the AdventureWorks2019 database. In SQL Server Management Studio, right-click the **AdventureWorks** database, select **Properties**, and then select **Query Store**. You will see something similar to the following:

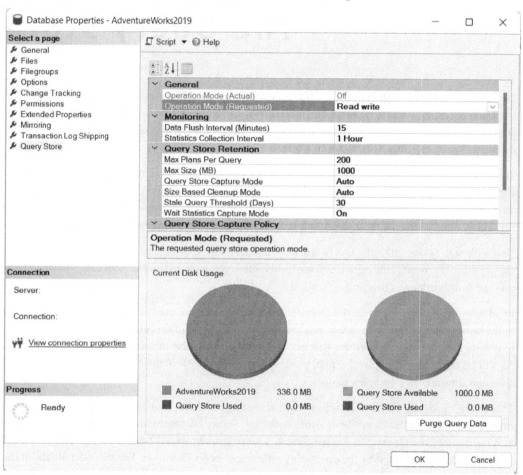

Figure 9.1 – Query Store configuration

To enable the Query Store, you must change **Operation Mode (Requested)** to **Read write**. If you click the **Script** button at the top of the **Database Properties** window, the following code will be generated:

```
USE master
GO
```

```
ALTER DATABASE AdventureWorks2019 SET QUERY_STORE = ON
GO
ALTER DATABASE AdventureWorks2019 SET QUERY_STORE (OPERATION_
MODE = READ_WRITE)
```

Click **OK** or run the produced code. In addition, you can use the same method to change any of the listed Query Store properties. You can use the following catalog view to see the currently defined Query Store properties while connected to the **AdventureWorks2019** database:

```
SELECT * FROM sys.database_query_store_options
```

To start testing the Query Store, we need some query activity. Run the following random queries that have been taken from *Chapter 3* and *Chapter 4*. The query and plan information will be available in the Query Store immediately once the query has been optimized and executed:

```
SELECT TerritoryID, COUNT(*)
FROM Sales.SalesOrderHeader
GROUP BY TerritoryID
ORDER BY TerritoryID
SELECT * FROM Sales.SalesOrderdetail s
JOIN Production.Product p ON s.ProductID = p.ProductID
WHERE SalesOrderID = 43659
OPTION (MERGE JOIN)
SELECT h.SalesOrderID, s.SalesOrderDetailID, OrderDate
FROM Sales.SalesOrderHeader h
JOIN Sales.SalesOrderDetail s ON h.SalesOrderID =
s.SalesOrderID
SELECT e.BusinessEntityID, TerritoryID
FROM HumanResources.Employee AS e
JOIN Sales.SalesPerson AS s ON e.BusinessEntityID =
s.BusinessEntityID
SELECT SalesOrderID, SUM(LineTotal)FROM Sales.SalesOrderDetail
GROUP BY SalesOrderID
SELECT c.CustomerID, COUNT(*)
FROM Sales.Customer c JOIN Sales.SalesOrderHeader s
ON c.CustomerID = s.CustomerID
WHERE c.TerritoryID = 4
GROUP BY c.CustomerID
SELECT DISTINCT pp.LastName, pp.FirstName
```

```
FROM Person.Person pp JOIN HumanResources.Employee e
ON e.BusinessEntityID = pp.BusinessEntityID
JOIN Sales.SalesOrderHeader soh
ON pp.BusinessEntityID = soh.SalesPersonID
JOIN Sales.SalesOrderDetail sod
ON soh.SalesOrderID = soh.SalesOrderID
JOIN Production.Product p
ON sod.ProductID = p.ProductID
WHERE ProductNumber = 'BK-M18B-44'
SELECT soh.SalesOrderID, sod.SalesOrderDetailID, SalesReasonID
FROM Sales.SalesOrderHeader soh
JOIN Sales.SalesOrderDetail sod
ON soh.SalesOrderID = soh.SalesOrderID
JOIN Sales.SalesOrderHeaderSalesReason sohsr
ON sohsr.SalesOrderID = soh.SalesOrderID
WHERE soh.SalesOrderID = 43697
```

Now, we can start inspecting the query and plan information that's available. To see the available choices, expand or refresh the **Query Store** folder in SQL Server Management Studio, as shown in the following screenshot:

Figure 9.2 – The Query Store folder

Select **Top Resource Consuming Queries** to open the **Top Resource Consuming Queries** pane. A sample can be seen in the following screenshot:

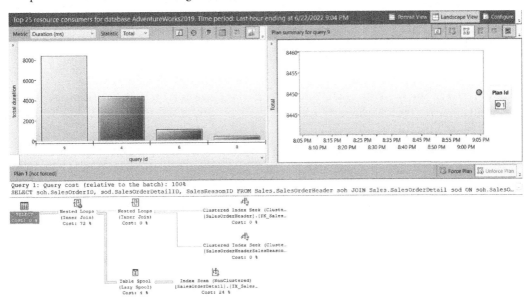

Figure 9.3 – The Top Resource Consuming Queries pane

Spend some time becoming familiar with the feature. For example, you can select different metrics such as duration, execution count, CPU time, logical reads, logical writes, physical reads, CLR time, DOP, memory consumption, row count, log memory used, tempdb memory used, and wait time. You could also inspect the available query plans and optionally force or unforce any of them. Several other choices are available, such are for viewing the information in a different format or configuring the time interval.

Selecting **Regressed queries** will take you to the **Regressed Queries** pane. Since we just enabled the Query Store, we may not have any regressed queries yet. The **Regressed queries** pane will show you similar information to the **Top Resource Consuming Queries** pane.

Try a few more queries, as shown here. Create or alter our test procedure once again:

```
CREATE OR ALTER PROCEDURE test (@pid int)
AS
SELECT * FROM Sales.SalesOrderDetail
WHERE ProductID = @pid
```

Run each query 100 times:

```
EXEC test @pid = 897
GO 100
EXEC test @pid = 870
GO 100
```

Now, you can run **Queries With High Variation** to get the **Queries With High Variation** pane, which is partially shown in the following screenshot:

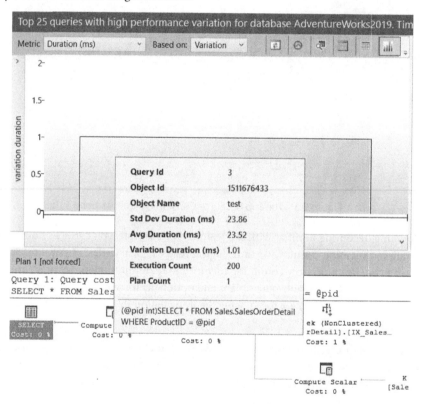

Figure 9.4 – A partial view of the Queries With High Variation pane

Finally, select **Query Waits Statistics**, which will open the **Query Waits Statistics** pane, which is partially shown in the following screenshot. Wait statistics in the Query Store are only available starting with SQL Server 2017 and can be individually enabled by running the following statement:

```
ALTER DATABASE AdventureWorks2019 SET QUERY_STORE = ON (WAIT_
STATS_CAPTURE_MODE = ON)
```

Wait statistics was also enabled by default when we enabled the Query Store in SQL Server 2022 at the beginning of this chapter, something you can verify by looking at the `wait_stats_capture_mode` column of the `sys.database_query_store_options` catalog view:

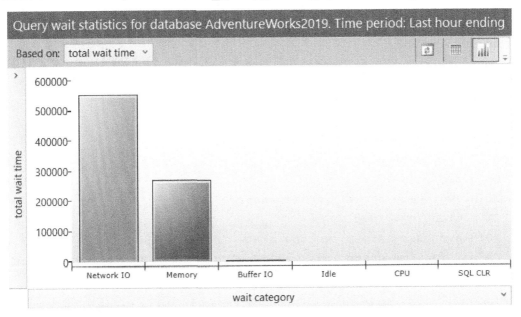

Figure 9.5 – A partial view of the Query Wait Statistics pane

Now that we have learned what the Query Store is and how it can be used, let's learn how to use queries to work with it.

Querying the Query Store

So far, we have only been using the Query Store user interface directly in SQL Server Management Studio. It won't be long after you start working with the Query Store that you will need to query the Query Store tables directly. As a quick introduction on how to access such tables, I will cover two examples here. For more details, please refer to the SQL Server documentation.

One of my favorites is the following query to collect queries that have timed out or finished because of an error. But first, let's create at least one example. Run the following query. Since it is running an expensive `CROSS JOIN`, it will take too long to finish. Cancel the query after running it for a few seconds:

```
SELECT * FROM Sales.SalesOrderDetail sod1 CROSS JOIN Sales.
SalesOrderDetail sod2
```

Now, you can run the following report to list all the queries that timed out or finished because of an error:

```
SELECT rs.avg_logical_io_reads, qt.query_sql_text,
 q.query_id, execution_type_desc, qt.query_text_id, p.plan_id,
rs.runtime_stats_id,
 rsi.start_time, rsi.end_time, rs.avg_rowcount, rs.count_
executions
FROM sys.query_store_query_text AS qt
JOIN sys.query_store_query AS q
ON qt.query_text_id = q.query_text_id
JOIN sys.query_store_plan AS p
ON q.query_id = p.query_id
JOIN sys.query_store_runtime_stats AS rs
ON p.plan_id = rs.plan_id
JOIN sys.query_store_runtime_stats_interval AS rsi
ON rsi.runtime_stats_interval_id = rs.runtime_stats_interval_id
WHERE execution_type_desc IN ('Aborted', 'Exception')
```

Finally, let's look at a typical query that lists the most expensive queries by CPU time. Keep in mind that using the Query Store for this kind of report has multiple advantages over DMVs such as sys. dm_exec_query_stats. For example, the Query Store captures the history of the plans for every query. The listed DMV only provides information about the plans that are currently in the plan cache. Some plans are never cached at all or some may be evicted because of memory pressure or some other reasons:

```
SELECT TOP 20
 p.query_id query_id,
 qt.query_sql_text query_text,
CONVERT(float, SUM(rs.avg_cpu_time * rs.count_executions))
total_cpu_time,
SUM(rs.count_executions) count_executions,
COUNT(DISTINCT p.plan_id) num_plans
FROM sys.query_store_runtime_stats rs
JOIN sys.query_store_plan p ON p.plan_id = rs.plan_id
JOIN sys.query_store_query q ON q.query_id = p.query_id
JOIN sys.query_store_query_text qt ON q.query_text_id =
qt.query_text_id
```

```
GROUP BY p.query_id, qt.query_sql_text
ORDER BY total_cpu_time DESC
```

Finally, you may never need to disable the Query Store. If you do need to do this, run the following command:

```
ALTER DATABASE AdventureWorks2019 SET QUERY_STORE = OFF
```

With these examples, you have learned how to use queries to work with the Query Store.

Summary

This chapter covered the Query Store, a query performance troubleshooting feature that collects information about queries, plans, and runtime statistics and can be used to find performance differences due to execution plan changes.

New with SQL Server 2022, the Query Store can be used to implement query hints and can be enabled on secondary replicas. Query store hints can be used to change the behavior of a query without the need to change the query's text. The Query Store can be enabled on secondary replicas used by Always On availability groups. This can help in scenarios where you want to troubleshoot query performance on read-only workloads running on such secondary replicas.

Finally, as covered in the next chapter, the Query Store plays a very important role in the new intelligent query processing features that are available. This is because it is required by the memory grant feedback, cardinality estimation feedback, and degree of parallelism feedback features to persist information on queries and plans. In addition, it may be used by the cardinality estimation feedback feature to implement a Query Store hint.

10
Intelligent Query Processing

This chapter covers intelligent query processing—a family of features whose purpose is to improve the performance of existing workloads with no application changes or minimal implementation effort. Originally, SQL Server 2017 introduced three of those features under the name of adaptive query processing, and several features have been added to the latest two releases, up to SQL Server 2022. One of those features, memory grant feedback, has been improved with every release.

In general, you can make these features available by enabling the applicable database compatibility level for the database, which could be either 140, 150, or 160 for SQL Server 2017, SQL Server 2019, and SQL Server 2022, respectively. However, as of SQL Server 2022, some of the new features require the query store to be enabled, for example, to persist the information of queries and plans. Every intelligent query processing feature can be disabled if you found a problem or a performance regression, either at the database level by changing the database compatibility level, or at the query level by using a specifically documented hint.

At this moment, intelligent query processing covers 13 features, and we will cover the most important ones in this chapter, including memory grant feedback persistence and percentile, cardinality estimation feedback, the degree of parallelism feedback, interleaved execution, table variable deferred compilation, adaptive joins, and query compilation replay. You can refer to the official SQL Server documentation for more details about these features or other additional intelligent query processing features.

In this chapter, we will cover the following topics:

- Overview of intelligent query processing
- Parameter-sensitive plan optimization
- Memory grant feedback
- Cardinality estimation feedback
- Degree of parallelism feedback

- Interleaved execution
- Table variable deferred compilation
- Adaptive joins

Overview of intelligent query processing

As mentioned in the previous chapter, it is strongly recommended that you enable the query store to get help on troubleshooting query performance problems. In addition, starting with SQL Server 2022, the query store is required to persist the information of queries and plans for some of the new intelligent query processing features. *Figure 10.1*, which is taken from the official SQL Server documentation, shows all of these features, including the version of SQL Server on which they were released:

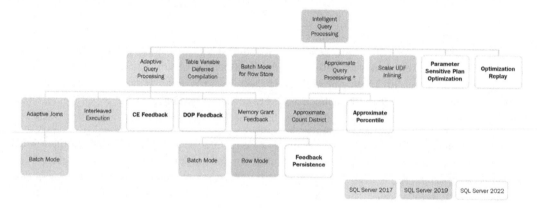

Figure 10.1 – The features of intelligent query processing

As suggested earlier, a specific compatibility level is required to enable most of these intelligent query processing features. *Table 10.1* shows a summary of the database compatibility level required for the features introduced with SQL Server 2022. In addition, cardinality estimation feedback, memory grant feedback persistence and percentile, compilation replay, and the degree of parallelism feedback require the query store to be enabled. Approximate percentile, query compilation replay, and the degree of parallelism feedback are enabled automatically in SQL Server 2022 with any database compatibility level. This is summarized in *Table 10.1*:

All compatibility levels	Compatibility level 140	Compatibility level 160
Approximate percentile	Memory grant feedback percentile	Parameter-sensitive plan optimization
Query compilation replay	Memory grant feedback persistence	Cardinality estimation feedback
The degree of parallelism feedback		

Table 10.1: The minimum compatibility level requirement of SQL Server 2022 features

As expected with any SQL Server feature, all intelligent query processing features introduced with SQL Server 2017 and SQL Server 2019 are available in the later versions, assuming their corresponding database compatibility level has been enabled. However, as of SQL Server 2022, one feature, memory grant feedback, includes the enhancement from the last two releases earlier, even with the original compatibility level of 140. More details on memory grant feedback will be discussed next.

Finally, all of these intelligent query processing features are available on any edition of SQL Server. As a reminder, although not directly related to intelligent query processing features, as covered earlier in the book starting with SQL Server 2016 Service Pack 1, for the first time in the product history, SQL Server provided a consistent programmability surface area for developers across all SQL Server editions. This means that previously existing Enterprise Edition-only features, such as in-memory OLTP, columnstore indexes, partitioning, database snapshots, compression, and more, were made available to any edition of SQL Server.

Parameter-sensitive plan optimization

Without a doubt, one of the most important intelligent query processing features introduced with SQL Server 2022 is parameter-sensitive plan optimization. Parameter-sensitive plan optimization was covered in detail in *Chapter 8*, Understanding *Plan Caching*, where we also covered parameter sniffing. As we learned, getting an execution plan tailored to the current parameters of a query naturally improves the performance of your applications. This saves optimization time and CPU resources because the query does not need to be optimized again. However, although the query optimizer and the plan cache work well together most of the time, some performance problems can occasionally appear.

Given that the query optimizer can produce different execution plans for syntactically identical queries, depending on their parameters, caching and reusing only one of these plans may create a performance issue for alternate instances of this query that would benefit from a better plan. Parameter-sensitive plan optimization helps with this problem by automatically enabling multiple active cached plans for a single parameterized statement. A different cached plan could be used depending on the parameter and expected data size. For more details about parameter-sensitive plan optimization, please refer to *Chapter 8*, Understanding *Plan Caching*.

Memory grant feedback

The memory grant feedback feature was introduced with SQL Server 2017 and has been improved and enhanced in the following two releases. The original release was memory grant feedback for batch mode, and its row mode version was introduced in SQL Server 2019. This feature helped to adjust memory grant sizes for both batch and row mode operators. SQL Server 2022 improves on this feature by adding persistence and percentile capabilities.

Let's start by explaining why this feature is needed. We need to remember that SQL Server uses the buffer pool to store the pages read from disk, and this memory buffer pool uses most of the memory available to a SQL Server instance. However, a memory grant is additional memory that is allocated to a query, and it is only required for operations such as sorting or hashing. This additional memory is only required for the duration of the query. Sorting and hashing operations were covered in *Chapter 4, The Execution Engine*, where we indicated that memory is required to store the rows to be sorted by the **Sort** operator, or to store the hash data of Hash Join and Hash Aggregate operations. As a reminder, a hash join requires two inputs, the build input and the probe input, but only the former requires memory. In some very rare cases, a memory grant is also required for parallel plans with multiple range scans.

As you might have guessed, finding the adequate size for a memory grant will be estimated by the query optimizer. Getting an incorrect estimation can lead to two different performance problems. First, underestimating a memory grant will lead to a query not having enough memory and needing to use disk space on tempdb, in other words, performing expensive spills to disk, which will also lead to additional query processing. Second, overestimating the required memory will lead to memory waste, and such wasted memory can lead to reduced concurrency, especially when this overestimation is happening in multiple queries at the same time. Although the processes obtaining the excessive memory grant will perform as expected, other processes requesting memory might have to wait until some memory is released.

Persistence and percentile

SQL Server 2022 has improved the memory grant feedback feature in a couple of ways. The original memory grant feedback feature, either batch or row, was adjusted in size based only on the most recent query execution, that is, the most recently used grant. In addition, in the first two releases, the memory grant feedback was usually disabled for parameter-sensitive queries.

The second limitation was that this memory grant size adjustment was only stored in the query plan inside the plan cache. So, if the plan was evicted from the cache, the memory information was lost and the memory grant feedback process would have to start again, impacting the performance of the first executions. As covered in *Chapter 8*, Understanding *Plan Caching*, a plan can be evicted from the plan cache for multiple reasons including memory pressure or by executing several commands. In addition, some operations or commands can clear the entire plan cache for a database or SQL Server instance. Two examples could be a database failing over within an availability group or a SQL Server instance being restarted.

SQL Server first improves on the original feature by persisting the memory grant size information along with other query information in the query store. In this way, the grant information will survive across cache evictions or even server restarts. In the second improvement, the memory grant adjustments are now based on the recent history of executions, instead of just the most recently used grant. SQL Server inspects the entire history of memory grant adjustments and will consider the 90th percentile of it, plus an additional buffer.

Although using a history of grant adjustments can make almost every query execution easier and reduce or eliminate spills to disks, it can also waste memory in cases when only a small amount of memory is needed, as we will see in the following example. For this example, we might need more data than is available on AdventureWorks2019. So, let's use the same table and test the stored procedure, as we did in *Chapter 8*, Understanding *Plan Caching*, so we can show big memory variations:

```
CREATE TABLE dbo.SalesOrderDetail (
    SalesOrderID int NOT NULL,
    SalesOrderDetailID int NOT NULL,
    CarrierTrackingNumber nvarchar(25) NULL,
    OrderQty smallint NOT NULL,
    ProductID int NOT NULL,
    SpecialOfferID int NOT NULL,
    UnitPrice money NOT NULL,
    UnitPriceDiscount money NOT NULL,
    LineTotal money,
    rowguid uniqueidentifier ROWGUIDCOL NOT NULL,
    ModifiedDate datetime NOT NULL)
```

Run the next INSERT statement exactly as it is:

```
INSERT INTO dbo.SalesOrderDetail (
    SalesOrderID,
    SalesOrderDetailID,
    CarrierTrackingNumber,
    OrderQty,
    ProductID,
    SpecialOfferID,
    UnitPrice,
    UnitPriceDiscount,
    LineTotal,
    rowguid,
    ModifiedDate)
SELECT * FROM Sales.SalesOrderDetail
WHERE ProductID = 897
-- WHERE ProductID = 870
-- GO 10
```

This will only insert two rows with ProductID 897. Now change the last three lines to look like the following:

```
-- WHERE ProductID = 897
WHERE ProductID = 870
GO 10
```

This will insert all of the records with ProductID 870 10 times for a total of 46,880 rows. Now we will create our test procedure:

```
CREATE OR ALTER PROCEDURE test (@pid int)
AS
SELECT * FROM dbo.SalesOrderDetail
WHERE ProductID = @pid
ORDER BY OrderQty
```

Since the persistence and percentile improvements have been incorporated into the original memory grant feedback release, you need at least a compatibility level of 140. Additionally, we need to enable the query store:

```
ALTER DATABASE AdventureWorks2019 SET COMPATIBILITY_LEVEL = 160
ALTER DATABASE AdventureWorks2019 SET QUERY_STORE = ON
ALTER DATABASE AdventureWorks2019 SET QUERY_STORE CLEAR ALL
```

Use the following code to start with a clean buffer pool and a clean plan cache:

```
DBCC FREEPROCCACHE
DBCC DROPCLEANBUFFERS
```

You could start testing the feature by running a few executions of our test procedure. For example, let's start with ProductID 897, which only returns a couple of rows:

```
EXEC test @pid = 897
```

You could inspect the graphical or XML plan to look for the memory grant information. Although your values might vary, you will get something similar to the following:

```
<MemoryGrantInfo SerialRequiredMemory="512"
SerialDesiredMemory="544" RequiredMemory="512"
DesiredMemory="544" RequestedMemory="1024" GrantWaitTime="0"
GrantedMemory="1024" MaxUsedMemory="16" MaxQueryMemory="195760"
LastRequestedMemory="0" IsMemoryGrantFeedbackAdjusted="No:
First Execution" />
```

In addition to all the memory information, we will inspect the value of
`IsMemoryGrantFeedbackAdjusted`. In this case, "`No: First Execution`"
means that the memory grant feedback did not adjust the memory, as this is the first
optimization and execution. Run it a second time:

```
EXEC test @pid = 897
```

This time, we get the following:

```
<MemoryGrantInfo SerialRequiredMemory="512"
SerialDesiredMemory="544" RequiredMemory="512"
DesiredMemory="544" RequestedMemory="1024" GrantWaitTime="0"
GrantedMemory="1024" MaxUsedMemory="16" MaxQueryMemory="208192"
LastRequestedMemory="1024" IsMemoryGrantFeedbackAdjusted="No:
Accurate Grant" />
```

Now, `IsMemoryGrantFeedbackAdjusted` shows that this is an accurate grant, so there is
no need to trigger the memory grant feedback yet. Now let's run the version returning 46,880 rows:

```
EXEC test @pid = 870
```

As expected, the current memory grant will not be enough to run this query, and we will get the
following warning on the Sort operator:

```
Operator used tempdb to spill data during execution with spill
level 1 and 1 spilled thread(s), Sort wrote 452 to and read 452
pages from tempdb with granted memory 1024KB and used memory
1024KB
```

The plan, showing the Sort warning, can be seen in *Figure 10.2*:

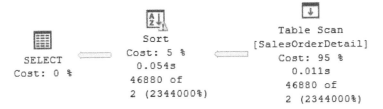

Figure 10.2 – Sort with a spill to tempdb

Additionally, you could inspect the `Warnings` element on the XML plan, which contains all the
information about the previous warning:

```
<Warnings>
  <SpillToTempDb SpillLevel="1" SpilledThreadCount="1" />
```

```
   <SortSpillDetails GrantedMemoryKb="1024" UsedMemoryKb="1024"
WritesToTempDb="452" ReadsFromTempDb="452" />
</Warnings>
```

If you run this query once more, you will get additional memory and the warning on the Sort operator will disappear.

Finally, and as expected for our extreme example, once the memory grant is stable, running our original test, which only returns two rows, will get us a warning on the SELECT operator:

```
EXEC test @pid = 897
```

This results in the following output:

```
The query memory grant detected "Excessive Grant", which may
impact the reliability. Grant size: Initial 8056 KB, Final 8056
KB, Used 16 KB
```

In the same way as before, the following warning can be seen on the XML plan:

```
<Warnings>
   <MemoryGrantWarning GrantWarningKind="Excessive Grant"
RequestedMemory="8056" GrantedMemory="8056" MaxUsedMemory="16"
/>
</Warnings>
```

Let's try a new exercise with multiple executions to inspect the value of IsMemoryGrantFeedbackAdjusted. Run the following code to start a clean test:

```
ALTER DATABASE AdventureWorks2019 SET QUERY_STORE CLEAR ALL
DBCC FREEPROCCACHE
DBCC DROPCLEANBUFFERS
```

Run the following to execute our test procedure with two different parameters:

```
EXEC test @pid = 897
GO 2
EXEC test @pid = 870
GO 3
EXEC test @pid = 897
GO 3
```

Look up the `IsMemoryGrantFeedbackAdjusted` value on the eight resulting execution plans, which might be easier to see on the XML plan. You might get something like the following, where each entry corresponds to each different plan in order:

```
IsMemoryGrantFeedbackAdjusted="No: First Execution"
IsMemoryGrantFeedbackAdjusted="No: Accurate Grant"
IsMemoryGrantFeedbackAdjusted="No: Accurate Grant"
IsMemoryGrantFeedbackAdjusted="Yes: Adjusting"
IsMemoryGrantFeedbackAdjusted="Yes: Stable"
IsMemoryGrantFeedbackAdjusted="Yes: Stable "
IsMemoryGrantFeedbackAdjusted="Yes: Stable "
IsMemoryGrantFeedbackAdjusted="No: Percentile Adjusting "
IsMemoryGrantFeedbackAdjusted="No: Percentile Adjusting "
```

As mentioned earlier, "`No: First Execution`" means that the memory grant feedback did not adjust the memory as this is the first optimization and execution. When we try the second execution with the same parameter, we now get "`No: Accurate Grant`", which means that this is an accurate grant, so there is no need to trigger the memory grant feedback yet. Bear in mind that these two first executions only return two rows each.

However, when we use the parameter of 870, which returns 46,880 rows each, things change a bit. First, "`Yes: Adjusting`" means that the memory grant feedback has been applied and could be later adjusted. On the other side, "`Yes: Stable`" means that the granted memory is now stable.

Finally, when we run again the procedure with the parameter of 897, we can see that the memory grant percentile-adjusting feature has been triggered. This memory grant feedback process will continue until it gets to a stable point.

Although we tested this feature with two extreme examples, while implementing the feature in your environment, you should validate that, in fact, you are getting the required memory and are not getting `SpillToTempDb` warnings. If you need to disable any or both of those features, you can use the following statements for memory grant feedback persistence and percentile, respectively:

```
ALTER DATABASE SCOPED CONFIGURATION SET MEMORY_GRANT_FEEDBACK_
PERSISTENCE = OFF
ALTER DATABASE SCOPED CONFIGURATION SET MEMORY_GRANT_FEEDBACK_
PERCENTILE = OFF
```

With that, we have learned all about memory grant feedback. Now we will move on to another new core SQL Server 2022 feature, that is, cardinality estimation feedback.

Cardinality estimation feedback

As mentioned in *Chapter 6, Understanding Statistics*, the cardinality estimator estimates the number of rows to be processed by each operator in a query execution plan. Similar to the concept of memory grant feedback, and also based on the query store, cardinality estimation feedback is another intelligent query processing feature introduced with SQL Server 2022, which can learn and adjust based on the history of previous query executions. As we learned in *Chapter 6, Understanding Statistics*, the cardinality estimator uses different model assumptions to perform cardinality estimations. In addition, starting with SQL Server 2014, SQL Server has two different cardinality estimators to choose from.

The cardinality estimator feedback feature works by analyzing repeating queries. If an existing model assumption appears incorrect or produces a suboptimal query plan, the cardinality estimator will identify and use a model assumption that better fits a given query and data distribution. The cardinality estimator feedback is based on USE HINT query hints. Now, let's look at an example; later, we will show you the model assumptions covered in the current release of the cardinality estimator feedback feature.

So, AdventureWorks2019 might not have the size or complexity for a good example, but let me show you the concept anyway. We will take a look at the so-called correlation model assumptions. We analyzed the following query in the cardinality estimator section of *Chapter 6, Understanding Statistics*, where we saw how two different models provided two different cardinality estimates, of the 388.061 and 292.269 rows, for the old and new cardinality estimator, respectively.

Let's review this again. Test this with the old cardinality estimator and validate an estimated value of 292.269 rows, as shown in *Figure 10.3*:

```
ALTER DATABASE AdventureWorks2019 SET COMPATIBILITY_LEVEL = 110
SELECT City, PostalCode FROM Person.Address WHERE City =
'Burbank' OR PostalCode = '91502'
```

Try the new cardinality estimator on the same query and validate 388.061:

```
ALTER DATABASE AdventureWorks2019 SET COMPATIBILITY_LEVEL = 160
SELECT City, PostalCode FROM Person.Address WHERE City =
'Burbank' OR PostalCode = '91502'
```

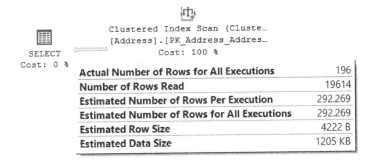

Figure 10.3 – Cardinality estimator model assumption

Essentially, this means that the cardinality estimator applies two different models, out of a total of three possibilities for correlation model assumptions. You can force any of those three models using a hint such as in the following three queries. You might not want to use these hints directly in your code, so I include them here just for illustration purposes. You can test the following code using a compatibility level of 160 and validate their three different estimations for the same query predicates:

```
SELECT City, PostalCode FROM Person.Address WHERE City =
'Burbank' OR PostalCode = '91502' -- estimates 388.061
OPTION(USE HINT('ASSUME_FULL_INDEPENDENCE_FOR_FILTER_
ESTIMATES'))


SELECT * FROM Person.Address WHERE City = 'Burbank' OR
PostalCode = '91502' -- estimates 292.269
OPTION(USE HINT('ASSUME_PARTIAL_CORRELATION_FOR_FILTER_
ESTIMATES'))


SELECT City, PostalCode FROM Person.Address WHERE City =
'Burbank' OR PostalCode = '91502' -- estimates 196
OPTION(USE HINT('ASSUME_MIN_SELECTIVITY_FOR_FILTER_ESTIMATES'))
```

By default, the old and new cardinality estimators apply the first two models, respectively. The third model returns an estimation of 196 rows. Unfortunately for our testing, even when the cardinality estimation improves, meaning it is getting close to the actual number of rows in our test query, because of the database simplicity, all three choices still produce the same execution plan.

Let's try the cardinality estimator feedback feature anyway. The feature is enabled by default using the latest compatibility level. We will need the query store, too. Run the following code to set up our test:

```
ALTER DATABASE AdventureWorks2019 SET COMPATIBILITY_LEVEL = 160
ALTER DATABASE AdventureWorks2019 SET QUERY_STORE = ON
```

```
ALTER DATABASE AdventureWorks2019 SET QUERY_STORE CLEAR ALL
ALTER DATABASE SCOPED CONFIGURATION CLEAR PROCEDURE_CACHE
DBCC DROPCLEANBUFFERS
```

Additionally, let's configure an extended events session with the following events and start it using SQL Server Management Studio. Also, use the **Watch Live Data** feature to see the captured events. For more details on how to do this, you can refer to *Chapter 2*:

```
CREATE EVENT SESSION test ON SERVER
ADD EVENT sqlserver.query_feedback_analysis,
ADD EVENT sqlserver.query_feedback_validation
```

Run our query multiple times and see the events that have been captured:

```
SELECT City, PostalCode FROM Person.Address WHERE City =
'Burbank' OR PostalCode = '91502'
GO 30
```

You might catch the data, as shown in *Figure 10.4*, on `query_feedback_analysis` on **Watch Live Data**:

Field	Value
check_queue_size	0
feedback_hint	OPTION(USE HINT('ASSUME_FULL_INDEPENDENCE_FOR_FILTER_ESTIMATES'))
max_check_queue_size	1044284
max_validation_queue_size	1253140
plan_id	1
query_id	1
validation_queue_size	0

Figure 10.4 – The query_feedback_analysis event

Essentially, this means that the cardinality estimation feedback feature is going to try the indicated model during the next execution. This is performed via the query store and using the specified hint, `ASSUME_FULL_INDEPENDENCE_FOR_FILTER_ESTIMATES`. This will be validated in the next execution, which will trigger a `query_feedback_validation` event. In our case, since there is no performance benefit, as the same plan is being used, the change is discarded and the original model assumption is used again.

However, assuming that this will get us a better performance, which you can validate by comparing the `original_cpu_time` and `feedback_validation_cpu_time` values of the `query_feedback_validation` event, the query store will keep the hint and it will be used for future execution.

So, in summary, you don't have to do anything to benefit from this feature. If you want to know whether it is being used in your environment, you can examine the listed events and, in addition, take a look at the `sys.query_store_query_hints` and `sys.query_store_plan_feedback` catalog views.

The current cardinality estimator feedback implements performance feedback using three different categories of model assumptions: correlated model assumptions, containment model assumptions, and optimizer row goals. We covered the correlated model assumptions in our previous example, which, as you can see, is used to estimate the selectivity of predicates within a specific table or view. The official SQL Server documentation currently defines these models as follows:

- **Fully independent**: In this model, the cardinality of predicates is calculated by multiplying the selectivity of all predicates. This is the default model for the old cardinality estimator.

- **Partially correlated**: In this model, the cardinality is calculated by using a variation on exponential backoff. This is the default model for the new cardinality estimator.

- **Fully correlated**: In this model, the cardinality is calculated by using the minimum selectivity of all the predicates.

In *Chapter 6, Understanding Statistics*, we learned how to calculate the cardinality for all these three cases.

In addition, current cardinality estimator feedback provides two models for join containment. They are defined in the official SQL Server documentation, as follows:

- **Simple containment**: This model assumes that join predicates are fully correlated. In this scenario, filter selectivity is calculated first, and then join selectivity is factored in.

- **Base containment**: This model assumes there is no correlation between join predicates and downstream filters.

Finally, by default, the cardinality estimator can detect performance problems with row goal optimizations and can, optionally, disable it if any inefficiency is detected. Row goal optimizations are used on queries with the TOP, IN, and EXISTS keywords, the FAST query hint, or the SET ROWCOUNT statement.

For more details about the cardinality estimator, please refer to *Chapter 6, Understanding Statistics*.

Degree of parallelism feedback

Based on the same concept as the memory feedback and cardinality estimation feedback features, and also relying on the query store, the degree of parallelism feedback works by identifying parallelism performance problems for repeating queries. The degree of parallelism feedback bases its decisions on the CPU time, the elapsed time, and the parallelism parallel-related waits.

Based on the feedback of recent query executions, the degree of parallelism feedback can automatically change the degree of parallelism and, again, monitor the performance of the query to see whether the change helps. The minimum value for a new query degree of parallelism that the feedback can recommend is 2, meaning the query cannot go to a serial plan. The maximum degree of parallelism is the max degree of parallelism server setting. As suggested, the feedback is persisted as it uses the query store.

Interleaved execution

Interleaved execution is a feature introduced with SQL Server 2017 and, in its current release, only supports multistatement table-valued functions. A well-known problem with multistatement table-valued functions is that they do not provide a cardinality estimate, which, in some cases, can create a performance problem as the query optimizer might not have good enough information to produce an efficient plan. With interleaved execution, SQL Server will pause query optimization, execute the multistatement table-valued function, and use an actual and accurate row count, to continue the query optimization.

Let's test the feature using the following multistatement table-valued function:

```
CREATE FUNCTION dbo.tvf_Sales(@year int)
RETURNS @Sales TABLE (
  SalesOrderID int,
  SalesOrderDetailID int,
  CarrierTrackingNumber nvarchar(25),
  OrderQty smallint,
  ProductID int,
  SpecialOfferID int,
  UnitPrice money,
  UnitPriceDiscount money,
  LineTotal money,
  rowguid uniqueidentifier ROWGUIDCOL,
  ModifiedDate datetime)
AS
BEGIN
  INSERT @Sales
  SELECT * FROM Sales.SalesOrderDetail
  WHERE YEAR(ModifiedDate) = @year
  RETURN
END
```

Since the feature is enabled by default, let's run the following code using a hint to disable it and see its original behavior:

```
SELECT * FROM dbo.tvf_Sales(2011) s
JOIN Sales.SalesOrderHeader h ON s.SalesOrderID =
h.SalesOrderID
OPTION (USE HINT('DISABLE_INTERLEAVED_EXECUTION_TVF'))
```

The plan from *Figure 10.5* is generated, which shows a default estimated number of rows of 100, as follows:

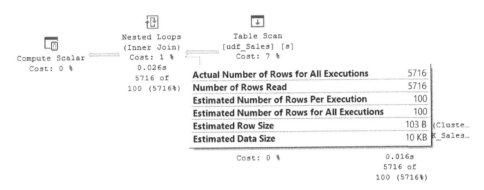

Actual Number of Rows for All Executions	5716
Number of Rows Read	5716
Estimated Number of Rows Per Execution	100
Estimated Number of Rows for All Executions	100
Estimated Row Size	103 B
Estimated Data Size	10 KB

Figure 10.5 – A plan with the interleaved execution feature disabled

As you might have noticed, this estimation of 100 takes the query optimizer to produce a Nested Loops operator. This might not be the best choice for the actual number of rows. Run the query again without the DISABLE_INTERLEAVED_EXECUTION_TVF hint:

```
SELECT * FROM dbo.tvf_Sales(2011) s
JOIN Sales.SalesOrderHeader h ON s.SalesOrderID =
h.SalesOrderID
```

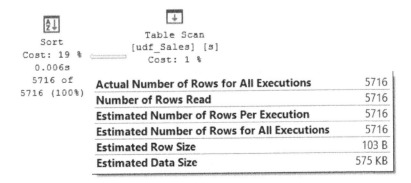

Actual Number of Rows for All Executions	5716
Number of Rows Read	5716
Estimated Number of Rows Per Execution	5716
Estimated Number of Rows for All Executions	5716
Estimated Row Size	103 B
Estimated Data Size	575 KB

Figure 10.6 – A plan using interleaved execution

The final plan, as shown in *Figure 10.6*, shows a correct and actual number of rows, which is used by the query optimizer to create a more efficient execution plan.

Table variable deferred compilation

Similar to multistatement table-valued functions, table variables have the limitation that they do not support optimizer statistics and just provide one-row guess estimates. Table variable deferred compilation provides a solution to this problem. As its name suggests, this feature defers the optimization of a statement that references a table variable. By using table variable deferred compilation, the query processor can use the actual cardinality instead of the original guess of one.

Let's translate our multistatement table-valued function example to a table variable using the following code. Since the scope of a table variable is a batch, you will need to run all three next statements, `DECLARE`, `INSERT` and `SELECT`, at the same time:

```
DECLARE @Sales TABLE (
  SalesOrderID int,
  SalesOrderDetailID int,
  CarrierTrackingNumber nvarchar(25),
  OrderQty smallint,
  ProductID int,
  SpecialOfferID int,
  UnitPrice money,
  UnitPriceDiscount money,
  LineTotal money,
  rowguid uniqueidentifier ROWGUIDCOL,
  ModifiedDate datetime)
```

Insert some data by running the following `INSERT` statement:

```
INSERT @Sales
SELECT * FROM Sales.SalesOrderDetail
```

In the same way as before, let's use a hint to disable this feature, so we can see the behavior before SQL Server 2019:

```
SELECT * FROM @Sales s
JOIN Sales.SalesOrderHeader h ON s.SalesOrderID =
h.SalesOrderID
WHERE YEAR(s.ModifiedDate) = 2011
OPTION (USE HINT('DISABLE_DEFERRED_COMPILATION_TV'))
```

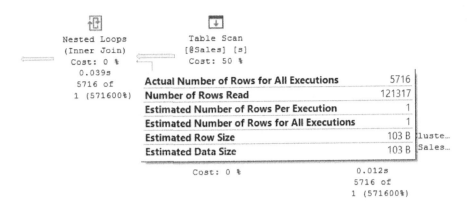

Figure 10.7 – A plan with table variable deferred compilation disabled

This will create the plan in *Figure 10.7*. Now run all three statements again removing the DISABLE_
DEFERRED_COMPILATION_TV hint, as shown in the following code:

```
SELECT * FROM @Sales s
JOIN Sales.SalesOrderHeader h ON s.SalesOrderID =
h.SalesOrderID
WHERE YEAR(s.ModifiedDate) = 2011
```

This will create the plan in *Figure 10.8*, which shows that the actual number of rows is used and more
likely will build an optimal query plan:

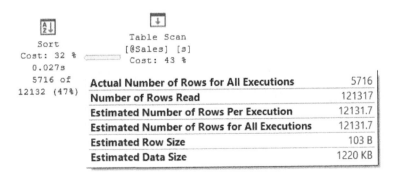

Figure 10.8 – A plan with table variable deferred compilation

Now, we will explore a feature introduced with SQL Server 2017, Adaptive joins.

Adaptive joins

Adaptive join is a feature released on the first version of intelligent query processing as part of the originally called adaptive query processing family of features. Additionally, adaptive query processing originally included memory grant feedback and interleaved execution. Although memory grant feedback started with batch mode and was later enhanced to include row mode, adaptive join remains a batch mode-only feature.

The main purpose of an adaptive join is to leave the decision of which physical join to utilize until the execution time when the number of rows needed to be processed is known. Only Nested Loops and Hash Joins are considered on the current release, and the choice is deferred until after the first input has been scanned.

This feature will be selected by the query optimizer only if the best choice for a join could be either a Nested Loops join or a hash join. If the best choice is a Merge Join operator, an adaptive join will not be considered at all. In addition, this feature assumes that the initial join is a hash join, so the execution will start by reading what is considered the build input. Depending on a calculated threshold, if a specific number of rows is met, execution will continue as a hash join; otherwise, it will use the existing rows already read by the build input to execute as a Nested Loops join. It is easier to understand by looking at an example. Let's create a new table. Drop the table if you still have a table with the same name:

```
CREATE TABLE dbo.SalesOrderDetail (
    SalesOrderID int NOT NULL,
    SalesOrderDetailID int NOT NULL,
    CarrierTrackingNumber nvarchar(25) NULL,
    OrderQty smallint NOT NULL,
    ProductID int NOT NULL,
    SpecialOfferID int NOT NULL,
    UnitPrice money NOT NULL,
    UnitPriceDiscount money NOT NULL,
    LineTotal money,
    rowguid uniqueidentifier ROWGUIDCOL NOT NULL,
    ModifiedDate datetime NOT NULL)
```

Insert some data on it:

```
INSERT INTO dbo.SalesOrderDetail (
    SalesOrderID,
    SalesOrderDetailID,
    CarrierTrackingNumber,
    OrderQty,
```

```
      ProductID,
      SpecialOfferID,
      UnitPrice,
      UnitPriceDiscount,
      LineTotal,
      rowguid,
      ModifiedDate)
SELECT * FROM Sales.SalesOrderDetail
GO 50
```

Create a columnstore index on our new table:

```
CREATE CLUSTERED COLUMNSTORE INDEX CIX_SalesOrderDetail
ON dbo.SalesOrderDetail
```

We are ready to run our query:

```
SELECT * FROM dbo.SalesOrderDetail sod
JOIN Sales.SalesOrderHeader soh
ON sod.SalesOrderID = soh.SalesOrderID
WHERE ProductID = 897
```

This will produce the query plan that is shown in *Figure 10.9*:

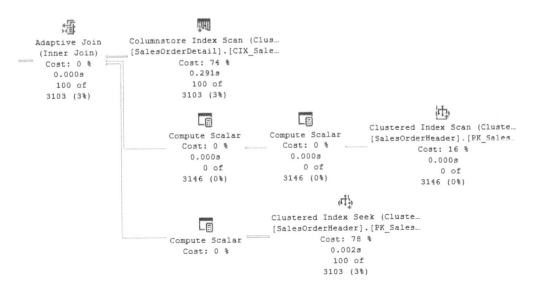

Figure 10.9 – A plan using adaptive joins

Notice the new Adaptive Join operator, which you can see has three inputs. The first or top input is the build input, which, as mentioned before, is executed as the build input assuming a hash join has been selected. The second or middle input is the input that would be executed if a hash join was finally selected. The third or bottom input is the input that would be executed if a Nested Loops join was selected.

By looking at the plan, you could figure out that the actual join type selected was Nested Loops. You can tell because the Clustered Index Seek operator shows that 100 out of 3,103 rows have been processed. The Clustered Index Scan operator shows 0 out of 3,146 rows, meaning it was not used. Finally, you can confirm this by looking at the Adaptive Join properties, where you can see the actual join type is Nested Loops. In addition, the Adaptive Threshold Rows property on the same operator has a value of 595.506 rows. The adaptive join will continue using a hash join if the build input is at or over this value. It will run as a Nested Loops join if the number of rows is lower.

Summary

In this chapter, we covered the most important intelligent query processing features of all three releases up to SQL Server 2022. Of course, new to SQL Server 2022 is that some of the features, such as memory grant feedback, cardinality estimation feedback, and the degree of parallelism feedback, now require the query store to persist the information of queries and plans. Memory grant feedback had the limitation that the feedback was lost when plans were evicted or SQL Server was restarted.

The first release of intelligent query processing, in SQL Server 2017, introduced three of those features under the name of adaptive query processing, and usually, you can make these features available by enabling the applicable database compatibility level of the database. Similarly, any intelligent query processing feature can be disabled if you find a performance regression, either at the database level, by changing the database compatibility level, or at the query level by using a specifically documented hint.

In this chapter, we covered memory grant feedback persistence and percentile capabilities, cardinality estimation feedback, the degree of parallelism feedback, interleaved execution, table variable deferred compilation, adaptive joins, and query compilation replay. Please refer to the official SQL Server documentation for more details about these features or other additional intelligent query processing features. In the next chapter, we will explore data warehouses and the various features around them.

11
An Introduction to Data Warehouses

Usually, when we read about high-performing applications in a SQL Server book or article, we assume they are only talking about transactional applications and, of course, **online transaction processing (OLTP)** databases. Although we have not mentioned data warehouses so far in this book, most of the content applies to both OLTP databases and data warehouse databases. The SQL Server query optimizer can automatically identify and optimize data warehouse queries without any required configuration, so the concepts explained in this book regarding query optimization, query operators, indexes, statistics, and more apply to data warehouses, too.

In this chapter, we will cover topics that are only specific to data warehouses. Additionally, describing what a data warehouse is provides us with the opportunity to define OLTP systems and what the differences between both are. We will describe how the query optimizer identifies data warehouse queries and cover some of the data warehouse optimizations introduced in the last few versions of SQL Server.

Bitmap filtering, an optimization used in star join queries and introduced with SQL Server 2008, can be used to filter out rows from a fact table very early during query processing, thus significantly improving the performance of data warehouse queries. Bitmap filtering is based on Bloom filters – a space-efficient probabilistic data structure originally conceived by Burton Howard Bloom in 1970.

Columnstore indexes, a feature introduced with SQL Server 2012, introduce us to two new paradigms: columnar-based storage and new batch-processing algorithms. Although columnstore indexes had some limitations when they were originally released—mostly, the fact that the indexes were not updatable and only nonclustered indexes could be created—these limitations have been addressed in later releases. The star join query optimization is an Enterprise Edition-only feature. Additionally, the xVelocity memory-optimized columnstore indexes started as an Enterprise Edition-only feature, but as of SQL Server 2016 Service Pack 1, are available on all the editions of the product.

In this chapter, we will cover the following topics:

- Data warehouses

- Star join query optimization

- Columnstore indexes

Data warehouses

Usually, the information within an organization is kept in one of two forms—in an operational system or in an analytical system—both of which have very different purposes. Although the purpose of an operational system, which is also known as an OLTP system, is to support the execution of a business process, the purpose of an analytic system or data warehouse is to help with the measurement of a business process and business decision-making. OLTP systems are based on small, high-performance transactions consisting of INSERT, DELETE, UPDATE, and SELECT statements, while a data warehouse is based on large and complex queries of aggregated data. The degree of normalization is another main difference between these systems: while an OLTP system will usually be in the third normal form, a data warehouse will use a denormalized dimensional model called a star schema. The third normal form used by OLTP systems helps with data integrity and data redundancy problems because update operations only need to be updated in one place. A data warehouse dimensional model is more appropriate for ad hoc complex queries.

We can see a summary of the differences between operational and analytic systems, as detailed in *Table 11.1*:

	Operational system	Analytic system
Purpose	Execution of a business process	Measurement of a business process
Primary interaction style	Insert, update, delete, and query	Query
Scope of interaction	Individual transaction	Aggregated transactions
Query patterns	Predictable and stable	Unpredictable and changing
Temporal focus	Current	Current and historic
Design optimization	Update concurrency	High-performance query
Design principle	**Entity-relationship** (**ER**) design in **third normal form** (**3NF**)	Dimensional design (star schema or cube)
Also known as	Transactional system and OLTP system	Data warehouse system and data mart

Table 11.1 – Comparing operational and analytic systems

A dimensional design, when implemented in a relational database such as SQL Server, is called a star schema. Data warehouses using a star schema use fact and dimension tables, where fact tables contain the business's facts or numerical measures, which can participate in calculations, and dimension tables contain the attributes or descriptions of the facts. Not everything that is numeric is a fact, which can be the case with numeric data such as phone numbers, age, and size information. Sometimes, additional normalization is performed within dimension tables in a star schema, which is called a snowflake schema.

SQL Server includes a sample data warehouse database, `AdventureWorksDW2019`, which follows a snowflake design and will be used in the examples for this chapter. *Figure 11.1* shows a diagram with some of the fact and dimension tables of `AdventureWorksDW2019`:

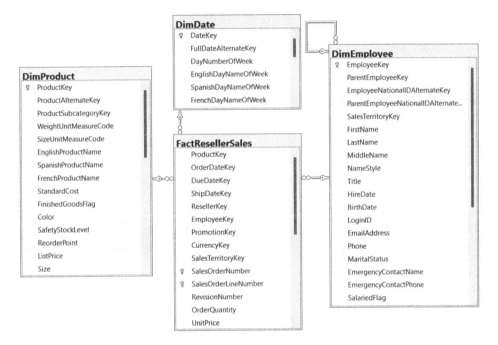

Figure 11.1 – Fact and dimension tables in `AdventureWorksDW2019`

Usually, fact tables are very large and can store millions or billions of rows, compared to dimension tables, which are significantly smaller. The size of data warehouse databases tends to range from hundreds of gigabytes to terabytes. Facts are stored as columns in a fact table, while related dimensions are stored as columns in dimension tables. Usually, fact tables have foreign keys to link them to the primary keys of the dimension tables. When used in queries, facts are usually aggregated or summarized, whereas dimensions are used as filters or query predicates. Additionally, a dimension table has a surrogate key, usually an integer, which is also the primary key of the table. For example, in `AdventureWorksDW2019`, the **DimCustomer** table has **CustomerKey**, which is also its primary key, and it is defined as an identity.

> **Note**
>
> More details about data warehousing and dimensional designs can be found in *The Data Warehouse Toolkit* (Wiley, 2013), by Ralph Kimball and Margy Ross, and *Star Schema: The Complete Reference*, by Christopher Adamson.

The world of data is rapidly evolving, and new trends such as increasing data volumes and new sources and types of data, along with the new requirement of support for near real-time processing, are changing the traditional data warehouse. In some cases, new approaches are being proposed in response to these trends.

Although SQL Server Enterprise Edition allows you to handle large data warehouses and contains the star join query optimizations and xVelocity memory-optimized columnstore indexes covered in this chapter, SQL Server is also available as an appliance that can allow companies to handle databases of up to 6 **petabytes** (**PB**) of data storage. Built on a **Multiple Parallel Processing** (**MPP**) architecture with preinstalled software, SQL Server Parallel Data Warehouse provides a highly scalable architecture to help with these large data warehouses. In April 2014, Microsoft announced the **Analytics Platform System** (**APS**), which is an appliance solution with hardware and software components that include SQL Server Parallel Data Warehouse and Microsoft's Hadoop distribution, HDInsight, which is based on the Hortonworks Data Platform.

Finally, in SQL Server 2022, Azure Synapse Link for SQL will allow you to get near real-time analytics over operational data. This new feature will allow you to run business intelligence, analytics, and machine learning scenarios on SQL Server 2022 operational data with minimum impact on source databases. Currently, Azure Synapse Link for SQL is in preview, and you can get more information about it by looking at `https://docs.microsoft.com/en-us/azure/synapse-analytics/synapse-link/sql-synapse-link-overview`.

Now that we have had a brief introduction to data warehouses, let's dive into a key feature in SQL Server for it.

Star join query optimization

Queries that join a fact table to dimension tables are called star join queries, and SQL Server includes special optimizations for this kind of query. A typical star join query joins a fact table with one or more dimension tables, groups by some columns of the dimension tables, and aggregates on one or more columns of the fact table. In addition to the filters applied when the tables are joined, other filters can be applied to the fact and dimension tables. Here is an example of a typical star join query in `AdventureWorksDW2019` showing all the characteristics that were just mentioned:

```
SELECT TOP 10 p.ModelName, p.EnglishDescription,
SUM(f.SalesAmount) AS SalesAmount
FROM FactResellerSales f JOIN DimProduct p
```

```
ON f.ProductKey = p.ProductKey
JOIN DimEmployee e
ON f.EmployeeKey = e.EmployeeKey
WHERE f.OrderDateKey >= 20030601
AND e.SalesTerritoryKey = 1
GROUP BY p.ModelName, p.EnglishDescription
ORDER BY SUM(f.SalesAmount) DESC
```

Sometimes, because data warehouse implementations do not completely specify the relationships between fact and dimension tables and do not explicitly define foreign key constraints in order to avoid the overhead of constraint enforcement during updates, SQL Server uses heuristics to automatically detect star join queries and can reliably identify fact and dimension tables. One such heuristic is to consider the largest table of the star join query as the fact table, which must have a specified minimum size, too. In addition, to qualify for a star join query, the join conditions must be inner joins and all the join predicates must be single-column equality predicates. It is worth noting that even in cases where these heuristics do not work correctly and one dimension table is incorrectly chosen as a fact table, a valid plan returning correct data is still selected, although it might not be an efficient one.

Based on the selectivity of a fact table, SQL Server can define three different approaches to optimize star join queries. For highly selective queries, which could return up to 10 percent of the rows of the table, SQL Server might produce a plan with Nested Loops Joins, Index Seeks, and bookmark lookups. For medium-selectivity queries, processing anywhere from 10 percent to 75 percent of the rows in a table, the query optimizer might recommend hash joins with bitmap filters, in combination with fact table scans or fact table range scans. Finally, for the least selective of the queries, returning more than 75 percent of the rows of the table, SQL Server might recommend regular hash joins with fact table scans. The choice of these operators and plans is not surprising for the most and least selective queries because this is their standard behavior, as explained in *Chapter 4, The Execution Engine*. However, what is new is the choice of hash joins and bitmap filtering for medium-selectivity queries; therefore, we will be looking at those optimizations next. But first, let's introduce bitmap filters.

Although bitmap filters are used on the star join optimization covered in this section, they have been used in SQL Server since version 7.0. Also, they might appear on other plans, an example of which was shown at the end of the *Parallelism* section in *Chapter 4, The Execution Engine*. Bitmap filters are based on Bloom filters, a space-efficient probabilistic data structure originally conceived by Burton Bloom in 1970. Bitmap filters are used in parallel plans, and they greatly improve the performance of these plans by performing a semi-join reduction early in the query before rows are passed through the parallelism operator. Although it is more common to see bitmap filters with hash joins, they could be used by Merge Join operators, too.

As explained in *Chapter 4, The Execution Engine*, a hash join operation has two phases: build and probe. In the build phase, all the join keys of the build or outer table are hashed into a hash table. A bitmap is created as a byproduct of this operation, and the bits in the array are set to correspond with hash values that contain at least one row. The bitmap is later examined when the probe or inner table is being read. If the bit is not set, the row cannot have a match in the outer table and is discarded.

Bitmap filters are used in star join queries to filter out rows from the fact table very early during query processing. This optimization was introduced in SQL Server 2008, and your existing queries can automatically benefit from it without any changes. This optimization is referred to as **optimized bitmap filtering** in order to differentiate it from the standard bitmap filtering that was available in previous versions of SQL Server. Although standard bitmap filtering can be used in plans with hash joins and Merge Join operations, as indicated earlier, optimized bitmap filtering is only allowed on plans with hash joins. The `Opt_` prefix in the name of a bitmap operator indicates an optimized bitmap filter is being used.

To filter out rows from the fact table, SQL Server builds the hash tables on the "build input" side of the hash join (which, in our case, is a dimension table), constructing a bitmap filter that is an array of bits, which is later used to filter out rows from the fact table that do not qualify for the hash joins. There might be some false positives, meaning that some of the rows might not participate in the join, but there are no false negatives. SQL Server then passes the bitmaps to the appropriate operators to help remove any nonqualifying rows from the fact table early in the query plan.

Multiple filters can be applied to a single operator, and optimized bitmap filters can be applied to exchange operators, such as Distribute Streams and Repartition Streams operators, and filter operators. An additional optimization while using bitmap filters is the in-row optimization, which allows you to eliminate rows even earlier during query processing. When the bitmap filter is based on not-nullable big or bigint columns, the bitmap filter could be applied directly to the table operation. An example of this is shown next.

For this example, let's run the following query:

```
SELECT TOP 10 p.ModelName, p.EnglishDescription,
SUM(f.SalesAmount) AS SalesAmount
FROM FactResellerSales f JOIN DimProduct p
ON f.ProductKey = p.ProductKey
JOIN DimEmployee e
ON f.EmployeeKey = e.EmployeeKey
WHERE f.OrderDateKey >= 20030601
AND e.SalesTerritoryKey = 1
GROUP BY p.ModelName, p.EnglishDescription
ORDER BY SUM(f.SalesAmount) DESC
```

With the current size of AdventureWorksDW2019, this query is not even expensive enough to generate a parallel plan because its cost is only 1.98374. Although we can do a little trick to simulate more records on this database, we encourage you to test this or similar queries in your data warehouse development or test environment.

To simulate a larger table with 100,000 rows and 10,000 pages, run the following statement:

```
UPDATE STATISTICS dbo.FactResellerSales WITH ROWCOUNT = 100000,
PAGECOUNT = 10000
```

> **Note**
>
> The undocumented ROWCOUNT and PAGECOUNT choices of the UPDATE STATISTICS statement were introduced in *Chapter 6, Understanding Statistics*. As such, they should not be used in a production environment. They will only be used in this exercise to simulate a larger table.

Clean the plan cache by running a statement such as the following:

```
DBCC FREEPROCCACHE
```

Then, run the previous star join query again. This time, we get a more expensive query and a different plan, which is partially shown in *Figure 11.2*:

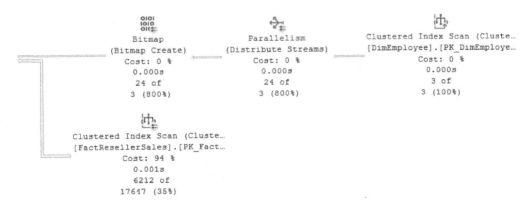

Figure 11.2 – A plan with an optimized bitmap filter

As explained earlier, you can see that a bitmap filter was created on the build input of the hash join, which, in this case, reads data from the `DimEmployee` dimension table. Looking at **Defined Values** in the bitmap operator's **Properties** window, you can see that, in this case, the name of the bitmap filter shows the `Opt_Bitmap1006` value. Now, look at the properties of the Clustered Index Scan operator, which are shown in *Figure 11.3*. Here, you can see that the previously created bitmap filter, `Opt_Bitmap1006`, is used in the **Predicate** section to filter out rows from the `FactResellerSales` fact table. Also, notice the `IN ROW` parameter, which shows that in-row optimization was also used, thus filtering out rows from the plan as early as possible (in this case, from the Clustered Index Scan operation):

```
[AdventureWorksDW2019].[dbo].[FactResellerSales].[OrderDateKey]
as [f].[OrderDateKey]>=(20030601) AND PROBE([Opt_Bitmap1006],
[AdventureWorksDW2019].[dbo].[FactResellerSales].[EmployeeKey]
as [f].[EmployeeKey],N'[IN ROW]')
```

Finally, run the following statement to correct the page and row count we just changed in the `FactResellerSales` table:

```
DBCC UPDATEUSAGE (AdventureWorksDW2019, 'dbo.
FactResellerSales') WITH COUNT_ROWS
```

Now that we have learned about star query optimization, we will explore another useful feature for data warehouses: columnstore indexes.

Columnstore indexes

When SQL Server 2012 was originally released, one of the main new features was columnstore indexes. By using a new column-based storage approach and new query-processing algorithms, memory-optimized columnstore indexes were designed to improve the performance of data warehouse queries by several orders of magnitude. Although the inability to update data was the biggest drawback when this feature was originally released back in 2012, this limitation was addressed in the following release. From SQL Server 2014 onward, it has the ability to directly update its data and even create a columnstore clustered index on it. The fact that columnstore indexes were originally limited to only nonclustered indexes was also considered a limitation because it required duplicated data on an already very large object such as a fact table. That is, all the indexed columns would be both on the base table and in the columnstore index.

As mentioned at the beginning of this chapter, in an OLTP system, transactions usually access one row or a few rows, whereas typical data warehouse star join queries access a large number of rows. In addition, an OLTP transaction usually accesses all of the columns in the row, which is opposite to a star join query, where only a few columns are required. This data access pattern showed that a columnar approach could benefit data warehouse workloads.

The traditional storage approach used by SQL Server is to store rows on data pages, which we call a "rowstore." Rowstores in SQL Server include heaps and B-tree structures, such as standard clustered and nonclustered indexes. Column-oriented storage such as the one used by columnstore indexes dedicates entire database pages to store data from a single column. Rowstores and columnstores are compared in *Figure 11.3*, where a rowstore contains pages with rows, with each row containing all its columns, and a columnstore contains pages with data for only one column, labeled C1, C2, and so on. Because the data is stored in columns, one question that is frequently asked is how a row is retrieved from this columnar storage. It is the position of the value in the column that indicates to which row this data belongs. For example, the first value on each page (C1, C2, and so on), as shown in *Figure 11.3*, belongs to the first row, the second value on each page belongs to the second row, and so on:

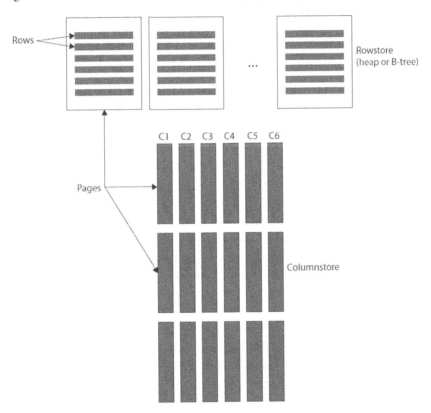

Figure 11.3 – Rowstore and columnstore data layout comparison

Column-oriented storage is not new and has been used before by some other database vendors. Columnstore indexes are based on Microsoft xVelocity technology, formerly known as VertiPaq, which is also used in **SQL Server Analysis Services (SSAS)**, Power Pivot for Excel, and SharePoint. Similar to the in-memory OLTP feature, as covered in *Chapter 7*, columnstore indexes are also an in-memory technology.

As mentioned earlier, columnstore indexes dedicate entire database pages to store data from a single column. Also, columnstore indexes are divided into segments, which consist of multiple pages, and each segment is stored in SQL Server as a separate BLOB. As indicated earlier, as of SQL Server 2014, it is now possible to define a columnstore index as a clustered index, which is a great benefit because there is no need for duplicated data. For example, in SQL Server 2012, a nonclustered columnstore index had to be created on a heap or regular clustered index, thus duplicating the data on an already large fact table.

Performance benefits

Columnstore indexes provide increased performance benefits based on the following:

- **Reduced I/O**: Because rowstore pages contain all the columns in a row, in a data warehouse without columnstore indexes, SQL Server has to read all of the columns, including the columns that are not required by the query. Typical star join queries use only between 10 percent and 15 percent of the columns in a fact table. Based on this, using a columnstore to only read those columns can represent savings of between 85 percent and 90 percent in disk I/O, compared to a rowstore.

- **Batch mode processing**: New query-processing algorithms are designed to process data in batches and are very efficient at handling large amounts of data. Batch mode processing is explained in more detail in the next section.

- **Compression**: Because data from the same column is stored contiguously on the same pages, usually, they will have similar or repeated values that can often be compressed more effectively. Compression can improve performance because fewer disk I/O operations are needed to read compressed data and more data can fit into memory. Columnstore compression is not the same as the row and page compression that has been available since SQL Server 2008 and, instead, uses the VertiPaq compression algorithms. However, one difference is that, in columnstore indexes, column data is automatically compressed and compression cannot be disabled, whereas row and page compression in rowstores is optional and has to be explicitly configured.

- **Segment elimination**: As indicated earlier, columnstore indexes are divided into segments, and SQL Server keeps the minimum and maximum values for each column segment in the `sys.column_store_segments` catalog view. This information can be used by SQL Server to compare against query filter conditions to identify whether a segment can contain the requested data, thus avoiding reading segments that are not needed and saving both I/O and CPU resources.

Because data warehouse queries using columnstore indexes can now be executed, in many cases, several orders of magnitude faster than with tables defined as rowstore, they can provide other benefits too, such as reducing or eliminating the need to rely on prebuilt aggregates such as OLAP cubes, indexed views, and summary tables. The only action required to benefit from these performance improvements is to define the columnstore indexes in your fact tables. There is no need to change your queries or use any specific syntax; the query optimizer will automatically consider the columnstore index—although, as always, whether or not it is used in a plan will be a cost-based decision. Additionally, columnstore indexes provide more flexibility to changes than building these prebuilt aggregates. If a query changes, the columnstore index will still be useful, and the query optimizer will automatically react to those query changes, whereas the prebuilt aggregate might no longer be able to support the new query or might require changes to accommodate it.

Batch mode processing

As covered in *Chapter 1, An Introduction to Query Tuning and Optimization*, when we talked about the traditional query-processing mode in SQL Server, you saw that operators request rows from other operators one row at a time—for example, using the GetRow() method. This row processing mode works fine for transactional OLTP workloads where queries are expected to produce only a few rows. However, for data warehouse queries, which process large amounts of rows to aggregate data, this one-row-at-a-time processing mode could become very expensive.

With columnstore indexes, SQL Server is not only providing columnar-based storage but is also introducing a query-processing mode that processes a large number of records, one batch at a time. A batch is stored as a vector in a separate area of memory and, typically, represents about 1,000 rows of data. This also means that query operators can now run in either row mode or batch mode. Starting with SQL Server 2012, only a few operators can run in either batch mode or row mode, and those operators include Columnstore Index Scan, Hash Aggregate, Hash Join, Project, and Filter. Another operator, Batch Hash Table Build, works only in batch mode; it is used to build a batch hash table for the memory-optimized columnstore index in a hash join. In SQL Server 2014, the number of batch mode operators has been expanded, and existing operators, especially the Hash Join operator, have been improved.

It is worth noting that a plan with both row- and batch-processing operators might have some performance degradation, as communication between row mode and batch mode operators is more expensive than the communication between operators running in the same mode. As a result, each transition has an associated cost that the query optimizer uses to minimize the number of these transitions in a plan. In addition, when both row- and batch-processing operators are present in the same plan, you should verify that most of the plan, or at least the most expensive parts of the plan, are executed in batch mode.

Plans will show both the estimated and the actual execution mode, which you will see in the examples later. Usually, the estimated and the actual execution mode should have the same value for the same operation. You can use this information to troubleshoot your plans and to make sure that batch processing is used. However, a plan showing an estimated execution mode of "batch" and an actual execution mode of "row" might be evidence of a performance problem.

Back in the SQL Server 2012 release, limitations on available memory or threads can cause one operation to dynamically switch from batch mode to row mode, thus degrading the performance of query execution. If the estimated plan showed a parallel plan and the actual plan switched to "serial," you could infer that not enough threads were available for the query. If the plan actually ran in parallel, you could tell that not having enough memory was the problem. In this version of SQL Server, some of these batch operators might use hash tables, which were required to fit entirely in memory. When not enough memory was available at execution time, SQL Server might dynamically switch the operation back to row mode, where standard hash tables can be used and could spill to disk if not enough memory is available. Switching to row execution due to memory limitations could also be caused by bad cardinality estimations.

This memory requirement has been eliminated starting with SQL Server 2014; the build hash table of Hash Join does not have to entirely fit in memory and can instead use spilling functionality. Although spilling to disk is not the perfect solution, it allows the operation to continue in batch mode instead of switching to row mode, as we would do in SQL Server 2012.

Finally, the Hash Join operator supported only inner joins in the initial release. This functionality was expanded in SQL Server 2014 to include the full spectrum of join types, such as inner, outer, semi, and anti-semi joins. UNION ALL and scalar aggregation were upgraded to support batch processing, too.

Creating columnstore indexes

Creating a nonclustered columnstore index requires you to define the list of columns to be included in the index, which is not needed if you are creating a clustered columnstore index. A clustered columnstore index includes all of the columns in the table and stores the entire table. You can create a clustered columnstore index from a heap, but you could also create it from a regular clustered index, assuming you want this rowstore clustered index to be replaced. However, although you can create clustered or nonclustered columnstore indexes on a table, in contrast to rowstores, only one columnstore index can exist at a time. For example, let's suppose you create the following clustered columnstore index using a small version of FactInternetSales2:

```
CREATE TABLE dbo.FactInternetSales2 (
ProductKey int NOT NULL,
OrderDateKey int NOT NULL,
DueDateKey int NOT NULL,
```

```
ShipDateKey int NOT NULL)
GO
CREATE CLUSTERED COLUMNSTORE INDEX csi_FactInternetSales2
ON dbo.FactInternetSales2
```

You can try to create the following nonclustered columnstore index in the same table:

```
CREATE NONCLUSTERED COLUMNSTORE INDEX ncsi_FactInternetSales2
ON dbo.FactInternetSales2
(ProductKey, OrderDateKey)
```

This would return the following error message:

```
Msg 35339, Level 16, State 1, Line 1
Multiple columnstore indexes are not supported.
```

Earlier versions of SQL Server will return the following message instead:

```
Msg 35303, Level 16, State 1, Line 1
CREATE INDEX statement failed because a nonclustered index
cannot be created on a table that has a clustered columnstore
index. Consider replacing the clustered columnstore index with
a nonclustered columnstore index.
```

In the same way, if you already have a nonclustered columnstore index and try to create a clustered columnstore index, you will get the following message:

```
Msg 35304, Level 16, State 1, Line 1
CREATE INDEX statement failed because a clustered columnstore
index cannot be created on a table that has a nonclustered
index. Consider dropping all nonclustered indexes and trying
again.
```

Drop the existing table before running the next exercise, as follows:

```
DROP TABLE FactInternetSales2
```

Now, let's look at the plans created by the columnstore indexes. Run the following code to create the FactInternetSales2 table inside the AdventureWorksDW2019 database:

```
USE AdventureWorksDW2019
GO
CREATE TABLE dbo.FactInternetSales2 (
ProductKey int NOT NULL,
OrderDateKey int NOT NULL,
DueDateKey int NOT NULL,
ShipDateKey int NOT NULL,
CustomerKey int NOT NULL,
PromotionKey int NOT NULL,
CurrencyKey int NOT NULL,
SalesTerritoryKey int NOT NULL,
SalesOrderNumber nvarchar(20) NOT NULL,
SalesOrderLineNumber tinyint NOT NULL,
RevisionNumber tinyint NOT NULL,
OrderQuantity smallint NOT NULL,
UnitPrice money NOT NULL,
ExtendedAmount money NOT NULL,
UnitPriceDiscountPct float NOT NULL,
DiscountAmount float NOT NULL,
ProductStandardCost money NOT NULL,
TotalProductCost money NOT NULL,
SalesAmount money NOT NULL,
TaxAmt money NOT NULL,
Freight money NOT NULL,
CarrierTrackingNumber nvarchar(25) NULL,
CustomerPONumber nvarchar(25) NULL,
OrderDate datetime NULL,
DueDate datetime NULL,
ShipDate datetime NULL
)
```

Run the following statement to create a clustered columnstore index:

```
CREATE CLUSTERED COLUMNSTORE INDEX csi_FactInternetSales2
ON dbo.FactInternetSales2
```

Now we can insert some records by copying data from an existing fact table:

```
INSERT INTO dbo.FactInternetSales2
SELECT * FROM AdventureWorksDW2019.dbo.FactInternetSales
```

We just tested that, as of SQL Server 2014, the columnstore indexes are now updatable and support the INSERT, DELETE, UPDATE, and MERGE statements, as well as other standard methods such as the bcp bulk-loading tool and SQL Server Integration Services. Trying to run the previous INSERT statement against a columnstore index on a SQL Server 2012 instance would return the following error message, which also describes one of the workarounds to insert data in a columnstore index in that version of SQL Server:

```
Msg 35330, Level 15, State 1, Line 1
INSERT statement failed because data cannot be updated in
a table with a columnstore index. Consider disabling the
columnstore index before issuing the INSERT statement, then
rebuilding the columnstore index after INSERT is complete.
```

We are ready to run a star join query to access our columnstore index:

```
SELECT d.CalendarYear,
SUM(SalesAmount) AS SalesTotal
FROM dbo.FactInternetSales2 AS f
JOIN dbo.DimDate AS d
ON f.OrderDateKey = d.DateKey
GROUP BY d.CalendarYear
ORDER BY d.CalendarYear
```

This query will produce the plan that is shown in *Figure 11.4*, which uses our columnstore index in batch execution mode. Additionally, the plan uses adaptive joins, which is a feature covered in the previous chapter:

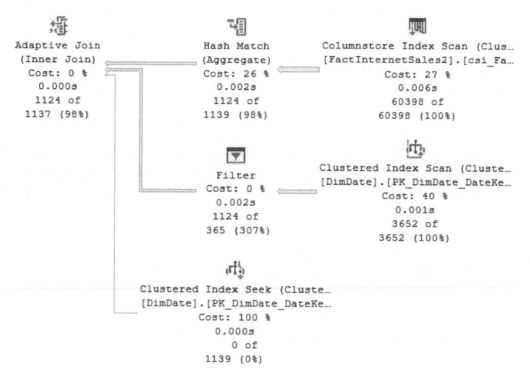

Figure 11.4 – A plan using a Columnstore Index Scan operator in batch mode

> **Note**
> Older versions of SQL Server required a large number of rows in order to run in batch execution mode. Even when they were able to use the columnstore index, a small table could only use row execution mode.

You can validate on the properties of the Columnstore Index Scan operator that the **Actual Execution Mode** value is **Batch** (see *Figure 11.5*). In the same way, the **Storage** property shows **ColumnStore**:

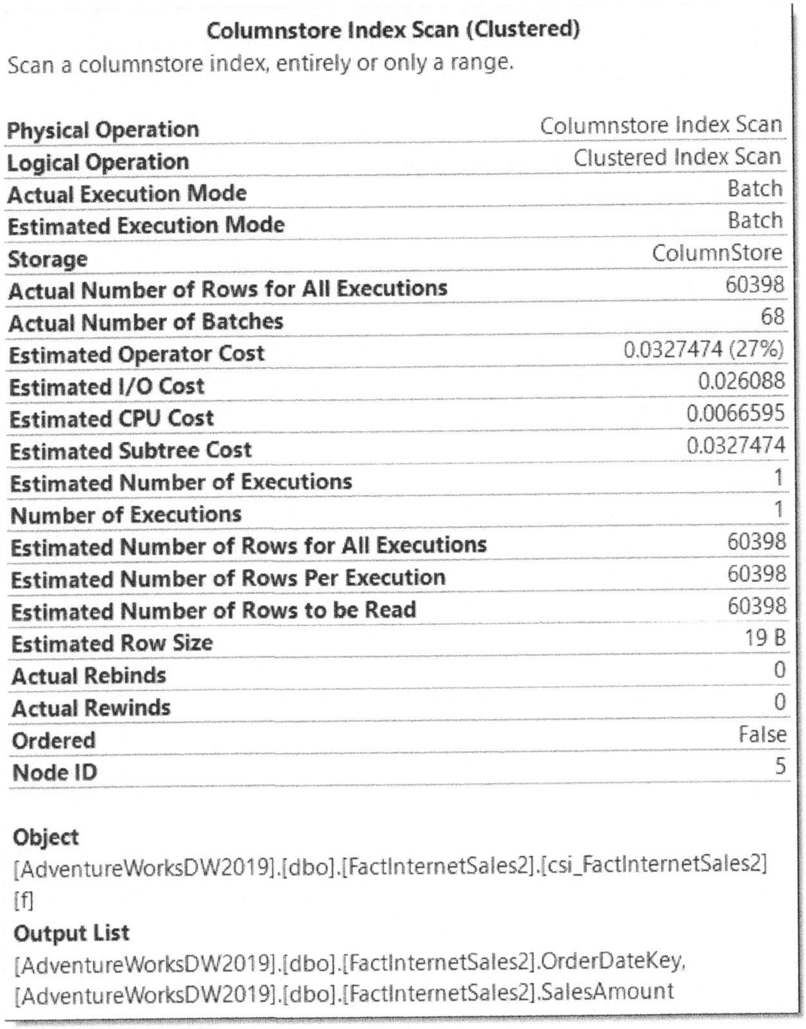

Columnstore Index Scan (Clustered)

Scan a columnstore index, entirely or only a range.

Physical Operation	Columnstore Index Scan
Logical Operation	Clustered Index Scan
Actual Execution Mode	Batch
Estimated Execution Mode	Batch
Storage	ColumnStore
Actual Number of Rows for All Executions	60398
Actual Number of Batches	68
Estimated Operator Cost	0.0327474 (27%)
Estimated I/O Cost	0.026088
Estimated CPU Cost	0.0066595
Estimated Subtree Cost	0.0327474
Estimated Number of Executions	1
Number of Executions	1
Estimated Number of Rows for All Executions	60398
Estimated Number of Rows Per Execution	60398
Estimated Number of Rows to be Read	60398
Estimated Row Size	19 B
Actual Rebinds	0
Actual Rewinds	0
Ordered	False
Node ID	5

Object
[AdventureWorksDW2019].[dbo].[FactInternetSales2].[csi_FactInternetSales2]
[f]
Output List
[AdventureWorksDW2019].[dbo].[FactInternetSales2].OrderDateKey,
[AdventureWorksDW2019].[dbo].[FactInternetSales2].SalesAmount

Figure 11.5 – The Columnstore Index Scan properties

Similar to a rowstore, you can use the ALTER INDEX REBUILD statement to remove any fragmentation of a columnstore index, as shown in the following code:

```
ALTER INDEX csi_FactInternetSales2 on FactInternetSales2
REBUILD
```

Because a fact table is a very large table, and an index rebuild operation in a columnstore index is an offline operation, you can partition it and follow the same recommendations you would for a large table in a rowstore. Here is a basic summary of the process:

- Rebuild the most recently used partition only. Fragmentation is more likely to occur only in partitions that have been modified recently.

- Rebuild only the partitions that have been updated after loading data or heavy DML operations.

Similar to dropping a regular clustered index, dropping a clustered columnstore index will convert the table back into a rowstore heap. To verify this, run the following query:

```
SELECT * FROM sys.indexes
WHERE object_id = OBJECT_ID('FactInternetSales2')
```

An output similar to the following will be shown:

Object_ID	Name	Index_ID	Type	Type_desc
1762105318	csi_FactInternetSales2	1	5	CLUSTERED COLUMNSTORE

Dropping the index running by using the next DROP INDEX statement and then running the previous query again will change index_id to 0 and type_desc to HEAP:

```
DROP INDEX FactInternetSales2.csi_FactInternetSales2
```

Hints

Finally, a couple of hints could be useful in cases where the query optimizer is not giving you a good plan when working with nonclustered columnstore indexes. One case is when the query optimizer ignores this index. In this case, you can use the INDEX hint to ask SQL Server to use the existing nonclustered columnstore index. To test it, create the following index in the existing FactInternetSales table:

```
CREATE NONCLUSTERED COLUMNSTORE INDEX csi_FactInternetSales
ON dbo.FactInternetSales (
ProductKey,
OrderDateKey,
DueDateKey,
ShipDateKey,
CustomerKey,
PromotionKey,
```

```
CurrencyKey,
SalesTerritoryKey,
SalesOrderNumber,
SalesOrderLineNumber,
RevisionNumber,
OrderQuantity,
UnitPrice,
ExtendedAmount,
UnitPriceDiscountPct,
DiscountAmount,
ProductStandardCost,
TotalProductCost,
SalesAmount,
TaxAmt,
Freight,
CarrierTrackingNumber,
CustomerPONumber,
OrderDate,
DueDate,
ShipDate
)
```

Assuming the columnstore index is not selected in the final execution plan, you could use the INDEX hint in the following way:

```
SELECT d.CalendarYear,
SUM(SalesAmount) AS SalesTotal
FROM dbo.FactInternetSales AS f
WITH (INDEX(csi_FactInternetSales))
JOIN dbo.DimDate AS d
ON f.OrderDateKey = d.DateKey
GROUP BY d.CalendarYear
ORDER BY d.CalendarYear
```

Another case is when for some reason you don't want to use an existing nonclustered columnstore index. In this case, the IGNORE_NONCLUSTERED_COLUMNSTORE_INDEX hint could be used, as shown in the following query:

```
SELECT d.CalendarYear,
SUM(SalesAmount) AS SalesTotal
FROM dbo.FactInternetSales AS f
JOIN dbo.DimDate AS d
ON f.OrderDateKey = d.DateKey
GROUP BY d.CalendarYear
ORDER BY d.CalendarYear
OPTION (IGNORE_NONCLUSTERED_COLUMNSTORE_INDEX)
```

Finally, drop the created columnstore index by running the following statement:

```
DROP INDEX FactInternetSales.csi_FactInternetSales
```

Summary

This chapter covered data warehouses and explained how operational and analytic systems serve very different purposes—one helping with the execution of a business process and the other helping with the measurement of such a business process. The fact that a data warehouse system is also used differently from an OLTP system created opportunities for a new database engine design, which was implemented using the columnstore indexes feature when SQL Server 2012 was originally released.

Because a typical star join query only uses between 10 percent and 15 percent of the columns in a fact table, a columnar-based approach was implemented, which seemed to be more appropriate than the traditional rowstore. Because processing one row at a time also did not seem to be efficient for the large number of rows processed by star join queries, a new batch-processing mode was implemented, too. Finally, following new hardware trends, columnstore indexes, same as with in-memory OLTP, were implemented as in-memory technologies.

Additionally. the SQL Server query optimizer is able to automatically detect and optimize data warehouse queries. One of the explained optimizations, using bitmap filtering, is based on a concept originally conceived in 1970. Bitmap filtering can be used to filter out rows from a fact table very early during query processing, thus improving the performance of star join queries. In the next and final chapter, we will learn how to understand various query hints.

12
Understanding Query Hints

Query optimization is an inherently complex problem, not only for SQL Server but also for other relational database systems. Even though query optimization research dates back to the early 1970s, challenges in some fundamental areas are still being addressed today. The first major impediment to a query optimizer finding an optimal plan is the fact that, for many queries, it is just not possible to explore the entire search space. An effect known as combinatorial explosion makes this exhaustive enumeration impossible because the number of possible plans grows very rapidly, depending on the number of tables joined in the query. To make searching a manageable process, heuristics are used to limit the search space (that is, the number of possible plans to be considered), as covered in *Chapter 3, The Query Optimizer*. However, if a query optimizer can't explore the entire search space, there is no way to prove that you can get an optimal plan, or even that the best plan is among the candidates being considered, whether it is selected or not. As a result, the set of plans a query optimizer must consider must be low cost.

This leads us to another major technical challenge for the query optimizer: accurate cost and cardinality estimation. Because a cost-based optimizer selects the execution plan with the lowest estimated cost, the quality of the plan selection is only as good as the accuracy of the optimizer's cost and cardinality estimations. Even supposing that optimization time is not a concern and that the query optimizer can analyze the entire search space without a problem, cardinality and cost estimation errors can still make a query optimizer select a nonoptimal plan. That is, the query optimizer may consider the best possible plan but, because of bad cost estimation, select a less efficient plan.

Cost estimation models are inherently inexact because they do not consider all the hardware conditions and must make certain assumptions about the environment. For example, the costing model assumes that every query starts with a cold cache (that is, that its data is read from disk and not from memory), and this assumption could lead to cost estimation errors in some cases. In addition, cost estimation relies on cardinality estimation, which is also inexact and has some known limitations, especially when it comes to estimating the intermediate results in a plan. Errors in intermediate results get magnified as more tables are joined and more estimation errors are included within the calculations. On top of all that, some operations are not covered by the mathematical model of the cardinality estimation component, which means the query optimizer must resort to guessing logic or heuristics to deal with these situations.

This chapter covers the following topics:

- Breaking down complex queries
- Hints
- Joins
- Aggregations
- FORCE ORDER
- The INDEX, FORCESCAN, and FORCESEEK hints
- FAST N
- The NOEXPAND and EXPAND VIEWS hints
- Plan guides
- USE PLAN

Breaking down complex queries

As we saw in *Chapter 3, The Query Optimizer*, in some cases, the SQL Server query optimizer may not be able to produce a good plan for a query with a large number of joins. The same is true for complex queries with both joins and aggregations. However, because it is rarely necessary to request all the data in a single query, a good solution for those cases could be to just break down a large and complex query into two or more simpler queries while storing the intermediate results in temporary tables. Breaking down complex queries this way offers several advantages:

- **Better plans**: Query performance is improved because the query optimizer can create efficient plans for simpler queries.

- **Better statistics**: Because one of the problems of some complex plans is being able to degrade intermediate statistics, breaking down these queries and storing the aggregated or intermediate results in temporary tables allows SQL Server to create new statistics, greatly improving the cardinality estimation of the remaining queries. It is worth noting that temporary tables should be used and not table variables, as the latter does not support statistics.

  Starting with SQL Server 2012 Service Pack 2, you can use trace flag 2453 to provide a better cardinality estimation while using table variables. For more details, see http://support.microsoft.com/kb/2952444.

- **No hints required**: Because using hints is a common practice to fix problems with complex plans, breaking down the query allows the query optimizer to create an efficient plan without requiring hints. This has the additional benefit that the query optimizer can automatically react to future data or schema changes. On the other hand, a query using hints would require future maintenance because the hint being used may no longer be helpful, or may even negatively impact its performance after such changes. Hints, which should be used only as a last resort when no other solution is available, will be covered later in this chapter.

In the paper *When to Break Down Complex Queries*, the author describes several problematic query patterns that the SQL Server query optimizer can't create good plans for. Although the paper was published in October 2011 and indicates that it applies to versions from SQL Server 2005 to SQL Server 2012, code-named **Denali**, we are still able to see the same behavior on the currently supported versions of the product, including SQL Server 2022.

> **Note**
>
> Denali was the codename for SQL Server 2012 and its name comes from the highest mountain peak in North America.

Here are some of these query patterns, which we will cover briefly:

- OR logic in the WHERE clause
- Joins on aggregated datasets
- Queries with a large number of very complex joins

> **Note**
>
> You can find the paper *When to Break Down Complex Queries* at https://techcommunity.microsoft.com/t5/datacat/when-to-break-down-complex-queries/ba-p/305154.

OR logic in the WHERE clause

The SQL Server query optimizer can identify and create efficient plans when using OR logic in the WHERE clause for the following cases:

- WHERE a.col1 = @val1 OR a.col1 = @val2
- WHERE a.col1 IN (@val1, @val2)
- WHERE a.col1 = @val1 OR a.col2 = @val2
- WHERE a.col1 = @val1 OR a.col2 IN (SELECT col2 FROM tab2)

As you'll notice, all the listed cases use the same or different columns but in the same table. Here is an example of a query showing the first case:

```
SELECT * FROM Sales.SalesOrderHeader
WHERE CustomerID = 11020 OR SalesPersonID = 285
```

In this query, SQL Server can use index seek operations on two indexes, `IX_SalesOrderHeader_CustomerID` and `IX_SalesOrderHeader_SalesPersonID`, and use an index union to solve both predicates. The efficient plan is shown in *Figure 12.1*. Once again, this chapter may show partial plans so that they are easier to read:

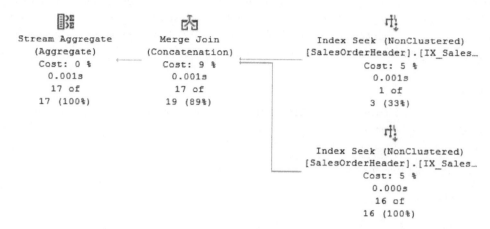

Figure 12.1 – A plan using WHERE a.col1 = @val1 OR a.col2 = @val2

However, poor plans may be created when filters on the OR operator evaluate different tables, basically following the WHERE `a.col1 = @val1 OR b.col2 = @val2` pattern.

Running the following two queries using a very selective predicate will create two plans using efficient Index Seek operators on the `IX_SalesOrderDetail_ProductID` and `IX_SalesOrderHeader_CustomerID` indexes, returning two and three records, respectively:

```
SELECT SalesOrderID FROM Sales.SalesOrderDetail
WHERE ProductID = 897
SELECT SalesOrderID FROM Sales.SalesOrderHeader
WHERE CustomerID = 11020
```

However, if we join both tables using the same selective predicates (and just for demonstration purposes), SQL Server will now return a very expensive plan for scanning the mentioned indexes, instead of using the more efficient seek operations shown previously:

```
SELECT sod.SalesOrderID FROM Sales.SalesOrderHeader soh
JOIN Sales.SalesOrderDetail sod
ON soh.SalesOrderID = sod.SalesOrderID
WHERE sod.ProductID = 897 OR soh.CustomerID = 11020
```

This can be seen in the following plan:

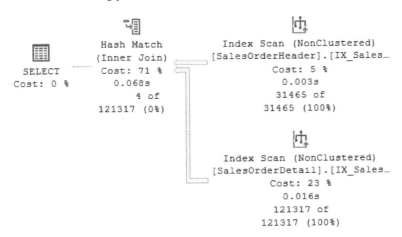

Figure 12.2 – A plan using WHERE a.col1 = @val1 OR b.col2 = @val2

This kind of query pattern can be fixed using the UNION clause instead of an OR condition, as shown here. This produces the same results and now allows you to perform seeks on all the indexes, resulting in a more efficient plan:

```
SELECT sod.SalesOrderID FROM Sales.SalesOrderHeader soh
JOIN Sales.SalesOrderDetail sod
ON soh.SalesOrderID = sod.SalesOrderID
WHERE sod.ProductID = 897
UNION
SELECT sod.SalesOrderID FROM Sales.SalesOrderHeader soh
JOIN Sales.SalesOrderDetail sod
ON soh.SalesOrderID = sod.SalesOrderID
WHERE soh.CustomerID = 11020
```

Although the query looks more complicated and redundant, it produces a very effective plan, as shown here:

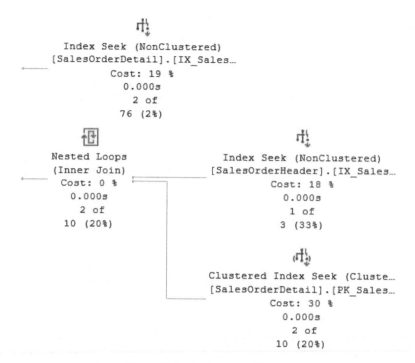

Figure 12.3 – A plan using UNION

Joins on aggregated datasets

The second query pattern occurs when the results of aggregations are joined in large and complex queries. As covered in *Chapter 6, Understanding Statistics*, statistics can provide a good cardinality estimation for operations being performed on the table that owns the statistics (for example, estimating the number of records returned by a filter operation). However, the query optimizer must use this estimate in an operation earlier in the plan, apply it to the next operation to get a new estimation, and so on. In some complex plans, these estimates can quickly degrade in accuracy.

By looking at any such complex query plan, you may notice that, near the beginning of the data flow, the estimated and actual number of rows are very similar, but after the aggregated intermediate result sets are joined to other aggregated intermediate result sets, the quality of the cardinality estimation may have degraded. When the query optimizer can't get a good estimate of the size of the dataset, it could make suboptimal decisions for joins, join orders, or other operations in the plan.

Solutions to these complex queries involve breaking down the queries, as mentioned at the beginning of this section. You can partition your queries by looking at the plan to find places where there are large differences in the number of estimated versus the actual number of rows. In addition, each aggregation in the complex query could be saved into a temporary table, which, again, would create better quality statistics that can be used for the remaining parts of the query. Finally, a query with a large number of very complex joins is another query pattern that can benefit from being broken down into two or more simpler queries, with the intermediate results being stored in temporary tables. The problem with queries that contain a large number of joins will be explained in more detail in the *Joins* section later in this chapter.

Hints

SQL is a declarative language; it only defines what data to retrieve from the database. It doesn't describe how the data should be fetched. That, as we know, is the job of the query optimizer, which analyzes several candidate execution plans for a given query, estimates the cost of each of these plans, and selects an efficient plan by choosing the cheapest of the choices considered.

But there may be cases when the selected execution plan is not performing as you have expected and, as part of your query troubleshooting process, you may try to find a better plan yourself. Before doing this, keep in mind that just because your query does not perform as you expected, this does not mean a better plan is always possible. Your plan may be an efficient one, but the query may be an expensive one to perform, or your system may be experiencing performance bottlenecks that are impacting the query's execution.

However, although the query optimizer does an excellent job most of the time, it does occasionally fail to produce an efficient plan, as you've seen throughout this book. That being said, even in cases where you're not getting an efficient plan, you should still try to distinguish between the times when problems arise because you're not providing the query optimizer with all the information it needs to do a good job and those when the problems are a result of a query optimizer limitation. Part of the focus of this book so far has been to help you provide the query optimizer with the information it needs to produce an efficient execution plan, such as the right indexes and good-quality statistics, as well as how to troubleshoot the cases where you are not getting a good plan. This chapter covers what to do if you hit a query optimizer limitation.

Having said that, there might be cases where the query optimizer may produce an inefficient plan, and as a result, we may be forced to resort to hints. Hints are essentially optimizer directives that allow us to take explicit control of the execution plan for a given query to improve its performance. In reaching for a hint, however, we are going against the declarative property of the SQL language and, instead, giving direct instructions to the query optimizer. Overriding the query optimizer is risky business; hints need to be used with caution, and only as a last resort when no other option is available to produce a viable plan.

With this warning in mind, we will review some of the hints SQL Server provides, should the need arise, as well as how and when they might be used. We will only focus on those hints we often see provide positive performance benefits in certain circumstances. Some other query hints, such as `OPTIMIZE FOR`, `OPTIMIZE FOR UNKNOWN`, and `RECOMPILE`, were covered in *Chapter 8*, Understanding *Plan Caching*, so they won't be touched on again in this chapter.

When to use hints

Hints are a powerful means by which we can force our decisions to overrule those of the query optimizer. However, you should only do so with extreme caution, because hints restrict the choices available to the query optimizer. They also make your code less flexible and will require additional maintenance. A hint should only be employed once you are certain you have no alternative options. At a minimum, before you reach for a hint, you should explore the following potential issues:

- **System performance problems**: You need to make sure your performance problem is not linked to other system-related issues, such as blocking or bottlenecks in server resources such as I/O, memory, and CPU.

- **Cardinality estimation errors**: The query optimizer often misses the correct plan because of cardinality estimation errors. Cardinality estimation errors can sometimes be fixed via solutions such as updating statistics, using a bigger sample for your statistics (or scanning the entire table), using computed columns, multicolumn statistics, filtered statistics, and so on. There might be cases where the cardinality estimation errors are caused by using features in which statistics are not supported at all, such as table variables and multistatement table-valued user-defined functions. In these particular instances, you may consider using standard or temporary tables if you are not getting an efficient plan. Statistics and cardinality estimation errors were covered in detail in *Chapter 6, Understanding Statistics*.

- **Additional troubleshooting**: You may need to perform additional troubleshooting before considering using hints. One of the obvious choices for improving the performance of your queries is providing the query optimizer with the right indexes. How to make sure that your indexes have been selected by the query optimizer was covered in *Chapter 5, Working with Indexes*. You may also consider some other, less obvious troubleshooting procedures, such as breaking your query down into steps or smaller pieces and storing any intermediate results in temporary tables, as shown earlier in this chapter. You can use this method as a troubleshooting procedure – for example, to find out which part of the original query is expensive so that you can focus on it. Alternatively, you can keep it as the final version of your query if these changes alone give you better performance.

As discussed earlier in this chapter, query optimizers have improved radically after more than 30 years of research, but still face some technical challenges. The SQL Server query optimizer will give you an efficient execution plan for most of your queries but will be increasingly challenged as the complexity of the query grows with more tables joined, plus the use of aggregations and other SQL features. If, after investigating the troubleshooting options and recommendations described previously and throughout this book, you still find that the query optimizer is not finding a good execution plan for your query, you may need to consider using hints to direct the query optimizer toward what you feel is the optimal execution path.

Always remember that, by applying a hint, you effectively disable some of the available transformation rules that the query optimizer usually has access to and thus restrict the available search space. Only transformation rules that help achieve the requested plan will be executed. For example, if you use hints to force a particular join order, the query optimizer will disable rules that reorder joins. Always try to use the least restrictive hint since this will retain as much flexibility as possible in your query and make maintenance somewhat easier. In addition, please be aware that hints cannot be used to generate an invalid plan or a plan that the query optimizer wouldn't normally consider during query optimization.

Furthermore, a hint that initially does a great job may actively hinder performance at a later point in time when some conditions change – for example, as a result of schema updates, changes in data, new versions of SQL Server, or after applying SQL Server service packs or cumulative updates. The hints may prevent the query optimizer from modifying the execution plan accordingly, and thus result in degraded performance. It is your responsibility to monitor and maintain your hinted queries to make sure they continue to perform well after such system changes or to remove those hints if they are no longer needed.

Also, remember that if you decide to use a hint to change a single section or physical operator of a plan, then after you apply the hint, the query optimizer will perform a completely new optimization. The query optimizer will obey your hint during the optimization process, but it still has the flexibility to change everything else in the plan, so the result of your tweaking may be unintended changes to other sections of the plan. Finally, note that the fact that your query is not performing as you hoped does not always mean that the query optimizer is not giving you a good enough execution plan. If the operation you are performing is simply expensive and resource-intensive, then it is possible that no amount of tuning or hinting will help you achieve the performance you would like.

Types of hints

SQL Server provides a wide range of hints, which can be classified as follows:

- Query hints tell the optimizer to apply the hint throughout the entire query. They are specified using the OPTION clause, which is included at the end of the query.

- Join hints apply to a specific join in a query and can be specified by using ANSI-style join hints.

- Table hints apply to a single table and are usually included by using the WITH keyword in the FROM clause.

Another useful classification is dividing hints into physical operator hints and goal-oriented hints:

- Physical operator hints, as the name suggests, request the use of a specific physical operator, join order, or aggregation placement. Most of the hints covered in this chapter are physical hints.

- A goal-oriented hint does not specify how to build the plan. Instead, it specifies a goal to achieve, leaving the query optimizer to find the best physical operators to achieve that goal. Goal-oriented hints are usually safer and require less knowledge about the internal workings of the query optimizer. Examples of goal-oriented hints include the OPTIMIZE FOR and FAST N hints.

New with SQL Server 2022, Query Store hints leverage the Query Store feature to provide a way to shape query plans without the need to change application code. Query Store hints can be used as a replacement for plan guides, which can be complex to use. Query Store hints were covered in *Chapter 9, The Query Store*. Plan guides will be covered at the end of this chapter.

Locking hints do not affect plan selection, so they will not be covered here. Plan guides, which allow you to apply a hint to a query without changing the code in your application, and the USE PLAN query hint, which allows you to force the query optimizer to use a specified execution plan for a query, will be covered later in this chapter.

In the next few sections, we will discuss hints that affect joins, join orders, aggregations, index scans or seeks, and views, as they are the most commonly used. For an entire list of SQL Server hints, please refer to the SQL Server documentation.

> **Note**
>
> Note that with a very simple and small database such as AdventureWorks2019, SQL Server will give you an optimal or good enough plan for the examples in this chapter without requiring any hints. However, we will be exploring alternative plans using hints for demonstration purposes only, some of which could be potentially more expensive than the unhinted version.

Joins

We can explicitly ask the query optimizer to use any of the available join physical algorithms: Nested Loop Join, Merge Join, and Hash Join. We could do this at the query level, in which case all the existing joins in the query will be affected, or we can request it at the join level, ensuring that only that specific join is impacted (although, as you will see later, this last choice will also impact the join order on the plan).

Let's focus on join hints at the query level first, in which case, the join algorithm is specified using the OPTION clause. You can also specify two of the three available joins, which asks the query optimizer to exclude the third physical join operator from consideration. The decision between which of the remaining two joins to use will be cost-based. For example, take a look at the following unhinted query:

```
SELECT *
FROM Production.Product AS p
JOIN Sales.SalesOrderDetail AS sod
ON p.ProductID = sod.ProductID
```

This will produce the following plan, which uses a Hash Join:

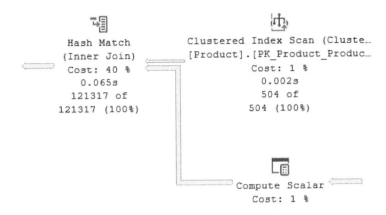

Figure 12.4 – An execution plan using a Hash Join

On the other hand, the following query will ask SQL Server to exclude a Hash Join by requesting either a Nested Loop Join or Merge Join. In this case, SQL Server chooses a more expensive plan with a Merge Join operator, also showing that the query optimizer was making the right decision in the first place:

```
SELECT *
FROM Production.Product AS p
JOIN Sales.SalesOrderDetail AS sod
ON p.ProductID = sod.ProductID
OPTION (LOOP JOIN, MERGE JOIN)
```

This plan is partially shown here:

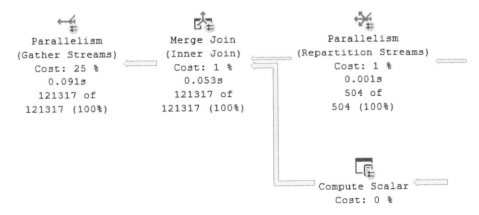

Figure 12.5 – An execution plan excluding a Hash Join

Join hints can not only force the joins we explicitly specify in our query text, but can also impact most of the joins introduced by the query optimizer, such as foreign key validation and cascading actions. Other joins, such as Nested Loop Joins, which are used in a bookmark lookup, cannot be changed because it would defeat the purpose of using the bookmark lookup in the first place. For example, in the following query, the hint to use a Merge Join will be ignored:

```
SELECT AddressID, City, StateProvinceID, ModifiedDate
FROM Person.Address
WHERE City = 'Santa Fe'
OPTION (MERGE JOIN)
```

This can be seen in the following plan

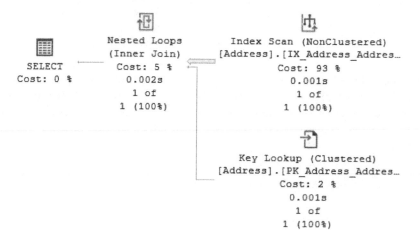

Figure 12.6 – Hint ignored in a bookmark lookup example

As mentioned earlier, hints cannot force the query optimizer to generate invalid plans, so the following query will not compile because both Merge and Hash Joins require an equality operator on the join predicate:

```
SELECT *
FROM Production.Product AS p
JOIN Sales.SalesOrderDetail AS sod
ON sod.ProductID > p.ProductID
WHERE p.ProductID > 900
OPTION (HASH JOIN)
```

Trying to execute the previous query will return the following error message:

```
Msg 8622, Level 16, State 1, Line 1
Query processor could not produce a query plan because of
the hints defined in this query. Resubmit the query without
specifying any hints and without using SET FORCEPLAN.
```

However, as mentioned previously, keep in mind that using a query-level hint will impact the entire query. If you need explicit control over each join in a query, you can use ANSI-style join hints, the benefit of which is that a join type can be individually selected for every join in the plan. However, be warned that using ANSI join hints will also add the behavior of the FORCE ORDER hint, which asks to preserve the join order and aggregation placement, as indicated by the query syntax. This behavior will be explained in the *FORCE ORDER* section, later in this chapter.

In the meantime, let me show you an example. The first query that was used in this section employs a Hash Join for accessing the Product table when used with no hints, which means that Product will be the build input and the SalesOrderDetail probe input. This plan was shown in *Figure 12.4*. The following query will use a hint to request a Nested Loop Join instead. Notice that the INNER keyword is required this time:

```
SELECT *
FROM Production.Product AS p
INNER LOOP JOIN Sales.SalesOrderDetail AS sod
ON p.ProductID = sod.ProductID
```

However, as mentioned earlier, the join order is impacted as well; the Product table will always be the outer input, and SalesOrderDetail will be the inner input. If we wanted to reverse the roles, we would need to explicitly rewrite the query, as shown here, in which case SalesOrderDetail will be the outer input and Product will be the inner input:

```
SELECT *
FROM Sales.SalesOrderDetail AS sod
INNER LOOP JOIN Production.Product AS p
ON p.ProductID = sod.ProductID
```

This can be seen in the following plan:

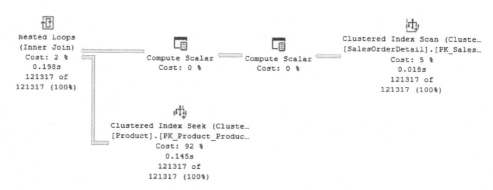

Figure 12.7 – An execution plan with ANSI-style join hints

In addition, the following warning is shown in the **Messages** tab when the code is executed using Management Studio, which indicates that not only was the join algorithm forced, but the join order was forced as well (that is, the tables were joined using the order specified in the query text):

```
Warning: The join order has been enforced because a local join
hint is used.
```

Aggregations

Just like join algorithms, aggregation algorithms can also be forced by using the GROUP hints. Specifically, the ORDER GROUP hint requests that the query optimizer use a Stream Aggregate algorithm, while the HASH GROUP hint requests a Hash Aggregate algorithm. These hints can only be specified at the query level, so they will impact all the aggregation operations in the query. To see the effects of this, take a look at the following unhinted query, which uses a Stream Aggregate operator:

```
SELECT SalesOrderID, COUNT(*)
FROM Sales.SalesOrderDetail
GROUP BY SalesOrderID
```

This produces the following plan:

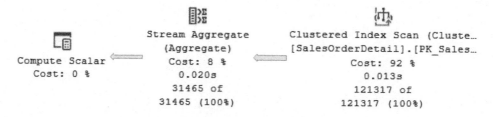

Figure 12.8 – A query using Stream Aggregate

Because the `SalesOrderDetail` table has a clustered index on the `SalesOrderID` column, and therefore the data is already sorted on the GROUP BY column, using a Stream Aggregate operator is the obvious choice. However, if we add a HASH GROUP hint to the previous query, as shown here, it will force a Hash Aggregate operator:

```
SELECT SalesOrderID, COUNT(*)
FROM Sales.SalesOrderDetail
GROUP BY SalesOrderID
OPTION (HASH GROUP)
```

This will produce the following plan, which, not surprisingly, makes the query more expensive than necessary:

Figure 12.9 – An execution plan with a HASH GROUP hint

On the other hand, a scalar aggregation will always use a Stream Aggregate operator. A hint to force a hash aggregate on a scalar aggregation, as shown in the following query, will simply be ignored in SQL Server 2012 and later. SQL Server 2008 R2 and earlier versions, however, will trigger compilation error 8622, as shown earlier, complaining about the hints defined in the query:

```
SELECT COUNT(*) FROM Sales.SalesOrderDetail
OPTION (HASH GROUP)
```

FORCE ORDER

The FORCE ORDER hint can give the user full control over the join and aggregation placement in an execution plan. Specifically, the FORCE ORDER hint asks the query optimizer to preserve the join order and aggregation placement as indicated by the query syntax. Also, notice that the ANSI-style join hints explained previously can give you control of the join order, in addition to control over the choice of the join algorithm. Both the FORCE ORDER and ANSI-style join hints are very powerful, and because of that, they need to be used with extreme caution. As explained earlier in this chapter, finding an optimum join order is a critical and challenging part of the query optimization process because the sheer number of possible join orders can be huge, even with queries involving only a few tables. What this boils down to is that, by using the FORCE ORDER hint, you are attempting to optimize the join order yourself. You can use the FORCE ORDER hint to obtain any query, such as a left-deep tree, bushy tree, or right-deep tree, all of which were explained in *Chapter 3, The Query Optimizer.*

The SQL Server query optimizer will usually produce a left-deep tree plan, but you can force bushy trees or right-deep trees by changing the location of the ON clause in the join predicate using subqueries, using parentheses, and so on. Be aware that forcing join order does not affect the simplification phase of query optimization, and some joins may still be removed if needed, as also explained in *Chapter 3, The Query Optimizer*.

If you do need to change the join order of a query for some reason, you can try starting with the join order recommended by the query optimizer and change only the part you think is suffering from a problem, such as cardinality estimation errors. You can also follow the practices that the query optimizer itself would follow, as explained in *Chapter 4, The Execution Engine*. For example, if you are forcing a Hash Join, select the smallest table as the build input; if you're forcing a Nested Loop Join, use small tables in the outer input and the tables with indexes as the inner input. You could also start by joining small tables first, or tables that can help filter out the most possible number of rows.

Let's look at an example:

```
SELECT LastName, FirstName, soh.SalesOrderID
FROM Person.Person p JOIN HumanResources.Employee e
ON e.BusinessEntityID = p.BusinessEntityID
JOIN Sales.SalesOrderHeader soh
ON p.BusinessEntityID = soh.SalesPersonID
WHERE ShipDate > '2008-01-01'
```

The following query, without hints, will produce the following plan:

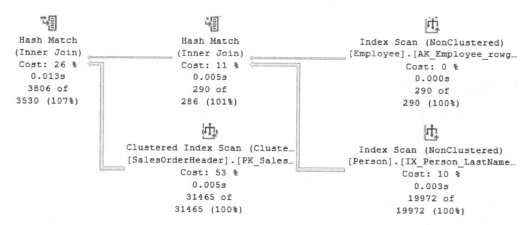

Figure 12.10 – An execution plan without hints

As you can see, the query optimizer does not follow the join order specified in the query syntax exactly (for example, the Person table is not accessed first). Instead, the query optimizer found a more efficient join order based on cost decisions. Now, let's see what happens if we add a FORCE ORDER hint to the same query:

```
SELECT LastName, FirstName, soh.SalesOrderID
FROM Person.Person p JOIN HumanResources.Employee e
ON e.BusinessEntityID = p.BusinessEntityID
JOIN Sales.SalesOrderHeader soh
ON p.BusinessEntityID = soh.SalesPersonID
WHERE ShipDate > '2008-01-01'
OPTION (FORCE ORDER)
```

This will produce the following plan:

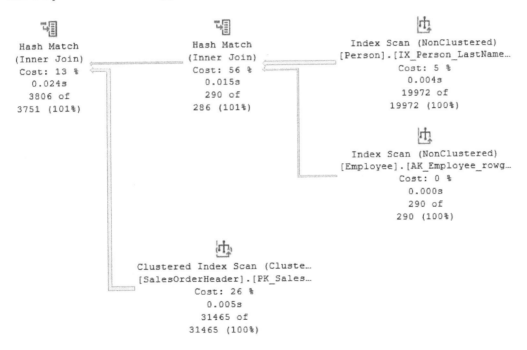

Figure 12.11 – An execution plan with the FORCE ORDER hint

In this query using the FORCE ORDER hint, the tables will be joined in the order specified in the query, and by default, a left-deep tree will be created. On the other hand, if you are using the FORCE ORDER hint in a query with ANSI joins, SQL Server will consider the location of the ON clauses to define the location of the joins. You can use this to create a right-deep tree, as shown in the following query:

```
SELECT LastName, FirstName, soh.SalesOrderID
FROM Person.Person p JOIN HumanResources.Employee e
JOIN Sales.SalesOrderHeader soh
ON e.BusinessEntityID = soh.SalesPersonID
ON e.BusinessEntityID = p.BusinessEntityID
WHERE ShipDate > '2008-01-01'
OPTION (FORCE ORDER)
```

This produces the following plan:

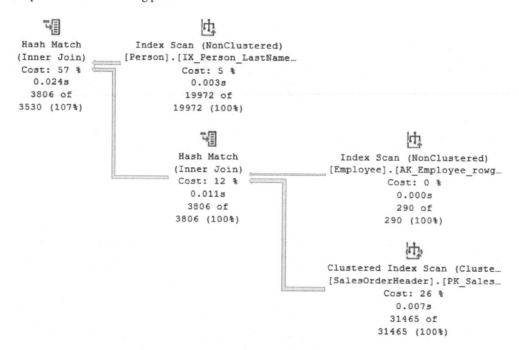

Figure 12.12 – Plan forcing a right-deep tree

Although the order in which the tables are joined is specified as Person, Employee, and SalesOrderHeader, the placement of the ON clauses defines that Employee and SalesOrderHeader are to be joined first, thus creating a right-deep tree.

In addition to taking control of join orders, as mentioned in the introduction to this section, FORCE ORDER can be used to force the order of aggregations. Consider the following unhinted example:

```
SELECT c.CustomerID, COUNT(*)
FROM Sales.Customer c
JOIN Sales.SalesOrderHeader o
ON c.CustomerID = o.CustomerID
GROUP BY c.CustomerID
```

This produces the following plan:

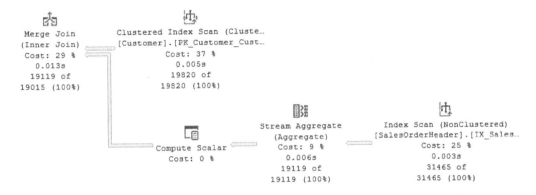

Figure 12.13 – A plan with aggregation before the join

As you can see, in this case, the query optimizer decided to perform the aggregation before the join. Remember that, as mentioned in *Chapter 3, The Query Optimizer*, and *Chapter 4, The Execution Engine*, the query optimizer may decide to perform aggregations before or after a join if this can improve the performance of the query. By adding a FORCE ORDER hint, as shown in the following query, you can cause the aggregation to be performed after the join:

```
SELECT c.CustomerID, COUNT(*)
FROM Sales.Customer c
JOIN Sales.SalesOrderHeader o
ON c.CustomerID = o.CustomerID
GROUP BY c.CustomerID
OPTION (FORCE ORDER)
```

This can be seen in the following plan:

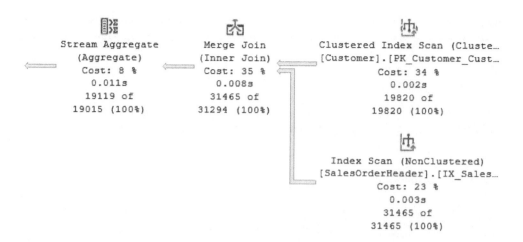

Figure 12.14 – The FORCE ORDER hint used with an aggregation

Finally, a related statement, SET FORCEPLAN, can also be used to preserve the join order, as indicated in the FROM clause of a query. However, it will only request Nested Loop Joins, unless other types of joins are required to construct a plan for the query, or the query includes a query hint or join hint. The difference between this statement and the hints shown so far is that SET FORCEPLAN needs to be turned on, and will stay in effect until it is explicitly turned off. For more information regarding the SET FORCEPLAN statement, please refer to the SQL Server documentation.

The INDEX, FORCESCAN, and FORCESEEK hints

The INDEX, FORCESCAN, and FORCESEEK hints are table hints, and we will consider each in turn. The INDEX hint can be used to request the query optimizer to use a specific index or indexes, an example of which was shown in our discussion of columnstore indexes in *Chapter 11, An Introduction to Data Warehouses*. Either the index ID or the name of the index can be used as a target for the query optimizer, but a name is the recommended way because we do not have control over the index ID values for nonclustered indexes. However, if you still want to use index ID values, they can be found on the index_id column of the sys.indexes catalog view, where index ID 0 is a heap, index ID 1 is a clustered index, and a value greater than 1 is a nonclustered index. On a query that uses a heap, using the INDEX(0) hint results in a Table Scan operator being used, whereas INDEX(1) returns an error message indicating that no such index exists. A query with a clustered index, however, can use both values: INDEX(0) will force a Clustered Index Scan, while INDEX(1) can use either a Clustered Index Scan or a Clustered Index Seek.

The FORCESCAN hint requests the query optimizer to use only an index scan operation as the access path to the referenced table or view and can be specified with or without an INDEX hint. On the other hand, the FORCESEEK hint can be used to force the query optimizer to use an Index Seek operation and can work on both clustered and nonclustered indexes. It can also work in combination with the INDEX hint, as you'll see later.

In addition to helping improve the performance of your queries, in some cases, you may want to consider using an INDEX hint to minimize lock contention or deadlocks. Notice that when you use an INDEX hint, your query becomes dependent on the existence of the specified index and will stop working if that index is removed. Using FORCESEEK without an available index will also result in an error, as shown later in this section.

You can also use the INDEX hint to avoid a bookmark lookup operation, as shown in the following example. Because the query optimizer estimates that only a few records will be returned by the next query, it decides to use an Index Seek and Key Lookup combination:

```
SELECT * FROM Sales.SalesOrderDetail
WHERE ProductID = 897
```

This can be seen in the following plan:

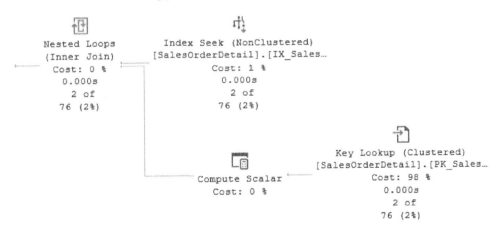

Figure 12.15 – A plan with a Nested Loop Join

However, suppose that you want to avoid a bookmark lookup operation; you can use the INDEX table hint to force a table scan instead, which could be the scan of either a heap or a clustered index. The following query will force the use of a Clustered Index Scan operator:

```
SELECT * FROM Sales.SalesOrderDetail WITH (INDEX(0))
WHERE ProductID = 897
```

This can be seen in the following plan:

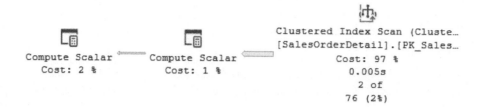

Figure 12.16 – A plan with an INDEX hint

The same behavior can be obtained by using the FORCESCAN hint, as shown in the following query:

```
SELECT * FROM Sales.SalesOrderDetail WITH (FORCESCAN)
WHERE ProductID = 897
```

Using INDEX(1) in this example would give a similar result because SQL Server cannot use the clustered index to perform an Index Seek operation; the clustered key is on SalesOrderID and SalesOrderDetailID, so the only viable choice is to scan the clustered index. Of course, you can also force the opposite operation. In the following example, the query optimizer estimates that a high number of records will be returned, so it decides to use a plan with a Clustered Index Scan:

```
SELECT * FROM Sales.SalesOrderDetail
WHERE ProductID = 870
```

Because we have an index on ProductID (IX_SalesOrderDetail_ProductID), we can force the plan to use such an index, as shown in the following query. The produced plan will use an Index Seek on the IX_SalesOrderDetail_ProductID index and a Key Lookup operation on the base table, which in this case is the clustered index:

```
SELECT * FROM Sales.SalesOrderDetail WITH (INDEX(IX_
SalesOrderDetail_ProductID))
WHERE ProductID = 870
```

You can also achieve a similar result by forcing a seek using the FORCESEEK table hint, which was introduced in SQL Server 2008. The following query will create the same plan, similar to the previous query:

```
SELECT * FROM Sales.SalesOrderDetail WITH (FORCESEEK)
WHERE ProductID = 870
```

You can even combine both hints to obtain the same plan, as shown in the following query. Keep in mind that using the INDEX hint does not necessarily mean that an Index Seek operation will be performed, so the FORCESEEK hint could help you achieve that:

```
SELECT * FROM Sales.SalesOrderDetail
WITH (INDEX(IX_SalesOrderDetail_ProductID), FORCESEEK)
WHERE ProductID = 870
```

Using FORCESEEK when SQL Server cannot perform an Index Seek operation will cause the query to not compile, as shown here, and will instead return error message 8622, shown earlier, complaining about the hints defined in the query:

```
SELECT * FROM Sales.SalesOrderDetail WITH (FORCESEEK)
WHERE OrderQty = 1
```

FAST N

FAST N is one of the so-called "goal-oriented hints." It does not indicate what physical operators to use; instead, it specifies what goal the plan is trying to achieve. This hint is used to optimize a query to retrieve the first *n* rows of results as quickly as possible. It can help in situations where only the first few rows returned by a query are relevant, and perhaps you won't be using the remaining records of the query at all. The price to pay for achieving this speed is that retrieving those remaining records may take longer than if you had used a plan without this hint. In other words, because the query is optimized to retrieve the first *n* records as soon as possible, retrieving all the records returned by the query may be very expensive.

The query optimizer usually accomplishes this FAST N goal by avoiding any blocking operators, such as Sort, Hash Join, and Hash Aggregation, so the client submitting the query does not have to wait before the first few records are produced. Let's look at an example. Run the following query:

```
SELECT * FROM Sales.SalesOrderDetail
ORDER BY ProductID
```

This will produce the following plan:

Figure 12.17 – A plan using a Sort operation

In this case, the Sort operator is the most effective way to get the records sorted by ProductID if you want to see the entire query output. However, because Sort is a blocking operator, SQL Server won't be able to produce any row until the entire sort operation has been completed. Now, supposing that your application wants to see a page that shows 20 records at a time, you can use the FAST hint to get these 20 records as quickly as possible, as shown in the following query:

```
SELECT * FROM Sales.SalesOrderDetail
ORDER BY ProductID
OPTION (FAST 20)
```

This time, the new plan, shown in *Figure 12.18*, scans an available nonclustered index while performing key lookups on the clustered table. Because this plan uses random I/O, it would be very expensive for the entire query, but it will achieve the goal of returning the first 20 records very quickly:

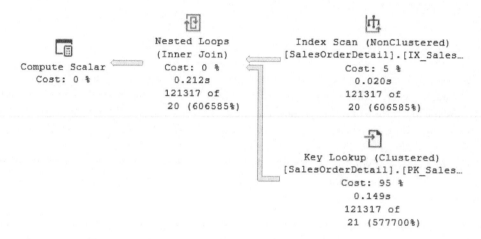

Figure 12.18 – A plan using a FAST N hint

There is also a FASTFIRSTROW hint, but it is not as flexible as FAST N because you can specify any number for N. Essentially, FASTFIRSTROW would be the same as specifying the FAST 1 hint.

The NOEXPAND and EXPAND VIEWS hints

Before talking about the NOEXPAND and EXPAND VIEWS hints, let's discuss the default behavior of queries when using indexed views so that you can see how these hints can change this behavior. As explained in *Chapter 3*, *The Query Optimizer*, SQL Server expands views in the early steps of query optimization during binding, when a view reference is expanded to include the view definition (for example, to directly include the tables used in the view). This behavior is the same for every edition of SQL Server. Later on in the optimization process, but only in Enterprise Edition, SQL Server may match the query to an existing indexed view. So, the view was expanded at the beginning but was later matched to an existing indexed view. The EXPAND VIEWS hint removes the matching step, thus making sure the views are expanded but not matched at the end of the optimization process. Therefore, this hint only has an effect in SQL Server Enterprise Edition.

On the other hand, the NOEXPAND hint asks SQL Server not to expand any views at all and to use the specified indexed view instead. This hint works in every SQL Server edition, and it is the only way (when using a SQL Server edition other than Enterprise) to ask SQL Server to match an existing indexed view. Here's an example. Create an indexed view on AdventureWorks2019 by running the following code:

```
CREATE VIEW v_test
WITH SCHEMABINDING AS
SELECT SalesOrderID, COUNT_BIG(*) as cnt
FROM Sales.SalesOrderDetail
GROUP BY SalesOrderID
GO
CREATE UNIQUE CLUSTERED INDEX ix_test ON v_test(SalesOrderID)
```

Next, run the following query:

```
SELECT SalesOrderID, COUNT(*)
FROM Sales.SalesOrderDetail
GROUP BY SalesOrderID
```

If you are using SQL Server Enterprise Edition (or the Enterprise Evaluation or Developer Edition, which share the same database engine edition), you will get the following plan, which matches the existing indexed view:

Figure 12.19 – A plan using an existing indexed view

Alternatively, you can use the EXPAND VIEWS hint, as shown in the following query, to avoid matching the index view:

```
SELECT SalesOrderID, COUNT(*)
FROM Sales.SalesOrderDetail
```

```
GROUP BY SalesOrderID
OPTION (EXPAND VIEWS)
```

This will result in the following plan:

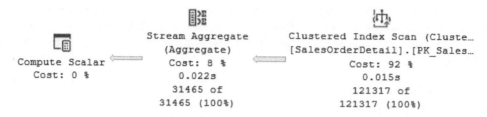

Figure 12.20 – A plan using the EXPAND VIEWS hint

Different from EXPAND VIEWS, which is a query hint, NOEXPAND is a table hint, and the following query shows how to use it to get the same results as our previous query. Note that the name of the indexed view is directly mentioned:

```
SELECT * FROM v_test WITH (NOEXPAND)
```

Not surprisingly, the plan selected will scan the v_test indexed view in a similar way to the plan shown in *Figure 12.19*.

Finally, drop the indexed view you just created:

```
DROP VIEW v_test
```

Plan guides

There might be situations where you need to apply a hint to a query but you are unable or unwilling to change your query code or your application. A common case where this occurs is if you are working with third-party code or applications that you cannot change.

Plan guides, a feature introduced with SQL Server 2005, can help you in these cases. Plan guides essentially work by keeping a list of queries on the server, along with the hints you want to apply to them, basically separating the hint specification from the query itself. To use a plan guide, you need to provide SQL Server with the query you want to optimize and either a query hint using the OPTION clause or an XML plan using the USE PLAN hint, which will be explained in the next section. When the query is optimized, SQL Server will apply the hint requested in the plan guide definition. You can also specify NULL as a hint in your plan guide to remove an existing hint in your application. Plan guides can also match queries in different contexts – for example, a stored procedure, a user-defined scalar function, or a standalone statement that is not part of any database object.

> **Note**
>
> As mentioned earlier in this chapter, starting with SQL Server 2022, you can use Query Store hints when code cannot be changed and as a replacement for plan guides. Query Store hints were covered in *Chapter 9, The Query Store*, and also used in *Chapter 10, Intelligent Query Processing*.

You can use the `sp_create_plan_guide` stored procedure to create a plan guide and `sp_control_plan_guide` to drop, enable, or disable plan guides. You can also see which plan guides are defined in your database by looking at the `sys.plan_guides` catalog view.

To make sure the query in the plan guide definition matches the query being executed, especially for standalone statements, you can use the Plan Guide Successful SQL trace event or the plan guide successful extended event, which will show whether an execution plan was successfully created using a plan guide. On the other hand, the Plan Guide Unsuccessful SQL trace event or plan guide unsuccessful extended event will show if SQL Server was unable to create an execution plan using a plan guide, meaning that the query was optimized without it. You could see the plan guide unsuccessful events, for example, if you try to use a plan guide to force a Merge or Hash Join with a nonequality operator in the join condition, as shown earlier in this chapter.

Let's look at an example of these events. Suppose we want to use plan guides to avoid a Merge or Hash Join in our previous query to avoid high memory usage. Before running this code, open a SQL Server Profiler session, connect it to your instance of SQL Server, select the blank template to start a new trace definition, select both **Plan Guide Successful** and **Plan Guide Unsuccessful** from the **Performance** section of the **Events** tab, and then start the trace.

Next, create the following stored procedure:

```
CREATE OR ALTER PROCEDURE test
AS
SELECT *
FROM Production.Product AS p
JOIN Sales.SalesOrderDetail AS sod
ON p.ProductID = sod.ProductID
```

Before creating a plan guide, execute the stored procedure and display its execution plan to verify that it is using a Hash Join operator:

```
EXEC test
```

Next, create a plan guide to force the query to use a Nested Loop Join:

```
EXEC sp_create_plan_guide
@name = N'plan_guide_test',
@stmt = N'SELECT *
```

```
FROM Production.Product AS p
JOIN Sales.SalesOrderDetail AS sod
ON p.ProductID = sod.ProductID',
@type = N'OBJECT',
@module_or_batch = N'test',
@params = NULL,
@hints = N'OPTION (LOOP JOIN)'
```

Now, if you execute the stored procedure again, you can verify that it is indeed using a Nested Loop Join operator, as shown in the following plan. However, notice that this is a more expensive plan because the query optimizer was originally choosing the right join type before using a hint:

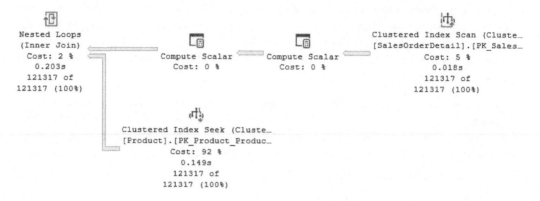

Figure 12.21 – A query using a plan guide

In addition, during this execution, SQL Server Profiler should capture a `Plan Guide Successful` event, showing that SQL Server was able to use the defined plan guide. The `TextData` column in `Profiler` will show the name of the plan guide, which in this case is `plan_guide_test`. You can also see whether an execution plan is using a plan guide by looking at the `PlanGuideName` property, which in this case will also show `plan_guide_test`.

When you create a plan guide, it is automatically enabled, but you can disable it or enable it again at any time. For example, the following statement will disable the previous plan guide, and the stored procedure will again use a Hash Join when executed:

```
EXEC sp_control_plan_guide N'DISABLE', N'plan_guide_test'
```

To enable the plan guide again, use the following statement:

```
EXEC sp_control_plan_guide N'ENABLE', N'plan_guide_test'
```

Finally, to clean up, drop both the plan guide and the stored procedure. Note that you need to drop the plan guide first because you cannot drop a stored procedure that is currently being referenced by a plan guide:

```
EXEC sp_control_plan_guide N'DROP', N'plan_guide_test'
DROP PROCEDURE test
```

USE PLAN

Finally, let's take a look at the USE PLAN query hint, which was also introduced with SQL Server 2005. The USE PLAN hint takes the use of hints to the extreme by allowing the user to specify an entire execution plan as a target to be used to optimize a query. This hint is useful when you know that a better plan than the query optimizer's suggestion exists. This can be the case, for example, when a better-performing plan was produced in the past, in a different system, or even in a previous version of SQL Server. The plan should be specified in XML format, and you will generally use SQL Server itself to generate the XML text for the desired plan since it can be extremely difficult to write an XML plan manually.

The USE PLAN hint can force most of the specified plan properties – including the tree structure, join order, join algorithms, aggregations, sorting and unions, and index operations such as scans, seeks, and intersections – so that only the transformation rules that can be useful in finding the desired plan are executed. In addition, starting with SQL Server 2008, USE PLAN supports UPDATE statements (INSERT, UPDATE, DELETE, and MERGE), which was not the case when the hint was first introduced in SQL Server 2005. Some statements that are still not supported include full-text and distributed queries, as well as queries with dynamic, keyset-driven, and forward-only cursors.

Suppose we have the same query we saw earlier in the *Plan guides* section, which produces a Hash Join:

```
SELECT *
FROM Production.Product AS p
JOIN Sales.SalesOrderDetail AS sod
ON p.ProductID = sod.ProductID
```

Also, suppose that you want SQL Server to use a different execution plan, which we can generate using a hint:

```
SELECT *
FROM Production.Product AS p
JOIN Sales.SalesOrderDetail AS sod
ON p.ProductID = sod.ProductID
OPTION (LOOP JOIN)
```

You can force this new plan to use a Nested Loop Join instead of a Hash Join. To accomplish that, display the new XML plan (by right-clicking the graphical plan and selecting **Show Execution Plan XML…**), copy it to an editor, replace any existing single quotes with double quotes, and then copy the plan to the query, as shown here:

```
SELECT *
FROM Production.Product AS p
JOIN Sales.SalesOrderDetail AS sod
ON p.ProductID = sod.ProductID
OPTION (USE PLAN N'<?xml version="1.0" encoding="utf-16"?>

...

</ShowPlanXML>')
```

Of course, the XML plan is too long to display here, so we have just displayed the start and end. Make sure that the query ends with `'`) after the XML plan. Running this `SELECT` statement will request SQL Server to try to use the indicated plan, and the query will be executed with a Nested Loop Join, as requested in the provided XML execution plan.

You can combine both plan guides and the `USE PLAN` query hint to force a specific execution plan in a situation where you don't want to change the text of the original query. The following and final query will use the same test procedure included in the *Plan guides* section, together with the XML plan that was generated (you may need to recreate the stored procedure if it was previously dropped). Note the use of two single quotes before the XML plan specification, meaning that, this time, the query text needs to end with `'`) :

```
EXEC sp_create_plan_guide
@name = N'plan_guide_test',
@stmt = N'SELECT *
FROM Production.Product AS p
JOIN Sales.SalesOrderDetail AS sod
ON p.ProductID = sod.ProductID',
@type = N'OBJECT',
@module_or_batch = N'test',
@params = NULL,
@hints = N'OPTION (USE PLAN N''<?xml version="1.0"
encoding="utf-16"?>

...

</ShowPlanXML>'')'
```

Finally, bear in mind that when the USE PLAN hint is used directly in a query, an invalid plan will make the query fail. However, when the USE PLAN hint is used in a plan guide, an invalid plan will simply compile the query without the requested hint, as mentioned in the previous section.

Summary

The SQL Server query processor typically selects a good execution plan for your queries, but there may still be cases when, even after extensive troubleshooting, you do not get good performance from a selected plan. Query optimization is an inherently complex problem, and despite several decades of query optimization research, challenges in some fundamental areas are still being addressed today.

This chapter provided recommendations on what to do when SQL Server is not giving you a good execution plan. One such methodology, which you can use in cases when the SQL Server query optimizer can't produce a good plan for complex queries, is to break these queries down into two or more simpler queries while storing the intermediate results in temporary tables.

Although hints can be used to improve the performance of a query in these cases by directly taking control of the execution plan selection, they should always be used with caution, and only as a last resort. You should also be aware that code that uses hints will require additional maintenance and is significantly less flexible to changes in your database or application or changes due to software upgrades.

Finally, we hope that this book has provided you with the knowledge needed to write better queries and to give the query processor the information it needs to produce efficient execution plans. At the same time, we hope you have learned more about how to get the information you need to diagnose and troubleshoot the cases when, despite your best efforts, you are not getting a good plan. In addition, having seen how the query processor works and some of the limitations this complex piece of software still faces today, you can be better prepared to decide when and how hints can be used to improve the performance of your queries.

Index

X

Packt.com

Subscribe to our online digital library for full access to over 7,000 books and videos, as well as industry leading tools to help you plan your personal development and advance your career. For more information, please visit our website.

Why subscribe?

- Spend less time learning and more time coding with practical eBooks and Videos from over 4,000 industry professionals

- Improve your learning with Skill Plans built especially for you

- Get a free eBook or video every month

- Fully searchable for easy access to vital information

- Copy and paste, print, and bookmark content

Did you know that Packt offers eBook versions of every book published, with PDF and ePub files available? You can upgrade to the eBook version at packt.com and as a print book customer, you are entitled to a discount on the eBook copy. Get in touch with us at customercare@packtpub.com for more details.

At www.packt.com, you can also read a collection of free technical articles, sign up for a range of free newsletters, and receive exclusive discounts and offers on Packt books and eBooks.

Other Books You May Enjoy

If you enjoyed this book, you may be interested in these other books by Packt:

A Definitive Guide to Apache ShardingSphere

Trista Pan , Zhang Liang , Yacine Si Tayeb

ISBN: 978-1-80323-942-2

- Assemble a custom solution using the software's pluggable architecture
- Discover how to use Database Plus features effectively
- Understand the difference between ShardingSphere-JDBC and ShardingSphere-Proxy
- Get to grips with ShardingSphere's pluggability mechanism
- Explore mainstream test models for databases and distributed databases
- Perform migrations from an on-premise database to a cloud-based database
- Reconfigure your data infrastructure and eliminate switching costs

The MySQL Workshop

Thomas Pettit , Scott Cosentino

ISBN: 978-1-83921-490-5

- Understand the concepts of relational databases and document stores
- Use SQL queries, stored procedures, views, functions, and transactions
- Connect to and manipulate data using MS Access, MS Excel, and Visual Basic for Applications (VBA)
- Read and write data in the CSV or JSON format using MySQL
- Manage data while running MySQL Shell in JavaScript mode
- Use X DevAPI to access a NoSQL interface for MySQL
- Manage user roles, credentials, and privileges to keep data secure
- Perform a logical database backup with mysqldump and mysqlpump

Packt is searching for authors like you

If you're interested in becoming an author for Packt, please visit authors.packtpub.com and apply today. We have worked with thousands of developers and tech professionals, just like you, to help them share their insight with the global tech community. You can make a general application, apply for a specific hot topic that we are recruiting an author for, or submit your own idea.

Share Your Thoughts

Now you've finished *SQL Server Query Tuning and Optimization*, we'd love to hear your thoughts! Scan the QR code below to go straight to the Amazon review page for this book and share your feedback or leave a review on the site that you purchased it from.

https://packt.link/r/1-803-24262-0

Your review is important to us and the tech community and will help us make sure we're delivering excellent quality content.

Made in the USA
Monee, IL
10 November 2022

17467497R00247